A Pocket Popper

David M the
Universit e
1969. Bor ity of
Cambridg of Economics, where
he was resea to Sir Karl Popper, and then at
Stanford University. He is the author of many learned articles on philosophical and logical subjects, and co-author of *Croquet and How to Play It* (1966).

A Pocket Popper

Edited by
David Miller

Fontana Press

First published in Great Britain
by Fontana Paperbacks 1983
Second impression, in Fontana Press, September 1987

Fontana Press is an imprint of
Fontana Paperbacks, part of
the Collins Publishing Group

Made and printed in Great Britain by
William Collins Sons & Co. Ltd, Glasgow

Contents

Editor's Introduction 9

Part I Theory of Knowledge

1 The Beginnings of Rationalism (1958) 25
2 The Defence of Rationalism (1945) 33
3 Knowledge without Authority (1960) 46
4 Knowledge: Subjective versus Objective (1967) 58
5 Evolutionary Epistemology (1973) 78
6 Two Kinds of Definitions (1945) 87
7 The Problem of Induction (1953, 1974) 101
8 The Problem of Demarcation (1974) 118

Part II Philosophy of Science

9 Scientific Method (1934) 133
10 Falsificationism versus Conventionalism (1934) 143
11 The Empirical Basis (1934) 152
12 The Aim of Science (1957) 162
13 The Growth of Scientific Knowledge (1960) 171
14 Truth and Approximation to Truth (1960) 181
15 Propensities, Probabilities, and the Quantum Theory (1957) 199

Part III Metaphysics

16 Metaphysics and Criticizability (1958) 209
17 Realism (1970) 220
18 Cosmology and Change (1958) 226

19 Natural Selection and Its Scientific Status (1977) 239
20 Indeterminism and Human Freedom (1965) 247
21 The Mind-Body Problem (1977) 265
22 The Self (1977) 276

Part IV Social Philosophy

23 Historicism (1936) 289
24 Piecemeal Social Engineering (1944) 304
25 The Paradoxes of Sovereignty (1945) 319
26 Marx's Theory of the State (1945) 326
27 Individualism versus Collectivism (1945) 338
28 The Autonomy of Sociology (1945) 345
29 The Rationality Principle (1967) 357
30 Against the Sociology of Knowledge (1945) 366

Notes 379
Editorial Note, Sources, and Acknowledgements 462
Bibliography 467
Index of Names 471
Index of Subjects 476

First thesis: We know a great deal. And we know not only many details of doubtful intellectual interest but also things which are of considerable practical significance and, what is even more important, which provide us with deep theoretical insight, and with a surprising understanding of the world.

Second thesis: Our ignorance is sobering and boundless. Indeed, it is precisely the staggering progress of the natural sciences (to which my first thesis alludes) which constantly opens our eyes anew to our ignorance, even in the field of the natural sciences themselves. This gives a new twist to the Socratic idea of ignorance. With each step forward, with each problem which we solve, we not only discover new and unsolved problems, but we also discover that where we believed that we were standing on firm and safe ground, all things are, in truth, insecure and in a state of flux.

K.R. POPPER

Editor's Introduction

We all make mistakes; to err is not distinctively human. But although many other living things, animals and even plants, do have a partial ability to anticipate some of their mistakes, to recognize them and even to learn from them, only human beings, it seems, actively assert themselves in this direction. Rather than wait for errors to reveal themselves, perhaps with disastrous consequences, we consciously and deliberately seek them out: we put our ideas and inventions to the test, we probe critically, we scrap what we find to be wrong and try again. Mingled with this critical attitude there is admittedly a distinctive human weakness: the feeling that we should be ashamed of our mistakes, and should regret making them, since they must be the result of our incompetence or our lack of mature insight. Yet such qualms are out of place and need to be firmly quashed, for there is no way known of systematically avoiding error; no way known, in particular, of avoiding it in our exploration of the unknown. Thus a reluctance to make mistakes typically degenerates into a wariness of new ideas, into a distaste for any kind of bold initiative. If we are in earnest to discover what the world is like, we must be fully prepared to correct mistakes; but if we are to correct them, we must be fully prepared to commit them first.

What ought to disturb us are not mistakes in general, but only those of them that we are powerless to correct. Indeed, we are plainly entitled to exclude from serious consideration proposals that we cannot criticize and therefore cannot put right. For once we embark on the venture of investigating the world and our involvement in it, we cannot shrink from scrutinizing every move we make and abandoning those that turn out to be mistaken. And if this is to work, we must from the start disallow ideas that cannot, if mistaken, be corrected. We can be indulgent towards the occurrence of errors; indeed, we must be, for whatever we do we shall not dodge them all. But incorrigible, irrevocable, or uncontrollable errors we cannot afford to commit. It is the perpetuation of errors that interferes with our understanding; and it is this, rather than their perpetration, that we must exert ourselves determinedly to avert.

The theme of the preceding remarks, that in the realm of errors cure is more important than prevention, forms the gist of the philosophy of human knowledge known as critical rationalism. This philosophy, though foreshadowed in a few particulars by a few earlier thinkers; for example by Hume, Kant, Whewell, and Peirce, has been elaborated almost exclusively in the last half century by Sir Karl Popper and by a small number of his students and followers. Its emphasis, unlike that of previous philosophies, is on guesswork as the way knowledge grows, and on criticism as the way it is controlled. Popper himself describes it by saying that knowledge evolves through a sequence of conjectures and refutations, of tentative solutions to problems, checked by searching and uncompromising tests. There is little place in critical rationalism for the preoccupying worries of traditional philosophy: whether our knowledge is securely founded, and if it is, how it is. This is not only because, in the eyes of critical rationalism, our knowledge is not securely founded, being freely aired rather than staidly grounded, but because nothing on earth would be gained if it were. What matters to a critical rationalist is whether the conjectures under debate are right, not whether there are reasons to suppose that they are. If a conjecture weathers all the objections we can raise against it, then there is no reason to suppose that it is not right. Nor, says the critical rationalist, is there any reason not to suppose that it is right: we may suppose what we like if there is no reason to think that it is wrong. And being right, as Popper was perhaps the first fully to appreciate (amazing as that may sound), is quite good enough; it is good enough both for abstract speculation about the universe we live in and for the practical business of living in that universe. Rarely, of course, do we know that we are right; but we don't need to know it if we are.

Arguments, according to critical rationalism, are always negative; they are always critical arguments, used only and needed only to unseat conjectures that have been earlier surmised. From this consideration follow several other propositions that are at the centre of Popper's philosophy. One, noted already, is that our conjectures have to be criticizable if they are to deserve to be entertained; for critical argument is the sole control that we have over our meditations and our dreams. Moreover, if we confine our arguments to those that turn on empirical facts, then our conjectures must be further restricted to those that are empirically falsifiable: to those that can clash, if the facts fall out that way, with the facts of experience. This is Popper's criterion of demarcation of empirical science from metaphysics (and from pseudoscience). But if our scientific conjectures, most of which say nothing about personal experience, though they do have implications for our common or shared experience, can conflict with the facts, then these facts can hardly be our personal inventions. Such is the simplicity of Popper's commonsense realism – a doctrine, one might add, against which no recognizably sensible argument has ever been adduced. The facts do not reside in our minds. Neither can our conjectures wholly do so if we are to subject them to any criticism: for we cannot chew over what we have already swallowed, or call into question what we have made our own. It is obvious that ideas are conceived in our minds, but their eventual linguistic formulation delivers them into a wider and a hostile world. Our scientific knowledge, that is to say, is not a variety of belief, a dispositional state of the human organism, but more like a separate human organ evolving under the pressure of unremitting criticism. By no means all human knowledge is like this, for we are animals as well as being humans, but critical rationalism will not begin to work if we cannot in some such manner distance ourselves from some of our unspoken preconceptions. Nor will it get far, least of all at the scientific level, unless we have a considerable ability to meddle effectively in the working of the world: if we cannot manipulate some physical bodies at will, we shall not be able to execute the experimental tests with which we wish to challenge our conjectures. So indeterminism, as much as realism and objectivism, is a necessary condition for the proper functioning of the critical method. To conclude this select list of the fellowship of critical rationalism, we may remark the paramount importance in the political arena of the principle of not running the risk of irrevocable and uncontrollable mistakes. It means that democratic political institutions must be concerned primarily with the safeguarding of freedom, especially the freedom to safeguard freedom, and thus with the prevention of irremovable tyranny. Likewise our social policy should direct itself chiefly at the remedying of identifiable social ills, in a way that minimizes, as far as possible, the danger of supplanting them with less easily eradicable injustices. A piecemeal approach to social reform is thus the straightforward application of critical rationalism to the discontents of social life. Popper prescribes revolutionary thinking in science because its products, imaginative new theories, are easily relinquished if they are mistaken. It is for exactly the same reason that he proscribes revolutionary activity in society. For its consequences, which are rarely possible to foresee, are almost always altogether impossible to overcome.

These simple and beautiful ideas, along with many others, are discussed, developed, and defended in the thirty selections from Popper's abundant writings that comprise the text of this book. Though anxious to display here their admirable and thoroughgoing unity I am not wanting to suggest that they were all thought up, let alone thought through, at one instant. Popper was in fact exercised at first by the problem of demarcation, the problem of discriminating between the achievements of physics and the other natural sciences on the one hand and the mere pretensions to scientific standing characteristic of psychoanalysis, Marxism, and astrology on the other. In recognizing that it was the falsifiability of scientific hypotheses that mattered, and still more the devotion of scientists to the task of exposing their hypotheses to the hazard of falsification, Popper sized up shrewdly the decisive role of negative arguments within science, and the sheer dispensability of arguments and experiments that presumed to lend hypotheses anything like positive support. Thus he came to solve Hume's problem of induction, one of the most vexatious enigmas of modern philosophy and one of the few, in my opinion, that has been unerringly untangled. These problems, of induction and demarcation, provided the subject matter of Popper's first book, *The Two Fundamental Problems of the Theory of Knowledge*, written in 1930-2 and still not translated into English. But at that time, as he admits, he 'wrongly identified the limits of science with those of arguability' (note 4 to selection 17). Several years were to elapse before this unduly modest assessment of the sovereignty of rational argument was to be strengthened and stiffened into an advocacy of the critical approach throughout.

Popper's enthusiasm for realism and for objectivism is apparent already in *The Logic of Scientific Discovery*, published in 1934, but these doctrines, especially the latter, have been expounded in depth only since the mid-1960s. The exploitation of his discoveries about scientific method in the analysis of social phenomena was immediate, of course, given his early unmasking of the pseudo-scientific swank of much Marxist talk; but a thorough study, culminating in the publication at the end of the war of *The Poverty of Historicism* and *The Open Society and Its Enemies*, was triggered only by the invasion of Austria in 1938. From these books grew a powerful series of arguments against determinism, against materialism, and against all similar attempts to belittle the ability of human beings to work, however hesitantly and unspectacularly, for the betterment of their individual condition in the world. It is one of the sublimest aspects of Popper's philosophy that, austerely rigorous though it is in its invocation of logical principles, it nonetheless exudes a deep sense of understanding of human imperfection. By insisting that the answer to our ignorance and to our fallibility lies not in pretending to know more than we do, or to know it more surely, but only in our own resolute efforts to improve things, Popper succeeds in restoring to human beings some of the dignity and the self-respect of which modern philosophy has sometimes seemed all too disposed to dispossess them.

An extensive and illuminating account of the path taken by Popper's thought from early youth until about 1970, of which the above is the merest glimpse, is to be found in his intellectual autobiography, *Unended Quest*. Popper was born in Vienna in 1902 into a prosperous and cultivated family: his father was a successful and scholarly lawyer, his mother a talented musician; and music has indeed been a commanding influence throughout his life. For nearly ten years after the First World War he was a student at the University of Vienna, reading mathematics and physics, psychology and philosophy; he received his doctorate in 1928 and in the next year qualified as a secondary school teacher in mathematics and physics. In 1934 the publication of *The Logic of Scientific Discovery* launched Popper's career as a philosopher. In December 1936 he accepted a lectureship at Canterbury College, Christchurch, New Zealand, and in January he and his wife left Austria for the antipodes. They remained there for the duration of the Second World War, returning to England after Popper's appointment in 1945 to a readership at the London School of Economics and Political Science. In the succeeding twenty three years as Professor of Logic and Scientific Method there he had a memorable impact on whole generations of students, who in his lectures and seminars were invited to share his own inextinguishable fascination with the open universe and the unlocking of its secrets. Popper retired in 1969; and, much honoured, he and his wife have continued to live modestly and unassumingly, as hardworking as ever, at Fallowfield, their home in Buckinghamshire. 'I do not think', Popper writes in *Unended Quest* (p.125), 'that I have had an unhappy hour as a philosopher since we returned to England.' For few philosophers has the thirst for understanding been so refreshingly unquenched.

The contents of the present book have not been arranged in a historical order. Rather, the book is divided into four parts, containing selections from Popper's writings on respectively the theory of knowledge, philosophy of science, metaphysics, and social philosophy, and the emphasis throughout is on the critical method and the pivotal part it plays in enhancing our knowledge of the world. Undeniably the book begins and ends in this vein. The first selection traces back to the first philosophers, the Milesian school of Thales, Anaximander, and Anaximenes, the rational attitude that Popper so warmly esteems, while the second defends a critical form of rationalism both from a logical and from a moral perspective. In this selection Popper acknowledges 'a certain priority of irrationalism' (p.36) in the assumption of the rationalist position itself, but in the light of his later work this seems a needlessly generous concession for him to make. In opting for the critical method we are not, to be sure, merely complying with the dictates of reason; but nor are we infringing them, and it is that that really counts. Critical rationalism, as W.W. Bartley has urged, is itself amenable to critical dissection. It is therefore a fully self-consistent position and one that by its own standards may rationally be adopted.

In selection 3 Popper strikes at the empiricist prejudice that every item of our knowledge derives from some person's sense experience. This presumption is quite sensationally amiss, in that almost all the knowledge we acquire we acquire through guessing, and what we learn from experience is only how wayward many of our guesses unfortunately are. Here it is stated very clearly that what matters is what we do with a hypothesis after it has been formulated; what prompted it, or what its pedigree is like, has no bearing on whether it is worth persevering with. This point is taken further in the next two selections, where our knowledge and its development are set firmly in a biological context. In selection 4 Popper concentrates on the impersonal status of that portion of our knowledge that has achieved linguistic expression; much of what we know, he suggests, not only is no longer part of us, it has emigrated to a world, called neutrally world 3, with its own problems and mysteries. In selection 5 this world 3 of objective knowledge is approached in a frankly Darwinian spirit; likened not metaphorically to a population of organisms, but almost literally to an astonishingly rapidly evolved human organ; and our objective knowledge is compared to that perhaps much greater residue of knowledge that is incorporated at the genetic and behavioural levels. New hypotheses, for instance, are seen as akin to chromosomal variants, and their criticism is seen as an unnaturally savage variation on Darwinian natural selection. A somewhat contrasting topic is broached in the next extract: that of the function, if any, performed by definitions in the organization of our knowledge. Here Popper forthrightly assails the undeservedly widespread dogma that definitions, and the precision fondly imagined to spring from them, are essential to any logical articulation of our thoughts, and even to plain clear thinking. His standpoint here is once more quite close to the core of critical rationalism, through its denial that there is any one correct place from which the exploration of the world should begin. Neither sensualistic observations nor essentialistic definitions furnish a dependable base from which an expedition may be confidently set in train.

The final two selections of Part I are devoted to the problems of induction and demarcation. Whereas on other issues I have inclined to rely on Popper's earlier writings, in these two cases I have taken excerpts from a relatively recent work, where many of the objections lodged against Popper's solutions to these problems are examined and responded to in detail. The problems themselves and their solutions are explained in these two selections with such elemental clarity that a further elucidation of them at this point is quite uncalled for.

In Part II of the book are treated a number of topics more specifically related to scientific knowledge, as well as some mildly technical matters involving truth, approximation to truth, content, and probability. The first three selections, 9-11, are from Popper's classic work, *The Logic of Scientific Discovery*; here are elaborated some of the methodological principles of falsificationism, here also are raised some pertinent questions concerning this method. For example, it is asked whether falsificationism itself is empirically falsifiable; whether it might be empty, given that a looming falsification can always be sidestepped; and whether the testing procedure it recommends, if dischargeable at all, has to fall back on test statements that are themselves incontestable. The answer given to each question is negative. Scientific method is presented as a store of methodological rules that we decide to conform to in the interests of what we take as the aim of science, not a collection of theses to be tested by an inspection of scientific behaviour; although falsifications can indeed always be scotched, we decide in advance not to avail ourselves of such manoeuvres; and included among the rules of method are rules for the acceptance of test statements as the result of a calculated, but reversible, decision to stop testing.

In selections 12 and 13 the aim of science is identified as one of providing increasingly deep and encompassing theoretical explanations, more and more adequate solutions to the problems that science itself generates. These desiderata of depth and content are shown to be starkly at odds with the pursuit of certainty or probability for our theories, and to be realizable only by something like the falsificationist programme. In the next selection truth is, innocuously enough one would think, offered as a further ingredient of what we want from science; and it is suggested that the best we can realistically hope for is to approach the truth gradually along a chain of better and better approximations. Tarski's theory of truth, and Popper's own unsuccessful stab at defining how it may be approximated, are also briefly sketched. Anyone who has difficulty in understanding why the problem of truth, which now seems so simple, was once so bewildering should at least look at Popper's notes on the liar and related paradoxes in selection 2; anyone who hopes that the problem of approximation to truth will be as magisterially resolved should consult the further literature indicated in note 11 to selection 14.

The final selection of Part II is a brief and rather condensed report on Popper's famous propensity interpretation of the singular probabilities that arise in modern physical theories, most notably in quantum mechanics. A subjectivistic reading, as measures of our ignorance, is usually imposed on these probabilities, but here Popper undertakes to understand them as quite objective constituents of the physical world. The selection concludes with the formulation of an unabashedly metaphysical hypothesis concerning these propensities and their operation throughout the natural order.

Part III of the book places before the reader a variety of metaphysical speculations, and proceeds to illustrate how such abstruse hypotheses can be critically evaluated. The significance of criticizability itself is dwelt on in selection 16, where one or two decidedly morose results of metaphysical excogitation are included among the examples of philosophical theories that are crippled when confronted with responsible criticism. Thereafter the metaphysical doctrines whose merits are appraised are rather more reputable. First, in selection 17, there is realism, a view so irredeemably interwoven with common sense as to set perhaps a minimum philosophical qualification for sanity. This is followed, in selection 18, by a charming historical essay on the engagement of the early Greek cosmologists with the problem of change, the problem of how a thing can change and at the same time remain the thing that has changed. It is perhaps worth remarking that although the existence of everyday objects is unquestionably a component of the commonsense realism that Popper subscribes to, no kind of permanence need be imputed to these objects, or to any others. I say this because, almost from the start, solutions to the problem of change have tried to forge a distinction between appearance, which is what changes, and reality, which is what stays the same; that this distinction would be a genuine forgery becomes all too apparent once we realize that illusions, however illusive they may be, are not for that reason not real. Appearance is a part of reality, not apart from it.

The next selection, selection 19, raises the question of whether Darwin's hypothesis of natural selection, of the survival of the fittest, properly belongs to science, or whether, being nearly tautological, it is a piece of metaphysics – albeit one that forms the kernel of a programme to guide scientific research, as Popper himself once contended. Popper acknowledges here that his previous assessment of the force of the hypothesis of natural selection was unkind, and he modifies it. Neither this hypothesis, nor evolutionary theory itself, is to be confounded with something that blatantly is without empirical content, the evolutionary philosophy of laws of progress criticized in selection 23. In selection 20 Popper tackles with some gusto the thorny problems of determinism in its various guises, in particular the problem of how to find room for human freedom between the extremes of rigid predetermination and utter chance. It is in this paper that Popper first sharply posed the problem, which he handsomely names after A.H.Compton, of how abstract world 3 entities can, without violating physical laws, have any physical influence on the physical world. Manifestly our theories do affect nature in some way; that railways and refrigerators, or copies of *Conjectures and Refutations*, have arrived in the world independently of the scientific and philosophical hypotheses they embody is itself a hypothesis that taxes the imagination beyond reason. Popper sees in this causal efficacy of world 3 inhabitants, an efficacy obviously mediated by human thinking, a key to the problems of the interrelation of mind and body, and of the unity of the self. The self, he tentatively suggests, emerges through interaction between the human animal and human language, and is sustained throughout its existence by those world 3 items with which it manages to remain in intellectual contact. These difficult questions are entered upon, with no pretence of providing complete or wholly satisfying answers, in selections 21 and 22.

The final part of the book, Part IV, is given over exclusively to problems of social and political philosophy, especially problems arising from the uneasy relationship of the individual subject to the state. Although Popper is unequivocally on the side of individual citizens in their ceaseless campaign not to be intimidated into submission and subservience, the idea that they would profit from the dismantling of the state is firmly resisted. On the contrary, it may be only the state that is able to shield them from being bullied by their neighbours, which may be just about as awful as being cowed by the state itself. This shows how vital it is that the state be kept in hand, and under some direction from the people for whom it is constituted. The state, that is, exists solely in the interests of its subjects; and it is definitely in their interests that it does exist. The actuality of human society is of even profounder significance, as Marx clearly perceived, for we would not be human beings at all if the social orchestration of our lives were to be silenced. If, as suggested in selection 22, our selves come into being through the medium of language, then the social origins of our individuality and of our humanity become quite plain; for quite plainly language is a social phenomenon. So even if political institutions might be purged from human life, social institutions assuredly could not be. But this must not be misinterpreted to mean that they are activated other than through the agency of individual humans; like the denizens of world 3 they possess the capacity to intercede in the world, but its realization is in our gift. It is we who run our institutions. Regrettably, this is often done quite unskilfully, and if we have any sense we will constantly be on the alert for unforeseen pitfalls. It is one of the underused truisms of Popper's social philosophy that our plans virtually always do slip up somewhere, not because of any satanic interference, but simply because we seldom know enough, or even very much, about how things will work out.

Part IV opens with a lengthy exposition and criticism of the methodological doctrine that Popper dubs historicism. According to this doctrine it is the duty of the social sciences to study society in a historical manner, as an entity that unfurls as time glides by: to contemplate it in its entirety and to foretell its destiny. Historicists frequently liken society to an organism, or to a biological species, and its career to the evolutionary process, but as selection 23 makes evident, even in biology there is no law of evolutionary unfolding; Darwin's hypothesis of natural selection, in particular, must not be misrepresented as such a law. In selection 24 Popper goes on to rebut some of the practical repercussions of the historicist mythology, in particular the holistic fallacy that the management of society can be done only on the grand scale; that it is the whole of society that we must endeavour to reshape. Against this he proposes that the main business of social engineering must be the elimination of specific sources of misery. It is not only that these are relatively easily picked out; in addition, the courses of action appropriate to their clearance can quite often be monitored with some degree of success.

Selection 25 shows that the question of who should rule, which Plato first marked out as fundamental for political theory, inevitably leads to paradoxical answers; it must be disregarded therefore and replaced by the question of how tyrants are to be dismissed before they do too much damage, and in particular before they make their own removal impossible without force. Once again, the accent is on setting things right, not on not getting them wrong. For one of the few lessons that we must not fail to learn from history is that few rulers decline to misuse the powers with which we entrust them. Nevertheless, it does seem to be possible to set up political institutions that offer some protection against oppression; 'democracy', for Popper, is just a label for such institutions. Our only hope, he makes clear in selection 26, where he combats Marx's aspersions on the efficacy of political power in the theatre of economic forces, is in founding and fostering democratic institutions, despite the incursions they make, for the sake of individual liberty, upon individual liberty. It must be repeated that the state, and its institutions, exist for the sake of the individual; and our rulers remain trustees of our individual liberty, however much they may betray that trust. Plato's contrary opinion, that individuals must sacrifice themselves entirely to the common interest, and his suggestion that this is true altruism or selflessness, are demolished in selection 27. The confusion of individualism with selfishness, of which Plato took full advantage, has since ancient times been an invaluable boon to totalitarian ways of thinking.

In the final three selections the inextricable entwinement of the individual with society is discussed still further. Selection 28 endorses Marx's judgement that the individual is always constrained by social laws, and that social transactions cannot be reduced to the laws of individual psychology. Although the individual is the one who acts, individuals interact. The laws governing these interactions cannot be spun out in psychological terms any more than the laws of gravitational interaction can be accounted for by the intrinsic or essential properties of Newtonian corpuscles (see note 3 to selection 12). Popper proposes that social and historical explanations must have recourse to what he calls situational logic. This topic is continued in selection 29, where he defends the view that the principle that agents act adequately to the situation as they see it is, though false, a principle that needs to be accommodated in every social explanation. Finally, in selection 30, we come to the social aspects of science. The objectivity of science, Popper observes, and even its rationality, are in the hands not of individual scientists alone, but of scientists in a scientific community. Criticism, especially, is irremediably social in character, since we are ordinarily as blind to our own failings as we are attentive to those of others. Social interaction is therefore as crucial to the prosperity of critical rationalism as are the individual qualities of imagination, resourcefulness, courage, determination, and willingness to learn. The flourishing of Western cosmology, philosophy, and science, as chronicled in the first selection, was the direct result of the creation of a critical tradition.

There is, it need hardly be said, more in the selections in this book than I have been able to mention here; and there is far more in Popper's writings than I have been able to pack into 440 pages. This absentee bonanza includes not only a wealth of historical commentary on Plato, on Marx, and on the mind-body problem, for instance, and of technical contributions to logic, probability theory, and quantum theory, here barely touched on; but also a great number of variations and amplifications on the dominant themes here represented, as well as on related motifs of epistemology, philosophy of science, metaphysics, and social philosophy. It is therefore presumably admissible in winding up this introduction to an introduction to Popper's thought to draw explicit attention to his principal publications, listed in the bibliography on pp.467f. below, and also to several books where his ideas are expounded and examined; to commend their further study, and to express a hope for their continued criticism and clarification. Critical rationalism may perhaps not be quite right; but neither, after all, may it be quite wrong. It would be nice to know.

In conclusion I am delighted to have the opportunity to record my thanks to Bill Bartley, Jack Birner, Larry Briskman, Roger James, Bryan Magee, Anthony O'Hear, and Tom Settle, who unsparingly criticized some of my more raw outlines for the book, made concrete suggestions concerning what I could not intelligently leave out, advised me on the tricky problem of what to name it, and in other ways ensured that the book is very much better than it otherwise might have been. No one but myself is to blame for the final outcome. To Briskman I am especially grateful, since he has for several years now read drafts of almost everything I have written, and has been unfaltering in his willingness to overwhelm me with detailed and hardheaded criticism. As documented in the editorial note at the end of the book, I owe thanks also to Popper's publishers for consenting to the republication of material of which they have custody. But most of all I am indebted to Karl and Hennie Popper, who have in a number of ways helped to lighten my editorial labours and have generously encouraged this attempt to place a book of selections before the general public. Popper also wrote the stuff, and for that I can't thank him enough.

David Miller
22 September 1982

Part I Theory of Knowledge

1 The Beginnings of Rationalism (1958)

I Back to the Presocratics

'Back to Methuselah' was a progressive programme, compared with 'Back to Thales' or 'Back to Anaximander': what Shaw offered us was an improved expectation of life – something that was in the air, at any rate when he wrote it. I have nothing to offer you, I am afraid, that is in the air today; for what I want to return to is the simple straightforward *rationality* of the Presocratics. Wherein does this much discussed 'rationality' of the Presocratics lie? The simplicity and boldness of their questions is part of it, but my thesis is that the decisive point is the critical attitude which, as I shall try to show, was first developed in the Ionian School.

The questions which the Presocratics tried to answer were primarily cosmological questions, but there were also questions of the theory of knowledge. It is my belief that philosophy must return to cosmology and to a simple theory of knowledge. There is at least one philosophical problem in which all thinking men are interested: the problem of understanding the world in which we live; and thus ourselves (who are part of that world) and our knowledge of it. All science is cosmology, I believe, and for me the interest of philosophy, no less than of science, lies solely in its bold attempt to add to our knowledge of the world, and to the theory of our knowledge of the world. I am interested in Wittgenstein, for example, not because of his linguistic philosophy, but because his *Tractatus* was a cosmological treatise (although a crude one), and because his theory of knowledge was closely linked with his cosmology.

For me, both philosophy and science lose all their attraction when they give up that pursuit – when they become specialisms and cease to see, and to wonder at, the riddles of our world. Specialization may be a great temptation for the scientist. For the philosopher it is the mortal sin.

II The Tradition of Critical Discussion

The early history of Greek philosophy, especially the history from Thales to Plato, is a splendid story. It is almost too good to be true. In every generation we find at least one new philosophy, one new cosmology of staggering originality and depth. How was this possible? Of course one cannot explain originality and genius. But one can try to throw some light on them. What was the secret of the ancients? I suggest that it was a *tradition – the tradition of critical discussion*.

I will try to put the problem more sharply. In all or almost all civilizations we find something like religious and cosmological teaching, and in many societies we find schools. Now schools, especially primitive schools, all have, it appears, a characteristic structure and function. Far from being places of critical discussion they make it their task to impart a definite doctrine, and to preserve it, pure and unchanged. It is the task of a school to hand on the tradition, the doctrine of its founder, its first master, to the next generation, and to this end the most important thing is to keep the doctrine inviolate. A school of this kind never admits a new idea. New ideas are heresies, and lead to schisms; should a member of the school try to change the doctrine, then he is expelled as a heretic. But the heretic claims, as a rule, that his is the true doctrine of the founder. Thus not even the inventor admits that he has introduced an invention; he believes, rather, that he is returning to the true orthodoxy which has somehow been perverted.

In this way all changes of doctrine – if any – are surreptitious changes. They are all presented as restatements of the true sayings of the master, of his own words, his own meaning, his own intentions.

It is clear that in a school of this kind we cannot expect to find a history of ideas, or even the material for such a history. For new ideas are not admitted to be new. Everything is ascribed to the master. All we might reconstruct is a history of schisms, and perhaps a history of the defence of certain doctrines against the heretics.

There cannot, of course, be any rational discussion in a school of this kind. There may be arguments against dissenters and heretics, or against some competing schools. But in the main it is with assertion and dogma and condemnation rather than argument that the doctrine is defended.

The great example of a school of this kind among the Greek philosophical schools is the Italian school founded by Pythagoras. Compared with the Ionian school, or with that of Elea, it had the character of a religious order, with a characteristic way of life and a secret doctrine. The story that a member, Hippasus of Metapontum, was drowned at sea because he revealed the secret of the irrationality of certain square roots, is characteristic of the atmosphere surrounding the Pythagorean school, whether or not there is any truth in this story.

But among Greek philosophic schools the early Pythagoreans were an exception. Leaving them aside, we could say that the character of Greek philosophy, and of the philosophical schools, is strikingly different from the dogmatic type of school here described. [In selection 18] I show this by an example: *the story of the problem of change is the story of a critical debate, of a rational discussion*. New ideas are propounded as such, and arise as the result of open criticism. There are few, if any, surreptitious changes. Instead of anonymity we find a history of ideas and of their originators.

Here is a unique phenomenon, and it is closely connected with the astonishing freedom and creativeness of Greek philosophy. How can we explain this phenomenon? *What we have to explain is the rise of a tradition*. It is a tradition that allows or encourages critical discussions between various schools and, more surprisingly still, within one and the same school. For nowhere outside the Pythagorean school do we find a school devoted to the preservation of a doctrine. Instead we find changes, new ideas, modifications, and outright criticism of the master.

(In Parmenides we even find, at an early date, a most remarkable phenomenon – that of a philosopher who propounds *two* doctrines, one which he says is true, and one which he himself describes as false. Yet he makes the false doctrine not simply an object of condemnation or of criticism; rather he presents it as the best possible account of the delusive opinion of mortal men, and of the world of mere appearance – the best account which a mortal man can give.)

How and where was this critical tradition founded? This is a problem deserving serious thought. This much is certain: Xenophanes who brought the Ionian tradition to Elea was fully conscious of the fact that his own teaching was purely conjectural, and that others might come who would know better. I shall come back to this point in section III below.

If we look for the first signs of this new critical attitude, this new freedom of thought, we are led to Anaximander's criticism of Thales. [See selection 18 below.] Here is a most striking fact: Anaximander criticizes his master and kinsman, one of the Seven Sages, the founder of the Ionian school. He was, according to tradition, only about fourteen years younger than Thales, and he must have developed his criticism and his new ideas while his master was alive. (They seem to have died within a few years of each other.) But there is no trace in the sources of a story of dissent, of any quarrel, or of any schism.

This suggests, I think, that it was Thales who founded the new tradition of freedom – based upon a new relation between master and pupil – and who thus created a new type of school, utterly different from the Pythagorean school. He seems to have been able to tolerate criticism. And what is more, he seems to have created the tradition that one ought to tolerate criticism.

Yet I like to think that he did even more than this. I can hardly imagine a relationship between master and pupil in which the master merely tolerates criticism without actively encouraging it. It does not seem to me possible that a pupil who is being trained in the dogmatic attitude would ever dare to criticize the dogma (least of all that of a famous sage) and to voice his criticism. And it seems to me an easier and simpler explanation to assume that the master encouraged a critical attitude – possibly not from the outset, but only after he was struck by the pertinence of some questions asked, without any critical intention, by the pupil.

However this may be, the conjecture that Thales actively encouraged criticism in his pupils would explain the fact that the critical attitude towards the master's doctrine became part of the

Ionian school tradition. I like to think that Thales was the first teacher who said to his pupils: 'This is how I see things – how I believe that things are. Try to improve upon my teaching.' (Those who believe that it is 'unhistorical' to attribute this undogmatic attitude to Thales may again be reminded of the fact that only two generations later we find a similar attitude consciously and clearly formulated in the fragments of Xenophanes.) At any rate, there is the historical fact that the Ionian school was the first in which pupils criticized their masters, in one generation after the other. There can be little doubt that the Greek tradition of philosophical criticism had its main source in Ionia.

It was a momentous innovation. It meant a break with the dogmatic tradition which permits only *one* school doctrine, and the introduction in its place of a tradition that admits a *plurality* of doctrines which all try to approach the truth by means of critical discussion.

It thus leads, almost by necessity, to the realization that our attempts to see and to find the truth are not final, but open to improvement; that our knowledge, our doctrine, is conjectural; that it consists of guesses, of hypotheses, rather than of final and certain truths; and that criticism and critical discussion are our only means of getting nearer to the truth. It thus leads to the tradition of bold conjectures and of free criticism, the tradition which created the rational or scientific attitude, and with it our Western civilization, the only civilization which is based upon science (though of course not upon science alone).

In this rationalist tradition bold changes of doctrine are not forbidden. On the contrary, innovation is encouraged, and is regarded as success, as improvement, if it is based on the result of a critical discussion of its predecessors. The very boldness of an innovation is admired; for it can be controlled by the severity of its critical examination. This is why changes of doctrine, far from being made surreptitiously, are traditionally handed down together with the older doctrines and the names of the innovators. And the material for a history of ideas becomes part of the school tradition.

To my knowledge the critical or rationalist tradition was invented only once. It was lost after two or three centuries, perhaps owing to the rise of the Aristotelian doctrine of *epistēmē*, of certain and demonstrable knowledge (a development of the Eleatic and Heraclitean distinction between certain truth and mere guesswork). It was rediscovered and consciously revived in the Renaissance, especially by Galileo Galilei.

III Critical Rationalism

I now come to my most central contention. It is this. The rationalist tradition, the tradition of critical discussion, represents the only practicable way of expanding our knowledge – conjectural or hypothetical knowledge, of course. There is no other way. More especially, there is no way that starts from observation or experiment. In the development of science observations and experiments play only the role of critical arguments. And they play this role alongside other, non-observational arguments. It is an important role; but the significance of observations and experiments depends *entirely* upon the question whether or not they may be used to *criticize theories*.

According to the theory of knowledge here outlined there are in the main only two ways in which theories may be superior to others: they may explain more; and they may be better tested – that is, they may be more fully and more critically discussed, in the light of all we know, of all the objections we can think of, and especially also in the light of observational or experimental tests which were designed with the aim of criticizing the theory.

There is only one element of rationality in our attempts to know the world: it is the critical examination of our theories. These theories themselves are guesswork. We do not know, we only guess. If you ask me, 'How do you know?' my reply would be, 'I don't; I only propose a guess. If you are interested in my problem, I shall be most happy if you criticize my guess, and if you offer counterproposals, I in turn will try to criticize them.'

This, I believe, is the true theory of knowledge (which I wish to submit for your criticism): the true description of a practice which arose in Ionia and which is incorporated in modern science (though there are many scientists who still believe in the Baconian myth of induction): the theory that knowledge proceeds by way of *conjectures and refutations*.

Two of the greatest men who clearly saw that there was no such thing as an inductive procedure, and who clearly understood what I regard as the true theory of knowledge, were Galileo and Einstein. Yet the ancients also knew it. Incredible as it sounds, we find a clear recognition and formulation of this theory of rational knowledge almost immediately after the practice of critical discussion had begun. Our oldest extant fragments in this field are those of Xenophanes. I will present here five of them in an order that suggests that it was the boldness of his attack and the gravity of his problems which made him conscious of the fact that all our knowledge was guesswork, yet that we may nevertheless, by searching for that knowledge 'which is the better', find it in the course of time. Here are the five fragments from Xenophanes's writings.

The Ethiops say that their gods are flat-nosed and black
While the Thracians say that theirs have blue eyes and red hair.

Yet if cattle or horses or lions had hands and could draw
And could sculpture like men, then the horses would draw their gods
Like horses, and cattle like cattle, and each would then shape
Bodies of gods in the likeness, each kind, of its own.

The gods did not reveal, from the beginning,
All things to us; but in the course of time,
Through seeking, men find that which is the better. . . .

These things are, we conjecture, like the truth.

But as for certain truth, no man has known it,
Nor will he know it; neither of the gods,
Nor yet of all the things of which I speak.
And even if by chance he were to utter
The final truth, he would himself not know it:
For all is but a woven web of guesses.

To show that Xenophanes was not alone I may also repeat here two of Heraclitus's sayings which I have quoted before in a different context. Both express the conjectural character of human knowledge, and the second refers to its daring, to the need to anticipate boldly what we do not know.

> It is not in the nature or character of man to possess true knowledge, though it is in the divine nature. . . . He who does not expect the unexpected will not detect it: for him it will remain undetectable, and unapproachable.

My last quotation is a very famous one from Democritus:

> But in fact, nothing do we know from having seen it; for the truth is hidden in the deep.

This is how the critical attitude of the Presocratics foreshadowed, and prepared for, the ethical rationalism of Socrates: his belief that the search for truth through critical discussion was a way of life – the best he knew.[1]

2 The Defence of Rationalism (1945)

I

The issue between rationalism and irrationalism is of long standing. Although Greek philosophy undoubtedly started off as a rationalist undertaking, there were streaks of mysticism even in its first beginnings. It is the yearning for the lost unity and shelter of tribalism which expresses itself in these mystical elements within a fundamentally rational approach.[1] An open conflict between rationalism and irrationalism broke out for the first time in the Middle Ages, as the opposition between scholasticism and mysticism. In the seventeenth, eighteenth, and nineteenth centuries, when the tide of rationalism, of intellectualism, and of 'materialism' was rising, irrationalists had to pay some attention to it, to argue against it; and by exhibiting its limitations, and exposing the immodest claims and dangers of pseudorationalism (which they did not distinguish from rationalism in our sense), some of these critics, notably Burke, have earned the gratitude of all true rationalists. But the tide has now turned, and 'profoundly significant allusions ... and allegories' (as Kant puts it) have become the fashion of the day. An oracular irrationalism has established (especially with Bergson and the majority of German philosophers and intellectuals) the habit of ignoring or at best deploring the existence of such an inferior being as a rationalist. To them the rationalists – or the 'materialists', as they often say – and especially, the rationalist scientist, are the poor in spirit, pursuing soulless and largely mechanical activities, and completely unaware of the deeper problems of human destiny and of its philosophy. And the rationalists usually reciprocate by dismissing irrationalism as sheer nonsense. Never before has the break been so complete. And the break in the diplomatic relations of the philosophers proved its significance when it was followed by a break in the diplomatic relations of the states.

In this issue, I am entirely on the side of rationalism. This is so much the case that even where I feel that rationalism has gone too far I still sympathize with it, holding as I do that an excess in this direction (as long as we exclude the intellectual immodesty of Plato's pseudorationalism) is harmless indeed as compared with an excess in the other. In my opinion, the only way in which excessive rationalism is likely to prove harmful is that it tends to undermine its own position and thus to further an irrationalist reaction. It is only this danger which induces me to examine the claims of an excessive rationalism more closely and to advocate a modest and self-critical rationalism which recognizes certain limitations. Accordingly, I shall distinguish in what follows between two rationalist positions, which I label 'critical rationalism' and 'uncritical rationalism' or 'comprehensive rationalism'.

Uncritical or comprehensive rationalism can be described as the attitude of the person who says 'I am not prepared to accept anything that cannot be defended by means of argument or experience'. We can express this also in the form of the principle that any assumption which cannot be supported either by argument or by experience is to be discarded.[2] Now it is easy to see that this principle of an uncritical rationalism is inconsistent; for since it cannot, in its turn, be supported by argument or by experience, it implies that it should itself be discarded. (It is analogous to the paradox of the liar,[3] i.e. to a sentence which asserts its own falsity.) Uncritical rationalism is therefore logically untenable; and since a purely logical argument can show this, uncritical rationalism can be defeated by its own chosen weapon, argument.

This criticism may be generalized. Since all argument must proceed from assumptions, it is plainly impossible to demand that all assumptions should be based on argument. The demand raised by many philosophers that we should start with no assumption whatever and never assume anything without 'sufficient reason', and even the weaker demand that we should start with a very small set of assumptions ('categories'), are both in this form inconsistent. For they themselves rest upon the truly colossal assumption that it is possible to start without, or with only a few assumptions, and still to obtain results that are worth while. (Indeed, this principle of avoiding all presuppositions is not, as some may think, a counsel of perfection, but a form of the paradox of the liar.[4])

Now all this is a little abstract, but it may be restated in connection with the problem of rationalism in a less formal way. The rationalist attitude is characterized by the importance it attaches to argument and experience. But neither logical argument nor experience can establish the rationalist attitude; for only those who are ready to consider argument or experience, and who have therefore adopted this attitude already, will be impressed by them. That is to say, a rationalist attitude must be first adopted if any argument or experience is to be effective, and it cannot therefore be based upon argument or experience. (And this consideration is quite independent of the question whether or not there exist any convincing rational arguments which favour the adoption of the rationalist attitude.) We have to conclude from this that no rational argument will have a rational effect on a man who does not want to adopt a rational attitude. Thus a comprehensive rationalism is untenable.

But this means that whoever adopts the rationalist attitude does so because he has adopted, consciously or unconsciously, some proposal, or decision, or belief, or behaviour; an adoption which may be called 'irrational'. Whether this adoption is tentative or leads to a settled habit, we may describe it as an irrational *faith in reason*. So rationalism is necessarily far from comprehensive or self-contained. This has frequently been overlooked by rationalists who thus exposed themselves to a beating in their own field and by their own favourite weapon whenever an irrationalist took the trouble to turn it against them. And indeed it did not escape the attention of some enemies of rationalism that one can always refuse to accept arguments, either all arguments or those of a certain kind; and that such an attitude can be carried through without becoming logically inconsistent. This led them to see that the uncritical rationalist who believes that rationalism is self-contained and can be established by argument must be wrong. Irrationalism is logically superior to uncritical rationalism.

Then why not adopt irrationalism? Many who started as rationalists but were disillusioned by the discovery that a too comprehensive rationalism defeats itself have indeed practically capitulated to irrationalism. (This is what has happened to Whitehead,[5] if I am not quite mistaken.) But such panic action is entirely uncalled for. Although an uncritical and comprehensive rationalism is logically untenable, and although a comprehensive irrationalism is logically tenable, this is no reason why we should adopt the latter. For there are other tenable attitudes, notably that of critical rationalism which recognizes the fact that the fundamental rationalist attitude results from an (at least tentative) act of faith – from faith in reason. Accordingly, our choice is open. We may choose some form of irrationalism, even some radical or comprehensive form. But we are also free to choose a critical form of rationalism, one which frankly admits its origin in an irrational decision (and which, to that extent, admits a certain priority of irrationalism).

II

The choice before us is not simply an intellectual affair, or a matter of taste. It is a moral decision.[6] For the question whether we adopt some more or less radical form of irrationalism, or whether we adopt that minimum concession to irrationalism which I have termed 'critical rationalism', will deeply affect our whole attitude towards other men, and towards the problems of social life. Rationalism is closely connected with the belief in the unity of mankind. Irrationalism, which is not bound by any rules of consistency, may be combined with any kind of belief, including a belief in the brotherhood of man; but the fact that it may easily be combined with a very different belief, and especially the fact that it lends itself easily to the support of a romantic belief in the existence of an elect body, in the division of men into leaders and led, into natural masters and natural slaves, shows clearly that a moral decision is involved in the choice between it and a critical rationalism.

As I have said before (in *The Open Society and Its Enemies*, chapter 5), and now again in my analysis of the uncritical version of rationalism, arguments cannot *determine* such a fundamental moral decision. But this does not imply that our choice cannot be *helped* by any kind of argument whatever. On the contrary, whenever we are faced with a moral decision of a more abstract kind, it is most helpful to analyse carefully the consequences which are likely to result from the alternatives between which we have to choose. For only if we can visualize these consequences in a concrete and practical way, do we really know what our decision is about; otherwise we decide blindly. In order to illustrate this point, I may quote a passage from Shaw's *Saint Joan*. The speaker is the Chaplain; he has stubbornly demanded Joan's death; but when he sees her at the stake, he breaks down: 'I meant no harm. I did not know what it would be like. . . . I did not know what I was doing. . . . If I had known, I would have torn her from their hands. You dont know: you havnt seen: it is so easy to talk when you dont know. You madden yourself with words. . . . But when it is brought home to you; when you see the thing you have done; when it is blinding your eyes, stifling your nostrils, tearing your heart, then – then – O God, take away this sight from me!' There were, of course, other figures in Shaw's play who knew exactly what they were doing, and yet decided to do it; and who did not regret it afterwards. Some people dislike seeing their fellow men burning at the stake, and others do not. This point (which was neglected by many Victorian optimists) is important, for it shows that a rational analysis of the consequences of a decision does not make the decision rational; the consequences do not determine our decision; it is always we who decide. But an analysis of the concrete consequences, and their clear realization in what we call our 'imagination', makes the difference between a blind decision and a decision made with open eyes; and since we use our imagination very little,[7] we only too often decide blindly. This is especially so if we are intoxicated by an oracular philosophy, one of the most powerful means of maddening ourselves with words – to use Shaw's expression.

The rational and imaginative analysis of the consequences of a moral theory has a certain analogy in scientific method. For in science, too, we do not accept an abstract theory because it is convincing in itself; we rather decide to accept or reject it after we have investigated those concrete and practical consequences which can be more directly tested by experiment. But there is a fundamental difference. In the case of a scientific theory, our decision depends upon the results of experiments. If these confirm the theory, we may accept it until we find a better one. If they contradict the theory, we reject it. But in the case of a moral theory, we can only confront its consequences with our conscience. And while the verdict of experiments does not depend upon ourselves, the verdict of our conscience does.

I hope I have made it clear in which sense the analysis of consequences may influence our decision without determining it. And in presenting the consequences of the two alternatives between which we must decide, rationalism and irrationalism, I warn the reader that I shall be partial. So far, in presenting the two alternatives of the moral decision before us – it is, in many senses, the most fundamental decision in the ethical field – I have tried to be impartial, although I have not hidden my sympathies. But now I am going to present those considerations of the consequences of the two alternatives which appear to me most telling, and by which I myself have been influenced in rejecting irrationalism and accepting the faith in reason.

Let us examine the consequences of irrationalism first. The irrationalist insists that emotions and passions rather than reason are the mainsprings of human action. To the rationalist's reply that, though this may be so, we should do what we can to remedy it, and should try to make reason play as large a part as it possibly can, the irrationalist would rejoin (if he condescends to a discussion) that this attitude is hopelessly unrealistic. For it does not consider the weakness of 'human nature', the feeble intellectual endowment of most men and their obvious dependence upon emotions and passions.

It is my firm conviction that this irrational emphasis upon emotion and passion leads ultimately to what I can only describe as crime. One reason for this opinion is that this attitude, which is at best one of resignation towards the irrational nature of human beings, at worst one of scorn for human reason, must lead to an appeal to violence and brute force as the ultimate arbiter in any dispute. For if a dispute arises, then this means that those more constructive emotions and passions which might in principle help to get over it, reverence, love, devotion to a common cause, etc., have shown themselves incapable of solving the problem. But if that is so, then what is left to the irrationalist except the appeal to other and less constructive emotions and passions, to fear, hatred, envy, and ultimately, to violence? This tendency is very much strengthened by another and perhaps even more important attitude which also is in my opinion inherent in irrationalism, namely, the stress on the inequality of men.

It cannot, of course, be denied that human individuals are, like all other things in our world, in very many respects very unequal. Nor can it be doubted that this inequality is of great importance and even in many respects highly desirable.[8] (The fear that the development of mass production and collectivization may react upon men by destroying their inequality or individuality is one of the nightmares[9] of our times.) But all this simply has no bearing upon the question whether or not we should decide to treat men, especially in political issues, as equals, or as much like equals as is possible; that is to say, as possessing equal rights, and equal claims to equal treatment; and it has no bearing upon the question whether we ought to construct political institutions accordingly. 'Equality before the law' is *not a fact but a political demand*[10] *based upon a moral decision*; and it is quite independent of the theory – which is probably false – that 'all men are born equal'. Now I do not intend to say that the adoption of this humanitarian attitude of impartiality is a direct consequence of a decision in favour of rationalism. But a tendency towards impartiality is closely related to rationalism, and can hardly be excluded from the rationalist creed. Again, I do not intend to say that an irrationalist could not consistently adopt an equalitarian or impartial attitude; and even if he could not do so consistently, he is not bound to be consistent. But I do wish to stress the fact that the irrationalist attitude can hardly avoid becoming entangled with the attitude that is opposed to equalitarianism. This fact is connected with its emphasis upon emotions and passions; for we cannot feel the same emotions towards everybody. Emotionally, we all divide men into those who are near to us, and those who are far from us. The division of mankind into friend and foe is a most obvious emotional division; and this division is even recognized in the Christian commandment, 'Love thy enemies!' Even the best Christian who really lives up to this commandment (there are not many, as is shown by the attitude of the average good Christian towards 'materialists' and 'atheists'), even he cannot feel equal love for all men. We cannot really love 'in the abstract'; we can love only those whom we know. Thus the appeal even to our best emotions, love and compassion, can only tend to divide mankind into different categories. And this will be more true if the appeal is made to lesser emotions and passions. Our 'natural' reaction will be to divide mankind into friend and foe; into those who belong to our tribe, to our emotional community, and those who stand outside it; into believers and unbelievers; into compatriots and aliens; into class comrades and class enemies; and into leaders and led.

I have mentioned before that the theory that our thoughts and opinions are dependent upon our class situation, or upon our national interests, must lead to irrationalism. I now wish to emphasize the fact that the reverse is also true. The abandonment of the rationalist attitude, of the respect for reason and argument and the other fellow's point of view, the stress upon the 'deeper' layers of human nature, all this must lead to the view that thought is merely a somewhat superficial manifestation of what lies within these irrational depths. It must nearly always, I believe, produce an attitude which considers the person of the thinker instead of his thought. It must produce the belief that 'we think with our blood', or 'with our national heritage', or 'with our class'. This view may be presented in a materialist form or in a highly spiritual fashion; the idea that we 'think with our race' may perhaps be replaced by the idea of elect or inspired souls who 'think by God's grace'. I refuse, on moral grounds, to be impressed by these differences; for the decisive similarity between all these intellectually immodest views is that they do not judge a thought on its own merits. By thus abandoning reason, they split mankind into friends and foes; into the few who share in reason with the gods, and the many who don't (as Plato says); into the few who stand near and the many who stand far; into those who speak the untranslatable language of our own emotions and passions and those whose tongue is not our tongue. Once we have done this, political equalitarianism becomes practically impossible.

Now the adoption of an anti-equalitarian attitude in political life, i.e. in the field of problems concerned with the power of man over man, is just what I should call criminal. For it offers a justification of the attitude that different categories of people have different rights; that the master has the right to enslave the slave; that some men have the right to use others as their tools. Ultimately, it will be used, as in Plato,[11] to justify murder.

I do not overlook the fact that there are irrationalists who love mankind, and that not all forms of irrationalism engender criminality. But I hold that he who teaches that not reason but love should rule opens the way for those who rule by hate. (Socrates, I believe, saw something of this when he suggested[12] that mistrust or hatred of argument is related to mistrust or hatred of man.) Those who do not see this connection at once, who believe in a direct rule of emotional love, should consider that love as such certainly does not promote impartiality. And it cannot do away with conflict either. That love as such may be unable to settle a conflict can be shown by considering a harmless test case, which may pass as representative of more serious ones. Tom likes the theatre and Dick likes dancing. Tom lovingly insists on going to a dance while Dick wants for Tom's sake to go to the theatre. This conflict cannot be settled by love; rather, the greater the love, the stronger will be the conflict. There are only two solutions; one is the use of emotion, and ultimately of violence, and the other is the use of reason, of impartiality, of reasonable compromise. All this is not intended to indicate that I do not appreciate the difference between love and hate, or that I think that life would be worth living without love. (And I am quite prepared to admit that the Christian idea of love is not meant in a purely emotional way.) But I insist that no emotion, not even love, can replace the rule of institutions controlled by reason.

This, of course, is not the only argument against the idea of a rule of love. Loving a person means wishing to make him happy. (This, by the way, was Thomas Aquinas's definition of love.) But of all political ideals, that of making the people happy is perhaps the most dangerous one. It leads invariably to the attempt to impose our scale of 'higher' values upon others, in order to make them realize what seems to us of greatest importance for their happiness; in order, as it were, to save their souls. It leads to Utopianism and Romanticism. We all feel certain that everybody would be happy in the beautiful, the perfect community of our dreams. And no doubt, there would be heaven on earth if we could all love one another. But the attempt to make heaven on earth invariably produces hell [see selection 24 below]. It leads to intolerance. It leads to religious wars, and to the saving of souls through the Inquisition. And it is, I believe, based on a complete misunderstanding of our moral duties. It is our duty to help those who need our help; but it cannot be our duty to make others happy, since this does not depend on us, and since it would only too often mean intruding on the privacy of those towards whom we have such amiable intentions. The political demand for piecemeal (as opposed to Utopian) methods corresponds to the decision that the fight against suffering must be considered a duty, while the right to care for the happiness of others must be considered a privilege confined to the close circle of their friends. In their case, we may perhaps have a certain right to try to impose our scale of values – our preferences regarding music, for example. (And we may even feel it our duty to open to them a world of values which, we trust, can so much contribute to their happiness.) This right of ours exists only if, and because, they can get rid of us; because friendships can be ended. But the use of political means for imposing our scale of values upon others is a very different matter. Pain, suffering, injustice, and their prevention, these are the eternal problems of public morals, the 'agenda' of public policy (as Bentham would have said). The 'higher' values should very largely be considered as 'non-agenda', and should be left to the realm of *laissez-faire*. Thus we might say: help your enemies; assist those in distress, even if they hate you; but love only your friends.

This is only part of the case against irrationalism, and of the consequences which induce me to adopt the opposite attitude, that is, a critical rationalism. This latter attitude with its emphasis upon argument and experience, with its device 'I may be wrong and you may be right, and by an effort we may get nearer to the truth', is, as mentioned before, closely akin to the scientific attitude. It is bound up with the idea that everybody is liable to make mistakes, which may be found out by himself, or by others, or by himself with the assistance of the criticism of others. It therefore suggests the idea that nobody should be his own judge, and it suggests the idea of impartiality. (This is closely related to the idea of 'scientific objectivity' [as analysed in selection 30 below].) Its faith in reason is a faith not only in our own reason, but also – and even more – in that of others. Thus a rationalist, even if he believes himself to be intellectually superior to others, will reject all claims to authority[13] since he is aware that, if his intelligence is superior to that of others (which is hard for him to judge), it is so only in so far as he is capable of learning from criticism as well as from his own and other people's mistakes, and that one can learn in this sense only if one takes others and their arguments seriously. Rationalism is therefore bound up with the idea that the other fellow has a right to be heard, and to defend his arguments. It thus implies the recognition of the claim to tolerance, at least[14] of all those who are not intolerant themselves. One does not kill a man when one adopts the attitude of first listening to his arguments. (Kant was right when he based the 'Golden Rule' on the idea of reason. To be sure, it is impossible to prove the rightness of any ethical principle, or even to argue in its favour in just the manner in which we argue in favour of a scientific statement. Ethics is not a science. But although there is no 'rational scientific basis' of ethics, there is an ethical basis of science, and of rationalism.) The idea of impartiality leads also to that of responsibility; not only do we have to listen to arguments, but we have a duty to respond, to answer, where our actions affect others. Ultimately, in this way, rationalism is linked up with the recognition of the necessity of social institutions to protect freedom of criticism, freedom of thought, and thus the freedom of men. And it establishes something like a moral obligation towards the support of these institutions. This is why rationalism is closely linked up with the political demand for practical social engineering – piecemeal engineering, of course – in the humanitarian sense, with the demand for the rationalization of society,[15] for planning for freedom, and for its control by reason; not by 'science', not by a Platonic, a pseudorational authority, but by that Socratic reason which is aware of its limitations, and which therefore respects the other man and does not aspire to coerce him – not even into happiness. The adoption of rationalism implies, moreover, that there is a common medium of communication, a common language of reason; it establishes something like a moral obligation towards that language, the obligation to keep up its standards of clarity[16] and to use it in such a way that it can retain its function as the vehicle of argument. That is to say, to use it plainly; to use it as an instrument of rational communication, of significant information, rather than as a means of 'self-expression', as the vicious romantic jargon of most of our educationalists has it. (It is characteristic of the modern romantic hysteria that it combines a Hegelian collectivism concerning 'reason' with an excessive individualism concerning 'emotions': thus the emphasis on language as a means of self-expression instead of a means of communication. Both attitudes, of course, are parts of the revolt against reason.) And it implies the recognition that mankind is united by the fact that our different mother tongues, in so far as they are rational, can be translated into one another. It recognizes the unity of human reason.

A few remarks may be added concerning the relation of the rationalist attitude to the attitude of readiness to use what is usually called 'imagination'. It is frequently assumed that imagination has a close affinity with emotion and therefore with irrationalism, and that rationalism rather tends towards an unimaginative dry scholasticism. I do not know whether such a view may have some psychological basis, and I rather doubt it. But my interests are institutional rather than psychological, and from an institutional point of view (as well as from that of method) it appears that rationalism must encourage the use of imagination because it needs it, while irrationalism must tend to discourage it. The very fact that rationalism is critical, whilst irrationalism must tend towards dogmatism (where there is no argument, nothing is left but full acceptance or flat denial), leads in this direction. Criticism always demands a certain degree of imagination, whilst dogmatism suppresses it. Similarly, scientific research and technical construction and invention are inconceivable without a very considerable use of imagination; one must offer something new in these fields (as opposed to the field of oracular philosophy where an endless repetition of impressive words seems to do the trick). At least as important is the part played by imagination in the practical application of equalitarianism and of impartiality. The basic attitude of the rationalist, 'I may be wrong and you may be right', demands, when put into practice, and especially when human conflicts are involved, a real effort of our imagination. I admit that the emotions of love and compassion may sometimes lead to a similar effort. But I hold that it is humanly impossible for us to love, or to suffer with, a great number of people; nor does it appear to me very desirable that we should, since it would ultimately destroy either our ability to help or the intensity of these very emotions. But reason, supported by imagination, enables us to understand that men who are far away, whom we shall never see, are like ourselves, and that their relations to one another are like our relations to those we love. A direct emotional attitude towards the abstract whole of mankind seems to me hardly possible. We can love mankind only in certain concrete individuals. But by the use of thought and imagination, we may become ready to help all who need our help.

All these considerations show, I believe, that the link between rationalism and humanitarianism is very close, and certainly much closer than the corresponding entanglement of irrationalism with the anti-equalitarian and anti-humanitarian attitude. I believe that as far as possible this result is corroborated by experience. A rationalist attitude seems to be usually combined with a basically equalitarian and humanitarian outlook; irrationalism, on the other hand, exhibits in most cases at least some of the anti-equalitarian tendencies described, even though it may often be associated with humanitarianism also. My point is that the latter connection is anything but well founded.

3 Knowledge without Authority (1960)

I

This part of my lecture might be described as an attack on *empiricism*, as formulated for example in the following classical statement of Hume's: 'If I ask why you believe any particular matter of fact . . . , you must tell me some reason; and this reason will be some other fact, connected with it. But as you cannot proceed after this manner, *in infinitum*, you must at last terminate in some fact, which is present to your memory or senses; or must allow that your belief is entirely without foundation.'[1]

The problem of the validity of empiricism may be roughly put as follows: is observation the ultimate source of our knowledge of nature? And if not, what are the sources of our knowledge?

These questions remain, whatever I may have said about Bacon, and even if I should have managed to make those parts of his philosophy on which I have commented somewhat unattractive for Baconians and for other empiricists.

The problem of the source of our knowledge has recently been restated as follows. If we make an assertion, we must justify it; but this means that we must be able to answer the following questions.

> '*How do you know? What are the sources of your assertion?*'

This, the empiricist holds, amounts in its turn to the question,

> '*What observations* (or memories of observations) *underlie your assertion?*'

I find this string of questions quite unsatisfactory.

First of all, most of our assertions are not based upon observations, but upon all kinds of other sources. 'I read it in *The Times*' or perhaps 'I read it in the *Encyclopaedia Britannica*' is a more likely and a more definite answer to the question 'How do you know?' than 'I have observed it' or 'I know it from an observation I made last year'.

'But', the empiricist will reply, 'how do you think that *The Times* or the *Encyclopaedia Britannica* got their information? Surely, if you only carry on your inquiry long enough, you will end up with *reports of the observations of eyewitnesses* (sometimes called "protocol sentences" or – by yourself – "basic statements"). Admittedly', the empiricist will continue, 'books are largely made from other books. Admittedly, a historian, for example, will work from documents. But ultimately, in the last analysis, these other books, or these documents, must have been based upon observations. Otherwise they would have to be described as poetry, or invention, or lies, but not as testimony. It is in this sense that we empiricists assert that observation must be the ultimate source of our knowledge.'

Here we have the empiricist's case, as it is still put by some of my positivist friends.

I shall try to show that this case is as little valid as Bacon's; that the answer to the question of the sources of knowledge goes against the empiricist; and, finally, that this whole question of ultimate sources – sources to which one may appeal, as one might to a higher court or a higher authority – must be rejected as based upon a mistake.

First I want to show that if you actually went on questioning *The Times* and its correspondents about the sources of their knowledge, you would in fact never arrive at all those observations by eyewitnesses in the existence of which the empiricist believes. You would find, rather, that with every single step you take, the need for further steps increases in snowball-like fashion.

Take as an example the sort of assertion for which reasonable people might simply accept as sufficient the answer 'I read it in *The Times*'; let us say the assertion 'The Prime Minister has decided to return to London several days ahead of schedule'. Now assume for a moment that somebody doubts this assertion, or feels the need to investigate its truth. What shall he do? If he has a friend in the Prime Minister's office, the simplest and most direct way would be to ring him up; and if this friend corroborates the message, then that is that.

In other words, the investigator will, if possible, try to check, or to examine, *the asserted fact itself*, rather than trace the source of the information. But according to the empiricist theory, the assertion 'I have read it in *The Times*' is merely a first step in a justification procedure consisting in tracing the ultimate source. What is the next step?

There are at least two next steps. One would be to reflect that 'I have read it in *The Times*' is also an assertion, and that we might ask 'What is the source of your knowledge that you read it in *The Times* and not, say, in a paper looking very similar to *The Times*?' The other is to ask *The Times* for the sources of its knowledge. The answer to the first question may be 'But we have only *The Times* on order and we always get it in the morning', which gives rise to a host of further questions about sources which we shall not pursue. The second question may elicit from the editor of *The Times* the answer: 'We had a telephone call from the Prime Minister's office.' Now according to the empiricist procedure, we should at this stage ask next: 'Who is the gentleman who received the telephone call?' and then get his observation report; but we should also have to ask that gentleman: 'What is the source of your knowledge that the voice you heard came from an official in the Prime Minister's office?', and so on.

There is a simple reason why this tedious sequence of questions never comes to a satisfactory conclusion. It is this. Every witness must always make ample use, in his report, of his knowledge of persons, places, things, linguistic usages, social conventions, and so on. He cannot rely merely upon his eyes or ears, especially if his report is to be of use in justifying any assertion worth justifying. But this fact must of course always raise new questions as to the sources of those elements of his knowledge which are not immediately observational.

This is why the programme of tracing back all knowledge to its ultimate source in observation is logically impossible to carry through: it leads to an infinite regress. (The doctrine that truth is manifest cuts off the regress. This is interesting because it may help to explain the attractiveness of that doctrine.)

I wish to mention, in parentheses, that this argument is closely related to another – that all observation involves interpretation in the light of our theoretical knowledge, or that pure observational knowledge, unadulterated by theory, would, if at all possible, be utterly barren and futile. [See the last paragraph of selection 11, section I, below.[2]]

The most striking thing about the observationalist programme of asking for sources – apart from its tediousness – is its stark violation of common sense. For if we are doubtful about an assertion, then the normal procedure is to test it, rather than to ask for its sources; and if we find independent corroboration, then we shall often accept the assertion without bothering at all about sources.

Of course there are cases in which the situation is different. Testing an *historical* assertion always means going back to sources; but not, as a rule, to the reports of eyewitnesses.

Clearly, no historian will accept the evidence of documents uncritically. There are problems of genuineness, there are problems of bias, and there are also such problems as the reconstruction of earlier sources. There are, of course, also problems such as: was the writer present when these events happened? But this is not one of the characteristic problems of the historian. He may worry about the reliability of a report, but he will rarely worry about whether or not the writer of a document was an eyewitness of the event in question, even assuming that this event was of the nature of an observable event. A letter saying 'I changed my mind yesterday on this question' may be most valuable historical evidence, even though changes of mind are unobservable (and even though we may conjecture, in view of other evidence, that the writer was lying).

As to eyewitnesses, they are important almost exclusively in a court of law where they can be cross-examined. As most lawyers know, eyewitnesses often err. This has been experimentally investigated, with the most striking results. Witnesses most anxious to describe an event as it happened are liable to make scores of mistakes, especially if some exciting things happen in a hurry; and if an event suggests some tempting interpretation, then this interpretation, more often than not, is allowed to distort what has actually been seen.

Hume's view of historical knowledge was different: '... we believe', he writes in the *Treatise*, 'that CAESAR was kill'd in the senate-house on the *ides* of *March* ... because this fact is establish'd on the unanimous testimony of historians, who agree to assign this precise time and place to that event. Here are certain characters and letters present either to our memory or senses; which characters we likewise remember to have been us'd as the signs of certain ideas; and these ideas were either in the minds of such as were immediately present at that action, and receiv'd the ideas directly from its existence; or they were deriv'd from the testimony of others, and that again from another testimony . . . 'till we arrive at those who were eye-witnesses and spectators of the event.'[3]

It seems to me that this view must lead to the infinite regress described above. For the problem is, of course, whether 'the unanimous testimony of historians' is to be accepted, or whether it is, perhaps, to be rejected as the result of their reliance on a common yet spurious source. The appeal to 'letters present either to our memory or senses' cannot have any bearing on this or on any other relevant problem of historiography.

II

But what, then, are the sources of our knowledge?

The answer, I think, is this: there are all kinds of sources of our knowledge; but *none has authority*.

We may say that *The Times* can be a source of knowledge, or the *Encyclopaedia Britannica*. We may say that certain papers in the *Physical Review* about a problem in physics have more authority, and are more of the character of a source, than an article about the same problem in *The Times* or the *Encyclopaedia*. But it would be quite wrong to say that the source of the article in the *Physical Review* must have been wholly, or even partly, observation. The source may well be the discovery of an inconsistency in another paper, or say, the discovery of the fact that a hypothesis proposed in another paper could be tested by such and such an experiment; all these non-observational discoveries are 'sources' in the sense that they all add to our knowledge.

I do not, of course, deny that an experiment may also add to our knowledge, and in a most important manner. But it is not a source in any ultimate sense. It has always to be checked: as in the example of the news in *The Times* we do not, as a rule, question the eyewitness of an experiment, but, if we doubt the result, we may repeat the experiment, or ask somebody else to repeat it.

The fundamental mistake made by the philosophical theory of the ultimate sources of our knowledge is that it does not distinguish clearly enough between questions of origin and questions of validity. Admittedly, in the case of historiography, these two questions may sometimes coincide. The question of the validity of an historical assertion may be testable only, or mainly, in the light of the origin of certain sources. But in general the two questions are different; and in general we do not test the validity of an assertion or information by tracing its sources or its origin, but we test it, much more directly, by a critical examination of what has been asserted – of the asserted facts themselves.

Thus the empiricist's questions 'How do you know? What is the source of your assertion?' are wrongly put. They are not formulated in an inexact or slovenly manner, but *they are entirely misconceived*: they are questions that beg for an authoritarian answer.

III

The traditional systems of epistemology may be said to result from yes-answers or no-answers to questions about the sources of our knowledge. *They never challenge these questions, or dispute their legitimacy*; the questions are taken as perfectly natural, and nobody seems to see any harm in them.

This is quite interesting, for these questions are clearly authoritarian in spirit. They can be compared with that traditional question of political theory, 'Who should rule?', which begs for an authoritarian answer such as 'the best', or 'the wisest', or 'the people', or 'the majority'. (It suggests, incidentally, such silly alternatives as 'Who should be our rulers: the capitalists or the workers?', analogous to 'What is the ultimate source of knowledge: the intellect or the senses?') This political question is wrongly put and the answers which it elicits are paradoxical [see selection 25 below]. It should be replaced by a completely different question such as '*How can we organize our political institutions so that bad or incompetent rulers* (whom we should try not to get, but whom we so easily might get all the same) *cannot do too much damage?*' I believe that only by changing our question in this way can we hope to proceed towards a reasonable theory of political institutions.

The question about the sources of our knowledge can be replaced in a similar way. It has always been asked in the spirit of: 'What are the best sources of our knowledge – the most reliable ones, those which will not lead us into error, and those to which we can and must turn, in case of doubt, as the last court of appeal?' I propose to assume, instead, that no such ideal sources exist – no more than ideal rulers – and that *all* 'sources' are liable to lead us into error at times. And I propose to replace, therefore, the question of the sources of our knowledge by the entirely different question: '*How can we hope to detect and eliminate error?*'

The question of the sources of our knowledge, like so many authoritarian questions, is a *genetic* one. It asks for the origin of our knowledge, in the belief that knowledge may legitimize itself by its pedigree. The nobility of the racially pure knowledge, the untainted knowledge, the knowledge which derives from the highest authority, if possible from God: these are the (often unconscious) metaphysical ideas behind the question. My modified question, 'How can we hope to detect error?' may be said to derive from the view that such pure, untainted and certain sources do not exist, and that questions of origin or of purity should not be confounded with questions of validity, or of truth. This view may be said to be as old as Xenophanes. Xenophanes knew that our knowledge is guesswork, opinion – *doxa* rather than *epistēmē* – as shown by his verses [quoted on p.31 above]. Yet the traditional question of the authoritative sources of knowledge is repeated even today – and very often by positivists and by other philosophers who believe themselves to be in revolt against authority.

The proper answer to my question 'How can we hope to detect and eliminate error?' is, I believe, 'By *criticizing* the theories or guesses of others and – if we can train ourselves to do so – by *criticizing* our own theories or guesses.' (The latter point is highly desirable, but not indispensable; for if we fail to criticize our own theories, there may be others to do it for us.) This answer sums up a position which I propose to call 'critical rationalism'. It is a view, an attitude, and a tradition, which we owe to the Greeks. It is very different from the 'rationalism' or 'intellectualism' of Descartes and his school, and very different even from the epistemology of Kant. Yet in the field of ethics, of moral knowledge, it was approached by Kant with his *principle of autonomy*. This principle expresses his realization that we must not accept the command of an authority, however exalted, as the basis of ethics. For whenever we are faced with a command by an authority, it is for us to judge, critically, whether it is moral or immoral to obey. The authority may have power to enforce its commands, and we may be powerless to resist. But if we have the physical power of choice, then the ultimate responsibility remains with us. It is our own critical decision whether to obey a command; whether to submit to an authority.

Kant boldly carried this idea into the field of religion: '... in whatever way', he writes, 'the Deity should be made known to you, and even ... if He should reveal Himself to you: it is you ... who must judge whether you are permitted to believe in Him, and to worship Him.'[4]

In view of this bold statement, it seems strange that in his philosophy of science Kant did not adopt the same attitude of critical rationalism, of the critical search for error. I feel certain that it was only his acceptance of the authority of Newton's cosmology – a result of its almost unbelievable success in passing the most severe tests – which prevented Kant from doing so. If this interpretation of Kant is correct, then the critical rationalism (and also the critical empiricism) which I advocate merely put the finishing touch to Kant's own critical philosophy. And this was made possible by Einstein, who taught us that Newton's theory may well be mistaken in spite of its overwhelming success.

So my answer to the questions 'How do you know? What is the source or the basis of your assertion? What observations have led you to it?' would be: 'I do *not* know: my assertion was merely a guess. Never mind the source, or the sources, from which it may spring – there are many possible sources, and I may not be aware of half of them; and origins or pedigrees have in any case little bearing upon truth. But if you are interested in the problem which I tried to solve by my tentative assertion, you may help me by criticizing it as severely as you can; and if you can design some experimental test which you think might refute my assertion, I shall gladly, and to the best of my powers, help you to refute it.'

This answer applies, strictly speaking, only if the question is asked about some scientific assertion as distinct from an historical one. If my conjecture was an historical one, sources (in the non-ultimate sense) will of course come into the critical discussion of its validity. Yet fundamentally, my answer will be the same, as we have seen.

IV

It is high time now, I think, to formulate the epistemological results of this discussion. I will put them in the form of nine theses.

(1) There are no ultimate sources of knowledge. Every source, every suggestion, is welcome; and every source, every suggestion, is open to critical examination. Except in history, we usually examine the facts themselves rather than the sources of our information.

(2) The proper epistemological question is not one about sources; rather, we ask whether the assertion made is true – that is to say, whether it agrees with the facts. (That we may operate, without getting involved in antinomies, with the idea of objective truth in the sense of correspondence to the facts, has been shown by the work of Alfred Tarski.) And we try to find this out, as well as we can, by examining or testing the assertion itself; either in a direct way, or by examining or testing its consequences.

(3) In connection with this examination, all kinds of arguments may be relevant. A typical procedure is to examine whether our theories are consistent with our observations. But we may also examine, for example, whether our historical sources are mutually and internally consistent.

(4) Quantitatively and qualitatively by far the most important source of our knowledge – apart from inborn knowledge – is tradition. Most things we know we have learnt by example, by being told, by reading books, by learning how to criticize, how to take and to accept criticism, how to respect truth.

(5) The fact that most of the sources of our knowledge are traditional condemns anti-traditionalism as futile. But this fact must not be held to support a traditionalist attitude: every bit of our traditional knowledge (and even our inborn knowledge) is open to critical examination and may be overthrown. Nevertheless, without tradition, knowledge would be impossible.

(6) Knowledge cannot start from nothing – from a *tabula rasa* – nor yet from observation. The advance of knowledge consists, mainly, in the modification of earlier knowledge. Although we may sometimes, for example in archaeology, advance through a chance observation, the significance of the discovery will usually depend upon its power to modify our earlier theories.

(7) Pessimistic and optimistic epistemologies are about equally mistaken. The pessimistic cave story of Plato is the true one, and not his optimistic story of *anamnēsis* (even though we should admit that all men, like all other animals, and even all plants, possess inborn knowledge). But although the world of appearances is indeed a world of mere shadows on the walls of our cave, we all constantly reach out beyond it; and although, as Democritus said, the truth is hidden in the deep, we can probe into the deep. There is no criterion of truth at our disposal, and this fact supports pessimism. But we do possess criteria which, *if we are lucky*, may allow us to recognize error and falsity. Clarity and distinctness are not criteria of truth, but such things as obscurity or confusion *may* indicate error. Similarly coherence cannot establish truth, but incoherence and inconsistency do establish falsehood. And, when they are recognized, our own errors provide the dim red lights which help us in groping our way out of the darkness of our cave.

(8) Neither observation nor reason is an authority. Intellectual intuition and imagination are most important, but they are not reliable: they may show us things very clearly, and yet they may mislead us. They are indispensable as the main sources of our theories; but most of our theories are false anyway. The most important function of observation and reasoning, and even of intuition and imagination, is to help us in the critical examination of those bold conjectures which are the means by which we probe into the unknown.

(9) Every solution of a problem raises new unsolved problems; the more so the deeper the original problem and the bolder its solution. The more we learn about the world, and the deeper our learning, the more conscious, specific, and articulate will be our knowledge of what we do not know, our knowledge of our ignorance. For this, indeed, is the main source of our ignorance

– the fact that our knowledge can only be finite, while our ignorance must necessarily be infinite.

We may get a glimpse of the vastness of our ignorance when we contemplate the vastness of the heavens: though the mere size of the universe is not the deepest cause of our ignorance, it is one of its causes. 'Where I seem to differ from some of my friends', F.P. Ramsey wrote in a charming passage, 'is in attaching little importance to physical size. I don't feel the least humble before the vastness of the heavens. The stars may be large but they cannot think or love; and these are qualities which impress me far more than size does. I take no credit for weighing nearly seventeen stone.'[5] I suspect that Ramsey's friends would have agreed with him about the insignificance of sheer physical size; and I suspect that if they felt humble before the vastness of the heavens, this was because they saw in it a symbol of their ignorance.

I believe that it would be worth trying to learn something about the world even if in trying to do so we should merely learn that we do not know much. This state of learned ignorance might be a help in many of our troubles. It might be well for all of us to remember that, while differing widely in the various little bits we know, in our infinite ignorance we are all equal.

V

There is a last question I wish to raise.

If only we look for it we can often find a true idea, worthy of being preserved, in a philosophical theory which must be rejected as false. Can we find an idea like this in one of the theories of the ultimate sources of our knowledge?

I believe we can; and I suggest that it is one of the two main ideas which underlie the doctrine that the source of all our knowledge is super-natural. The first of these ideas is false, I believe, while the second is true.

The first, the false idea, is that we must *justify* our knowledge, or our theories, by *positive* reasons, that is, by reasons capable of establishing them, or at least of making them highly probable; at any rate, by better reasons than that they have so far withstood criticism. This idea implies, I suggest, that we must appeal to some ultimate or authoritative source of true knowledge; which still leaves open the character of that authority – whether it is human, like observation or reason, or super-human (and therefore super-natural).

The second idea – whose vital importance has been stressed by Russell – is that no man's authority can establish truth by decree; that we should submit to truth; that *truth is above human authority*.

Taken together these two ideas almost immediately yield the conclusion that the sources from which our knowledge derives must be super-human; a conclusion which tends to encourage self-righteousness and the use of force against those who refuse to see the divine truth.

Some who rightly reject this conclusion do not, unhappily, reject the first idea – the belief in the existence of ultimate sources of knowledge. Instead they reject the second idea – the thesis that truth is above human authority. They thereby endanger the idea of the objectivity of knowledge, and of common standards of criticism or rationality.

What we should do, I suggest, is to give up the idea of ultimate sources of knowledge, and admit that all human knowledge is human: that it is mixed with our errors, our prejudices, our dreams, and our hopes: that all we can do is to grope for truth even though it be beyond our reach. We may admit that our groping is often inspired, but we must be on our guard against the belief, however deeply felt, that our inspiration carries any authority, divine or otherwise. If we thus admit that there is no authority beyond the reach of criticism to be found within the whole province of our knowledge, however far it may have penetrated into the unknown, then we can retain, without danger, the idea that truth is beyond human authority. And we must retain it. For without this idea there can be no objective standards of inquiry; no criticism of our conjectures; no groping for the unknown; no quest for knowledge.

4 Knowledge: Subjective versus Objective (1967)

1 Three Theses on Epistemology and World 3

I might have challenged those who have heard of my adverse attitude towards Plato and Hegel by calling my lecture '*A theory of the Platonic World*', or '*A theory of the Objective Spirit*'.

The main topic of this lecture will be what I often call, for want of a better name, 'world 3'. To explain this expression I will point out that, without taking the words 'world' or 'universe' too seriously, we may distinguish the following three worlds or universes: first, the world of physical objects or of physical states; secondly, the world of states of consciousness, or of mental states, or perhaps of behavioural dispositions to act; and thirdly, the world of *objective contents of thought*, especially of scientific and poetic thoughts and of works of art.

Thus what I call 'world 3' has admittedly much in common with Plato's theory of Forms or Ideas, and therefore also with Hegel's Objective Spirit, though my theory differs radically, in some decisive respects, from Plato's and Hegel's. It has more in common still with Bolzano's theory of a universe of propositions-in-themselves and of truths-in-themselves, though it differs from Bolzano's also. My world 3 resembles most closely the universe of Frege's objective contents of thought.

It is not part of my view or of my argument that we might not enumerate our worlds in different ways, or not enumerate them at all. We might, especially, distinguish more than three worlds. My term 'world 3' is merely a matter of convenience.

In upholding an objective third world I hope to provoke those whom I call '*belief philosophers*': those who, like Descartes, Locke, Berkeley, Hume, Kant, or Russell, are interested in our subjective beliefs, and their basis or origin. Against these belief philosophers I urge that our problem is to find better and bolder theories; and that *critical preference* counts, but *not belief*.

I wish to confess, however, at the very beginning, that I am a realist: I suggest, somewhat like a naïve realist, that there are a physical world (world 1) and a world of states of consciousness (world 2), and that these two interact. And I believe that there is a third world, in a sense which I shall explain more fully.

Among the inmates of my 'world 3' are, more especially, *theoretical systems*; but inmates just as important are *problems* and *problem situations*. And I will argue that the most important inmates of this world are *critical arguments*, and what may be called – in analogy to a physical state or to a state of consciousness – *the state of a discussion* or *the state of a critical argument*; and, of course, the contents of journals, books, and libraries.

Most opponents of the thesis of an objective world 3 will of course admit that there are problems, conjectures, theories, arguments, journals, and books. But they usually say that all these entities are, essentially, symbolic or linguistic *expressions* of subjective mental states, or perhaps of behavioural dispositions to act; further, that these entities are means of *communication* – that is to say, symbolic or linguistic means to evoke in others similar mental states or behavioural dispositions to act.

Against this, I have often argued that one cannot relegate all these entities and their content to world 2.

Let me repeat one of my standard arguments[1] for the (more or less) *independent existence of world 3*.

I consider two thought experiments:

Experiment (1). All our machines and tools are destroyed, and all our subjective learning, including our subjective knowledge of machines and tools, and how to use them. But *libraries and our capacity to learn from them* survive. Clearly, after much suffering, our world may get going again.

Experiment (2). As before, machines and tools are destroyed, and our subjective learning, including our subjective knowledge of machines and tools, and how to use them. But this time, *all libraries are destroyed also*, so that our capacity to learn from books becomes useless.

If you think about these two experiments, the reality,

significance, and degree of autonomy of world 3 (as well as its effects on worlds 1 and 2) may perhaps become a little clearer to you. For in the second case there will be no re-emergence of our civilization for many millennia.

I wish to defend in this lecture three main theses, all of which concern epistemology. Epistemology I take to be the theory of *scientific knowledge*.

My first thesis is this. Traditional epistemology has studied knowledge or thought in a subjective sense – in the sense of the ordinary usage of the words 'I know' or 'I am thinking'. This, I assert, has led students of epistemology into irrelevances: while intending to study scientific knowledge, they studied in fact something which is of no relevance to scientific knowledge. For *scientific knowledge* simply is not knowledge in the sense of the ordinary usage of the words 'I know'. While knowledge in the sense of 'I know' belongs to what I call 'world 2', the world of *subjects*, scientific knowledge belongs to world 3, to the world of objective theories, objective problems, and objective arguments.

Thus my first thesis is that the traditional epistemology, of Locke, Berkeley, Hume, and even of Russell, is irrelevant, in a pretty strict sense of the word. It is a corollary of this thesis that a large part of contemporary epistemology is irrelevant also.

My first thesis involves the existence of two different senses of knowledge or of thought: (1) *knowledge or thought in the subjective sense*, consisting of a state of mind or of consciousness or a disposition to behave or to react, and (2) *knowledge or thought in an objective sense*, consisting of problems, theories, and arguments as such. Knowledge in this objective sense is totally independent of anybody's claim to know; it is also independent of anybody's belief, or disposition to assent; or to assert, or to act. Knowledge in the objective sense is *knowledge without a knower*: it is *knowledge without a knowing subject*.

Of thought in the objective sense Frege wrote: 'I understand by a *thought* not the subjective act of thinking but its *objective content*. . . .'[2]

The two senses of thought and their interesting interrelations can be illustrated by the following highly convincing quotation from Heyting, who says about Brouwer's act of inventing his theory of the continuum:[3]

'If recursive functions had been invented before, he [Brouwer] would perhaps not have formed the notion of a choice sequence which, I think, would have been unlucky.'

This quotation refers on the one hand to some *subjective thought processes* of Brouwer's and says that they might not have occurred (which would have been unfortunate) had the *objective problem situation* been different. Thus Heyting mentions certain possible *influences* upon Brouwer's subjective thought processes, and he also expresses his opinion regarding the value of these subjective thought processes. Now it is interesting that influences, *qua* influences, must be subjective: only Brouwer's subjective acquaintance with recursive functions could have had that unfortunate effect of preventing him from inventing free choice sequences.

On the other hand, the quotation from Heyting points to a certain objective relationship between the *objective contents* of two thoughts or theories: Heyting does not refer to the subjective conditions or the electrochemistry of Brouwer's brain processes, but to an *objective problem situation in mathematics* and its possible influences on Brouwer's subjective acts of thought which were bent on solving these objective problems. I would describe this by saying that Heyting's remark is about the objective or world 3 *situational logic* of Brouwer's invention, and that Heyting's remark implies that the world 3 situation may affect world 2. Similarly, Heyting's suggestion that it would have been unfortunate if Brouwer had not invented choice sequences is a way of saying that the *objective content* of Brouwer's thought was valuable and interesting; valuable and interesting, that is, in the way it changed the objective problem situation in world 3.

To put the matter simply, if I say 'Brouwer's thought was influenced by Kant' or even 'Brouwer rejected Kant's theory of space' then I speak at least partly about acts of thought in the subjective sense: the word 'influence' indicates a context of thought processes or acts of thinking. If I say, however, 'Brouwer's thought differs vastly from Kant's', then it is pretty clear that I speak mainly about contents. And, ultimately, if I say 'Brouwer's thoughts are incompatible with Russell's', then, by using a *logical term* such as '*incompatible*', I make it unambiguously clear that I am using the word 'thought' only in Frege's objective sense, and that I am speaking only about the objective content, or the logical content, of theories.

Just as ordinary language unfortunately has no separate terms for 'thought' in the sense of world 2 and in the sense of world 3, so it has no separate terms for the corresponding two senses of 'I know' and of 'knowledge'.

In order to show that both senses exist, I will first mention three subjective or world 2 examples:

(1) 'I *know* you are trying to provoke me, but I will not be provoked.'

(2) 'I *know* that Fermat's last theorem has not been proved, but I believe it will be proved one day.'

(3) From the entry 'Knowledge' in *The Oxford English Dictionary*: *knowledge* is a 'state of being aware or informed'.

Next I will mention three objective or world 3 examples:

(1) From the entry 'Knowledge' in *The Oxford English Dictionary*: *knowledge* is a 'branch of learning; a science; an art'.

(2) 'Taking account of the present state of *metamathematical knowledge*, it seems possible that Fermat's last theorem may be undecidable.'

(3) 'I certify that this thesis is an original and significant *contribution to knowledge*.'

These very trite examples have only the function of helping to clarify what I mean when I speak of 'knowledge in the objective sense'. My quoting *The Oxford English Dictionary* should not be interpreted either as a concession to language analysis or as an attempt to appease its adherents. It is not quoted in an attempt to prove that 'ordinary usage' covers 'knowledge' in the objective sense of my world 3. In fact, I was surprised to find in *The Oxford English Dictionary* examples of objective usages of 'knowledge'. (I was even more surprised to find some at least *partly* objective usages of 'know': 'to distinguish . . . to be acquainted with (a thing, a place, a person); . . . to understand'.) At any rate, my examples are not intended as arguments. They are intended solely as illustrations.

My *first thesis*, so far not argued but only illustrated, was that traditional epistemology with its concentration on world 2, or on knowledge in the subjective sense, is irrelevant to the study of scientific knowledge.

My *second thesis* is that what is relevant for epistemology is the study of scientific problems and problem situations, of scientific conjectures (which I take as merely another word for scientific hypotheses or theories), of scientific discussions, of critical arguments, and of the role played by evidence in arguments; and therefore of scientific journals and books, and of experiments and their evaluation in scientific arguments; or, in brief, that the study of a *largely autonomous* world 3 of objective knowledge is of decisive importance for epistemology.

An epistemological study as described in my second thesis shows that scientists very often do not claim that their conjectures are true, or that they 'know' them in the subjective sense of 'know', or that they believe in them. Although in general they do not claim to know, in developing their research programmes they act on the basis of guesses about what is and what is not fruitful, and what line of research promises further results in world 3, the world of objective knowledge. In other words, scientists act on the basis of a guess or, if you like, of a *subjective belief* (for we may so call the subjective basis of an action) concerning what is promising of impending *growth in world 3, the world of objective knowledge*.

This, I suggest, furnishes an argument in favour both of my *first thesis* (of the irrelevance of a subjectivist epistemology) and of my *second thesis* (of the relevance of an objectivist epistemology).

But I have a *third thesis*. It is this. An objectivist epistemology which studies world 3 can help to throw an immense amount of light upon world 2, the world of subjective consciousness, especially upon the subjective thought processes of scientists; but *the converse is not true*.

These are my three main theses.

In addition to my three main theses, I offer three supporting theses.

The first of these is that world 3 is a natural product of the human animal, comparable to a spider's web.

The second supporting thesis (and an almost crucial thesis, I think) is that world 3 is largely *autonomous*, even though we constantly act upon it and are acted upon by it: it is autonomous in spite of the fact that it is our product and that it has a strong feedback effect upon us; that is to say, upon us *qua* inmates of world 2 and even of world 1.

The third supporting thesis is that it is through this interaction between ourselves and world 3 that objective knowledge grows, and that there is a close analogy between the growth of knowledge and biological growth; that is, the evolution of plants and animals.

II A Biological Approach to World 3

In the present section I shall try to defend the existence of an autonomous world 3 by a kind of biological or evolutionary argument.

A biologist may be interested in the behaviour of animals; but he may also be interested in some of the *non-living structures* which animals produce, such as spiders' webs, or nests built by wasps or ants, the burrows of badgers, dams constructed by beavers, or paths made by animals in forests.

I will distinguish between two main categories of problems arising from the study of these structures. The first category consists of problems concerned with *the methods used* by the animals, or *the ways the animals behave* when constructing these structures. This first category thus consists *of problems concerned with the acts of production*; with the behavioural dispositions of the animal; and with the relationships between the animal and the product. The second category of problems is concerned with the *structures themselves*. It is concerned with the chemistry of the materials used in the structure; with their geometrical and physical properties; with their evolutionary changes, depending upon special environmental conditions; and with their dependence upon or their adjustments to these environmental conditions. *Very* important also is the *feedback relation* from the properties of the structure to the behaviour of the animals. In dealing with this second category of problems – that is, with the structures themselves – we shall also have to look upon the structures from the point of view of their biological *functions*. Thus some problems of the first category will admittedly arise when we discuss problems of the second category; for example 'How was this nest built?' and 'What aspects of its structure are typical (and thus presumably traditional or inherited) and what aspects are variants adjusted to special conditions?'

As my last example of a problem shows, problems of the first category – that is, problems concerned with the production of the structure – will sometimes be suggested by problems of the second category. This must be so, since both categories of problems are dependent upon *the fact that such objective structures exist*, a fact which itself belongs to the second category. Thus the existence of the *structures themselves* may be said to create both categories of problems. We may say that the second category of problems – problems connected with the structures themselves – is more fundamental: all that it presupposes from the first category is the bare fact that the structures are somehow *produced by* some animals.

Now these simple considerations may of course also be applied to products of *human* activity, such as houses, or tools, and also to works of art. Especially important for us, they apply to what we call 'language', and to what we call 'science'.[4]

The connection between these biological considerations and the topic of my present lecture can be made clear by reformulating my three main theses. My first thesis can be put by saying that in the present problem situation in philosophy, few things are as important as the awareness of the distinction between the two categories of problems – production problems on the one hand and problems connected with the produced structures themselves on the other. My second thesis is that we should realize that the second category of problems, those concerned with the products in themselves, is in almost every respect more important than the first category, the problems of production. My third thesis is that the problems of the second category are basic for understanding the production problems: contrary to first impressions, we can learn more about production behaviour by studying the products themselves than we can learn about the products by studying production behaviour. This third thesis may be described as an anti-behaviouristic and anti-psychologistic thesis.

In their application to what may be called 'knowledge' my three theses may be formulated as follows.

(1) We should constantly be aware of the distinction between problems connected with our personal contributions to the production of scientific knowledge on the one hand, and problems connected with the structure of the various products, such as scientific theories or scientific arguments, on the other.

(2) We should realize that the study of the products is vastly more important than the study of the production, even for an understanding of the production and its methods.

(3) We can learn more about the heuristics and the methodology and even about the psychology of research by studying theories, and the arguments offered for or against them, than by any direct behaviouristic or psychological or sociological approach. In general, we may learn a great deal about behaviour and psychology from the study of the products.

In what follows I will call the approach from the side of the products – the theories and the arguments – the 'objective' approach or the 'world 3' approach. And I will call the behaviourist, the psychological, and the sociological approach to scientific knowledge the 'subjective' approach or the 'world 2' approach.

The appeal of the subjective approach is largely due to the fact that it is *causal*. For I admit that the objective structures for which I claim priority are caused by human behaviour. Being causal, the subjective approach may seem to be more scientific than the objective approach which, as it were, starts from effects rather than causes.

Though I admit that the objective structures are products of behaviour, I hold that the argument is mistaken. In all sciences, the ordinary approach is from the effects to the causes. The effect raises the problem – the problem to be explained, the explicandum – and the scientist tries to solve it by constructing an explanatory hypothesis.

My three main theses with their emphasis on the objective products are therefore neither teleological nor unscientific.

III The Objectivity and the Autonomy of World 3

One of the main reasons for the mistaken subjective approach to knowledge is the feeling that a book is nothing without a reader: only if it is understood does it really become a book; otherwise it is just paper with black spots on it.

This view is mistaken in many ways. A wasps' nest is a wasps' nest even after it has been deserted; even though it is never again used by wasps as a nest. A bird's nest is a bird's nest even if it was never lived in. Similarly a book remains a book – a certain type of product – even if it is never read (as may easily happen nowadays).

Moreover, a book, or even a library, need not even have been written by anybody: a series of books of logarithms, for example, may be produced and printed by a computer. It may be the best series of books of logarithms – it may contain logarithms up to, say, fifty decimal places. It may be sent out to libraries, but it may be found too cumbersome for use; at any rate, years may elapse before anybody uses it; and many figures in it (which represent mathematical theorems) may never be looked at as long as men live on earth. Yet each of these figures contains what I call 'objective knowledge'; and the question of whether or not I am entitled to call it by this name is of no interest.

The example of these books of logarithms may seem far-fetched. But it is not. I should say that almost every book is like this: it contains objective knowledge, true or false, useful or useless; and whether anybody ever reads it and really grasps its contents is almost accidental. A man who reads a book with understanding is a rare creature. But even if he were more common, there would always be plenty of misunderstandings and misinterpretations; and it is not the actual and somewhat accidental avoidance of such misunderstandings which turns black spots on white paper into a book, or an instance of knowledge in the objective sense. Rather, it is something more abstract. It is its possibility or potentiality of being understood, its dispositional character of being understood or interpreted, or misunderstood or misinterpreted, which makes a thing a book, And this potentiality or disposition may exist without ever being actualized or realized.

To see this more clearly, we may imagine that after the human race has perished, some books or libraries may be found by some civilized successors of ours (no matter whether these are terrestrial animals which have become civilized, or some visitors from outer space). These books may be deciphered. They may be those logarithm tables never read before, for argument's sake. This makes it quite clear that neither its composition by thinking animals nor the fact that it has not actually been read or understood is essential for making a thing a book, and that it is sufficient that it might be deciphered.

Thus I do admit that in order to belong to world 3, the world of objective knowledge, a book should – in principle, or virtually – be capable of being grasped (or deciphered, or understood, or 'known') by somebody. But I do not admit more.

We can thus say that there is a kind of Platonic (or Bolzano-esque) world 3 of books-in-themselves, theories-in-themselves, problems-in-themselves, problem-situations-in-themselves, arguments-in-themselves, and so on. And I assert that even though this world 3 is a human product, there are many theories-in-themselves and arguments-in-themselves and problem-situations-in-themselves which have never been produced or understood and may never be produced or understood by men.

The thesis of the existence of such a world of problem situations will strike many as extremely metaphysical and dubious. But it can be defended by pointing out its biological analogue. For example, it has its full analogue in the realm of birds' nests. Some years ago I got a present for my garden – a nesting-box for birds. It was a human product, of course, not a bird's product – just as our logarithm table was a computer's product rather than a human product. But in the context of the bird's world, it was part of an objective problem situation, and an objective opportunity. For some years the birds did not even seem to notice the nesting-box. But after some years, it was carefully inspected by some blue tits who even started building in it, but gave up very soon. Obviously, here was a graspable opportunity, though not, it appears, a particularly valuable one. At any rate, here was a problem situation. And the problem may be solved in another year by other birds. If it is not, another box may prove more adequate. On the other hand, a most adequate box may be removed before it is ever used. The question of the adequacy of the box is clearly an objective one; and whether the box is ever used is partly accidental. So it is with all ecological niches. They are potentialities and may be studied as such in an objective way, up to a point independently of the question of whether these potentialities will ever be actualized by any living organism. A bacteriologist knows how to prepare such an ecological niche for the culture of certain bacteria or moulds. It may be perfectly adequate for its purpose. Whether it will ever be used and inhabited is another question.

A large part of the objective world 3 of actual and potential theories and books and arguments arises as an unintended byproduct of the actually produced books and arguments. We may also say that it is a byproduct of human language. Language itself, like a bird's nest, is an unintended byproduct of actions which were directed at other aims.

How does an animal path in the jungle arise? Some animal may break through the undergrowth in order to get to a drinking place. Other animals find it easiest to use the same track. Thus it may be widened and improved by use. It is not planned – it is an unintended consequence of the need for easy or swift movement. This is how a path is originally made – perhaps even by men – and how language and any other institutions which are useful may arise, and how they may owe their existence and development to their usefulness. They are not planned or intended, and there was perhaps no need for them before they came into existence. But they may create a new need, or a new set of aims: the aim-structure of animals or men is not 'given', but it develops, with the help of some kind of feedback mechanism, out of earlier aims, and out of results which were or were not aimed at.[5]

In this way, a whole new universe of possibilities or potentialities may arise: a world which is to a large extent *autonomous*.

A very obvious example is a garden. Even though it may have been planned with great care, it will as a rule turn out partly in unexpected ways. But even if it turns out as planned, some unexpected interrelationships between the planned objects may give rise to a whole universe of possibilities, of possible new aims, and of new *problems*.

The world of language, of conjectures, theories, and arguments – in brief, the universe of objective knowledge – is one of the most important of these man-created, yet at the same time largely autonomous, universes.

The idea of *autonomy* is central to my theory of world 3: although world 3 is a human product, a human creation, it creates in its turn, as do other animal products, its own *domain of autonomy*.

There are countless examples. Perhaps the most striking ones, and at any rate those which should be kept in mind as our standard examples, may be found in the theory of natural numbers.

Pace Kronecker, I agree with Brouwer that the sequence of natural numbers is a human construction. But although we create this sequence, it creates its own autonomous problems in its turn. The distinction between odd and even numbers is not created by us: it is an unintended and unavoidable consequence of our creation. Prime numbers, of course, are similarly unintended autonomous and objective facts; and in their case it is obvious that there are many facts here for us to *discover*: there are conjectures like Goldbach's. And these conjectures, though they refer indirectly to objects of our creation, refer directly to problems and facts which have somehow emerged from our creation and which we cannot control or influence: they are hard facts, and the truth about them is often hard to discover.

This exemplifies what I mean when I say that world 3 is largely autonomous, though created by us.

But the autonomy is only partial: the new problems lead to new creations or constructions – such as recursive functions, or Brouwer's free choice sequences – and may thus add new objects to world 3. And every such step will create *new unintended facts*; *new unexpected problems*; and often also *new refutations*.[6]

There is also a most important feedback effect from our creations upon ourselves; from world 3 upon world 2. For the new emergent problems stimulate us to new creations.

The process can be described by the following somewhat oversimplified schema:[7]

$$P_1 \rightarrow TT \rightarrow EE \rightarrow P_2.$$

That is, we start from some problem P_1, proceed to a tentative solution or tentative theory TT, which may be (partly or wholly) mistaken; in any case it will be subject to error-elimination, EE, which may consist of critical discussion or experimental tests; at any rate, new problems P_2 arise from our own creative activity; and these new problems are not in general intentionally created by us, they emerge autonomously from the field of new relationships which we cannot help bringing into existence with every action, however little we intend to do so.

The autonomy of world 3, and the feedback of world 3 upon world 2 and even world 1, are among the most important facts of the growth of knowledge.

Following up our biological considerations, it is easy to see that they are of general importance for the theory of Darwinian evolution: they explain how we can lift ourselves by our own bootstraps. Or in more highbrow terminology, they help to explain 'emergence'.

IV **Language, Criticism, and World 3**

The most important of human creations, with the most important feedback effects upon ourselves and especially upon our brains, are the higher functions of human language; more especially, the *descriptive function* and the *argumentative function*.

Human languages share with animal languages the two lower functions of language: (1) self-expression and (2) signalling. The self-expressive function or symptomatic function of language is obvious: all animal language is symptomatic of the state of some organism. The signalling or release function is likewise obvious: we do not call any symptom linguistic unless we assume that it can release a response in another organism.

All animal languages and all linguistic phenomena share these two lower functions. But human language has many other functions (for example, the advisory, hortative, and fictional functions). Strangely enough, the most important of the higher functions have been overlooked by almost all philosophers. The explanation of this strange fact is that the two lower functions are always present when the higher ones are present, so that it is always possible to 'explain' every linguistic phenomenon, in terms of the lower functions, as an '*expression*' or a '*communication*'.

The two most important higher functions of human languages

are (3) the *descriptive* function and (4) the *argumentative* function.[8]

With the descriptive function of human language, the regulative idea of *truth* emerges, that is, of a description which fits the facts. Further regulative or evaluative ideas are content, truth content, and verisimilitude.[9]

The argumentative function of human language presupposes the descriptive function: arguments are, fundamentally, about descriptions: they criticize descriptions from the point of view of the regulative ideas of truth; content; and verisimilitude.

Now two points are all-important here:

(1) Without the development of an exosomatic descriptive language – a language which, like a tool, develops outside the body – there can be *no object* for our critical discussion. But with the development of a descriptive language (and further, of a written language), a linguistic world 3 can emerge; and it is only in this way, and only in world 3, that the problems and standards of rational criticism can develop.

(2) It is to this development of the higher functions of language that we owe our humanity, our reason. For our powers of reasoning are nothing but powers of critical argument.

This second point shows the futility of all theories of human language that focus on *expression and communication*. As we shall see [in selections 20 and 21 below], the human organism which, it is often said, is intended to express itself, depends in its structure very largely upon the emergence of the two higher functions of language.

With the evolution of the argumentative function of language, criticism becomes the main instrument of further growth. (Logic may be regarded as *the organon of criticism*.[10]) The autonomous world of the higher functions of language becomes the world of science. And the schema, originally valid for the animal world as well as for primitive man,

$$P_1 \rightarrow TT \rightarrow EE \rightarrow P_2$$

becomes the schema of the growth of knowledge through error-elimination by way of systematic *rational criticism*. It becomes the schema of the search for truth and content by means of rational discussion. It describes the way in which we lift ourselves by our bootstraps. It gives a rational description of evolutionary emergence, and of our *self-transcendence by means of selection and rational criticism*.

To sum up, although the meaning of 'knowledge', like that of all words, is unimportant, it is important to distinguish between different senses of the word.

(1) Subjective knowledge, which consists of certain inborn dispositions to act, and of their acquired modifications.

(2) Objective knowledge; for example, scientific knowledge which consists of conjectural theories, open problems, problem situations, and arguments.

All work in science is work directed towards the growth of objective knowledge. We are workers who are adding to the growth of objective knowledge as masons work on a cathedral.

Our work is fallible, like all human work. We constantly make mistakes, and there are objective standards of which we may fall short – standards of truth, of content, of validity, and other standards.

Language, the formulation of problems, the emergence of new problem situations, competing theories, mutual criticism by way of argument: all these are indispensable means to scientific growth. The most important functions or dimensions of human language are the descriptive and the argumentative functions (which animal languages do not possess). The growth of these functions is, of course, of our making, though they are unintended consequences of our actions. It is only within a language thus enriched that critical argument and knowledge in the objective sense become possible.

The repercussion, or the feedback effects, of the evolution of world 3 upon ourselves – our brains, our traditions (if anybody were to start where Adam started, he would not get further than Adam did), our dispositions to act (that is, our beliefs),[11] and our actions, can hardly be overrated.

As opposed to all this, *traditional epistemology* is interested in world 2: in knowledge as a certain kind of belief – justifiable belief, such as belief based upon perception. As a consequence, this kind of belief philosophy cannot explain (and does not even try to explain) the decisive phenomenon that scientists criticize their theories and so kill them. *Scientists try to eliminate their false theories, they try to let them die in their stead. The believer – whether animal or man – perishes with his false beliefs.*

v Historical Remarks

(i) *Plato and Neo-Platonism* For all we know, Plato was the discoverer of world 3. As Whitehead remarked, all Western philosophy consists of footnotes to Plato.

I will make only three brief remarks on Plato, two of them critical.

(1) Plato discovered not only world 3, but part of the influence or feedback of world 3 upon ourselves: he realized that we try to grasp the ideas of his world 3; also that we use them as explanations.

(2) Plato's world 3 was divine; it was unchanging and, of course, true. Thus there is a big gap between his and my world 3: my world 3 is manmade and changing. It contains not only true theories but also false ones, and especially open problems, conjectures, and refutations.

And while Plato, the great master of dialectical argument, saw in it merely a way of leading to world 3, I regard arguments as among the most important inmates of world 3; not to speak of open problems.

(3) Plato believed that world 3, the world of Forms or Ideas, would provide us with ultimate explanations (that is, explanation by essences [see p.165 below]). Thus he writes for example (*Phaedo*, 100 C): 'I think that if anything else apart from the idea of absolute beauty is beautiful, then it is beautiful *for the sole reason* that it has some share in the idea of absolute beauty. *And this kind of explanation applies to everything.*'

This is a theory of *ultimate explanation*; that is to say, of an explanation whose explicans is neither capable nor in need of further explanation. And it is a theory of *explanation by essences*; that is, by hypostatized words.

As a result, Plato envisaged the objects of world 3 as something like non-material things or, perhaps, like stars or constellations – to be gazed at, and intuited, though not liable to be touched by our minds. This is why the inmates of world 3 – the Forms or Ideas – became concepts of things, or essences or natures of things, rather than theories or arguments or problems.

This had the most far-reaching consequences for the history of philosophy. From Plato until today, most philosophers have either been nominalists[12] or else what I have called essentialists. They are more interested in the (essential) meaning of words than in the truth and falsity of theories.

I often present the problem in the form of a table.

	IDEAS	
	that is	
DESIGNATIONS *or* TERMS *or* CONCEPTS		STATEMENTS *or* PROPOSITIONS *or* THEORIES
	may be formulated in	
WORDS		ASSERTIONS
	which may be	
MEANINGFUL		TRUE
	and their	
MEANING		TRUTH
	may be reduced, by way of	
DEFINITIONS		DERIVATIONS
	to that of	
UNDEFINED CONCEPTS		PRIMITIVE PROPOSITIONS
	The attempt to establish (rather than reduce) by these means their	
MEANING		TRUTH
	leads to an infinite regress	

My thesis is that *the left side of this table is unimportant*, as compared to the right side: what should interest us are theories; truth; argument. If so many philosophers and scientists still think that concepts and conceptual systems (and problems of their meaning, or the meaning of words) are comparable in importance to theories and theoretical systems (and problems of their truth, or the truth of statements), then they are still suffering from Plato's main error.[13] For concepts are partly means of formulating theories, partly means of summing up theories. In any case their significance is mainly instrumental; and they may always be replaced by other concepts.

Contents and objects of thought seem to have played an important part in Stoicism and in neo-Platonism: Plotinus preserved Plato's separation between the empirical world and Plato's world of Forms or Ideas. Yet, like Aristotle,[14] Plotinus destroyed the transcendence of Plato's world by placing it into the consciousness of God.

Plotinus criticized Aristotle for failing to distinguish between the First Hypostasis (Oneness) and the Second Hypostasis (the divine intellect). Yet he followed Aristotle in identifying God's acts of thought with their own contents or objects; and he elaborated this view by taking the Forms or Ideas of Plato's intelligible world to be the immanent states of consciousness of the divine intellect.[15]

(ii) *Hegel* Hegel was a Platonist (or rather a neo-Platonist) of sorts and, like Plato, a Heraclitean of sorts. He was a Platonist whose world of Ideas was changing, evolving. Plato's 'Forms' or 'Ideas' were objective, and had nothing to do with conscious ideas in a subjective mind; they inhabited a divine, an unchanging, heavenly world (super-lunar in Aristotle's sense). By contrast Hegel's Ideas, like those of Plotinus, were conscious phenomena: thoughts thinking themselves and inhabiting some kind of consciousness, some kind of mind or 'Spirit'; and together with this 'Spirit' they were changing or evolving. The fact that Hegel's 'Objective Spirit' and 'Absolute Spirit' are subject to change is the only point in which his Spirits are more similar to my 'world 3' than is Plato's world of Ideas (or Bolzano's world of 'statements-in-themselves').

The most important differences between Hegel's 'Objective Spirit' and 'Absolute Spirit' and my 'world 3' are these:

(1) According to Hegel, though the Objective Spirit (comprising artistic creation) and Absolute Spirit (comprising philosophy) both consist of human productions, man is not creative. It is the hypostatized Objective Spirit, it is the divine self-consciousness of the Universe, that moves man: 'individuals . . . are instruments', instruments of the Spirit of the Epoch, and their work, their 'substantial business', is 'prepared and appointed independently of them'.[16]

Thus what I have called the autonomy of world 3, and its

feedback effect, become with Hegel omnipotent: it is only one of the aspects of his system in which his theological background manifests itself. As against this I assert that the individual creative element, the relation of give-and-take between a man and his work, is of the greatest importance. In Hegel this degenerates into the doctrine that the great man is something like a medium in which the Spirit of the Epoch expresses itself.

(2) In spite of a certain superficial similarity between Hegel's dialectic and my evolutionary schema

$$P_1 \rightarrow TT \rightarrow EE \rightarrow P_2$$

there is a fundamental difference. My schema works through error-elimination, and on the scientific level through conscious criticism under the regulative idea of the search for truth.

Criticism, of course, consists in the search for contradictions and in their elimination: the difficulty created by the demand for their elimination constitutes the new problem (P_2). Thus the elimination of error leads to the objective growth of our knowledge – of knowledge in the objective sense. It leads to the growth of objective verisimilitude: it makes possible the approximation to (absolute) truth.

Hegel, on the other hand, is a relativist.[17] He does not see our task as the search for contradictions, with the aim of eliminating them, for he thinks that contradictions are as good as (or better than) non-contradictory theoretical systems: they provide the mechanism by which the Spirit propels itself. Thus rational criticism plays no part in the Hegelian automatism, any more than does human creativity.[18]

(3) While Plato lets his hypostatized Ideas inhabit some divine heaven, Hegel personalizes his Spirit into some divine consciousness: the Ideas inhabit it as human ideas inhabit some human consciousness. His doctrine is, throughout, that the Spirit is not only conscious, but a self. As against this, my world 3 has no similarity whatever to human consciousness; and though its first inmates are products of human consciousness, they are totally different from conscious ideas or from thoughts in the subjective sense.

5 Evolutionary Epistemology (1973)

I

I now turn to progress in science. I will be looking at progress in science from a biological or evolutionary point of view. I am far from suggesting that this is the most important point of view for examining progress in science. But the biological approach offers a convenient way of introducing the two leading ideas of the first half of my talk. They are the ideas of *instruction* and of *selection*.

From a biological or evolutionary point of view, science, or progress in science, may be regarded as a means used by the human species to adapt itself to the environment: to invade new environmental niches, and even to invent new environmental niches.[1] This leads to the following problem.

We can distinguish between three levels of adaptation: genetic adaptation; adaptive behavioural learning; and scientific discovery, which is a special case of adaptive behavioural learning. My main problem in this part of my talk will be to inquire into the similarities and dissimilarities between the strategies of progress or adaptation on the *scientific* level and on those two other levels: the *genetic* level and the *behavioural* level. And I will compare the three levels of adaptation by investigating the role played on each level by *instruction* and by *selection*.

II

In order not to lead you blindfolded to the result of this comparison I will anticipate at once my main thesis. It is a thesis asserting the *fundamental similarity of the three levels*, as follows.

On all three levels – genetic adaptation, adaptive behaviour, and scientific discovery – the mechanism of adaptation is fundamentally the same.

This can be explained in some detail.

Adaptation on all three levels starts from an inherited *structure* which is basic. On the genetic level it is *the gene structure of the organism*. To it corresponds, on the behavioural level, *the innate repertoire* of the types of behaviour which are available to the organism; and on the scientific level, *the dominant scientific conjectures or theories*. These *structures* are always transmitted by *instruction*, on all three levels: by the replication of the coded genetic instruction on the genetic and the behavioural levels; and by social tradition and imitation on the behavioural and the scientific levels. On all three levels, the *instruction* comes from *within the structure*. If mutations or variations or errors occur, then these are new instructions, which also arise *from within the structure*, rather than *from without*, from the environment.

These inherited structures are exposed to certain pressures, or challenges, or problems: to selection pressures; to environmental challenges; to theoretical problems. In response, variations of the genetically or traditionally inherited *instructions* are produced,[2] by methods which are at least partly *random*. On the genetic level, these are mutations and recombinations of the coded instruction; on the behavioural level, they are tentative variations and recombinations within the repertoire; on the scientific level, they are new and revolutionary tentative theories. On all three levels we get new tentative trial instructions; or, briefly, tentative trials.

It is important that these tentative trials are changes that originate *within* the individual structure in a more or less random fashion – on all three levels. The view that they are *not* due to instruction from without, from the environment, is supported (if only weakly) by the fact that very similar organisms may sometimes respond in very different ways to the same new environmental challenge.

The next stage is that of *selection* from the available mutations and variations: those of the new tentative trials which are badly adapted are eliminated. *This is the stage of the elimination of error*. Only the more or less well adapted trial instructions survive and are inherited in their turn. Thus we may speak of *adaptation by 'the method of trial and error'* or better, by 'the method of trial and the elimination of error'. The elimination of error, or of badly adapted trial instructions, is also called '*natural selection*': it is a kind of 'negative feedback'. It operates on all three levels.

It is to be noted that in general *no equilibrium state of adaptation* is reached by any one application of the method of trial and the elimination of error, or by natural selection. First, because no perfect or optimal trial solutions to the problem are likely to be offered; secondly – and this is more important – because the emergence of new structures, or of new instructions, involves a change in the environmental situation. New elements of the environment may become relevant; and in consequence, new pressures, new challenges, new problems may arise, as a result of the structural changes which have arisen from within the organism.

On the genetic level the change may be a mutation of a gene, with a consequent change of an enzyme. Now the network of enzymes forms the more intimate environment of the gene structure. Accordingly, there will be a change in this intimate environment; and with it, new relationships between the organism and the more remote environment may arise; and further, new selection pressures.

The same happens on the behavioural level; for the adoption of a new kind of behaviour can be equated in most cases with the adoption of a new ecological niche. As a consequence, new selection pressures will arise, and new genetic changes.

On the scientific level, the tentative adoption of a new conjecture or theory may solve one or two problems, but it invariably opens up many *new* problems; for a new revolutionary theory functions exactly like a new and powerful sense organ. If the progress is significant then the new problems will differ from the old problems: the new problems will be on a radically different level of depth. This happened, for example, in relativity; it happened in quantum mechanics; and it happens right now, most dramatically, in molecular biology. In each of these cases, new horizons of unexpected problems were opened up by the new theory.

This, I suggest, is the way in which science progresses. And our progress can best be gauged by comparing our old problems with our new ones. If the progress that has been made is great, then the new problems will be of a character undreamt of before. There will be deeper problems; and besides, there will be more of them. The further we progress in knowledge, the more clearly we can discern the vastness of our ignorance. (The realization of our ignorance has become pinpointed as a result, for example, of the astonishing revolution brought about by molecular biology.)

I will now sum up my thesis.

On all the three levels which I am considering, the genetic, the behavioural, and the scientific levels, we are operating with inherited structures which are passed on by instruction; either through the genetic code or through tradition. On all the three levels, new structures and new instructions arise by trial changes from *within the structure*: by tentative trials which are subject to natural selection or the elimination of error.

III

So far I have stressed the *similarities* in the working of the adaptive mechanism on the three levels. This raises an obvious problem: what about the *differences*?

The main difference between the genetic and the behavioural levels is this. Mutations on the genetic level are not only random but completely 'blind', in two senses. First, they are in no way goal-directed. Secondly, the survival of a mutation cannot influence the further mutations, not even the frequencies or probabilities of their occurrence; though admittedly, the *survival* of a mutation may sometimes determine what kind of mutations may possibly *survive* in future cases. On the behavioural level, trials are also more or less random, but they are no longer completely 'blind' in either of the two senses mentioned. First, they are goal-directed; and secondly, animals may learn from the outcome of a trial: they may learn to avoid the type of trial behaviour which has led to a failure. (They may even avoid it in cases in which it could have succeeded.) Similarly, they may also learn from success; and successful behaviour may be repeated, even in cases in which it is not adequate. However, a certain degree of 'blindness' is inherent in all trials.[3]

Behavioural adaptation is usually an intensely active process: the animal – especially the young animal at play – and even the plant, are actively investigating the environment.[4]

This activity, which is largely genetically programmed, seems to me to mark an important difference between the genetic level and the behavioural level. I may here refer to the experience which the *Gestalt* psychologists call 'insight'; an experience that accompanies many behavioural discoveries.[5] However, it must not be overlooked that even a discovery accompanied by 'insight' may be *mistaken*: every trial, even one with 'insight', is of the nature of a conjecture or a hypothesis. Köhler's apes, it will be remembered, sometimes hit with 'insight' on what turned out to be a mistaken attempt to solve their problem; and even great mathematicians are sometimes misled by intuition. Thus animals and men have to try out their hypotheses; they have to use the method of trial and of error-elimination.

On the other hand I agree with Köhler and Thorpe[6] that the trials of problem-solving animals are in general not completely blind. Only in extreme cases, when the problem which confronts the animal does not yield to the making of hypotheses, will the animal resort to more or less blind and random attempts in order to get out of a disconcerting situation. Yet even in these attempts, goal-directedness is usually discernible, in sharp contrast to the blind randomness of genetic mutations and recombinations.

Another difference between genetic change and adaptive behavioural change is that the former *always* establishes a rigid and almost invariable genetic structure. The latter, admittedly, leads *sometimes* also to a fairly rigid behaviour pattern which is dogmatically adhered to; radically so in the case of 'imprinting' (Konrad Lorenz); but in other cases it leads to a flexible pattern which allows for differentiation or modification; for example, it may lead to exploratory behaviour, or to what Pavlov called the 'freedom reflex'.[7]

On the scientific level, discoveries are revolutionary and creative. Indeed, a certain creativity may be attributed to all levels, even to the genetic level: new trials, leading to new environments and thus to new selection pressures, create new and revolutionary results on all levels, even though there are strong conservative tendencies built into the various mechanisms of instruction.

Genetic adaptation can of course operate only within the time span of a few generations – at the very least, say, one or two generations. In organisms which replicate very quickly this may be a short time span; and there may be simply no room for behavioural adaptation. More slowly reproducing organisms are compelled to invent behavioural adaptation in order to adjust themselves to quick environmental changes. They thus need a behavioural repertoire, with types of behaviour of greater or lesser latitude or range. The repertoire, and the latitude of the available types of behaviour, can be assumed to be genetically programmed; and since, as indicated, a new type of behaviour may be said to involve the choice of a new environmental niche, new types of behaviour may indeed be genetically creative, for they may in their turn determine new selection pressures and thereby indirectly decide upon the future evolution of the genetic structure.[8]

On the level of scientific discovery two new aspects emerge. The most important one is that scientific theories can be formulated linguistically, and that they can even be published. Thus they become objects outside ourselves: objects open to investigation. As a consequence, they are now open to *criticism*. Thus we can get rid of a badly fitting theory before the adoption of the theory makes us unfit to survive: by criticizing our theories we can let our theories die in our stead. This is of course immensely important.

The other aspect is also connected with language. It is one of the novelties of human language that it encourages story telling, and thus *creative imagination*. Scientific discovery is akin to explanatory story telling, to myth making and to poetic imagination. The growth of imagination enhances of course the need for some control, such as, in science, interpersonal criticism – the friendly-hostile co-operation of scientists which is partly based on competition and partly on the common aim to get nearer to the truth. This, and the role played by instruction and tradition, seem to me to exhaust the main sociological elements inherently involved in the progress of science; though more could be said of course about the social obstacles to progress, or the social dangers inherent in progress.

IV

I have suggested that progress in science, or scientific discovery, depends on *instruction and selection*: on a conservative or traditional or historical element, and on a revolutionary use of trial and the elimination of error by criticism, which includes severe empirical examinations or tests; that is, attempts to probe into the possible weaknesses of theories, attempts to refute them.

Of course, the individual scientist may wish to establish his theory rather than to refute it. But from the point of view of progress in science, this wish can easily mislead him. Moreover, if he does not himself examine his favourite theory critically, others will do so for him. The only results which will be regarded by them as supporting the theory will be the failures of interesting attempts to refute it; failures to find counterexamples where such counterexamples would be most expected, in the light of the best of the competing theories. Thus it need not create a great obstacle to science if the individual scientist is biased in favour of a pet theory. Yet I think that Claude Bernard was very wise when he wrote: 'Those who have an excessive faith in their ideas are not well fitted to make discoveries.'[9]

All this is part of the critical approach to science, as opposed to the inductivist approach; or of the Darwinian or eliminationist or selectionist approach as opposed to the Lamarckian approach which operates with the idea of *instruction from without*, or from the environment, while the critical or selectionist approach only allows *instruction from within* – from within the structure itself.

In fact, I contend that *there is no such thing as instruction from without the structure*, or the passive reception of a flow of information which impresses itself on our sense organs. All observations are theory-impregnated: there is no pure, disinterested, theory-free observation. (To see this, we may try, using a little imagination, to compare human observation with that of an ant or a spider.)

Francis Bacon was rightly worried about the fact that our theories may prejudice our observations. This led him to advise scientists that they should avoid prejudice by purifying their minds of all theories. Similar recipes are still given.[10] But to attain objectivity we cannot rely on the empty mind: objectivity rests on criticism, on critical discussion, and on the critical examination of experiments. [See selection 11, section II, and selection 30 below.] And we must recognize, particularly, that our very sense organs incorporate what amount to prejudices. I have stressed before (in section II) that theories are like sense organs. Now I wish to stress that our sense organs are like theories. They *incorporate* adaptive theories (as has been shown in the case of rabbits and cats). And these theories are the result of natural selection.

V

However, not even Darwin or Wallace, not to mention Spencer, saw that there is no instruction from without. They did not operate with purely selectionist arguments. In fact, they frequently argued on Lamarckian lines.[11] In this they seem to have been mistaken. Yet it may be worth while to speculate about possible limits to Darwinism; for we should always be on the look-out for possible alternatives to any dominant theory.

I think that two points might be made here. The first is that the argument against the genetic inheritance of acquired characteristics (such as mutilations) depends upon the existence of a genetic mechanism in which there is a fairly sharp distinction between the gene structure and the remaining part of the organism: the soma. But this genetic mechanism must itself be a late product of evolution, and it was undoubtedly preceded by various other mechanisms of a less sophisticated kind. Moreover, certain very special kinds of mutilations *are* inherited; more particularly, mutilations of the gene structure by radiation. Thus if we assume that the primeval organism was a naked gene then we can even say that every non-lethal mutilation to this organism would be inherited. What we cannot say is that this fact contributes in any way to an explanation of genetic adaptation, or of genetic learning, except indirectly, via natural selection.

The second point is this. We may consider the very tentative conjecture that, as a somatic response to certain environmental pressures, some chemical mutagen is produced, increasing what is called the spontaneous mutation rate. This would be a kind of semi-Lamarckian effect, even though *adaptation* would still proceed only by the elimination of mutations; that is, by natural selection. Of course, there may not be much in this conjecture, as it seems that the spontaneous mutation rate suffices for adaptive evolution.[12]

These two points are made here merely as a warning against too dogmatic an adherence to Darwinism. Of course, I do conjecture that Darwinism is right, even on the level of scientific discovery; and that it is right even beyond this level: that it is right even on the level of artistic creation. We do not discover new facts or new effects by copying them, or by inferring them inductively from observation; or by any other method of instruction by the environment. We use, rather, the method of trial and the elimination of error. As Ernst Gombrich says, 'making comes before matching':[13] the active production of a new trial structure comes before its exposure to eliminating tests.

VI

I suggest therefore that we conceive the way science progresses somewhat on the lines of Niels Jerne's and Sir Macfarlane Burnet's theories of antibody formation.[14] Earlier theories of antibody formation assumed that the antigen works as a negative template for the formation of the antibody. This would mean that there is *instruction from without*, from the invading antibody. The fundamental idea of Jerne was that the instruction or information which enables the antibody to recognize the antigen is, literally, inborn: that it is part of the gene structure, though possibly subject to a repertoire of mutational variations. It is conveyed by the genetic code, by the chromosomes of the specialized cells which produce the antibodies; and the immune reaction is a result of growth-stimulation given to these cells by the antibody/antigen complex. Thus these cells are *selected* with the help of the invading environment (that is, with the help of the antigen), rather than instructed. (The analogy with the selection – and the modification – of scientific theories is clearly seen by Jerne, who in this connection refers to Kierkegaard, and to Socrates in the *Meno*.)

With this remark I conclude my discussion of the biological aspects of progress in science.

6 Two Kinds of Definitions (1945)

> The chief danger to our philosophy, apart from laziness and woolliness, is *scholasticism*, . . . which is treating what is vague as if it were precise. . . .
>
> F. P. RAMSEY[1]

The problem of definitions and of the 'meaning of terms' is the most important source of Aristotle's regrettably still prevailing intellectual influence, of all that verbal and empty scholasticism that haunts not only the Middle Ages, but our own contemporary philosophy; for even a philosophy as recent as that of L. Wittgenstein suffers, as we shall see, from this influence. The development of thought since Aristotle could, I think, be summed up by saying that every discipline, as long as it used the Aristotelian method of definition, has remained arrested in a state of empty verbiage and barren scholasticism, and that the degree to which the various sciences have been able to make any progress depended on the degree to which they have been able to get rid of this essentialist method. (This is why so much of our 'social science' still belongs to the Middle Ages.) The discussion of this method will have to be a little abstract, owing to the fact that the problem has been so thoroughly muddled by Plato and Aristotle, whose influence has given rise to such deep-rooted prejudices that the prospect of dispelling them does not seem very bright. In spite of all that, it is perhaps not without interest to analyse the source of so much confusion and verbiage.

Aristotle followed Plato in distinguishing between *knowledge* and *opinion*.[2] Knowledge, or science, according to Aristotle, may be of two kinds – either demonstrative or intuitive. *Demonstrative knowledge* is also a knowledge of 'causes'. It consists of statements that can be demonstrated – the conclusions – together with their syllogistic demonstrations (which exhibit the 'causes' in their 'middle terms'). *Intuitive knowledge* consists in grasping the 'indivisible form' or essence or essential nature of a thing (if it is 'immediate', i.e. if its 'cause' is identical with its essential nature); it is the originative source of all science since it grasps the original basic premisses of all demonstrations.

Undoubtedly, Aristotle was right when he insisted that we must not attempt to prove or demonstrate *all* our knowledge. Every proof must proceed from premisses; the proof as such, that is to say, the derivation from the premisses, can therefore never finally settle the truth of any conclusion, but only show that the conclusion must be true *provided* the premisses are true. If we were to demand that the premisses should be proved in their turn, the question of truth would only be shifted back by another step to a new set of premisses, and so on, to infinity. It was in order to avoid such an infinite regress (as the logicians say) that Aristotle taught that we must assume that there are premisses which are indubitably true, and which do not need any proof; and these he called 'basic premisses'. If we take for granted the methods by which we derive conclusions from these basic premisses, then we could say that, according to Aristotle, the whole of scientific knowledge is contained in the basic premisses, and that it would all be ours if only we could obtain an encyclopaedic list of the basic premisses. But how to obtain these basic premisses? Like Plato, Aristotle believed that we obtain all knowledge ultimately by an intuitive grasp of the essences of things. 'We can know a thing only by knowing its essence', Aristotle writes, and 'to know a thing is to know its essence'. A 'basic premiss' is, according to him, nothing but a statement describing the essence of a thing. But such a statement is just what he calls[3] a definition. Thus *all 'basic premisses of proofs' are definitions.*

What does a definition look like? An example of a definition would be: 'A puppy is a young dog.' The subject of such a definition sentence, the term 'puppy', is called the *term to be defined (or defined term)*; the words 'young dog' are called the *defining formula.* As a rule, the defining formula is longer and more complicated than the defined term, and sometimes very much so.

Aristotle considers[4] the term to be defined as a name of the essence of a thing, and the defining formula as the description of that essence. And he insists that the defining formula must give an exhaustive description of the essence or the essential properties of the thing in question; thus a statement like 'A puppy has four legs', although true, is not a satisfactory definition, since it does not exhaust what may be called the essence of puppiness, but holds true of a horse also; and similarly the statement 'A puppy is brown', although it may be true of some, is not true of all puppies; and it describes what is not an essential but merely an accidental property of the defined term.

But the most difficult question is how we can get hold of definitions or basic premisses, and make sure that they are correct – that we have not erred, not grasped the wrong essence. Although Aristotle is not very clear on this point, there can be little doubt that, in the main, he again follows Plato. Plato taught[5] that we can grasp the Ideas with the help of some kind of unerring *intellectual intuition*; that is to say, we visualize or look at them with our 'mental eye', a process which he conceived as analogous to seeing, but dependent purely upon our intellect, and excluding any element that depends upon our senses. Aristotle's view is less radical and less inspired than Plato's, but in the end it amounts to the same.[6] For although he teaches that we arrive at the definition only after we have made many observations, he admits that sense experience does not in itself grasp the universal essence, and that it cannot, therefore, fully determine a definition. Eventually he simply postulates that we possess an intellectual intuition, a mental or intellectual faculty which enables us unerringly to grasp the essences of things, and to know them. And he further assumes that if we know an essence intuitively, we must be capable of describing it and therefore of defining it. (His arguments in the *Posterior Analytics* in favour of this theory are surprisingly weak. They consist merely in pointing out that our knowledge of the basic premisses cannot be demonstrative, since this would lead to an infinite regress, and that the basic premisses must be at least as true and as certain as the conclusions based upon them. 'It follows from this', he writes, 'that there cannot be demonstrative knowledge of the primary premisses; and since nothing but intellectual intuition can be more true than demonstrative knowledge, it follows that it must be intellectual intuition that grasps the basic premisses.' In the *De Anima*, and in the theological part of the *Metaphysics*, we find more of an argument; for here we have a *theory* of intellectual intuition – that it comes into contact with its object, the essence, and that it even becomes one with its object. 'Actual knowledge is identical with its object.')

Summing up this brief analysis, we can give, I believe, a fair description of the Aristotelian ideal of perfect and complete knowledge if we say that he saw the ultimate aim of all inquiry in the compilation of an encyclopaedia containing the intuitive definitions of all essences, that is to say, their names together with their defining formulae; and that he considered the progress of knowledge as consisting in the gradual accumulation of such an encyclopaedia, in expanding it as well as in filling up the gaps in it and, of course, in the syllogistic derivation from it of 'the whole body of facts' which constitute demonstrative knowledge.

Now there can be little doubt that all these essentialist views stand in the strongest possible contrast to the methods of modern science. (I have the empirical sciences in mind, not perhaps pure mathematics.) First, although in science we do our best to find the truth, we are conscious of the fact that we can never be sure whether we have got it. We have learnt in the past, from many disappointments, that we must not expect finality. And we have learnt not to be disappointed any longer if our scientific theories are overthrown; for we can, in most cases, determine with great confidence which of any two theories is the better one. We can therefore know that we are making progress; and it is this knowledge that to most of us atones for the loss of the illusion of finality and certainty. In other words, we know that our scientific theories must always remain hypotheses, but that, in many important cases, we can find out whether or not a new hypothesis is superior to an old one. For if they are different, then they will lead to different predictions, which can often be tested experimentally; and on the basis of such a crucial experiment, we can sometimes find out that the new theory leads to satisfactory results where the old one breaks down. Thus we can say that in our search for truth, we have replaced scientific certainty by scientific progress. And this view of scientific method is corroborated by the development of science. For science does not develop by a gradual encyclopaedic accumulation of essential information, as Aristotle thought, but by a much more revolutionary method; it progresses by bold ideas, by the advancement of new and very strange theories (such as the theory that the earth is not flat, or that 'metrical space' is not flat), and by the overthrow of the old ones.

But this view of scientific method [developed in selections 9-14 below] means that in science there is no '*knowledge*', in the sense in which Plato and Aristotle understood the word, in the sense which implies finality; in science, we never have sufficient reason for the belief that we have attained the truth. What we usually call 'scientific knowledge' is, as a rule, not knowledge in this sense, but rather information regarding the various competing hypotheses and the way in which they have stood up to various tests; it is, using the language of Plato and Aristotle, information concerning the latest, and the best tested, scientific '*opinion*'. This view means, furthermore, that we have no proofs in science (excepting, of course, pure mathematics and logic). In the empirical sciences, which alone can furnish us with information about the world we live in, proofs do not occur, if we mean by 'proof' an argument which establishes once and for ever the truth of a theory. (What may occur, however, are refutations of scientific theories.) On the other hand, pure mathematics and logic, which permit of proofs, give us no information about the world, but only develop the means of describing it. Thus we could say (as I have pointed out elsewhere[7]): 'In so far as a scientific statement speaks about reality, it must be falsifiable; and in so far as it is not falsifiable, it does not speak about reality.' But although proof does not play any part in the empirical sciences, argument still does; indeed, its part is at least as important as that played by observation and experiment.

The role of definitions in science, especially, is also very different from what Aristotle had in mind. Aristotle taught that in a definition we have first pointed to the essence – perhaps by naming it – and that we then describe it with the help of the defining formula; just as in an ordinary sentence like 'This puppy is brown', we first point to a certain thing by saying 'this puppy', and then describe it as 'brown'. And he taught that by thus describing the essence to which the term points which is to be defined, we determine or explain the *meaning*[8] of the term also.

Accordingly, the definition may at one time answer two very closely related questions. The one is 'What is it?', for example, 'What is a puppy?'; it asks what the essence is which is denoted by the defined term. The other is 'What does it mean?', for example, 'What does "puppy" mean?'; it asks for the meaning of a term (namely, of the term that denotes the essence). In the present context, it is not necessary to distinguish between these two questions; rather, it is important to see what they have in common; and I wish, especially, to draw attention to the fact that *both questions are raised by the term that stands, in the definition, on the left side and answered by the defining formula which stands on the right side*. This fact characterizes the essentialist view, from which the scientific method of definition radically differs.

While we may say that the essentialist interpretation reads a definition 'normally', that is to say, from *the left to the right*, we can say that a *definition*, as it is *normally used in modern science*, *must be read back to front, or from the right to the left*; for it starts with the defining formula, and asks for a short label for it. Thus the scientific view of the definition 'A puppy is a young dog' would be that it is an answer to the question '*What shall we call* a young dog?' rather than an answer to the question '*What is* a puppy?' (Questions like '*What is* life?' or '*What is* gravity?' do not play any role in science.) The scientific use of definitions, characterized by the approach 'from the right to the left', may be called its *nominalist* interpretation, as opposed to its Aristotelian or *essentialist* interpretation.[9] In modern science, only[10] nominalist definitions occur, that is to say, shorthand symbols or labels are introduced in order to cut a long story short. And we can at once see from this that definitions do *not* play any very important part in science. For shorthand symbols can always, of course, be replaced by the longer expressions, the defining formulae, for which they stand. In some cases this would make our scientific language very cumbersome; we should waste time and paper. But we should never lose the slightest piece of factual information. Our 'scientific knowledge', in the sense in which this term may be properly used, remains entirely unaffected if we eliminate all definitions; the only effect is upon our language, which would lose, not precision, but merely brevity. (This must not be taken to mean that in science there cannot be an urgent practical need for introducing definitions, for brevity's sake.) There could hardly be a greater contrast than that between this view of the part played by definitions, and Aristotle's view. For Aristotle's essentialist definitions are the principles from which all our knowledge is derived; they thus contain all our knowledge; and they serve to substitute a long formula for a short one. As opposed to this, the scientific or nominalist definitions do not contain any knowledge whatever, not even any 'opinion'; they do nothing but introduce new arbitrary shorthand labels; they cut a long story short.

In practice, these labels are of the greatest usefulness. In order to see this, we only need to consider the extreme difficulties that would arise if a bacteriologist, whenever he spoke of a certain strain of bacteria, had to repeat its whole description (including the methods of dyeing, etc., by which it is distinguished from a number of similar species). And we may also understand, by a similar consideration, why it has so often been forgotten, even by scientists, that scientific definitions must be read 'from the right to the left', as explained above. For most people, when first studying a science, say bacteriology, must try to find out the meanings of all these new technical terms with which they are faced. In this way, they really *learn* the definition 'from the left to the right', substituting, as if it were an essentialist definition, a very long story for a very short one. But this is merely a psychological accident, and a teacher or writer of a textbook may indeed proceed quite differently; that is to say, he may introduce a technical term only after the need for it has arisen.

So far I have tried to show that the scientific or nominalist use of definitions is entirely different from Aristotle's essentialist method of definitions. But it can also be shown that the essentialist view of definitions is simply untenable in itself. In order not to prolong this discussion unduly, I shall criticize two only of the essentialist doctrines; two doctrines which are of significance because some influential modern schools are still based upon them. One is the esoteric doctrine of intellectual intuition, and the other the very popular doctrine that 'we must define our terms', if we wish to be precise.

Aristotle held with Plato that we possess a faculty, intellectual intuition, by which we can visualize essences and find out which definition is the correct one, and many modern essentialists have repeated this doctrine. Other philosophers, following Kant, maintain that we do not possess anything of the sort. My opinion is that we can readily admit that we possess something which may be described as 'intellectual intuition'; or more precisely, that certain of our intellectual experiences may be thus described. Everybody who 'understands' an idea, or a point of view, or an arithmetical method, for instance, multiplication, in the sense that he has 'got the feel of it', might be said to understand that thing intuitively; and there are countless intellectual experiences of that kind. But I would insist, on the other hand, that these experiences, important as they may be for our scientific endeavours, can never serve to establish the truth of any idea or theory, however strongly somebody may feel, intuitively, that it must be true, or that it is 'self-evident'.[11] Such intuitions cannot even serve as an argument, although they may encourage us to look for arguments. For somebody else may have just as strong an intuition that the same theory is false. The way of science is paved with discarded theories which were once declared self-evident; Francis Bacon, for example, sneered at those who denied the self-evident truth that the sun and the stars rotated round the earth, which was obviously at rest. Intuition undoubtedly plays a great part in the life of a scientist, just as it does in the life of a poet. It leads him to his discoveries. But it may also lead him to his failures. And it always remains his private affair, as it were. Science does not ask how he has got his ideas, it is only interested in arguments that can be tested by everybody. The great mathematician, Gauss, described this situation very neatly once when he exclaimed: 'I have got my result; but I do not know yet how to get it.' All this applies, of course, to Aristotle's doctrine of intellectual intuition of so-called essences, which was propagated by Hegel, and in our own time by E. Husserl and his numerous pupils; and it indicates that the 'intellectual intuition of essences' or 'pure phenomenology', as Husserl calls it, is a method of neither science nor philosophy. (The much debated question whether it is a new invention, as the pure phenomenologists think, or perhaps a version of Cartesianism or Hegelianism, can be easily decided; it is a version of Aristotelianism.)

The second doctrine to be criticized has even more important connections with modern views; and it bears especially upon the problem of verbalism. Since Aristotle, it has become widely known that one cannot prove all statements, and that an attempt to do so would break down because it would lead only to an infinite regression of proofs. But neither he[12] nor, apparently, a great many modern writers seems to realize that the analogous attempt to define the meaning of all our terms must, in the same way, lead to an infinite regression of definitions. The following passage from Crossman's *Plato To-day* is characteristic of a view which by implication is held by many contemporary philosophers of repute, for example, by Wittgenstein:[13] '. . . if we do not know precisely the meaning of the words we use, we cannot discuss anything profitably. Most of the futile arguments on which we all waste time are largely due to the fact that we each have our own vague meaning for the words we use and assume that our opponents are using them in the same sense. If we defined our terms to start with, we could have far more profitable discussions. Again, we have only to read the daily papers to observe that propaganda (the modern counterpart of rhetoric) depends largely for its success on confusing the meaning of the terms. If politicians were compelled by law to define any term they wished to use, they would lose most of their popular appeal, their speeches would be shorter, and many of their disagreements would be found to be purely verbal.' This passage is very characteristic of one of the prejudices which we owe to Aristotle, of the prejudice that language can be made more precise by the use of definitions. Let us consider whether this can really be done.

First, we can see clearly that if 'politicians' (or anybody else) 'were compelled by law to define any term they wished to use', their speeches would not be shorter, but infinitely long. For a definition cannot establish the meaning of a term any more than a logical derivation can establish the truth of a statement; both can only shift this problem back. The derivation shifts the problem of truth back to the premises, the definition shifts the problem of meaning back to the defining terms (i.e., the terms that make up the defining formula).[14] But these, for many reasons, are likely to be just as vague and confusing as the terms we started with; and in any case, we should have to go on to define them in turn; which leads to new terms which too must be defined. And so on, to infinity. One sees that the demand that all our terms should be defined is just as untenable as the demand that all our statements should be proved.

At first sight this criticism may seem unfair. It may be said that what people have in mind, if they demand definitions, is the elimination of the ambiguities so often connected with words such as[15] 'democracy', 'liberty', 'duty', 'religion', etc.; that it is clearly impossible to define all our terms, but possible to define some of these more dangerous terms and to leave it at that; and that the defining terms have just to be accepted, i.e., that we must stop after a step or two in order to avoid an infinite regression. This defence, however, is untenable. Admittedly, the terms mentioned are much misused. But I deny that the attempt to define them can improve matters. It can only make matters worse. That by 'defining their terms' even once, and leaving the defining terms undefined, the politicians would not be able to make their speeches shorter, is clear; for any essentialist definition, i.e. one that 'defines our terms' (as opposed to the nominalist one which introduces new technical terms), means the substitution of a long story for a short one, as we have seen. Besides, the attempt to define terms would only increase the vagueness and confusion. For since we cannot demand that all the defining terms should be defined in their turn, a clever politician or philosopher could easily satisfy the demand for definitions. If asked what he means by 'democracy', for example, he could say 'the rule of the general will' or 'the rule of the spirit of the people'; and since he has now given a definition, and so satisfied the highest standards of precision, nobody will dare to criticize him any longer. And, indeed, how could he be criticized, since the demand that 'rule' or 'people' or 'will' or 'spirit' should be defined in their turn, puts us well on the way to an infinite regression so that everybody would hesitate to raise it? But should it be raised in spite of all that, then it can be equally easily satisfied. On the other hand, a quarrel about the question whether the definition was correct, or true, can only lead to an empty controversy about words.

Thus the essentialist view of definition breaks down, even if it does not, with Aristotle, attempt to establish the 'principles' of our knowledge, but only makes the apparently more modest demand that we should 'define the meaning of our terms'.

But undoubtedly, the demand that we speak clearly and without ambiguity is very important, and must be satisfied. Can the nominalist view satisfy it? And can nominalism escape the infinite regression?

It can. For the nominalist position there is no difficulty which corresponds to the infinite regression. As we have seen, science does not use definitions in order to determine the meaning of its terms, but only in order to introduce handy shorthand labels. And it does not depend on definitions; all definitions can be omitted without loss to the information imparted. It follows from this that in science, *all the terms that are really needed must be undefined terms*. How then do the sciences make sure of the meanings of their terms? Various replies to this question have been suggested,[16] but I do not think that any of them is satisfactory. The situation seems to be this. Aristotelianism and related philosophies have told us for such a long time how important it is to get a precise knowledge of the meaning of our terms that we are all inclined to believe it. And we continue to cling to this creed in spite of the unquestionable fact that philosophy, which for twenty centuries has worried about the meaning of its terms, is not only full of verbalism but also appallingly vague and ambiguous, while a science like physics which worries hardly at all about terms and their meaning, but about facts instead, has achieved great precision. This, surely, should be taken as indicating that, under Aristotelian influence, the importance of the meaning of terms has been grossly exaggerated. But I think that it indicates even more. For not only does this concentration on the problem of meaning fail to establish precision; it is itself the main source of vagueness, ambiguity, and confusion.

In science, we take care that the statements we make should never *depend* upon the meaning of our terms. Even where the terms are defined, we never try to derive any information from the definition, or to base any argument upon it. This is why our terms make so little trouble. We do not overburden them. We try to attach to them as little weight as possible. We do not take their 'meaning' too seriously. We are always conscious that our terms are a little vague (since we have learnt to use them only in practical applications) and we reach precision not by reducing their penumbra of vagueness, but rather by keeping well within it, by carefully phrasing our sentences in such a way that the possible shades of meaning of our terms do not matter. This is how we avoid quarrelling about words.

The view that the precision of science and of scientific language depends upon the precision of its terms is certainly very plausible, but it is none the less, I believe, a mere prejudice. The precision of a language depends, rather, just upon the fact that it takes care not to burden its terms with the task of being precise. A term like 'sand-dune' or 'wind' is certainly very vague. (How many inches high must a little sand-hill be in order to be called 'sand-dune'? How quickly must the air move in order to be called 'wind'?) However, for many of the geologist's purposes, these terms are quite sufficiently precise; and for other purposes, when a higher degree of differentiation is needed, he can always say 'dunes between 4 and 30 feet high' or 'wind of a velocity of between 20 and 40 miles an hour'. And the position in the more exact sciences is analogous. In physical measurements, for instance, we always take care to consider the range within which there may be an error; and precision does not consist in trying to reduce this range to nothing, or in pretending that there is no such range, but rather in its explicit recognition.

Even where a term has made trouble, as for instance the term 'simultaneity' in physics, it was not because its meaning was imprecise or ambiguous, but rather because of some intuitive theory which induced us to burden the term with too much meaning, or with too 'precise' a meaning, rather than with too little. What Einstein found in his analysis of simultaneity was that, when speaking of simultaneous events, physicists made a false assumption which would have been unchallengeable were there signals of infinite velocity. The fault was not that they did not mean anything, or that their meaning was ambiguous, or the term not precise enough; what Einstein found was, rather, that the elimination of a theoretical assumption, unnoticed so far because of its intuitive self-evidence, was able to remove a difficulty which had arisen in science. Accordingly, he was not really concerned with a question of the meaning of a term, but rather with the truth of a theory. It is very unlikely that it would have led to much if someone had started, apart from a definite physical problem, to improve the concept of simultaneity by analysing its 'essential meaning', or even by analysing what physicists 'really mean' when they speak of simultaneity.

I think we can learn from this example that we should not attempt to cross our bridges before we come to them. And I also think that the preoccupation with questions concerning the meaning of terms, such as their vagueness or their ambiguity, can certainly not be justified by an appeal to Einstein's example. Such a preoccupation rests, rather, on the assumption that much depends upon the meaning of our terms, and that we operate with this meaning; and therefore it must lead to verbalism and scholasticism. From this point of view, we may criticize a doctrine like that of Wittgenstein,[17] who holds that while science investigates matters of fact, it is the business of philosophy to clarify the meaning of terms, thereby purging our language, and eliminating linguistic puzzles. It is characteristic of the views of this school that they do not lead to any chain of argument that could be rationally criticized; the school therefore addresses its subtle analyses[18] exclusively to the small esoteric circle of the initiated. This seems to suggest that any preoccupation with meaning tends to lead to that result which is so typical of Aristotelianism: scholasticism and mysticism.

Let us consider briefly how these two typical results of Aristotelianism have arisen. Aristotle insisted that demonstration or proof, and definition, are the two fundamental methods of obtaining knowledge. Considering the doctrine of proof first, it cannot be denied that it has led to countless attempts to prove more than can be proved; medieval philosophy is full of this scholasticism and the same tendency can be observed, on the Continent, down to Kant. It was Kant's criticism of all attempts to prove the existence of God which led to the romantic reaction of Fichte, Schelling, and Hegel. The new tendency is to discard proofs, and with them, any kind of rational argument. With the romantics, a new kind of dogmatism becomes fashionable, in philosophy as well as in the social sciences. It confronts us with its dictum. And we can *take it or leave it*. This romantic period of an oracular philosophy, called by Schopenhauer the 'age of dishonesty', is described by him as follows:[19] 'The character of honesty, that spirit of undertaking an inquiry together with the reader, which permeates the works of all previous philosophers, disappears here completely. Every page witnesses that these so-called philosophers do not attempt to teach, but to bewitch the reader.'

A similar result was produced by Aristotle's doctrine of definition. First it led to a good deal of hairsplitting. But later, philosophers began to feel that one cannot argue about definitions. In this way, essentialism not only encouraged verbalism, but it also led to the disillusionment with argument, that is, with reason. Scholasticism and mysticism and despair in reason, these are the unavoidable results of the essentialism of Plato and Aristotle. And Plato's open revolt against freedom becomes, with Aristotle, a secret revolt against reason.

As we know from Aristotle himself, essentialism and the theory of definition met with strong opposition when they were first proposed, especially from Socrates's old companion Antisthenes, whose criticism seems to have been most sensible.[20] But this opposition was unfortunately defeated. The consequences of this defeat for the intellectual development of mankind can hardly be overrated.

7 The Problem of Induction (1953, 1974)

I

For a brief formulation of the problem of induction we can turn to Born, who writes: '. . . no observation or experiment, however extended, can give more than a finite number of repetitions'; therefore, 'the statement of a law – B depends on A – always transcends experience. Yet this kind of statement is made everywhere and all the time, and sometimes from scanty material.'[1]

In other words, the logical problem of induction arises from (1) Hume's discovery (so well expressed by Born) that it is impossible to justify a law by observation or experiment, since it 'transcends experience'; (2) the fact that science proposes and uses laws 'everywhere and all the time'. (Like Hume, Born is struck by the 'scanty material', i.e. the few observed instances upon which the law may be based.) To this we have to add (3) *the principle of empiricism* which asserts that in science only observation and experiment may decide upon the *acceptance or rejection* of scientific statements, including laws and theories.

These three principles, (1), (2), and (3), appear at first sight to clash; and this apparent clash constitutes the *logical problem of induction*.

Faced with this clash, Born gives up (3), the principle of empiricism (as Kant and many others, including Bertrand Russell, have done before him), in favour of what he calls a 'metaphysical principle'; a metaphysical principle which he does not even attempt to formulate; which he vaguely describes as a 'code or rule of craft'; and of which I have never seen any formulation which even looked promising and was not clearly untenable.

But in fact the principles (1) to (3) do not clash. We can see this the moment we realize that the acceptance by science of a law or of a theory is *tentative only*; which is to say that all laws and theories are conjectures, or tentative *hypotheses* (a position which I have sometimes called 'hypotheticism'); and that we may reject a law or theory on the basis of new evidence, without necessarily discarding the old evidence which originally led us to accept it. (I do not doubt that Born and many others would agree that theories are accepted only tentatively. But the widespread belief in induction shows that the far-reaching implications of this view are rarely seen.)

The principle of empiricism (3) can be fully preserved, since the fate of a theory, its acceptance or rejection, is decided by observation and experiment – by the results of tests. So long as a theory stands up to the severest tests we can design, it is accepted; if it does not, it is rejected. But it is never inferred, in any sense, from the empirical evidence. There is neither a psychological nor a logical induction. *Only the falsity of the theory can be inferred from empirical evidence, and this inference is a purely deductive one.*

Hume showed that it is not possible to infer a theory from observation statements; but this does not affect the possibility of refuting a theory by observation statements. The full appreciation of this possibility makes the relation between theories and observations perfectly clear.

This solves the problem of the alleged clash between the principles (1), (2), and (3), and with it Hume's problem of induction.

II

Hume's problem of induction has almost always been badly formulated by what may be called the philosophical tradition. I will first give a few of these bad formulations, which I shall call the *traditional formulations of the problem of induction*. I shall replace them, however, by what I regard as better formulations.

Typical examples of formulations of the problem of induction that are both traditional and bad are the following.

What is the justification for the belief that the future will resemble the past? What is the justification of so-called *inductive inferences*?

By an inductive inference is here meant an inference from repeatedly *observed instances* to some as yet *unobserved instances*. It is of comparatively minor significance whether such an inference from the observed to the unobserved is, from the point of view of time, predictive or retrodictive; whether we infer that the sun will rise tomorrow or that it did rise 100,000 years ago. Of course, from a pragmatic point of view, one might say that it is the predictive type of inference which is the more important. No doubt usually it is.

There are various other philosophers who also regard as misconceived this traditional problem of induction. Some say that it is misconceived because no justification is needed for inductive inference; no more in fact than for deductive inference. Inductive inference is inductively valid just as deductive inference is deductively valid. I think it was Professor Strawson who was the first to say this.

I am of a different opinion. I hold with Hume that there simply is no such logical entity as an inductive inference; or, that all so-called inductive inferences are logically invalid – and even *inductively* invalid, to put it more sharply [see the end of this selection]. We have many examples of deductively valid inferences, and even some partial criteria of deductive validity; but no example of an inductively valid inference exists.[2] And I hold, incidentally, that this result can be found in Hume, even though Hume, at the same time, and in sharp contrast to myself, *believed in the psychological power of induction*; not as a valid procedure, but as a procedure which animals and men successfully make use of, as a matter of fact and of biological necessity.

I take it as an important task to make clear, even at the cost of some repetition, where I agree and where I disagree with Hume.

I agree with Hume's opinion that induction is invalid and in no sense justified. Consequently neither Hume nor I can accept the traditional formulations which uncritically ask for the justification of induction; such a request is uncritical because it is blind to the possibility that induction is invalid in *every sense*, and therefore *unjustifiable*.

I disagree with Hume's opinion (the opinion incidentally of almost all philosophers) that induction is a fact and in any case needed. I hold that neither animals nor men use any procedure like induction, or any argument based on the repetition of instances. The belief that we use induction is simply a mistake. It is a kind of optical illusion.

What we do use is a method of trial and the elimination of error; however misleadingly this method may look like induction, its logical structure, if we examine it closely, totally differs from that of induction. Moreover, it is a method which does not give rise to any of the difficulties connected with the problem of induction.

Thus it is not because induction can manage without justification that I am opposed to the traditional problem; on the contrary, it would urgently need justification. But the need cannot be satisfied. Induction simply does not exist, and the opposite view is a straightforward mistake.

III

There are many ways to present my own non-inductivist point of view. Perhaps the simplest is this. I will try to show that the whole apparatus of induction becomes unnecessary once we admit the general fallibility of human knowledge or, as I like to call it, the *conjectural character of human knowledge*.

Let me point this out first for the best kind of human knowledge we have; that is, for scientific knowledge. I assert that scientific knowledge is essentially conjectural or hypothetical.

Take as an example classical Newtonian mechanics. There never was a more successful theory. If repeated observational success could establish a theory, it would have established Newton's theory. Yet Newton's theory was superseded in the field of astronomy by Einstein's theory, and in the atomic field by quantum theory. And almost all physicists think now that Newtonian classical mechanics is no more than a marvellous conjecture, a strangely successful hypothesis, and a staggeringly good approximation to the truth.

I can now formulate my central thesis, which is this. Once we fully realize the implications of the conjectural character of human knowledge, then the problem of induction changes its character completely: there is no need any longer to be disturbed by Hume's negative results, since there is no need any longer to ascribe to human knowledge a *validity* derived from repeated observations. Human knowledge possesses no such validity. On the other hand, we can explain all our achievements in terms of the method of trial and the elimination of error. To put it in a nutshell, our conjectures are our trial balloons, and we test them by criticizing them and by trying to replace them – by trying to show that there can be better or worse conjectures, and that they can be improved upon. The place of the problem of induction is usurped by the problem of the comparative goodness or badness of the rival conjectures or theories that have been proposed.

The main barrier to accepting the conjectural character of human knowledge, and to accepting that it contains the solution of the problem of induction, is a doctrine which may be called the commonsense theory of human knowledge or the *bucket theory of the human mind.*[3]

IV

I think very highly of common sense. In fact, I think that all philosophy must start from commonsense views and from their critical examination.

For our purposes here I want to distinguish two parts of the commonsense view of the world and draw attention to the fact that they clash with one another.

The first is commonsense realism; this is the view that there is a real world, with real people, animals and plants, cars and stars in it. I think that this view is true and immensely important, and I believe that no valid criticism of it has ever been proposed. [See also selection 17 below.]

A very different part of the commonsense view of the world is the commonsense *theory of knowledge*. The problem is the problem of how we get knowledge about the world. The commonsense solution is: by opening our eyes and ears. *Our senses are the main if not the only sources of our knowledge of the world.*

This second view I regard as thoroughly mistaken, and as insufficiently criticized (in spite of Leibniz and Kant). I call it the bucket theory of the mind, because it can be summed up by the diagram overleaf.

What allegedly enters the bucket through our senses are the elements, the atoms or molecules, of knowledge. Our knowledge then consists of an accumulation, a digest, or perhaps a synthesis of the elements offered to us by our senses.

Both halves of commonsense philosophy, commonsense realism and the commonsense theory of knowledge, were held by Hume; he found, as did Berkeley before him, that there is a clash between them. For the commonsense theory of knowledge is liable to lead to a kind of anti-realism. If knowledge results from sensations, then sensations are the only *certain* elements of knowledge, and we can have no good reason to believe that anything but sensation exists.

Hume, Berkeley, and Leibniz were all believers in a principle of sufficient reason. For Berkeley and Hume the principle took the form: if you do not have sufficient reasons for holding a belief, then this fact is itself a sufficient reason for abandoning this belief. Genuine knowledge consisted for both Berkeley and Hume essentially of belief, backed by sufficient reasons: but this led them to the position that knowledge consists, more or less, of sensations on their own.

Thus for these philosophers the real world of common sense does not really exist; according to Hume, even we ourselves do not fully exist. All that exist are sensations, impressions, and memory images. [See also selection 22, section I, below.]

This anti-realistic view can be characterized by various names, but the most usual name seems to be 'idealism'. Hume's idealism appeared to him to be a strict refutation of commonsense realism. But though he felt *rationally* obliged to regard commonsense realism as a mistake, he himself admitted that he was in practice quite unable to disbelieve in commonsense realism for more than an hour.

Thus Hume experienced very strongly the clash between the two parts of commonsense philosophy: realism, and the commonsense theory of knowledge. And although he was aware that emotionally he was unable to give up realism, he looked on this fact as a mere consequence of irrational custom or habit; he was convinced that a consistent adherence to the more critical results of the theory of knowledge ought to make us abandon realism.[4] Fundamentally, Hume's idealism has remained the mainstream of British empiricism.

V

Hume's two problems of induction – the logical problem and the psychological problem – can best be presented, I think, against the background of the commonsense theory of induction. This theory is very simple. Since all knowledge is supposed to be the result of past observation, so especially is all expectational knowledge such as that the sun will rise tomorrow, or that all men are bound to die, or that bread nourishes. All this has to be the result of past observation.

It is to Hume's undying credit that he dared to challenge the commonsense view of induction, even though he never doubted that it must be largely true. He believed that induction by repetition was logically untenable – that rationally, or logically, *no amount* of observed instances can have the slightest bearing upon unobserved instances. This is Hume's negative solution of the problem of induction, a solution which I fully endorse.

But Hume held, at the same time, that although induction was rationally invalid, it was a psychological fact, and that we all rely on it.

Thus Hume's two problems of induction were:

(1) The logical problem: *Are we rationally justified in reasoning from repeated instances of which we have had experience to instances of which we have had no experience?*

Hume's unrelenting answer was: No, we are not justified, however great the number of repetitions may be. And he added that it did not make the slightest difference if, in this problem, we ask for the justification not of *certain* belief, but of *probable* belief. Instances of which we have had experience do not allow us to reason or argue about the *probability* of instances of which we have had no experience, any more than to the *certainty* of such instances.

(2) The following psychological question: *How is it that nevertheless all reasonable people expect and believe that instances of which they have had no experience will conform to those of which they have had experience?* Or in other words, why do we all have *expectations*, and why do we hold on to them with such great *confidence*, or such strong belief?

Hume's answer to this psychological problem of induction was: *Because of 'custom or habit'; or in other words, because of the irrational but irresistible power of the law of association*. We are *conditioned by repetition*; a conditioning mechanism without which, Hume says, we could hardly survive.

My own view is that Hume's answer to the logical problem is right and that his answer to the psychological problem is, in spite of its persuasiveness, quite mistaken.

VI

The answers given by Hume to the logical and psychological problems of induction lead immediately to an irrationalist conclusion. According to Hume, all our knowledge, especially all our scientific knowledge, is just irrational habit or custom, and it is rationally totally indefensible.

Hume himself thought of this as a form of scepticism; but it was rather, as Bertrand Russell pointed out, an unintended surrender to irrationalism. It is an amazing fact that a peerless critical genius, one of the most rational minds of all ages, not only came to disbelieve in reason, but became a champion of unreason, of irrationalism.

Nobody has felt this paradox more strongly than Bertrand Russell, an admirer and, in many respects, even a late disciple of Hume. Thus in the Hume chapter in *A History of Western Philosophy*, published in 1946, Russell says about Hume's treatment of induction: 'Hume's philosophy . . . represents the bankruptcy of eighteenth-century reasonableness' and, 'It is therefore important to discover whether there is any answer to Hume within a philosophy that is wholly or mainly *empirical*. If not, *there is no intellectual difference between sanity and insanity*. The lunatic who believes that he is a poached egg is to be condemned solely on the ground that he is in a minority . . . .'

Russell goes on to assert that if induction (or the principle of induction) is rejected, 'every attempt to arrive at general scientific laws from particular observations is fallacious, and Hume's scepticism is inescapable for an empiricist.'

And Russell sums up his view of the situation created by the clash between Hume's two answers, by the following dramatic remark:

'*The growth of unreason throughout the nineteenth century and what has passed of the twentieth* is a natural sequel to Hume's destruction of empiricism.'[5]

This last quotation of Russell's goes *perhaps* too far. I do not wish to overdramatize the situation; and although I sometimes feel that Russell is right in his emphasis, at other moments I doubt it.

Yet the following quotation from Professor Strawson seems to me to support Russell's grave opinion: '[If] . . . there is a problem of induction, and . . . Hume posed it, it must be added that he solved it . . . [;] our acceptance of the "basic canons" [of induction] . . . is forced upon us by Nature. . . . Reason is, and ought to be the slave of the passions.'[6]

However this may be, I assert that I have an answer to Hume's psychological problem which completely removes the clash between the logic and the psychology of knowledge; and with it, it removes all of Hume's and Strawson's reasoning against reason.

VII

My own way of avoiding Hume's irrationalist consequences is very simple. I solve the psychological problem of induction (and also such formulations as the pragmatic problem) in a manner which satisfies the following '*principle of the primacy of the logical solution*', or, more briefly, the '*principle of transference*'. The principle runs like this: the solution of the logical problem of induction, far from clashing with those of the psychological or pragmatic problems, can, with some care, be directly transferred to them. As a result, there is no clash, and there are no irrationalist consequences.

The logical problem of induction itself needs some reformulation to start with.

First, it must be formulated in terms not only of 'instances' (as by Hume) but of universal regularities or laws. Regularities or laws are presupposed by Hume's own term 'instance'; for an instance is an instance *of* something – *of* a regularity or *of* a law. (Or, rather, it is an instance of many regularities or many laws.)

Secondly, we must widen the scope of reasoning from instances to laws so that we can take heed also of counterinstances.

In this way, we arrive at a reformulation of Hume's *logical problem of induction* along the following lines:

Are we rationally justified in reasoning from instances or from counterinstances of which we have had experience to the truth or falsity of the corresponding laws, or to instances of which we have had no experience?

This is a purely logical problem. It is essentially merely a slight extension of Hume's logical problem of induction formulated here earlier, in section v.

The answer to this problem is: as implied by Hume, we certainly are not justified in reasoning from an instance to the truth of the corresponding law. But to this negative result a second result, equally negative, may be added: we *are* justified in reasoning from a counterinstance to the *falsity* of the corresponding universal law (that is, of any law of which it is a counterinstance). Or in other words, from a purely logical point of view, the acceptance of *one* counterinstance to 'All swans are white' implies the falsity of the law 'All swans are white' – that law, that is, whose counterinstance we accepted. Induction is logically invalid; but refutation or falsification is a logically valid way of arguing from a single counterinstance to – or, rather, against – the corresponding law.

This shows that I continue to agree with Hume's negative logical result; but I extend it.

This logical situation is completely independent of any question of whether we would, in practice, accept a single counterinstance – for example, a solitary black swan – in refutation of a so far highly successful law. I do not suggest that we would necessarily be so easily satisfied; we might well suspect that the black specimen before us was not a swan. And in practice, anyway, we would be most reluctant to accept an isolated counterinstance. But this is a different question [see section IV of selection 10 below]. Logic forces us to reject even the most successful law the moment we accept one single counterinstance.

Thus we can say: Hume was right in his negative result that there can be no logically valid positive argument leading in the inductive direction. But there is a further negative result; there are logically valid negative arguments leading in the inductive direction: *a counterinstance may disprove a law.*

VIII

Hume's negative result establishes for good that all our universal laws or theories remain for ever guesses, conjectures, hypotheses. But the second negative result concerning the force of counterinstances by no means rules out the possibility of a positive theory of how, by purely rational arguments, we can *prefer* some competing conjectures to others.

In fact, we can erect a fairly elaborate *logical theory of preference* – preference from the point of view of the search for truth.

To put it in a nutshell, Russell's desperate remark that if with Hume we reject all positive induction, 'there is no intellectual difference between sanity and insanity' is mistaken. For the rejection of induction does not prevent us from preferring, say, Newton's theory to Kepler's, or Einstein's theory to Newton's: during our rational critical discussion of these theories we *may* have accepted the existence of counterexamples to Kepler's theory which do not refute Newton's, and of counterexamples to Newton's which do not refute Einstein's. Given the acceptance of these counterexamples we can say that Kepler's and Newton's theories are certainly false; whilst Einstein's may be true or it may be false: that we don't know. Thus there may exist *purely intellectual* preferences for one or the other of these theories; and we are very far from having to say with Russell that all the difference between science and lunacy disappears. Admittedly, Hume's argument still stands, and therefore the difference between a scientist and a lunatic is not that the first bases his theories securely upon observations while the second does not, or anything like that. Nevertheless we may now see that there *may be* a difference: it *may be* that the lunatic's theory is easily refutable by observation, while the scientist's theory has withstood severe tests.

What the scientist's and the lunatic's theories have in common is that both belong to *conjectural knowledge*. But some conjectures are much better than others; and this is a sufficient answer to Russell, and it is sufficient to avoid radical scepticism. For since it is possible for some conjectures to be *preferable* to others, it is also possible for our conjectural knowledge to improve, and to *grow*. (Of course, it is possible that a theory that is preferred to another at one time may fall out of favour at a later time so that the other is now preferred to it. But, on the other hand, this may not happen.)

We may *prefer* some competing theories to others on purely rational grounds. It is important that we are clear what the principles of preference or selection are.

In the first place they are governed by the idea of truth. We want, if at all possible, theories which are true, and for this reason we try to eliminate the false ones.

But we want more than this. We want new and interesting truth. We are thus led to the idea of *the growth of informative content*, and especially of *truth content*. That is, we are led to the following *principle of preference*: a theory with a great informative content is on the whole more interesting, even before it has been tested, than a theory with little content. Admittedly, we may have to abandon the theory with the greater content, or as I also call it, the bolder theory, if it does not stand up to tests. But even in this case we may have learned more from it than from a theory with little content, for falsifying tests can sometimes reveal new and unexpected facts and problems. [See also selection 13 below.]

Thus our logical analysis leads us direct to a theory of method, and especially to the following methodological rule: try out, and aim at, bold theories, with great informative content; and then let these bold theories compete, by discussing them critically and by testing them severely.

IX

My *solution* of the logical problem of induction was that we may have *preferences* for certain of the competing conjectures; that is, for those which are highly informative and which so far have stood up to eliminative criticism. These preferred conjectures are the result of selection, of the struggle for survival of the hypotheses under the strain of *criticism, which is artificially intensified selection pressure.*

The same holds for the psychological problem of induction. Here too we are faced with competing hypotheses, which may perhaps be called beliefs, and some of them are eliminated, while others survive, anyway for the time being. Animals are often eliminated along with their beliefs; or else they survive with them. Men frequently outlive their beliefs; but for as long as the beliefs survive (often a very short time), they form the (momentary or lasting) *basis of action.*

My thesis is that this Darwinian procedure of the selection of beliefs and actions can in no sense be described as irrational. In no way does it clash with the rational solution of the logical problem of induction. Rather, it is just the transference of the logical solution to the psychological field. (This does not mean, of course, that we never suffer from what are called 'irrational beliefs'.)

Thus with an application of the principle of transference to Hume's psychological problem Hume's irrationalist conclusions disappear.

X

In talking of preference I have so far discussed only the theoretician's preference – if he has any; and why it will be for the 'better', that is, more testable, theory, and for the better tested one. Of course, the theoretician may not have *any* preference: he may be discouraged by Hume's, and my, 'sceptical' solution to Hume's logical problem; he may say that, if he cannot *make sure* of finding the true theory among the competing theories, he is not interested in any method like the one described – not even if the method makes it reasonably certain that, *if* a true theory should be among the theories proposed, it will be among the surviving, the preferred, the corroborated ones. Yet a more sanguine or more dedicated or more curious 'pure' theoretician may well be encouraged, by our analysis, to propose again and again new competing theories in the hope that one of them may be true – even if we shall never be able to make sure of any one that it is true.

Thus the pure theoretician has more than one way of action open to him; and he will choose a method such as the method of trial and the elimination of error only if his curiosity exceeds his disappointment at the unavoidable uncertainty and incompleteness of all our endeavours.

It is different with him *qua* man of practical action. For a man of practical action has always to *choose* between some more or less definite alternatives, since *even inaction is a kind of action*.

But every action presupposes a set of expectations, that is, of theories about the world. Which theory shall the man of action choose? Is there such a thing as a *rational choice*?

This leads us to the *pragmatic problems of induction*, which to start with, we might formulate thus:

(1) Upon which theory should we rely for practical action, from a rational point of view?

(2) Which theory should we prefer for practical action, from a rational point of view?

My answer to (1) is: from a rational point of view, we should not 'rely' on any theory, for no theory has been shown to be true, or can be shown to be true (or 'reliable').

My answer to (2) is: we should *prefer* the best tested theory as a basis for action.

In other words, there is no 'absolute reliance'; but since we *have* to choose, it will be 'rational' to choose the best tested theory. This will be 'rational' in the most obvious sense of the word known to me: the best tested theory is the one which, in the light of our *critical discussion*, appears to be the best so far; and I do not know of anything more 'rational' than a well-conducted critical discussion.

Since this point appears not to have got home I shall try to restate it here in a slightly new way, suggested to me by David Miller. Let us forget momentarily about what theories we 'use' or 'choose' or 'base our practical actions on', and consider only the resulting *proposal* or *decision* (to do X; not to do X; to do nothing; or so on). Such a proposal can, we hope, be rationally criticized; and if we are rational agents we will want it to survive, if possible, the most testing criticism we can muster. *But such criticism will freely make use of the best tested scientific theories in our possession*. Consequently any proposal that ignores these theories (where they are relevant, I need hardly add) will collapse under criticism. Should any proposal remain, it will be rational to adopt it.

This seems to me all far from tautological. Indeed, it might well be challenged by challenging the italicized sentence in the last paragraph. Why, it might be asked, does rational criticism make use of the best tested although highly unreliable theories? The answer, however, is exactly the same as before. Deciding to criticize a practical proposal from the standpoint of modern medicine (rather than, say, in phrenological terms) is itself a kind of 'practical' decision (anyway it may have practical consequences). Thus the rational decision is always: adopt critical methods that have themselves withstood severe criticism.

There is, of course, an infinite regress here. But it is transparently harmless.

Now I do not particularly want to deny (or, for that matter, assert) that, in choosing the best tested theory as a basis for action, we 'rely' on it, in some sense of the word. It may therefore even be described as the *most* 'reliable' theory available, in some sense of this term. Yet this is not to say that it is 'reliable'. It is 'unreliable' at least in the sense that we shall always do well, even in practical action, to foresee the possibility that something may go wrong with it and with our expectations.

But it is not merely this trivial caution which we must derive from our negative reply to the pragmatic problem (1). Rather, it is of the utmost importance for the understanding of the whole problem, and especially of what I have called the traditional problem, that in spite of the 'rationality' of choosing the best tested theory as a basis of action, this choice is *not* 'rational' in the sense that it is based upon *good reasons in favour* of the expectation that it will in practice be a successful choice: *there can be no good reasons* in this sense, and this is precisely Hume's result. On the contrary, even if our physical theories should be true, it is perfectly possible that the world as we know it, with all its pragmatically relevant regularities, may completely disintegrate in the next second. This should be obvious to anybody today; but I said so[7] before Hiroshima: there are infinitely many possible causes of local, partial, or total disaster.

From a pragmatic point of view, however, most of these possibilities are obviously not worth bothering about because we cannot *do* anything about them: they are beyond the realm of action. (I do not, of course, include atomic war among those disasters which are beyond the realm of human action, although most of us think in just this way since we cannot do more about it than about an act of God.)

All this would hold even if we could be certain that our physical and biological theories were true. But we do not know it. On the contrary, we have very good reason to suspect even the best of them; and this adds, of course, further infinities to the infinite possibilities of catastrophe.

It is this kind of consideration which makes Hume's and my own negative reply so important. For we can now see very clearly why we must beware lest our theory of knowledge proves too much. More precisely, *no theory of knowledge should attempt to explain why we are successful in our attempts to explain things.*

Even if we assume that we have been successful – that our physical theories are true – we can learn from our cosmology how infinitely improbable this success is: our theories tell us that the world is almost completely empty, and that empty space is filled with chaotic radiation. And almost all places which are not empty are occupied either by chaotic dust, or by gases, or by very hot stars – all in conditions which seem to make the application of any physical method of acquiring knowledge impossible.

There are many worlds, possible and actual worlds, in which a search for knowledge and for regularities would fail. And even in the world as we actually know it from the sciences, the occurrence of conditions under which life, and a search for knowledge, could arise – and succeed – seems to be almost infinitely improbable. Moreover, it seems that if ever such conditions should appear, they would be bound to disappear again, after a time which, cosmologically speaking, is very short.

It is in this sense that induction is inductively invalid, as I said above. That is to say, any strong positive reply to Hume's logical problem (say, the thesis that induction is valid) would be paradoxical. For, on the one hand, if induction is the method of science, then modern cosmology is at least roughly correct (I do not dispute this); and on the other, modern cosmology teaches us that to generalize from observations taken, for the most part, in our incredibly idiosyncratic region of the universe would almost always be quite invalid. Thus if induction is 'inductively valid' it will almost always lead to false conclusions; and therefore it is inductively invalid.

8 The Problem of Demarcation (1974)

1 Science versus Non-science

I now turn to the *problem of demarcation*, and to explaining how this problem is related to the problems of empirical content and of testability.

The great scientists, such as Galileo, Kepler, Newton, Einstein, and Bohr (to confine myself to a few of the dead) represent to me a simple but impressive idea of science. Obviously, no such list, however much extended, would *define* scientist or science *in extenso*. But it suggests for me an oversimplification, one from which we can, I think, learn a lot. It is the working of great scientists which I have in my mind as my paradigm for science. Not that I lack respect for the lesser ones; there are hundreds of great men and great scientists who come into the almost heroic category.

But with all respect for the lesser scientists, I wish to convey here a heroic and romantic idea of science and its workers: men who humbly devoted themselves to the search for truth, to the growth of our knowledge; men whose life consisted in an adventure of bold ideas. I am prepared to consider with them many of their less brilliant helpers who were equally devoted to the search for truth – for great truth. But I do not count among them those for whom science is no more than a profession, a technique: those who are not deeply moved by great problems and by the oversimplifications of bold solutions.

It is science in this heroic sense that I wish to study. As a side result I find that we can throw a lot of light even on the more modest workers in applied science.

This, then, for me is science. I do not try to define it, for very good reasons. I only wish to draw a simple picture of the kind of men I have in mind, and of their activities. And the picture will be an oversimplification: these are men of bold ideas, but highly critical of their own ideas; they try to find whether their ideas are right by trying first to find whether they are not perhaps wrong. They work with bold conjectures and severe attempts at refuting their own conjectures.

My criterion of demarcation between science and non-science is a simple logical analysis of this picture. How good or bad it is will be shown by its fertility.

Bold ideas are new, daring, hypotheses or conjectures. And severe attempts at refutations are severe critical discussions and severe empirical tests.

When is a conjecture daring and when is it not daring, in the sense here proposed? Answer: it is daring if and only if it takes a great risk of being false – if matters could be otherwise, and seem at the time to be otherwise.

Let us consider a simple example. Copernicus's or Aristarchus's conjecture that the sun rather than the earth rests at the centre of the universe was an incredibly daring one. It was, incidentally, false; nobody accepts today the conjecture that the sun is (in the sense of Aristarchus and Copernicus) at rest in the centre of the universe. But this does not affect the boldness of the conjecture, nor its fertility. And one of its main consequences – that the earth does not rest at the centre of the universe but that it has (at least) a daily and an annual motion – is still fully accepted, in spite of some misunderstandings of relativity.[1]

But it is not the present acceptance of the theory which I wish to discuss, but its boldness. It was bold because it clashed with all then accepted views, *and* with the prima facie evidence of the senses. It was bold because it postulated a hitherto unknown hidden reality behind the appearances.

It was not bold in another very important sense: neither Aristarchus nor Copernicus suggested a feasible crucial experiment. In fact, they did not suggest that anything was wrong with the traditional appearances: they let the accepted appearances severely alone; they only reinterpreted them. They were not anxious to stick out their necks by predicting new observable appearances. (This is an oversimplification as far as Copernicus is concerned, but it is almost certainly true of Aristarchus.)

To the degree that this is so, Aristarchus's and Copernicus's theories may be described in my terminology as unscientific or metaphysical. To the degree that Copernicus did make a number of minor predictions, his theory is, in my terminology, scientific. But even as a metaphysical theory it was far from meaningless; and in proposing a new bold view of the universe it made a tremendous contribution to the advent of the new science.

Kepler went much further. He too had a bold metaphysical view, partly based upon the Copernican theory, of the reality of the world. But his view led him to many new detailed predictions of the appearances. At first these predictions did not tally with the observations. He tried to reinterpret the observations in the light of his theories; but his addiction to the search for truth was even greater than his enthusiasm for the metaphysical harmony of the world. Thus he felt forced to give up a number of his favoured theories, one by one, and to replace them by others which fitted the facts. It was a great and a heartrending struggle. The final outcome, his famous and immensely important three laws, he did not really like – except the third. But they stood up to his severest tests – they agreed with the detailed appearances, the observations which he had inherited from Tycho.

Kepler's laws are excellent approximations to what we think today are the true movements of the planets of our solar system. They are even excellent approximations to the movements of the distant binary star systems which have since been discovered. Yet they are merely *approximations* to what seems to be the truth; *they are not true*.

They have been tested in the light of new theories – of Newton's theory and of Einstein's – which predicted small deviations from Kepler's laws. (According to Newton, Kepler's laws are correct only for two-body systems [see also selection 12 below].) Thus the crucial experiments went against Kepler, very slightly, but sufficiently clearly.

Of these three theories – Kepler's, Newton's, and Einstein's – the latest and still the most successful is Einstein's; and it was this theory which led me into the philosophy of science. What impressed me so greatly about Einstein's theory of gravitation were the following points.

(1) It was a very bold theory. It greatly deviated in its fundamental outlook from Newton's theory which at that time was utterly successful. (The small deviation of the perihelion of Mercury did not seriously trouble anybody in the light of its other almost incredible successes. Whether it should have done is another matter.)

(2) From the point of view of Einstein's theory, Newton's theory was an excellent approximation, though false (just as from the point of view of Newton's theory, Kepler's and Galileo's theories were excellent approximations, though false). Thus it is not its truth which decides the scientific character of a theory.

(3) Einstein derived from his theory three important predictions of vastly different observable effects, two of which had not been thought of by anybody before him, and all of which contradicted Newton's theory, so far as they could be said to fall within the field of application of this theory at all.

But what impressed me perhaps most were the following two points.

(4) Einstein declared that these predictions were crucial: if they did not agree with his precise theoretical calculations, he would regard his theory as refuted.

(5) But even if they were observed as predicted, Einstein declared that *his theory was false*: he said that it would be a better approximation to the truth than Newton's, but he gave reasons why he would not, even if all predictions came out right, regard it as a true theory. He sketched a number of demands which a true theory (a unified field theory) would have to satisfy, and declared that his theory was at best an approximation to this so far unattained unified field theory.

It may be remarked in passing that Einstein, like Kepler, failed to achieve his scientific dream – or his metaphysical dream: it does not matter in this context what label we use. What we call today Kepler's laws or Einstein's theory of gravitation are results which in no way satisfied their creators, who each continued to work on his dream to the end of his life. And even of Newton a similar point can be made: he never believed that a theory of action at a distance could be a finally acceptable explanation of gravity.[2]

Einstein's theory was first tested by Eddington's famous eclipse experiment of 1919. In spite of his unbelief in the truth of his theory, his belief that it was merely a new important approximation towards the truth, Einstein never doubted the outcome of this experiment; the inner coherence, the inner logic of his theory convinced him that it was a step forward even though he thought that it could not be true. It has since passed a series of further tests, all very successfully. But some people still think the agreement between Einstein's theory and the observations may be the result of (incredibly improbable) accidents. It is impossible to rule this out; yet the agreement may rather be the result of Einstein's theory's being a fantastically good approximation to the truth.[3]

The picture of science at which I have so far only hinted may be sketched as follows.

There is a reality behind the world as it appears to us, possibly a many-layered reality, of which the appearances are the outermost layers. What the great scientist does is boldly to guess, daringly to conjecture, what these inner realities are like. This is akin to myth making. (Historically we can trace back the ideas of Newton via Anaximander to Hesiod, and the ideas of Einstein via Faraday, Boscovič, Leibniz, and Descartes to Aristotle and Parmenides.[4]) The boldness can be gauged by the distance between the world of appearance and the conjectured reality, the explanatory hypotheses.

But there is another, a special kind of boldness – *the boldness of predicting* aspects of the world of appearance which so far have been overlooked but which it must possess if the conjectured reality is (more or less) right, if the explanatory hypotheses are (approximately) true. It is this more special kind of boldness which I have usually in mind when I speak of bold scientific conjectures. It is the boldness of a conjecture which takes a real risk – the risk of being tested, and refuted; the risk of clashing with reality.

Thus my proposal was, and is, that it is this second boldness, together with the readiness to look out for tests and refutations, which distinguishes 'empirical' science from non-science, and especially from pre-scientific myths and metaphysics.

I will call this proposal (D): (D) for '*demarcation*'.

The italicized proposal (D) is what I still regard as the centre of my philosophy. But I have always been highly critical of any idea of my own; and so I tried at once to find fault with this particular idea, years before I published it. And I published it together with the main results of this criticism. My criticism led me to a sequence of refinements or improvements of the proposal (D): they were not later concessions, but they were published together with the proposal as parts of the proposal itself.[5]

II Difficulties with the Demarcation Proposal

(1) From the beginning I called my criterion of demarcation a *proposal*. This was partly because of my uneasiness about definitions and my dislike of them. Definitions are either abbreviations and therefore unnecessary, though perhaps convenient, or they are Aristotelian attempts to 'state the essence' of a word, and therefore unconscious conventional dogmas [see selection 6 above]. If I define 'science' by my criterion of demarcation (I admit that this is more or less what I am doing) than anybody could propose another definition, such as 'science is the sum total of true statements'. A discussion of the merits of such definitions can be pretty pointless. This is why I gave here first a description of great or heroic science and then a proposal for a criterion which allows us to demarcate – roughly – this kind of science. Any demarcation in my sense *must* be rough. (This is one of the great differences from any formal meaning criterion of any artificial 'language of science'.) For the transition between metaphysics and science is not a sharp one: what was a metaphysical idea yesterday can become a testable scientific theory tomorrow; and this happens frequently (I gave various examples in *The Logic of Scientific Discovery* and elsewhere: atomism is perhaps the best).

Thus one of the difficulties is that our criterion must not be too sharp; and in the chapter 'Degrees of Testability' of *The Logic of Scientific Discovery* I suggested (as a kind of second improvement of the criterion (D) of the foregoing section) that a theory is scientific to the degree to which it is testable.

This, incidentally, led later to one of the most fruitful discoveries of that book: that there are degrees of testability (or of scientific character), which can be identified with degrees of empirical content (or informative content).

(2) The formula (D) of the foregoing section is expressed in somewhat psychological language. It can be considerably improved if one speaks of *theoretical systems* or *systems of statements*, as I did throughout *The Logic of Scientific Discovery*. This leads at once to the recognition of one of the problems connected with the falsifiability criterion of demarcation: even if we can apply it to *systems* of statements, it may be difficult if not impossible to say which particular statement, or which subsystem of a system of statements, has been exposed to a particular experimental test. Thus we may describe a *system* as scientific or empirically testable, while being most uncertain about its constituent parts.

An example is Newton's theory of gravitation. It has often been asked whether Newton's laws of motion, or which of them, are masked definitions rather than empirical assertions.

My answer is as follows: Newton's theory is a system. *If we falsify it, we falsify the whole system.* We may perhaps put the blame on one of its laws or on another. But this means only that we *conjecture* that a certain change in the system will free it from falsification; or in other words, that we conjecture that a certain alternative system will be an improvement, a better approximation to the truth.

But this means: attributing the blame for a falsification to a certain subsystem is a typical hypothesis, a conjecture like any other, though perhaps hardly more than a vague suspicion if no definite alternative suggestion is being made. And the same applies the other way round: the decision that a certain subsystem is not to be blamed for the falsification is likewise a typical conjecture. The attribution or non-attribution of responsibility for failure is conjectural, like everything in science; and what matters is the proposal of a new alternative and competing conjectural system that is able to pass the falsifying test.

(3) Points (1) and (2) illustrate that however correct my criterion of bold conjectures and severe refutations may be, there are difficulties which must not be overlooked. A primitive difficulty of this kind may be described as follows. A biologist offers the conjecture that all swans are white. When black swans are discovered in Australia, he says that it is not refuted. He insists that

these black swans are a new kind of bird since it is *part of the defining property* of a swan that it is white. In other words, he can escape the refutation, though I think that he is likely to learn more if he admits that he was wrong.

In any case – and this is very important – the theory 'All swans are white' is refutable at least in the following clear logical sense: it must be declared refuted by anybody who accepts that there is at least one non-white swan.

(4) The principle involved in this example is a very primitive one, but it has a host of applications. For a long time chemists have been inclined to regard atomic weights, melting points, and similar properties as *defining properties* of materials: there can be no water whose freezing point differs from 0°C; it just would not be water, however similar in other respects it might be to water. But if this is so, then according to my criterion of demarcation 'Water freezes at 0°C' would not be a scientific or an empirical statement; it would be a tautology – part of a definition.

Clearly, there is a problem here: either my criterion of demarcation is refuted, or we have to admit the possibility of discovering water whose freezing point is other than 0°C.

(5) I plead of course for the second possibility, and I hold that from this simple example we can learn a lot about the advantages of my proposal (D). For let us assume we have discovered water with a different freezing point. Is this still to be called 'water'? *I assert that the question is totally irrelevant*. The scientific hypothesis was that a liquid (no matter what you call it) with a considerable list of chemical and physical properties freezes at 0°C. If any of these properties which have been conjectured to be constantly conjoined should not materialize then *we were wrong*; and thus *new and interesting problems open up*. The least of them is whether or not we should continue to call the liquid in question 'water': *this* is purely arbitrary or conventional. Thus my criterion of demarcation is not only not refuted by this example: it helps us to discover what is significant for science and what is arbitrary and irrelevant.

(6) As explained in the very first chapter of *The Logic of Scientific Discovery*, we can always adopt evasive tactics in the face of refutations. For historical reasons I originally called these tactics 'conventionalist stratagems [or twists]', but now call them

'*immunizing tactics or stratagems*':[6] we can always immunize a theory against refutation. There are many such evasive immunizing tactics; and if nothing better occurs to us, we can always deny the objectivity – or even the existence – of the refuting observation. (Remember the people who *refused* to look through Galileo's telescope.) Those intellectuals who are more interested in being right than in learning something interesting but unexpected are by no means rare exceptions.

(7) None of the difficulties so far discussed is terribly serious: it may seem that a little intellectual honesty would go a long way to overcome them. By and large this is true. But how can we describe this intellectual honesty in logical terms? I described it in *The Logic of Scientific Discovery*, as *a rule of method*, or a *methodological rule*: 'Do not try to evade falsification, but stick your neck out!'

(8) But I was yet a little more self-critical: I first noticed that such a rule of method is, necessarily, somewhat vague – as is the problem of demarcation altogether. Clearly, one can say that if you avoid falsification *at any price*, you give up empirical science in my sense. But I found that, in addition, supersensitivity with respect to refuting criticism was just as dangerous: there is a legitimate place for dogmatism, though a very limited place. He who gives up his theory too easily in the face of apparent refutations will never discover the possibilities inherent in his theory. *There is room in science for debate*: for attack and therefore also for defence. Only if we try to defend them can we learn all the different possibilities inherent in our theories. As always, science is conjecture. You have to conjecture when to stop defending a favourite theory, and when to try a new one.

(9) Thus I did not propose the simple rule: 'Look out for refutations, and never dogmatically defend your theory.' Still, it was much better advice than dogmatic defence at any price. The truth is that we must be constantly critical; self-critical with respect to our own theories, and self-critical with respect to our own criticism; and, of course, we must never evade an issue.

This, then, is roughly the *methodological form* of (D), of the criterion of demarcation. Propose theories which can be criticized. Think about possible decisive falsifying experiments – crucial experiments. But do not give up your theories too easily – not, at any rate, before you have critically examined your criticism.

III Empirical-scientific and Non-scientific Theories

The difficulties connected with my criterion of demarcation (D) are important, but must not be exaggerated. It is vague, since it is a methodological rule, and since the demarcation between science and non-science is vague. But it is more than sharp enough to make a distinction between many physical theories on the one hand, and metaphysical theories, such as psychoanalysis, or Marxism (in its present form), on the other. This is, of course, one of my main theses; and nobody who has not understood it can be said to have understood my theory.

The situation with Marxism is, incidentally, very different from that with psychoanalysis. Marxism was once a scientific theory: it predicted that capitalism would lead to increasing misery and, through a more or less mild revolution, to socialism; it predicted that this would happen first in the technically highest developed countries; and it predicted that the technical evolution of the 'means of production' would lead to social, political, and ideological developments, rather than the other way round.

But the (so-called) socialist revolution came first in one of the technically backward countries. And instead of the means of production producing a new ideology, it was Lenin's and Stalin's ideology that Russia must push forward with its industrialization ('Socialism is dictatorship of the proletariat plus electrification') which promoted the new development of the means of production.

Thus one might say that Marxism was once a science, but one which was refuted by some of the facts which happened to clash with its predictions (I have here mentioned just a few of these facts).[7]

However, Marxism is no longer a science; for it broke the methodological rule that we must accept falsification, and it immunized itself against the most blatant refutations of its predictions. Ever since then, it can be described only as non-science – as a metaphysical dream, if you like, married to a cruel reality.

Psychoanalysis is a very different case. It is an interesting psychological metaphysics (and no doubt there is some truth in it, as there is so often in metaphysical ideas), but it never was a science. There may be lots of people who are Freudian or Adlerian cases: Freud himself was clearly a Freudian case, and Adler an Adlerian case. But what prevents their theories from being scientific in the sense here described is, very simply, that they do not exclude any physically possible human behaviour. Whatever anybody may do is, in principle, explicable in Freudian or Adlerian terms. (Adler's break with Freud was more Adlerian than Freudian, but Freud never looked on it as a refutation of his theory.)

The point is very clear. Neither Freud nor Adler excludes any particular person's acting in any particular way, whatever the outward circumstances. Whether a man sacrificed his life to rescue a drowning child (a case of sublimation) or whether he murdered the child by drowning him (a case of repression) could not possibly be predicted or excluded by Freud's theory; *the theory was compatible with everything that could happen – even without any special immunization treatment.*

Thus while Marxism became nonscientific by its adoption of an immunizing strategy, psychoanalysis was immune to start with, and remained so.[8] In contrast, most physical theories are pretty free of immunizing tactics and *highly falsifiable to start with.* As a rule, *they exclude an infinity of conceivable possibilities.*

The main value of my criterion of demarcation was, of course, to point out these differences. And it led me to the theory that the empirical content of a theory could be measured by the number of possibilities which it excluded (provided a reasonably non-immunizing methodology was adopted).

IV Ad Hoc Hypotheses and Auxiliary Hypotheses

There is one important method of avoiding or evading refutations: it is the method of auxiliary hypotheses or *ad hoc* hypotheses.

If any of our conjectures goes wrong – if, for example, the planet Uranus does not move exactly as Newton's theory demands – *then we have to change the theory.* But there are in the main two kinds of changes; *conservative and revolutionary.* And among the more conservative changes there are again two: *ad hoc hypotheses* and *auxiliary hypotheses*.

In the case of the disturbances in the motion of Uranus the adopted hypothesis was partly revolutionary: what was conjectured was the existence of a new planet, something which did not affect Newton's laws of motion, but which did affect the much older 'system of the world'. The new conjecture was auxiliary rather than *ad hoc* for although there was only this one *ad hoc* reason for introducing it, it was *independently testable*: the position of the new planet (Neptune) was calculated, the planet was discovered optically, and it was found that it fully explained the anomalies of Uranus. Thus the auxiliary hypothesis stayed within the Newtonian theoretical framework, and the threatened refutation was transformed into a resounding success.

I call a conjecture '*ad hoc*' if it is introduced (like this one) to explain a particular difficulty, but if (in contrast to this one) *it cannot be tested independently*.

It is clear that, like everything in methodology, the distinction between an *ad hoc* hypothesis and a conservative auxiliary hypothesis is a little vague. Pauli introduced the hypothesis of the neutrino quite consciously as an *ad hoc* hypothesis. He had originally no hope that one day independent evidence would be found; at the time this seemed practically impossible. So we have an example here of an *ad hoc* hypothesis which, with the growth of knowledge, did shed its *ad hoc* character. And we have a warning here not to pronounce too severe an edict against *ad hoc* hypotheses: they may become testable after all, as may also happen to a metaphysical hypothesis. But in general, our criterion of testability warns us against *ad hoc* hypotheses; and Pauli was at first far from happy about the neutrino, which would in all likelihood have been abandoned in the end, had not new methods provided independent tests for its existence.

Ad hoc hypotheses – that is, at the time untestable auxiliary hypotheses – can save almost any theory from any *particular* refutation. But this does not mean that we can go on with an *ad hoc* hypothesis as long as we like. It may become testable; and a negative test may force us either to give it up or to introduce a new secondary *ad hoc* hypothesis, and so on, *ad infinitum*. This, in fact, is a thing we almost always avoid. (I say 'almost' because methodological rules are not hard and fast.)

Moreover, the possibility of making things up with *ad hoc* hypotheses must not be exaggerated: there are many refutations which cannot be evaded in this way, even though some kind of immunizing tactic such as ignoring the refutation is always possible.

Part II Philosophy of Science

9 Scientific Method (1934)

The theory to be developed in the following pages stands directly opposed to all attempts to operate with the ideas of inductive logic. It might be described as the theory of *the deductive method of testing*, or as the view that a hypothesis can only be empirically *tested* – and only *after* it has been advanced.

Before I can elaborate this view (which might be called 'deductivism', in contrast to 'inductivism'[1]) I must first make clear the distinction between the *psychology of knowledge* which deals with empirical facts, and the *logic of knowledge* which is concerned only with logical relations. For the belief in inductive logic is largely due to a confusion of psychological problems with epistemological ones. It may be worth noticing, by the way, that this confusion spells trouble not only for the logic of knowledge but for its psychology as well.

I Elimination of Psychologism

I said above that the work of the scientist consists in putting forward and testing theories.

The initial stage, the act of conceiving or inventing a theory, seems to me neither to call for logical analysis nor to be susceptible of it. The question how it happens that a new idea occurs to a man – whether it is a musical theme, a dramatic conflict, or a scientific theory – may be of great interest to empirical psychology; but it is irrelevant to the logical analysis of scientific knowledge. This latter is concerned not with *questions of fact* (Kant's *quid facti?*), but only with questions of *justification* or *validity* (Kant's *quid juris?*). Its questions are of the following kind. Can a statement be justified? And if so, how? Is it testable? Is it logically dependent on certain other statements? Or does it perhaps contradict them? In order that a statement may be logically examined in this way, it must already have been presented to us. Someone must have formulated it, and submitted it to logical examination.

Accordingly I shall distinguish sharply between the process of conceiving a new idea, and the methods and results of examining it logically. As to the task of the logic of knowledge – in contradistinction to the psychology of knowledge – I shall proceed on the assumption that it consists solely in investigating the methods employed in those systematic tests to which every new idea must be subjected if it is to be seriously entertained.

Some might object that it would be more to the purpose to regard it as the business of epistemology to produce what has been called a '*rational reconstruction*' of the steps that have led the scientist to a discovery – to the finding of some new truth. But the question is: what, precisely, do we want to reconstruct? If it is the processes involved in the stimulation and release of an inspiration which are to be reconstructed, then I should refuse to take it as the task of the logic of knowledge. Such processes are the concern of empirical psychology but hardly of logic. It is another matter if we want to reconstruct rationally the *subsequent tests* whereby the inspiration may be discovered to be a discovery, or become known to be knowledge. In so far as the scientist critically judges, alters, or rejects his own inspiration we may, if we like, regard the methodological analysis undertaken here as a kind of 'rational reconstruction' of the corresponding thought processes. But this reconstruction would not describe these processes as they actually happen: it can give only a logical skeleton of the procedure of testing. Still, this is perhaps all that is meant by those who speak of a 'rational reconstruction' of the ways in which we gain knowledge.

It so happens that my arguments here are quite independent of this problem. However, my view of the matter, for what it is worth, is that there is no such thing as a logical method of having new ideas, or a logical reconstruction of this process. My view may be expressed by saying that every discovery contains 'an irrational element', or 'a creative intuition', in Bergson's sense. In a similar way Einstein speaks of the 'search for those highly universal laws . . . from which a picture of the world can be obtained by pure deduction. There is no logical path', he says, 'leading to these . . . laws. They can only be reached by intuition, based upon something like an intellectual love ('*Einfühlung*') of the objects of experience.'[2]

II Deductive Testing of Theories

According to the view that will be put forward here, the method of critically testing theories, and selecting them according to the results of tests, always proceeds on the following lines. From a new idea, put up tentatively, and not yet justified in any way – an anticipation, a hypothesis, a theoretical system, or what you will – conclusions are drawn by means of logical deduction. These conclusions are then compared with one another and with other relevant statements, so as to find what logical relations (such as equivalence, derivability, compatibility, or incompatibility) exist between them.

We may if we like distinguish four different lines along which the testing of a theory could be carried out. First there is the logical comparison of the conclusions among themselves, by which the internal consistency of the system is tested. Secondly, there is the investigation of the logical form of the theory, with the object of determining whether it has the character of an empirical or scientific theory, or whether it is, for example, tautological. Thirdly, there is the comparison with other theories, chiefly with the aim of determining whether the theory would constitute a scientific advance should it survive our various tests. And finally, there is the testing of the theory by way of empirical applications of the conclusions which can be derived from it.

The purpose of this last kind of test is to find out how far the new consequences of the theory – whatever may be new in what it asserts – stand up to the demands of practice, whether raised by purely scientific experiments, or by practical technological applications. Here too the procedure of testing turns out to be deductive. With the help of other statements, previously accepted, certain singular statements – which we may call 'predictions' – are deduced from the theory; especially predictions that are easily testable or applicable. From among these statements, those are selected which are not derivable from the current theory, and more especially those which the current theory contradicts. Next we seek a decision as regards these (and other) derived statements by comparing them with the results of practical applications and experiments. If this decision is positive, that is, if the singular conclusions turn out to be acceptable, or *verified*, then the theory has, for the time being, passed its test: we have found no reason to discard it. But if the decision is negative, or in other words, if the conclusions have been *falsified*, then their falsification also falsifies the theory from which they were logically deduced.

It should be noticed that a positive decision can only temporarily support the theory, for subsequent negative decisions may always overthrow it. So long as a theory withstands detailed and severe tests and is not superseded by another theory in the course of scientific progress, we may say that it has 'proved its mettle' or that it is '*corroborated*'[3] by past experience.

Nothing resembling inductive logic appears in the procedure here outlined. I never assume that we can argue from the truth of singular statements to the truth of theories. I never assume that by force of 'verified' conclusions, theories can be established as 'true', or even as merely 'probable'. And a more detailed analysis of the methods of deductive testing shows that all the problems can be dealt with that are usually called '*epistemological*'. Those problems, more especially, to which inductive logic gives rise, can be eliminated without creating new ones in their place.

III Why Methodological Decisions are Indispensable

In accordance with my proposal made above, epistemology, or the logic of scientific discovery, should be identified with the theory of scientific method. The theory of method, in so far as it goes beyond the purely logical analysis of the relations between scientific statements, is concerned with *the choice of methods* – with decisions about the way in which scientific statements are to be dealt with. These decisions will of course depend in their turn upon the *aim* which we choose from among a number of possible aims. The decision here proposed for laying down suitable rules for what I call the 'empirical method' is closely connected with my criterion of demarcation [see selection 8, section I above]: I propose to adopt such rules as will ensure the testability of scientific statements; which is to say, their falsifiability.

What are rules of scientific method, and why do we need them? Can there be a theory of such rules, a methodology?

The way in which one answers these questions will largely depend upon one's attitude to science. Those who, like the positivists, see empirical science as a system of statements which satisfy certain *logical criteria*, such as meaningfulness or verifiability, will give one answer. A very different answer will be given by those who tend to see (as I do) the distinguishing characteristic of empirical statements in their susceptibility to revision – in the fact that they can be criticized, and superseded by better ones; and who regard it as their task to analyse the characteristic ability of science to advance, and the characteristic manner in which a choice is made, in crucial cases, between conflicting systems of theories.

I am quite ready to admit that there is a need for a purely logical analysis of theories, for an analysis which takes no account of how they change and develop. But this kind of analysis does not elucidate those aspects of the empirical sciences which I, for one, so highly prize. A system such as classical mechanics may be 'scientific' to any degree you like; but those who uphold it dogmatically – believing, perhaps, that it is their business to defend such a successful system against criticism as long as it is not *conclusively disproved* – are adopting the very reverse of that critical attitude which in my view is the proper one for the scientist. In point of fact, no conclusive disproof of a theory can ever be produced; for it is always possible to say that the experimental results are not reliable, or that the discrepancies which are asserted to exist between the experimental results and the theory are only apparent and that they will disappear with the advance of our understanding. (In the struggle against Einstein, both these arguments were often used in support of Newtonian mechanics, and similar arguments abound in the field of the social sciences.) If you insist on strict proof (or strict disproof) in the empirical sciences, you will never benefit from experience, and never learn from it how wrong you are.

If therefore we characterize empirical science merely by the formal or logical structure of its statements, we shall not be able to exclude from it that prevalent form of metaphysics which results from elevating an obsolete scientific theory into an incontrovertible truth.

Such are my reasons for proposing that empirical science should be characterized by its methods: by our manner of dealing with scientific systems: by what we do with them and what we do to them. Thus I shall try to establish the rules, or if you will the norms, by which the scientist is guided when he is engaged in research or in discovery, in the sense here understood.

IV The Naturalistic Approach to the Theory of Method

The hint I gave in the previous section as to the deepseated difference between my position and that of the positivists is in need of some amplification.

The positivist dislikes the idea that there should be meaningful problems outside the field of 'positive' empirical science – problems to be dealt with by a genuine philosophical theory. He dislikes the idea that there should be a genuine theory of knowledge, an epistemology or a methodology.[4] He wishes to see in the alleged philosophical problems mere 'pseudoproblems' or 'puzzles'. Now this wish of his – which, by the way, he does not express as a wish or a proposal but rather as a statement of fact – can always be gratified. For nothing is easier than to unmask a problem as 'meaningless' or 'pseudo'. All you have to do is to fix upon a conveniently narrow meaning for 'meaning', and you will soon be bound to say of any inconvenient question that you are unable to detect any meaning in it. Moreover, if you admit as meaningful none except problems in natural science, any debate about the concept of 'meaning' will also turn out to be meaningless. The dogma of meaning, once enthroned, is elevated forever above the battle. It can no longer be attacked. It has become (in Wittgenstein's own words) 'unassailable and definitive'.[5]

The controversial question whether philosophy exists, or has any right to exist, is almost as old as philosophy itself. Time and again an entirely new philosophical movement arises which finally unmasks the old philosophical problems as pseudoproblems, and which confronts the wicked nonsense of philosophy with the good sense of meaningful, positive, empirical, science. And time and again do the despised defenders of 'traditional philosophy' try to explain to the leaders of the latest positivistic assault that the main problem of philosophy is the critical analysis of the appeal to the authority of 'experience'[6] – precisely that 'experience' which every latest discoverer of positivism is, as ever, artlessly taking for granted. To such objections, however, the positivist only replies with a shrug: they mean nothing to him, since they do not belong to empirical science, which alone is meaningful. 'Experience' for him is a programme, not a problem (unless it is studied by empirical psychology).

I do not think positivists are likely to respond any differently to my own attempts to analyse 'experience' which I interpret as the method of empirical science. For only two kinds of statement exist for them: logical tautologies and empirical statements. If methodology is not logic, then, they will conclude, it must be a branch of some empirical science – the science, say, of the behaviour of scientists at work.

This view, according to which methodology is an empirical science in its turn – a study of the actual behaviour of scientists, or of the actual procedure of 'science' – may be described as '*naturalistic*'. A naturalistic methodology (sometimes called an 'inductive theory of science'[7]) has its value, no doubt. A student of the logic of science may well take an interest in it, and learn from it. But what I call 'methodology' should not be taken for an empirical science. I do not believe that it is possible to decide, by using the methods of an empirical science, such controversial questions as whether science actually uses a principle of induction or not. And my doubts increase when I remember that what is to be called a 'science' and who is to be called a 'scientist' must always remain a matter of convention or decision.

I believe that questions of this kind should be treated in a different way. For example, we may consider and compare two different systems of methodological rules; one with, and one without, a principle of induction. And we may then examine whether such a principle, once introduced, can be applied without giving rise to inconsistencies; whether it helps us; and whether we really need it. It is this type of inquiry which leads me to dispense with the principle of induction: not because such a principle is as a matter of fact never used in science, but because I think that it is not needed; that it does not help us; and that it even gives rise to inconsistencies.

Thus I reject the naturalistic view. It is uncritical. Its upholders fail to notice that whenever they believe themselves to have discovered a fact, they have only proposed a convention.[8] Hence the convention is liable to turn into a dogma. This criticism of the naturalistic view applies not only to its criterion of meaning, but also to its idea of science, and consequently to its idea of empirical method.

v Methodological Rules as Conventions

Methodological rules are here regarded as *conventions*. They might be described as the rules of the game of empirical science. They differ from the rules of pure logic rather as do the rules of chess, which few would regard as part of *pure* logic: seeing that the rules of pure logic govern transformations of linguistic formulae, the result of an inquiry into the rules of chess could perhaps be entitled 'The Logic of Chess', but hardly 'Logic' pure and simple. (Similarly, the result of an inquiry into the rules of the game of science – that is, of scientific discovery – may be entitled 'The Logic of Scientific Discovery'.)

Two simple examples of methodological rules may be given. They will suffice to show that it would be hardly suitable to place an inquiry into method on the same level as a purely logical inquiry.

(1) The game of science is, in principle, without end. He who decides one day that scientific statements do not call for any further test, and that they can be regarded as finally verified, retires from the game.

(2) Once a hypothesis has been proposed and tested, and has proved its mettle, it may not be allowed to drop out without 'good reason'. A 'good reason' may be, for instance: replacement of the hypothesis by another which is better testable; or the falsification of one of the consequences of the hypothesis.[9]

These two examples show what methodological rules look like. Clearly they are very different from the rules usually called 'logical'. Although logic may perhaps set up criteria for deciding whether a statement is testable, it certainly is not concerned with the question whether anyone exerts himself to test it.

[In selection 8] I tried to define empirical science with the help of the criterion of falsifiability; but as I was obliged to admit the justice of certain objections, I provided a methodological supplement to my definition. Just as chess might be defined by the rules proper to it, so empirical science may be defined by means of its methodological rules. In establishing these rules we may proceed systematically. First a supreme rule is laid down which serves as a kind of norm for deciding upon the remaining rules, and which is thus a rule of a higher type. It is the rule which says that the other rules of scientific procedure must be designed in such a way that they do not protect any statement in science against falsification.

Methodological rules are thus closely connected both with other methodological rules and with our criterion of demarcation. But the connection is not a strictly deductive or logical one.[10] It results, rather, from the fact that the rules are constructed with the aim of ensuring the applicability of our criterion of demarcation; thus their formulation and acceptance proceed according to a practical rule of a higher type. An example of this has been given above (rule 1): theories which we decide not to submit to any further test would no longer be falsifiable. It is this systematic connection between the rules which makes it appropriate to speak of a *theory* of method. Admittedly the pronouncements of this theory are, as our examples show, for the most part conventions of a fairly obvious kind. Profound truths are not to be expected of methodology.[11] Nevertheless it may help us in many cases to clarify the logical situation, and even to solve some far-reaching problems which have hitherto proved intractable. One of these, for example, is the problem of deciding whether a probability statement should be accepted or rejected.[12]

It has often been doubted whether the various problems of the theory of knowledge stand in any systematic relation to one another, and also whether they can be treated systematically. I hope to show that these doubts are unjustified. The point is of some importance. My only reason for proposing my criterion of demarcation is that it is fruitful: that a great many points can be clarified and explained with its help. 'Definitions are dogmas; only the conclusions drawn from them can afford us any new insight', says Menger.[13] This is certainly true of the definition of the concept 'science'. It is only from the consequences of my definition of empirical science, and from the methodological decisions which depend upon this definition, that the scientist will be able to see how far it conforms to his intuitive idea of the goal of his endeavours. [See also selection 12 below.]

The philosopher too will accept my definition as useful only if he can accept its consequences. We must satisfy him that these consequences enable us to detect inconsistencies and inadequacies in older theories of knowledge, and to trace these back to the fundamental assumptions and conventions from which they spring. But we must also satisfy him that our own proposals are not threatened by the same kind of difficulties. This method of detecting and resolving contradictions is applied also within science itself, but it is of particular importance in the theory of knowledge. It is by this method, if by any, that methodological conventions might be justified, and might prove their value.[14]

Whether philosophers will regard these methodological investigations as belonging to philosophy is, I fear, very doubtful, but this does not really matter much. Yet it may be worth mentioning in this connection that not a few doctrines which are metaphysical, and thus certainly philosophical, could be interpreted as typical hypostatizations of methodological rules. An example of this is what is called 'the principle of causality'.[15] Another example is the problem of objectivity. For the requirement of scientific objectivity can also be interpreted as a methodological rule: the rule that only such statements may be introduced into science as are intersubjectively testable [see selection 10, section II, selection 11, section II, and selection 30]. It might indeed be said that the majority of the problems of theoretical philosophy, and the most interesting ones, can be re-interpreted in this way as problems of method.

10 Falsificationism versus Conventionalism (1934)

The question whether there is such a thing as a falsifiable singular statement (or a 'basic statement') will be examined later. Here I shall assume a positive answer to this question; and I shall examine how far my criterion of demarcation is applicable to theoretical systems – if it is applicable at all. A critical discussion of a position usually called 'conventionalism' will raise first some problems of method, to be met by taking certain *methodological decisions*. Next I shall try to characterize the logical properties of those systems of theories which are falsifiable – falsifiable, that is, if our methodological proposals are adopted.

I Some Conventionalist Objections

Objections are bound to be raised against my proposal to adopt falsifiability as our criterion for deciding whether or not a theoretical system belongs to empirical science. They will be raised, for example, by those who are influenced by the school of thought known as 'conventionalism'.[1] Some of these objections have already been touched upon [in section v of the previous selection]; they will now be considered a little more closely.

The source of the conventionalist philosophy would seem to be wonder at the austerely beautiful *simplicity of the world* as revealed in the laws of physics. Conventionalists seem to feel that this simplicity would be incomprehensible, and indeed miraculous, if we were bound to believe, with the realists, that the laws of nature reveal to us an inner, a structural, simplicity of our world beneath its outer appearance of lavish variety. Kant's idealism sought to explain this simplicity by saying that it is our own intellect which imposes its laws upon nature. Similarly, but even more boldly, the conventionalist treats this simplicity as our own creation. For him, however, it is not the effect of the laws of our intellect imposing themselves upon nature, thus making nature simple; for he does not believe that nature is simple. Only the '*laws of nature*' are simple; and these, the conventionalist holds, are our own free creations; our inventions; our arbitrary decisions and conventions. For the conventionalist, theoretical natural science is not a picture of nature but merely a logical construction. It is not the properties of the world which determine this construction; on the contrary it is this construction which determines the properties of an artificial world: a world of concepts implicitly defined by the natural laws which we have chosen. It is only *this* world of which science speaks.

According to this conventionalist point of view, laws of nature are not falsifiable by observation; for they are needed to determine what an observation and, more especially, what a scientific measurement is. It is these laws, laid down by us, which form the indispensable basis for the regulation of our clocks and the correction of our so-called 'rigid' measuring rods. A clock is called 'accurate' and a measuring rod 'rigid' only if the movements measured with the help of these instruments satisfy the axioms of mechanics which we have decided to adopt.[2]

The philosophy of conventionalism deserves great credit for the way it has helped to clarify the relations between theory and experiment. It recognized the importance, so little noticed by inductivists, of the part played by our actions and operations, planned in accordance with conventions and deductive reasoning, in conducting and interpreting our scientific experiments. I regard conventionalism as a system which is self-contained and defensible. Attempts to detect inconsistencies in it are not likely to succeed. Yet in spite of all this I find it quite unacceptable. Underlying it is an idea of science, of its aims and purposes, which is entirely different from mine. Whilst I do not demand any final certainty from science (and consequently do not get it), the conventionalist seeks in science 'a system of knowledge based upon ultimate grounds', to use a phrase of Dingler's. This goal is attainable; for it is possible to interpret any given scientific system as a system of implicit definitions. And periods when science develops slowly will give little occasion for conflict – unless purely academic – to arise between scientists inclined towards conventionalism and others who may favour a view like the one I advocate. It will be quite otherwise in a time of crisis. Whenever the 'classical' system of the day is threatened by the results of new experiments which might be interpreted as falsifications according to my point of view, the system will appear unshaken to the conventionalist. He will explain away the inconsistencies which may have arisen; perhaps by blaming our inadequate mastery of the system. Or he will eliminate them by suggesting *ad hoc* the adoption of certain auxiliary hypotheses, or perhaps of certain corrections to our measuring instruments.

In such times of crisis this conflict over the aims of science will become acute. We, and those who share our attitude, will hope to make new discoveries; and we shall hope to be helped in this by a newly erected scientific system. Thus we shall take the greatest interest in the falsifying experiment. We shall hail it as a success, for it has opened up new vistas into a world of new experiences. And we shall hail it even if these new experiences should furnish us with new arguments against our own most recent theories. But the newly rising structure, the boldness of which we admire, is seen by the conventionalist as a monument to the 'total collapse of science', as Dingler puts it. In the eyes of the conventionalist one principle only can help us to select a system as the chosen one from among all other possible systems: it is the principle of selecting the simplest system – the simplest system of implicit definitions; which of course means in practice the 'classical' system of the day.[3]

Thus my conflict with the conventionalists is not one that can be ultimately settled merely by a detached theoretical discussion. And yet it is possible I think to extract from the conventionalist mode of thought certain interesting arguments against my criterion of demarcation; for instance the following. I admit, a conventionalist might say, that the theoretical systems of the natural sciences are not verifiable, but I assert that they are not falsifiable either. For there is always the possibility of '. . .attaining, for any chosen axiomatic system, what is called its "correspondence with reality"';[4] and this can be done in a number of ways (some of which have been suggested above). Thus we may introduce *ad hoc* hypotheses. Or we may modify the so-called 'ostensive definitions' (or the 'explicit definitions' which may replace them). Or we may adopt a sceptical attitude as to the reliability of the experimenter whose observations, which threaten our system, we may exclude from science on the ground that they are insufficiently supported, unscientific, or not objective, or even on the ground that the experimenter was a liar. (This is the sort of attitude which the physicist may sometimes quite rightly adopt towards alleged occult phenomena.) In the last resort we can always cast doubt on the acumen of the theoretician (for example if he does not believe, as does Dingler, that the theory of electricity will one day be derived from Newton's theory of gravitation).

Thus, according to the conventionalist view, it is not possible to divide systems of theories into falsifiable and non-falsifiable ones; or rather, such a distinction will be ambiguous. As a consequence, our criterion of falsifiability must turn out to be useless as a criterion of demarcation.

II Methodological Rules

These objections of an imaginary conventionalist seem to me incontestable, just like the conventionalist philosophy itself. I admit that my criterion of falsifiability does not lead to an unambiguous classification. Indeed, it is impossible to decide, by analysing its logical form, whether a system of statements is a conventional system of irrefutable implicit definitions, or whether it is a system which is empirical in my sense; that is, a refutable system. Yet this only shows that my criterion of demarcation cannot be applied immediately to a *system of statements* – a fact I have already pointed out [in selection 8, section II, and selection 9, section V]. The question whether a given *system* should as such be regarded as a conventionalist or an empirical one is therefore misconceived. *Only with reference to the methods applied* to a theoretical system is it at all possible to ask whether we are dealing with a conventionalist or an empirical theory. The only way to avoid conventionalism is by taking a *decision*: the decision not to apply its methods. We decide that if our system is threatened we will never save it by any kind of *conventionalist stratagem*. Thus we shall guard against exploiting the ever open possibility just mentioned of '...attaining, for any chosen ... system, what is called its "correspondence with reality"'.

A clear appreciation of what may be gained (and lost) by conventionalist methods was expressed, a hundred years before Poincaré, by Black who wrote: 'A nice adaptation of conditions will make almost any hypothesis agree with the phenomena. This will please the imagination but does not advance our knowledge.'[5]

In order to formulate methodological rules which prevent the adoption of conventionalist stratagems, we should have to acquaint ourselves with the various forms these stratagems may take, so as to meet each with the appropriate anti-conventionalist countermove. Moreover we should agree that, whenever we find that a system has been rescued by a conventionalist stratagem, we shall test it afresh, and reject it, as circumstances may require.

The four main conventionalist stratagems have already been listed at the end of the previous section. The list makes no claim to completeness: it must be left to the investigator, especially in the fields of sociology and psychology (the physicist may hardly need the warning) to guard constantly against the temptation to employ new conventionalist stratagems – a temptation to which psychoanalysts, for example, often succumb.

As regards *auxiliary hypotheses* we propose to lay down the rule that only those are acceptable whose introduction does not diminish the degree of falsifiability or testability of the system in question, but, on the contrary, increases it.[6] If the degree of falsifiability is increased, then introducing the hypothesis has actually strengthened the theory: the system now rules out more than it did previously: it prohibits more. We can also put it like this. The introduction of an auxiliary hypothesis should always be regarded as an attempt to construct a new system; and this new system should then always be judged on the issue of whether it would, if adopted, constitute a real advance in our knowledge of the world. An example of an auxiliary hypothesis which is eminently acceptable in this sense is Pauli's exclusion principle. An example of an unsatisfactory auxiliary hypothesis would be the contraction hypothesis of Fitzgerald and Lorentz which had no falsifiable consequences but merely[7] served to restore the agreement between theory and experiment – mainly the findings of Michelson and Morley. An advance was here achieved only by the theory of relativity which predicted new consequences, new physical effects, and thereby opened up new possibilities for testing, and for falsifying, the theory. Our methodological rule may be qualified by the remark that we need not reject, as conventionalistic, every auxiliary hypothesis that fails to satisfy these standards. In particular, there are *singular* statements which do not really belong to the theoretical system at all. They are sometimes called 'auxiliary hypotheses', and although they are introduced to assist the theory, they are quite harmless. (An example would be the assumption that a certain observation or measurement which cannot be repeated may have been due to error. [See selection 11, section II.])

Changes in *explicit definitions*, whereby the concepts of an axiom system are given a meaning in terms of a system of lower level universality, are permissible if useful; but they must be regarded as modifications of the system, which thereafter has to be re-examined as if it were new. As regards undefined universal names, two possibilities must be distinguished. (1)There are some undefined concepts which only appear in statements of the highest level of universality, and whose use is established by the fact that we know in what logical relation other concepts stand to them. They can be eliminated in the course of deduction (an example is 'energy').[8] (2) There are other undefined concepts which occur in statements of lower levels of universality also, and whose meaning is established by usage (e.g. 'movement', 'mass point', 'position'). In connection with these, we shall forbid surreptitious alterations of usage, and otherwise proceed in conformity with our methodological decisions, as before.

As to the two remaining points (which concern the competence of the experimenter or theoretician) we shall adopt similar rules. Intersubjectively testable experiments are either to be accepted, or to be rejected in the light of counterexperiments. The bare appeal to logical derivations to be discovered in the future can be disregarded.

III Logical Investigation of Falsifiability

Only in the case of systems which would be falsifiable if treated in accordance with our rules of empirical method is there any need to guard against conventionalist strategems. Let us assume that we have successfully banned these stratagems by our rules: we may now ask for a *logical* characterization of such falsifiable systems. We shall attempt to characterize the falsifiability of a theory by the logical relations holding between the theory and the class of basic statements.

The character of the singular statements which I call 'basic statements' will be discussed more fully [in the next selection], and also the question whether they, in their turn, are falsifiable. Here we shall assume that falsifiable basic statements exist. It should be borne in mind that when I speak of 'basic statements', I am not referring to a system of *accepted* statements. The system of basic statements, as I use the term, is to include, rather, *all self-consistent singular statements* of a certain logical form – all conceivable singular statements of fact, as it were. Thus the system of all basic statements will contain many statements which are mutually incompatible.

As a first attempt one might perhaps try calling a theory 'empirical' whenever singular statements can be deduced from it. This attempt fails, however, because in order to deduce singular statements from a theory, we always need other singular statements – the initial conditions that tell us what to substitute for the variables in the theory. As a second attempt, one might try calling a theory 'empirical' if singular statements are derivable with the help of other singular statements serving as initial conditions. But this will not do either; for even a non-empirical theory, for example a tautological one, would allow us to derive some singular statements from other singular statements. (According to the rules of logic we can for example say: from the conjunction of 'Twice two is four' and 'Here is a black raven' there follows, among other things, 'Here is a raven'.) It would not even be enough to demand that from the theory together with some initial conditions we should be able to deduce *more* than we could deduce from those initial conditions alone. This demand would indeed exclude tautological theories, but it would not exclude synthetic metaphysical statements. (For example from 'Every occurrence has a cause' and 'A catastrophe is occurring here', we can deduce 'This catastrophe has a cause'.)

In this way we are led to the demand that the theory should allow us to deduce, roughly speaking, more *empirical* singular statements than we can deduce from the initial conditions alone.[9] This means that we must base our definition upon a particular class of singular statements; and this is the purpose for which we need the basic statements. Seeing that it would not be very easy to say in detail how a complicated theoretical system helps in the deduction of singular or basic statements, I propose the following definition. A theory is to be called 'empirical' or 'falsifiable' if it divides the class of all possible basic statements unambiguously into the following two non-empty subclasses. First, the class of all those basic statements with which it is inconsistent (or which it rules out, or prohibits): we call this the class of the *potential falsifiers* of the theory; and secondly, the class of those basic statements which it does not contradict (or which it 'permits'). We can put this more briefly by saying: a theory is falsifiable if the class of its potential falsifiers is not empty.

It may be added that a theory makes assertions only about its potential falsifiers. (It asserts their falsity.) About the 'permitted' basic statements it says nothing. In particular, it does not say that they are true.[10]

IV Falsifiability and Falsification

We must clearly distinguish between falsifiability and falsification. We have introduced falsifiability solely as a criterion for the empirical character of a system of statements. As to falsification, special rules must be introduced which will determine under what conditions a system is to be regarded as falsified.

We say that a theory is falsified only if we have accepted basic statements which contradict it. [See selection 9, section v.] This condition is necessary, but not sufficient; for non-reproducible single occurrences are of no significance to science. Thus a few stray basic statements contradicting a theory will hardly induce us to reject it as falsified. We shall take it as falsified only if we discover a *reproducible effect* which refutes the theory. In other words, we only accept the falsification if a low-level empirical hypothesis which describes such an effect is proposed and corroborated. This kind of hypothesis may be called a *falsifying hypothesis*. The requirement that the falsifying hypothesis must be empirical, and so falsifiable, only means that it must stand in a certain logical relationship to possible basic statements; thus this requirement only concerns the logical form of the hypothesis. The rider that the hypothesis should be corroborated refers to tests which it ought to have passed – tests which confront it with accepted basic statements.[11]

Thus the basic statements play two different roles. On the one hand, we have used the system of all *logically possible* basic statements in order to obtain with its help the logical characterization for which we were looking – that of the form of empirical statements. On the other hand, the *accepted* basic statements are the basis for the corroboration of hypotheses. If accepted basic statements contradict a theory, then we take them as providing sufficient grounds for its falsification only if they corroborate a falsifying hypothesis at the same time.

11 The Empirical Basis (1934)

We have now reduced the question of the falsifiability of theories to that of the falsifiability of those singular statements which I have called basic statements. But what kind of singular statements are these basic statements? How can they be falsified? To the practical research worker, these questions may be of little concern. But the obscurities and misunderstandings which surround the problem make it advisable to discuss it here in some detail.

I Perceptual Experiences as Empirical Basis: Psychologism

The doctrine that the empirical sciences are reducible to sense perceptions, and thus to our experiences, is one which many accept as obvious beyond all question. However, this doctrine stands or falls with inductive logic, and is here rejected along with it. I do not wish to deny that there is a grain of truth in the view that mathematics and logic are based on thinking, and the factual sciences on sense perceptions. But what is true in this view has little bearing on the epistemological problem. And indeed, there is hardly a problem in epistemology which has suffered more severely from the confusion of psychology with logic than this problem of the basis of statements of experience.

The problem of the basis of experience has troubled few thinkers so deeply as Fries.[1] He taught that, if the statements of science are not to be accepted *dogmatically*, we must be able to *justify* them. If we demand justification by reasoned argument, in the logical sense, then we are committed to the view that *statements can be justified only by statements*. The demand that *all* statements are to be logically justified (described by Fries as a 'predilection for proofs') is therefore bound to lead to an *infinite regress*. Now, if we wish to avoid the danger of dogmatism as well as an infinite regress, then it seems as if we could only have recourse to *psychologism*, i.e.

the doctrine that statements can be justified not only by statements but also by perceptual experience. Faced with this *trilemma* – dogmatism vs. infinite regress vs. psychologism – Fries, and with him almost all epistemologists who wished to account for our empirical knowledge, opted for psychologism. In sense experience, he taught, we have 'immediate knowledge':[2] by this immediate knowledge, we may justify our 'mediate knowledge' – knowledge expressed in the symbolism of some language. And this mediate knowledge includes, of course, the statements of science.

Usually the problem is not explored as far as this. In the epistemologies of sensationalism and positivism it is taken for granted that empirical scientific statements 'speak of our experiences'.[3] For how could we ever reach any knowledge of facts if not through sense perception? Merely by taking thought a man cannot add an iota to his knowledge of the world of facts. Thus perceptual experience must be the sole 'source of knowledge' of all the empirical sciences. All we know about the world of facts must therefore be expressible in the form of statements *about our experiences*. Whether this table is red or blue can be found out only by consulting our sense experience. By the immediate feeling of conviction which it conveys, we can distinguish the true statement, the one whose terms agree with experience, from the false statement, whose terms do not agree with it. Science is merely an attempt to classify and describe this perceptual knowledge, these immediate experiences whose truth we cannot doubt; *it is the systematic presentation of our immediate convictions*.

This doctrine founders in my opinion on the problems of induction and of universals. For we can utter no scientific statement that does not go far beyond what can be known with certainty 'on the basis of immediate experience'. (This fact may be referred to as the 'transcendence inherent in any description'.) Every description uses *universal* names (or symbols, or ideas); every statement has the character of a theory, of a hypothesis. The statement, 'Here is a glass of water' cannot be verified by any observational experience. The reason is that the *universals* which appear in it cannot be correlated with any specific sense experience. (An 'immediate experience' is *only once* 'immediately given'; it is unique.) By the word 'glass', for example, we denote physical bodies which exhibit a certain *lawlike behaviour*, and the same holds for the word 'water'. Universals cannot be reduced to classes of experiences; they cannot be 'constituted'.[4]

II The Objectivity of the Empirical Basis

I propose to look at science in a way which is slightly different from that favoured by the various psychologistic schools: I wish to *distinguish sharply between objective science on the one hand, and 'our knowledge' on the other*.

I readily admit that only observation can give us 'knowledge concerning facts', and that we can (as Hahn says) 'become aware of facts only by observation'. But this awareness, this knowledge of ours, does not justify or establish the truth of any statement. I do not believe, therefore, that the question which epistemology must ask is, '. . . on what does our *knowledge* rest? . . . or more exactly, how can I, having had the *experience S*, justify my description of it, and defend it against doubt?'[5] This will not do, even if we change the term 'experience' into 'protocol sentence'. In my view, what epistemology has to ask is, rather: how do we test scientific statements by their deductive consequences? (Or, more generally: how can we best criticize our theories (our hypotheses, our guesses), rather than defend them against doubt? [See also selection 3, section III.]) And *what kind* of consequences can we select for this purpose if they in their turn are to be intersubjectively testable?

By now, this kind of objective and non-psychological approach is pretty generally accepted where logical or tautological statements are concerned. Yet not so long ago it was held that logic was a science dealing with mental processes and their laws – the laws of our thought. On this view there was no other justification to be found for logic than the alleged fact that we just could not think in any other way. A logical inference seemed to be justified because it was experienced as a necessity of thought, as a feeling of being compelled to think along certain lines. In the field of logic, this kind of psychologism is now perhaps a thing of the past. Nobody would dream of justifying the validity of a logical inference, or of defending it against doubts, by writing beside it in the margin the following protocol sentence. 'Protocol: In checking this chain of inferences today, I experienced an acute feeling of conviction.'

The position is very different when we come to *empirical statements of science*. Here everybody believes that these are grounded on experiences such as perceptions; or in the formal mode of speech, on protocol sentences. Most people would see that any attempt to base logical statements on protocol sentences is a case of psychologism. But curiously enough, when it comes to empirical statements, the same kind of thing goes today by the name of 'physicalism'. Yet whether statements of logic are in question or statements of empirical science, I think the answer is the same: our *knowledge*, which may be described vaguely as a system of *dispositions*, and which may be of concern to psychology, may be in both cases linked with feelings of belief or of conviction: in the one case, perhaps, with the feeling of being compelled to think in a certain way; in the other with that of 'perceptual assurance'. But all this interests only the psychologists. It does not even touch upon problems like those of the logical connections between scientific statements, which alone interest the epistemologist.

(There is a widespread belief that the statement 'I see that this table here is white', possesses some profound advantage over the statement 'This table here is white', from the point of view of epistemology. But from the point of view of evaluating its possible objective tests, the first statement, in speaking about me, does not appear more secure than the second statement, which speaks about the table here.)

There is only one way to make sure of the validity of a chain of logical reasoning. This is to put it in the form in which it is most easily testable: we break it up into many small steps, each easy to check by anybody who has learnt the mathematical or logical technique of transforming sentences. If after this anybody still raises doubts then we can only beg him to point out an error in the steps of the proof, or to think the matter over again. In the case of the empirical sciences, the situation is much the same. Any empirical scientific statement can be presented (by describing experimental arrangements, etc.) in such a way that anyone who has learnt the relevant technique can test it. If, as a result, he rejects the statement, then it will not satisfy us if he tells us all about his feelings of doubt or about his feelings of conviction as to his perceptions. What he must do is to formulate an assertion which contradicts our own, and give us his instructions for testing it. If he fails to do this we can only ask him to take another and perhaps a more careful look at our experiment, and think again.

An assertion which owing to its logical form is not testable can at best operate, within science, as a stimulus: it can suggest a problem. In the field of logic and mathematics, this may be exemplified by Fermat's problem, and in the field of natural history, say, by reports about seaserpents. In such cases science does not say that the reports are unfounded; that Fermat was in error or that all the records of observed seaserpents are lies. Instead, it suspends judgement.

Science can be viewed from various standpoints, not only from that of epistemology; for example, we can look at it as a biological or as a sociological phenomenon. As such it might be described as a tool, or an instrument, comparable perhaps to some of our industrial machinery. Science may be regarded as a means of production – as the last word in 'roundabout production'.[6] Even from this point of view science is no more closely connected with 'our experience' than other instruments or means of production. And even if we look at it as gratifying our intellectual needs, its connection with our experiences does not differ in principle from that of any other objective structure. Admittedly it is not incorrect to say that science is '. . . an instrument' whose purpose is '. . . to predict from immediate or given experiences later experiences, and even as far as possible to control them'.[7] But I do not think that this talk about experiences contributes to clarity. It has hardly more point than, say, the not incorrect characterization of an oil derrick by the assertion that its purpose is to give us certain experiences: not oil, but rather the sight and smell of oil; not money, but rather the feeling of having money.

III Basic Statements

It has already been briefly indicated what role the basic statements play within the epistemological theory I advocate. We need them in order to decide whether a theory is to be called falsifiable, i.e.

empirical. And we also need them for the corroboration of falsifying hypotheses, and thus for the falsification of theories. [See selection 10, sections III and IV respectively.]

Basic statements must therefore satisfy the following conditions. (1) From a universal statement without initial conditions, no basic statement can be deduced.[8] On the other hand, (2) a universal statement and a basic statement can contradict each other. Condition (2) can only be satisfied if it is possible to derive the negation of a basic statement from the theory which it contradicts. From this and condition (1) it follows that a basic statement must have a logical form such that its negation cannot be a basic statement in its turn.

There is a familiar example of statements whose logical form is different from that of their negations. These are universal statements and existential statements: they are negations of one another, and they differ in their logical form. *Singular* statements can be constructed in an analogous way. The statement: 'There is a raven in the spacetime region *k*' may be said to be different in its logical form – and not only in its linguistic form – from the statement 'There is no raven in the spacetime region *k*'. A statement of the form 'There is a so-and-so in the region *k*' or 'Such-and-such an event is occurring in the region *k*' may be called a '*singular* existential statement' or a '*singular* there-is statement'. And the statement which results from negating it, i.e. 'There is no so-and-so in the region *k*' or 'No event of such-and-such a kind is occurring in the region *k*', may be called a '*singular* non-existence statement', or a '*singular* there-is-not statement'.

We may now lay down the following rule concerning basic statements: *basic statements have the form of singular existential statements*. This rule means that basic statements will satisfy condition (1), since a singular existential statement can never be deduced from a strictly universal statement, i.e. from a strict non-existence statement. They will also satisfy condition (2), as can be seen from the fact that from every singular existential statement a purely existential statement can be derived simply by omitting any reference to any individual spacetime region; and as we have seen, a purely existential statement may indeed contradict a theory.

It should be noticed that the conjunction of two basic

statements, *d* and *r*, which do not contradict each other, is in turn a basic statement. Sometimes we may even obtain a basic statement by joining one basic statement to another statement which is not basic. For example, we may form the conjunction of the basic statement, *r*, 'There is a pointer at the place *k*' with the singular non-existence statement $\bar{p}$, 'There is no pointer in motion at the place *k*'. For clearly, the conjunction $r \cdot \bar{p}$ ('*r-and-non-p*') of the two statements is equivalent to the singular existential statement 'There is a pointer at rest at the place *k*'. This has the consequence that, if we are given a theory *t* and the initial conditions *r*, from which we deduce the prediction *p*, then the statement $r \cdot \bar{p}$ will be a falsifier of the theory, and so a basic statement. (On the other hand, the conditional statement '$r \rightarrow p$' i.e. 'If *r* then *p*', is no more basic than the negation $\bar{p}$, since it is equivalent to the negation of a basic statement, viz. to the negation of $r \cdot \bar{p}$.)

These are the formal requirements for basic statements; they are satisfied by all singular existential statements. In addition to these, a basic statement must also satisfy a material requirement – a requirement concerning the event which, as the basic statement tells us, is occurring at the place *k*. This event must be an '*observable*' event; that is to say, basic statements must be testable, intersubjectively, by 'observation'. Since they are singular statements, this requirement can of course only refer to observers who are suitably placed in space and time (a point which I shall not elaborate).

No doubt it will now seem as though in demanding observability, I have, after all, allowed psychologism to slip back quietly into my theory. But this is not so. Admittedly, it is possible to interpret the concept of an *observable event* in a psychologistic sense. But I am using it in such a sense that it might just as well be replaced by 'an event involving position and movement of macroscopic physical bodies'. Or we might lay it down, more precisely, that every basic statement either must be itself a statement about relative positions of physical bodies, or must be equivalent to some basic statement of this 'mechanistic' or 'materialistic' kind. (That this stipulation is practicable is connected with the fact that a theory which is intersubjectively testable will also be intersensually[9] testable. This is to say that tests involving the perception of one of our senses can, in principle, be replaced by tests involving other senses.) Thus the charge that, in appealing to observability, I have stealthily re-admitted psychologism would have no more force than the charge that I have admitted mechanism or materialism. This shows that my theory is really quite neutral and that neither of these labels should be pinned to it. I say all this only so as to save the term 'observable', as I use it, from the stigma of psychologism. (Observations and perceptions may be psychological but observability is not.) I have no intention of *defining* the term 'observable' or 'observable event', though I am quite ready to elucidate it by means of either psychologistic or mechanistic examples. I think that it should be introduced as an undefined term which becomes sufficiently precise in use: as a primitive concept whose use the epistemologist has to learn, much as he has to learn the use of the term 'symbol', or as the physicist has to learn the use of the term 'mass point'.

Basic statements are therefore – in the material mode of speech – statements asserting that an observable event is occurring in a certain individual region of space and time.

IV The Relativity of Basic Statements. Resolution of Fries's Trilemma

Every test of a theory, whether resulting in its corroboration or falsification, must stop at some basic statement or other which we *decide to accept*. If we do not come to any decision, and do not accept some basic statement or other, then the test will have led nowhere. But considered from a logical point of view, the situation is never such that it compels us to stop at this particular basic statement rather than at that, or else give up the test altogether. For any basic statement can again in its turn be subjected to tests, using as a touchstone any of the basic statements which can be deduced from it with the help of some theory, either the one under test, or another. This procedure has no natural end. Thus if the test is to lead us anywhere, nothing remains but to stop at some point or other and say that we are satisfied, for the time being.

It is fairly easy to see that we arrive in this way at a procedure according to which we stop only at a kind of statement that is especially easy to test. For it means that we are stopping at statements about whose acceptance or rejection the various investigators are likely to reach agreement. And if they do not agree, they will simply continue with the tests, or else start them all over again. If this too leads to no result, then we might say that the statements in question were not intersubjectively testable, or that we were not, after all, dealing with observable events. If some day it should no longer be possible for scientific observers to reach agreement about basic statements this would amount to a failure of language as a means of universal communication. It would amount to a new 'Babel of Tongues': scientific discovery would be reduced to absurdity. In this new Babel, the soaring edifice of science would soon lie in ruins.

Just as a logical proof has reached a satisfactory shape when the difficult work is over, and everything can be easily checked, so, after science has done its work of deduction or explanation, we stop at basic statements which are easily testable. Statements about personal experiences – i.e. protocol sentences – are clearly *not* of this kind; thus they will not be very suitable to serve as statements at which we stop. We do of course make use of records or protocols, such as certificates of tests issued by a department of scientific and industrial research. These, if the need arises, can be re-examined. Thus it may become necessary, for example, to test the reaction times of the experts who carry out the tests (i.e. to determine their personal equations). But in general, and especially '. . .in critical cases' we do stop at easily testable statements, and *not*, as Carnap recommends, at perception or protocol sentences; i.e. we *do not* '. . .stop just at these ... because the intersubjective testing of statements about perceptions ... is relatively complicated and difficult'.[10]

What is our position now in regard to Fries's trilemma, the choice between dogmatism, infinite regress, and psychologism? [See section I above.] The basic statements at which we stop, which we decide to accept as satisfactory, and as sufficiently tested, have admittedly the character of *dogmas*, but only in so far as we may desist from justifying them by further arguments (or by further tests). But this kind of dogmatism is innocuous since, should the need arise, these statements can easily be tested further. I admit that this too makes the chain of deduction in principle infinite. But this kind of '*infinite regress*' is also innocuous since in our theory there is no question of trying to prove any statements by means of it. And finally, as to *psychologism*: I admit, again, that the decision to accept a basic statement, and to be satisfied with it, is causally connected with our experiences – especially with our *perceptual experiences*. But we do not attempt to *justify* basic statements by these experiences. Experiences can *motivate a decision*, perhaps decisively, and hence an acceptance or a rejection of a statement, but a basic statement cannot be *justified* by them – no more than by thumping the table.[11]

12 The Aim of Science (1957)

To speak of 'the aim' of scientific activity may perhaps sound a little naïve; for clearly, different scientists have different aims, and science itself (whatever that may mean) has no aims. I admit all this. And yet it seems that when we speak of science we do feel, more or less clearly, that there is something characteristic of scientific activity; and since scientific activity looks pretty much like a rational activity, and since a rational activity must have some aim, the attempt to describe the aim of science may not be entirely futile.

I suggest that it is the aim of science to find *satisfactory explanations*, of whatever strikes us as being in need of explanation. By an *explanation* (or a causal explanation) is meant a set of statements of which one describes the state of affairs to be explained (the *explicandum*) while the others, the explanatory statements, form the 'explanation' in the narrower sense of the word (the *explicans* of the *explicandum*).

We may take it, as a rule, that the *explicandum* is more or less well known to be true, or assumed to be so known. For there is little point in asking for an explanation of a state of affairs which may turn out to be entirely imaginary. (Flying saucers may represent such a case: the explanation needed may not be of flying saucers, but of reports of flying saucers; yet should flying saucers exist, then no further explanation of the *reports* would be required.) The *explicans*, on the other hand, which is the object of our search, will as a rule not be known: it will have to be discovered. Thus, scientific explanation, whenever it is a discovery, will be *the explanation of the known by the unknown*.[1]

The *explicans*, in order to be satisfactory (satisfactoriness may be a matter of degree), must fulfil a number of conditions. First, it must logically entail the *explicandum*. Secondly, the *explicans* ought to be true, although it will not, in general, be known to be true; in any case, it must not be known to be false even after the most critical examination. If it is not known to be true (as will usually be the case) there must be *independent* evidence in its favour. In other words, it must be *independently* testable; and we shall regard it as more satisfactory the greater the severity of the independent tests it has survived.

I still have to elucidate my use of the expression 'independent', with its opposites, '*ad hoc*', and (in extreme cases) 'circular'.

Let *a* be an *explicandum*, known to be true. Since *a* trivially follows from *a* itself, we could always offer *a* as an explanation of itself. But this would be highly unsatisfactory, even though we should know in this case that the *explicans* is true, and that the *explicandum* follows from it. *Thus we must exclude explanations of this kind because of their circularity.*

Yet the kind of circularity I have here in mind is a matter of degree. Consider the following dialogue: 'Why is the sea so rough today?' – 'Because Neptune is very angry' – 'By what evidence can you support your statement that Neptune is very angry?' – 'Oh, don't you *see* how *very* rough the sea is? And is it not always rough when Neptune is angry?' This explanation is found unsatisfactory because (just as in the case of the fully circular explanation) the only evidence for the *explicans* is the *explicandum* itself.[2] The feeling that this kind of almost circular or *ad hoc* explanation is highly unsatisfactory, and the corresponding requirement that explanations of this kind should be avoided are, I believe, among the main motive forces of the development of science: dissatisfaction is among the first fruits of the critical or rational approach.

In order that the *explicans* should not be *ad hoc*, it must be rich in content: it must have a variety of testable consequences, and among them, especially, testable consequences which are different from the *explicandum*. It is these different testable consequences which I have in mind when I speak of *independent* tests, or of *independent* evidence.

Although these remarks may perhaps help to elucidate somewhat the intuitive idea of an independently testable *explicans*, they are still quite insufficient to characterize a satisfactory and independently testable explanation. For if *a* is our *explicandum* – let *a* be again 'The sea is rough today' – then we can always offer a highly unsatisfactory *explicans* which is completely *ad hoc* even though it has independently testable consequences. We can even choose these consequences as we like. We may choose, say, 'These plums are juicy' and 'All ravens are black'. Let *b* be their conjunction. Then we can take as *explicans* simply the conjunction of *a* and *b*: it will satisfy all our requirements so far stated.

Only if we require that explanations shall make use of universal statements or laws of nature (supplemented by initial conditions) can we make progress towards realizing the idea of independent, or not *ad hoc*, explanations. For universal laws of nature *may* be statements with a rich content, so that *they may be independently tested* everywhere, and at all times. Thus if they are used as explanations, they *may* not be *ad hoc* because they *may* allow us to interpret the *explicandum* as an instance of a reproducible effect. All this is only true, however, if we confine ourselves to universal laws which are testable, that is to say, falsifiable.

The question 'What kind of explanation may be satisfactory?' thus leads to the reply: an explanation in terms of testable and falsifiable universal laws and initial conditions. And an explanation of this kind will be the more satisfactory the more highly testable these laws are and the better they have been tested. (This applies also to the initial conditions.)

In this way, the conjecture that it is the aim of science to find satisfactory explanations leads us further to the idea of improving the degree of satisfactoriness of the explanations by improving their degree of testability, that is to say, by proceeding to better testable theories; which means proceeding to theories of ever richer content, of higher degrees of universality, and of higher degrees of precision. [See notes 3 and 6 to selection 10 above.] This, no doubt, is fully in keeping with the actual practice of the theoretical sciences.

We may arrive at fundamentally the same result also in another way. If it is the aim of science to explain, then it will also be its aim to explain what so far has been accepted as an *explicans*; for example, a law of nature. Thus the task of science constantly renews itself. We may go on for ever, proceeding to explanations of a higher and higher level of universality – unless, indeed, we were to arrive at an *ultimate explanation*; that is to say, at an explanation which is neither capable of any further explanation, nor in need of it.

But are there ultimate explanations? The doctrine which I have called 'essentialism' amounts to the view that science must seek ultimate explanations in terms of essences: if we can explain the behaviour of a thing in terms of its essence – of its essential properties – then no further question can be raised, and none need be raised (except perhaps the theological question of the Creator of the essences). Thus Descartes believed that he had explained physics in terms of the *essence of a physical body* which, he taught, was extension; and some Newtonians, following Roger Cotes, believed that the *essence of matter* was its inertia and its power to attract other matter, and that Newton's theory could be derived from, and thus ultimately explained by, these essential properties of all matter. Newton himself was of a different opinion. It was a hypothesis concerning the ultimate or essentialist causal explanation of gravity itself which he had in mind when he wrote in the *Scholium generale* at the end of the *Principia*: 'So far I have explained the phenomena ... by the force of gravity, but I have not yet ascertained *the cause of gravity itself ... and I do not arbitrarily* [*or ad hoc*] invent hypotheses.'[3]

I do not believe in the essentialist doctrine of ultimate explanation. In the past, critics of this doctrine have been, as a rule, instrumentalists: they interpreted scientific theories as *nothing but* instruments for prediction, without any explanatory power. I do not agree with them either. But there is a third possibility, a 'third view', as I have called it. It has been well described as a 'modified essentialism' – with emphasis upon the word 'modified'.[4]

This 'third view' which I uphold modifies essentialism in a radical manner. First of all, I reject the idea of an ultimate explanation: I maintain that every explanation may be further explained, by a theory or conjecture of a higher degree of universality. There can be no explanation which is not in need of a further explanation, for none can be a self-explanatory description of an essence (such as an essentialist definition of body, as suggested by Descartes). Secondly, I reject all *what-is questions*: questions asking what a thing is, what is its essence, or its true nature. For we must give up the view, characteristic of essentialism, that in every single thing there is an essence, an inherent nature or principle (such as the spirit of wine in wine), which necessarily causes it to be what it is, and thus to act as it does. This animistic view explains nothing; but it has led essentialists (like Newton) to shun relational properties, such as gravity, and to believe, on grounds felt to be *a priori* valid, that a satisfactory explanation must be in terms of inherent properties (as opposed to relational properties). The third and last modification of essentialism is this. We must give up the view, closely connected with animism (and characteristic of Aristotle as opposed to Plato), that it is the essential properties inherent *in each individual or singular thing* which may be appealed to as the explanation of this thing's behaviour. For this view completely fails to throw any light whatever on the question why different individual things should behave in like manner. If it is said, 'because their essences are alike', the new question arises: *why should there not be as many different essences as there are different things?*

Plato tried to solve precisely this problem by saying that like individual things are the offspring, and thus copies, of the same original 'Form', which is therefore something 'outside' and 'prior' and 'superior' to the various individual things; and indeed, we have as yet no better theory of likeness. Even today, we appeal to their common origin if we wish to explain the likeness of two men, or of a bird and a fish, or of two beds, or two motor cars, or two languages, or two legal procedures; that is to say, we explain similarity in the main genetically; and if we make a metaphysical system out of this, it is liable to become a historicist philosophy. Plato's solution was rejected by Aristotle; but since Aristotle's version of essentialism does not contain even a hint of a solution, it seems that he never quite grasped the problem.[5]

By choosing explanations in terms of universal laws of nature, we offer a solution to precisely this last (Platonic) problem. For we conceive all individual things, and all singular facts, to be subject to these laws. The laws (which in their turn *are* in need of further explanation) thus explain regularities or similarities of individual things or singular facts or events. And these laws are not inherent in the singular things. (Nor are they Platonic Ideas outside the world.) Laws of nature are conceived, rather, as (conjectural) descriptions of the structural properties of nature – of our world itself.

Here then is the similarity between my own view (the 'third view') and essentialism; although I do not think that we can ever describe, by our universal laws, an *ultimate* essence of the world, I do not doubt that we may seek to probe deeper and deeper into the structure of our world or, as we might say, into properties of the world that are more and more essential, or of greater and greater depth.

Every time we proceed to explain some conjectural law or theory by a new conjectural theory of a higher degree of universality, we are discovering more about the world, trying to penetrate deeper into its secrets. And every time we succeed in falsifying a theory of this kind, we make a new important discovery. For these falsifications are most important. They teach us the unexpected; and they reassure us that, although our theories are made by ourselves, although they are our own inventions, they are none the less genuine assertions about the world; for they can *clash* with something we never made.

Our 'modified essentialism' is, I believe, helpful when the question of the logical form of natural laws is raised. It suggests that our laws or our theories must be *universal*, that is to say, must make assertions about the world – about all spatiotemporal regions of the world. It suggests, moreover, that our theories make assertions about structural or relational properties of the world; and that the properties described by an explanatory theory must be, in some sense or other, deeper than those to be explained. I believe that this word 'deeper' defies any attempt at exhaustive logical analysis, but that it is nevertheless a guide to our intuitions. (This is so in mathematics: all its theorems are logically equivalent, in the presence of the axioms, and yet there is a great difference in 'depth' which is hardly susceptible of logical analysis.) The 'depth' of a scientific theory seems to be most closely related to its simplicity and so to the wealth of its content. (It is otherwise with the depth of a mathematical theorem, whose content may be taken to be nil.) Two ingredients seem to be required: a rich content, and a certain coherence or compactness (or 'organicity') of the state of affairs described. It is this latter ingredient which, although it is intuitively fairly clear, is so difficult to analyse, and which the essentialists were trying to describe when they spoke of essences, in contradistinction to a mere accumulation of accidental properties. I do not think we can do much more than refer here to an intuitive idea, nor that we need do much more. For in the case of any particular theory proposed, it is the wealth of its content, and thus its degree of testability, which decide its interest, and the results of actual tests which decide its fate. From the point of view of method, we may look upon its depth, its coherence, and even its beauty, as a mere guide or stimulus to our intuition and to our imagination.

Nevertheless, there does seem to be something like a *sufficient* condition for depth, or for degrees of depth, which can be logically analysed. I shall try to explain this with the help of an example from the history of science.

It is well known that Newton's dynamics achieved a unification of Galileo's terrestrial and Kepler's celestial physics. It is often said that Newton's dynamics can be induced from Galileo's and Kepler's laws, and it has even been asserted that it can be strictly deduced from them.[6] But this is not so; from a logical point of view, Newton's theory, strictly speaking, contradicts both Galileo's and Kepler's (although these latter theories can of course be obtained as approximations, once we have Newton's theory to work with). For this reason it is impossible to derive Newton's theory from either Galileo's or Kepler's or both, whether by deduction or induction. For neither a deductive nor an inductive inference can ever proceed from consistent premisses to a conclusion that formally contradicts the premisses from which we started.

I regard this as a very strong argument against induction. Here, however, I am not so much interested in the impossibility of induction as in *the problem of depth*. And regarding this problem, we can indeed learn something from our example. Newton's theory unifies Galileo's and Kepler's. But far from being a mere conjunction of these two theories – which play the part of *explicanda* for Newton's – it *corrects them while explaining them*. The original explanatory task was the deduction of the earlier results. Yet this task is discharged, not by deducing these earlier results but by deducing something better in their place: new results which, under the special conditions of the older results, come numerically very close to these older results, and at the same time correct them. Thus the empirical success of the old theory may be said to corroborate the new theory; and in addition, the corrections may be tested in their turn – and perhaps refuted, or else corroborated. What is brought out strongly, by the logical situation which I have sketched, is the fact that the new theory cannot possibly be *ad hoc* or circular. Far from repeating its *explicandum*, the new theory contradicts it, and corrects it. In this way, even the evidence of the *explicandum* itself becomes independent evidence for the new theory. (Incidentally, this analysis allows us to *explain the value of metrical theories*, and of measurement; and it thus helps us to avoid the mistake of accepting measurement and precision as ultimate and irreducible values.)

I suggest that whenever in the empirical sciences a new theory of a higher level of universality successfully explains some older theory *by correcting it*, then this is a sure sign that the new theory has penetrated deeper than the older ones. The demand that a new theory should contain the old one approximately, for appropriate values of the parameters of the new theory, may be called (following Bohr) the '*principle of correspondence*'.

Fulfilment of this demand is a sufficient condition of depth, as I said before. That it is not a necessary condition may be seen from the fact that Maxwell's electromagnetic wave theory did not correct, in this sense, Fresnel's wave theory of light. It meant an increase in depth, no doubt, but in a different sense: 'The old question of the direction of the vibrations of polarized light became pointless. The difficulties concerning the boundary conditions for the boundaries between two media were solved by the very foundations of the theory. No *ad hoc* hypotheses were needed any longer for eliminating longitudinal light waves. Light pressure, so important in the theory of radiation, and only lately determined experimentally, could be derived as one of the consequences of the theory.'[7] This brilliant passage, in which Einstein sketches some of the major achievements of Maxwell's theory and compares it with Fresnel's, may be taken as an indication that there are other sufficient conditions of depth which are not covered by my analysis.

The task of science, which, I have suggested, is to find satisfactory explanations, can hardly be understood if we are not realists. For a satisfactory explanation is one which is not *ad hoc*; and this idea – the *idea of independent evidence* – can hardly be understood without the idea of discovery, of progressing to deeper layers of explanation: without the idea that there is something for us to discover, and something to discuss critically.

And yet it seems to me that within methodology we do not have to presuppose metaphysical realism; nor can we, I think, derive much help from it, except of an intuitive kind. For once we have been told that the aim of science is to explain, and that the most satisfactory explanation will be the one that is most severely testable and most severely tested, we know all that we need to know as methodologists. That the aim is realizable we cannot assert, neither with nor without the help of metaphysical realism which can give us only some intuitive encouragement, some hope, but no assurance of any kind. And although a rational treatment of methodology may be said to depend upon an assumed, or conjectured, aim of science, it certainly does not depend upon the metaphysical and most likely false assumption that the true structural theory of the world (if any) is discoverable by man, or expressible in human language.

If the picture of the world which modern science draws comes anywhere near to the truth – in other words, if we have anything like 'scientific knowledge' – then the conditions obtaining almost everywhere in the universe make the discovery of structural laws of the kind we are seeking – and thus the attainment of 'scientific knowledge' – almost impossible. For almost all regions of the universe are filled by chaotic radiation, and almost all the rest by matter in a similar chaotic state. In spite of this, science has been miraculously successful in proceeding towards what I have suggested should be regarded as its aim. [See also the end of selection 7 above.] This strange fact cannot, I think, be explained without proving too much. But it can encourage us to pursue that aim, even though we may not get any further encouragement to believe that we can actually attain it; neither from metaphysical realism nor from any other source.

13 The Growth of Scientific Knowledge (1960)

I

In this paper [this selection and the next] I wish to solve some of the problems, old as well as new, which are connected with the notions of scientific progress and of discrimination among competing theories. The new problems I wish to discuss are mainly those connected with the notions of objective truth, and of getting nearer to the truth – notions which seem to me of great help in analysing the growth of knowledge.

Although I shall confine my discussion to the growth of knowledge in science, my remarks are applicable without much change, I believe, to the growth of pre-scientific knowledge also – that is to say, to the general way in which men, and even animals, acquire new factual knowledge about the world. The method of learning by trial and error – of learning from our mistakes – seems to be fundamentally the same whether it is practised by lower or by higher animals, by chimpanzees or by men of science. My interest is not merely in the theory of scientific knowledge, but rather in the theory of knowledge in general. Yet the study of the growth of scientific knowledge is, I believe, the most fruitful way of studying the growth of knowledge in general. For the growth of scientific knowledge may be said to be the growth of ordinary human knowledge *writ large*.[1]

But is there any danger that our need to progress will go unsatisfied, and that the growth of scientific knowledge will come to an end? In particular, is there any danger that the advance of science will come to an end because science has completed its task? I hardly think so, thanks to the infinity of our ignorance. Among the real dangers to the progress of science is not the likelihood of its being completed, but such things as lack of imagination (sometimes a consequence of lack of real interest); or a misplaced faith in formalization and precision (which will be discussed below in section v); or authoritarianism in one or another of its many forms.

Since I have used the word 'progress' several times, I had better make quite sure, at this point, that I am not mistaken for a believer in a historical law of progress. Indeed I have before now [see selection 23 below] struck various blows against the belief in a law of progress, and I hold that even science is not subject to the operation of anything resembling such a law. The history of science, like the history of all human ideas, is a history of irresponsible dreams, of obstinacy, and of error. But science is one of the very few human activities – perhaps the only one – in which errors are systematically criticized and fairly often, in time, corrected. This is why we can say that, in science, we often learn from our mistakes, and why we can speak clearly and sensibly about making progress there. In most other fields of human endeavour there is change, but rarely progress (unless we adopt a very narrow view of our possible aims in life); for almost every gain is balanced, or more than balanced, by some loss. And in most fields we do not even know how to evaluate change.

Within the field of science we have, however, a *criterion of progress*: even before a theory has ever undergone an empirical test we may be able to say whether, provided it passes certain specified tests, it would be an improvement on other theories with which we are acquainted. This is my first thesis.

To put it a little differently, I assert that we *know* what a good scientific theory should be like, and – even before it has been tested – what kind of theory would be better still, provided it passes certain crucial tests. And it is this (metascientific) knowledge which makes it possible to speak of progress in science, and of a rational choice between theories.

II

Thus it is my first thesis that we can know of a theory, even before it has been tested, that *if* it passes certain tests it will be better than some other theory.

My first thesis implies that we have a criterion of relative *potential* satisfactoriness, or of *potential* progressiveness, which can be applied to a theory even before we know whether or not it will turn out, by the passing of some crucial tests, to be satisfactory *in fact*.

This criterion of relative potential satisfactoriness (which I formulated some time ago,[2] and which, incidentally, allows us to grade theories according to their degree of relative potential satisfactoriness) is extremely simple and intuitive. It characterizes as preferable the theory which tells us more; that is to say, the theory which contains the greater amount of empirical information or *content*; which is logically stronger; which has the greater explanatory and predictive power; and which can therefore be *more severely tested* by comparing predicted facts with observations. In short, we prefer an interesting, daring, and highly informative theory to a trivial one.

All these properties which, it thus appears, we desire in a theory can be shown to amount to one and the same thing: to a higher degree of empirical *content* or of testability.

III

My study of the *content* of a theory (or of any statement whatsoever) was based on the simple and obvious idea that the informative content of the *conjunction*, $a \cdot b$, of any two statements, a, and b, will always be greater than, or at least equal to, that of either of its components.

Let a be the statement 'It will rain on Friday'; b the statement 'It will be fine on Saturday'; and $a \cdot b$ the statement 'It will rain on Friday and it will be fine on Saturday': it is then obvious that the informative content of this last statement, the conjunction $a \cdot b$, will exceed that of its component a and also that of its component b. And it will also be obvious that the probability of $a \cdot b$ (or, what is the same, the probability that $a \cdot b$ will be true) will be no greater than that of either of its components.

Writing $Ct(a)$ for 'the content of the statement a', and $Ct(a \cdot b)$ for 'the content of the conjunction a and b', we have

$$(1) \qquad Ct(a) \leqq Ct(a \cdot b) \geqq Ct(b).$$

This contrasts with the corresponding law of the calculus of probability,

$$(2) \qquad p(a) \geqq p(a \cdot b) \leqq p(b),$$

where the inequality signs of (1) are inverted. Together these two laws, (1) and (2), state that with increasing content, probability decreases, and vice versa; or in other words, that content increases with increasing *im*probability. (This analysis is of course in full agreement with the general idea of the logical *content* of a statement as the class of *all those statements which are logically entailed* by it. We may also say that a statement *a* is logically stronger than a statement *b* if its content is greater than that of *b* – that is to say, if it entails more than *b*.)

This trivial fact has the following inescapable consequence: if growth of knowledge means that we operate with theories of increasing content, it must also mean that we operate with theories of decreasing probability (in the sense of the calculus of probability). Thus if our aim is the advancement or growth of knowledge, then a high probability (in the sense of the calculus of probability) cannot possibly be our aim as well: *these two aims are incompatible.*

I found this trivial though fundamental result about thirty years ago, and I have been preaching it ever since. Yet the prejudice that a high probability must be something highly desirable is so deeply ingrained that my trivial result is still held by many to be 'paradoxical'.[3] Despite this simple result the idea that a high degree of probability (in the sense of the calculus of probability) must be something highly desirable seems to be so obvious to most people that they are not prepared to consider it critically. Dr Bruce Brooke-Wavell has therefore suggested to me that I should stop talking in the context of 'probability' and should base my arguments on a 'calculus of content' and of 'relative content'; or in other words, that I should not speak about science aiming at improbability, but merely say that it aims at maximum content. I have given much thought to this suggestion, but I do not think that it would help: a head-on collision with the widely accepted and deeply ingrained probabilistic prejudice seems unavoidable if the matter is really to be cleared up. Even if, as would be easy enough,

I were to base my own theory upon the calculus of content, or of logical strength, it would still be necessary to explain that the probability calculus, in its ('logical') application to propositions or statements, is nothing but a *calculus of the logical weakness or lack of content of these statements* (either of absolute logical weakness or of relative logical weakness). Perhaps a head-on collision would be avoidable if people were not so generally inclined to assume uncritically that a high probability must be an aim of science, and that, therefore, the theory of induction must explain to us how we can attain a high degree of probability for our theories. (And it then becomes necessary to point out that there is something else – 'truthlikeness' or 'verisimilitude' – with a calculus totally different from the calculus of probability with which it seems to have been confused.)

To avoid these simple results, all kinds of more or less sophisticated theories have been designed. I believe I have shown that none of them is successful. But what is more important, they are quite unnecessary. One merely has to recognize that the property which we cherish in theories and which we may perhaps call 'verisimilitude' or 'truthlikeness' [see the next selection] is *not* a probability *in the sense of the calculus of probability* of which (2) is an inescapable theorem.

It should be noted that the problem before us is not a problem of words. I do not mind what you call 'probability', and I do not mind if you call those degrees for which the so-called 'calculus of probability' holds by any other name. I personally think that it is most convenient to reserve the term 'probability' for whatever may satisfy the well-known rules of this calculus (which Laplace, Keynes, Jeffreys, and many others have formulated, and for which I have given various formal axiom systems[4]). If (and only if) we accept this terminology, then there can be no doubt that the absolute probability of a statement *a* is simply the *degree of its logical weakness, or lack of informative content*, and that the relative probability of a statement *a*, given a statement *b*, is simply the degree of the relative weakness, or the relative *lack* of *new* informative content in statement *a*, assuming that we are already in possession of the information *b*.

Thus if we aim, in science, at a high informative content – if the growth of knowledge means that we know more, that we know *a* and *b*, rather than *a* alone, and that the content of our theories thus increases – then we have to admit that we also aim at a low probability, in the sense of the calculus of probability.

And since a low probability means a high probability of being falsified, it follows that a high degree of falsifiability, or refutability, or testability, is one of the aims of science – in fact, precisely the same aim as a high informative content.

The criterion of potential satisfactoriness is thus testability, or improbability: only a highly testable or improbable theory is worth testing, and is actually (and not merely potentially) satisfactory if it withstands severe tests – especially those tests to which we could point as crucial for the theory before they were ever undertaken.

It is possible in many cases to compare the severity of tests objectively. It is even possible, if we find it worth while, to define a measure of the severity of tests. By the same method we can define the explanatory power and the degree of corroboration of a theory.[5]

IV

The thesis that the criterion here proposed actually dominates the progress of science can easily be illustrated with the help of historical examples. The theories of Kepler and Galileo were unified and superseded by Newton's logically stronger and better testable theory, and similarly Fresnel's and Faraday's by Maxwell's. Newton's theory, and Maxwell's, in their turn, were unified and superseded by Einstein's. In each such case the progress was towards a more informative and therefore logically less probable theory: towards a theory which was more severely testable because it made predictions which, in a purely logical sense, were more easily refutable.

A theory which is not in fact refuted by testing those new and bold and improbable predictions to which it gives rise can be said to be corroborated by these severe tests. I may remind you in this connection of Galle's discovery of Neptune, of Hertz's discovery of electromagnetic waves, of Eddington's eclipse observations, of Elsasser's interpretation of Davisson's maxima as interference fringes of de Broglie waves, and of Powell's observations of the first Yukawa mesons.

All these discoveries represent corroborations by severe tests – by predictions which were highly improbable in the light of our previous knowledge (previous to the theory which was tested and corroborated). Other important discoveries have also been made while testing a theory, though they did not lead to its corroboration but to its refutation. A recent and important case is the refutation of parity. But Lavoisier's classical experiments which show that the volume of air decreases while a candle burns in a closed space, or that the weight of burning iron filings increases, do not establish the oxygen theory of combustion; yet they tend to refute the phlogiston theory.

Lavoisier's experiments were carefully thought out; but even most so-called 'chance discoveries' are fundamentally of the same logical structure. For these so-called 'chance discoveries' are as a rule refutations of theories which were consciously or unconsciously held: they are made when some of our expectations (based upon these theories) are unexpectedly disappointed. Thus the catalytic property of mercury was discovered when it was accidentally found that in its presence a chemical reaction had been speeded up which had not been expected to be influenced by mercury. But neither Örsted's nor Röntgen's nor Becquerel's nor Fleming's discovery was really accidental, even though each had accidental components: every one of these men was searching for an effect of the kind he found.

We can even say that some discoveries, such as Columbus's discovery of America, corroborate one theory (of the spherical earth) while refuting at the same time another (the theory of the size of the earth, and with it, of the nearest way to India); and that they were chance discoveries to the extent to which they contradicted all expectations, and were not consciously undertaken as tests of those theories which they refuted.

V

The stress I am laying upon change in scientific knowledge, upon its growth, or its progressiveness, may to some extent be contrasted with the current ideal of science as an axiomatized deductive system. This ideal has been dominant in European epistemology from Euclid's Platonizing cosmology (for this is, I believe, what

Euclid's *Elements* were really intended to be) to that of Newton, and further to the systems of Boscovič, Maxwell, Einstein, Bohr, Schrödinger, and Dirac. It is an epistemology that sees the final task and end of scientific activity in the construction of an axiomatized deductive system.

As opposed to this, I now believe that these most admirable deductive systems should be regarded as stepping stones rather than as ends:[6] as important stages on our way to richer, and better testable, scientific knowledge.

Regarded thus as means or stepping stones, they are certainly quite indispensable, for we are bound to develop our theories in the form of deductive systems. This is made unavoidable by the logical strength, by the great informative content, which we have to demand of our theories if they are to be better and better testable. The wealth of their consequences has to be unfolded deductively; for as a rule, a theory cannot be tested except by testing, one by one, some of its more remote consequences; consequences, that is, which cannot immediately be seen upon inspecting it intuitively.

Yet it is not the marvellous deductive unfolding of the system which makes a theory rational or empirical but the fact that we can examine it critically; that is to say, subject it to attempted refutations, including observational tests; and the fact that, in certain cases, a theory may be able to withstand those criticisms and those tests – among them tests under which its predecessors broke down, and sometimes even further and more severe tests. It is in the rational choice of the new theory that the rationality of science lies, rather than in the deductive development of the theory.

Consequently there is little merit in formalizing and elaborating a deductive non-conventional system beyond the requirements of the task of criticizing and testing it, and of comparing it critically with competitors. This critical comparison, though it has, admittedly, some minor conventional and arbitrary aspects, is largely non-conventional, thanks to the criterion of progress. It is this critical procedure which contains both the rational and the empirical elements of science. It contains those choices, those rejections, and those decisions, which show that we have learnt from our mistakes, and thereby added to our scientific knowledge.

VI

Yet perhaps even this picture of science – as a procedure whose rationality consists in the fact that we learn from our mistakes – is not quite good enough. It may still suggest that science progresses from theory to theory and that it consists of a sequence of better and better deductive systems. Yet what I really wish to suggest is that science should be visualized as *progressing from problems to problems* – to problems of ever increasing depth. For a scientific theory – an explanatory theory – is, if anything, an attempt to solve a scientific problem, that is to say, a problem concerned or connected with the discovery of an explanation.

Admittedly, our expectations, and thus our theories, may precede, historically, even our problems. *Yet science starts only with problems*. Problems crop up especially when we are disappointed in our expectations, or when our theories involve us in difficulties, in contradictions; and these may arise either within a theory, or between two different theories, or as the result of a clash between our theories and our observations. Moreover, it is only through a problem that we become conscious of holding a theory. It is the problem which challenges us to learn; to advance our knowledge; to experiment; and to observe.

Thus science starts from problems, and not from observations; though observations may give rise to a problem, especially if they are *unexpected*; that is to say, if they clash with our expectations or theories. The conscious task before the scientist is always the solution of a problem through the construction of a theory which solves the problem; for example, by explaining unexpected and unexplained observations. Yet every worthwhile new theory raises new problems; problems of reconciliation, problems of how to conduct new and previously unthought-of observational tests. And it is mainly through the new problems which it raises that it is fruitful.

Thus we may say that the most lasting contribution to the growth of scientific knowledge that a theory can make are the new problems which it raises, so that we are led back to the view of science and of the growth of knowledge as always starting from, and always ending with, problems – problems of an ever increasing depth, and an ever increasing fertility in suggesting new problems.

14 Truth and Approximation to Truth (1960)

I

[In the preceding selection] I have spoken about science, its progress, and its criterion of progress, without even mentioning *truth*. Perhaps surprisingly, this can be done without falling into pragmatism or instrumentalism: it is perfectly possible to argue in favour of the intuitive satisfactoriness of the criterion of progress in science without ever speaking about the truth of its theories. In fact, before I became acquainted with Tarski's theory of truth,[1] it appeared to me safer to discuss the criterion of progress without getting too deeply involved in the highly controversial problem connected with the use of the word 'true'.

My attitude at the time was this: although I accepted, as almost everybody does, the objective or absolute or correspondence theory of truth – truth as correspondence with the facts – I preferred to avoid the topic. For it appeared to me hopeless to try to understand clearly this strangely elusive idea of a correspondence between a statement and a fact.

In order to recall why the situation appeared so hopeless we only have to remember, as one example among many, Wittgenstein's *Tractatus* with its surprisingly naïve picture theory, or projection theory, of truth. In this book a proposition was conceived as a picture or projection of the fact which it was intended to describe and as having the same structure (or 'form') as that fact; just as a gramophone record is indeed a picture or a projection of a sound, and shares some of its structural properties.[2]

Another of these unavailing attempts to explain this correspondence was due to Schlick, who gave a beautifully clear and truly devastating criticism[3] of various correspondence theories – including the picture or projection theory – but who unfortunately produced in his turn another one which was no better. He interpreted the correspondence in question as a one-to-one correspondence between our designations and the designated objects, although counterexamples abound (designations applying to many objects, objects designated by many designations) which refute this interpretation.

All this was changed by Tarski's theory of truth and of the correspondence of a statement with the facts. Tarski's greatest achievement, and the real significance of his theory for the philosophy of the empirical sciences, is that he rehabilitated the correspondence theory of absolute or objective truth which had become suspect. He vindicated the free use of the intuitive idea of truth as correspondence to the facts. (The view that his theory is applicable only to formalized languages is, I think, mistaken. It is applicable to any consistent and even to a 'natural' language, if only we learn from Tarski's analysis how to dodge its inconsistencies; which means, admittedly, the introduction of some 'artificiality' – or caution – into its use.)

I may perhaps explain the way in which Tarski's theory of truth can be regarded, from an intuitive point of view, as a simple elucidation of the idea of *correspondence to the facts*. I shall have to stress this almost trivial point because, in spite of its triviality, it will be crucial for my argument.

The highly intuitive character of Tarski's ideas seems to become more evident (as I have found in teaching) if we first decide explicitly to take 'truth' as a synonym for 'correspondence to the facts', and then (forgetting all about 'truth') *proceed to explain the idea of 'correspondence to the facts'*.

Thus we shall first consider the following two formulations, each of which states very simply (in a metalanguage) under what conditions a certain assertion (of an object language) corresponds to the facts.

(1) The statement, or the assertion, '*Snow is white*' corresponds to the facts if, and only if, snow is, indeed, white.

(2) The statement, or the assertion, 'Grass is red' corresponds to the facts if, and only if, grass is, indeed, red.

These formulations (in which the word 'indeed' is only inserted for ease, and may be omitted) sound, of course, quite trivial. But it was left to Tarski to discover that, in spite of their apparent triviality, they contained the solution of the problem of explaining correspondence to the facts.

The decisive point is Tarski's discovery that, in order to speak of correspondence to the facts, as do (1) and (2), we must use a metalanguage in which we can *speak about two things: statements; and the facts to which they refer*. (Tarski calls such a metalanguage 'semantical'; a metalanguage in which we can speak about an object language but not about the facts to which it refers is called 'syntactical'.) Once the need for a (semantical) metalanguage is realized, everything becomes clear. (Note that while (3) '"John called" *is true*' is essentially a statement belonging to such a metalanguage, (4) '*It is true that* John called' may belong to the same language as 'John called'. Thus the phrase '*It is true that*' – which, like double negation, is logically redundant – differs widely from the metalinguistic predicate '*is true*'. The latter is needed for general remarks such as, 'If the conclusion is not true, the premisses cannot all be true' or 'John once made a true statement'.)

I have said that Schlick's theory was mistaken, yet I think that certain comments he made (*loc. cit.*) about his own theory throw some light on Tarski's. For Schlick says that the problem of truth shared the fate of some others whose solutions were not easily seen because they were mistakenly supposed to lie on a very deep level, while actually they were fairly plain and, at first sight, unimpressive. Tarski's solution may well appear unimpressive at first sight. Yet its fertility and its power are impressive indeed.

II

Thanks to Tarski's work, the idea of objective or absolute truth – that is truth as correspondence with the facts – appears to be accepted today with confidence by all who understand it. The difficulties in understanding it seem to have two sources: first, the combination of an extremely simple intuitive idea with a certain amount of complexity in the execution of the technical programme to which it gives rise; secondly, the widespread but mistaken dogma that a satisfactory theory of truth would have to be a theory of *true belief* – of well-founded, or rational belief. Indeed, the three rivals of the correspondence theory of truth – the coherence theory which mistakes consistency for truth, the evidence theory which mistakes 'known to be true' for 'true', and the pragmatic or instrumentalist theory which mistakes usefulness for truth – these are all subjectivist (or 'epistemic') theories of truth, in contradistinction to Tarski's objectivist (or 'metalogical') theory. They are subjectivist in the sense that *they all stem from the fundamental subjectivist position which can conceive of knowledge only as a special kind of mental state, or as a disposition, or as a special kind of belief*, characterized, for example, by its history or by its relation to other beliefs.

If we start from our subjective experience of believing, and thus look upon knowledge as a special kind of belief, then we may indeed have to look upon truth – that is, true knowledge – as some even more special kind of belief: as one that is well founded or justified. This would mean that there should be some more or less effective criterion, if only a partial one, of well-foundedness; some symptom by which to differentiate the experience of a well-founded belief from other experiences of belief. It can be shown that all subjectivist theories of truth aim at such a criterion: they try to define truth in terms of the sources or origins of our beliefs [see selection 3 above], or in terms of our operations of verification, or of some set of rules of acceptance, or simply in terms of the quality of our subjective convictions. They all say, more or less, that truth is what we are justified in believing or in accepting, in accordance with certain rules or criteria, of origins or sources of our knowledge, or of reliability, or stability, or biological success, or strength of conviction, or inability to think otherwise.

The objectivist theory of truth leads to a very different attitude. This may be seen from the fact that it allows us to make assertions such as the following: a theory may be true even though nobody believes it, and even though we have no reason for accepting it, or for believing that it is true; and another theory may be false, although we have comparatively good reasons for accepting it.

Clearly, these assertions would appear to be self-contradictory from the point of view of any subjectivist or epistemic theory of truth. But within the objectivist theory, they are not only consistent, but quite obviously true.

A similar assertion which the objectivist correspondence theory would make quite natural is this: even if we hit upon a true theory, we shall as a rule be merely guessing, and it may well be impossible for us to know that it *is* true.

An assertion like this was made, apparently for the first time, by Xenophanes who lived 2,500 years ago [see p.31 above]; which shows that the objectivist theory of truth is very old indeed – antedating Aristotle, who also held it. But only with Tarski's work has the suspicion been removed that the objectivist theory of truth as correspondence with the facts may be either self-contradictory (because of the paradox of the liar), or empty (as Ramsey suggested), or barren, or at the very least redundant, in the sense that we can do without it (as I once thought myself).

In my theory of scientific progress I might perhaps do without it, up to a point. Since Tarski, however, I no longer see any reason why I should try to avoid it. And if we wish to elucidate the difference between pure and applied science, between the search for knowledge and the search for power or for powerful instruments, then we cannot do without it. For the difference is that, in the search for knowledge, we are out to find true theories, or at least theories which are nearer than others to the truth – which correspond better to the facts; whereas in the search for theories that are merely powerful instruments for certain purposes, we are, in many cases, quite well served by theories which are known to be false.[4]

So one great advantage of the theory of objective or absolute truth is that it allows us to say – with Xenophanes – that we search for truth, but may not know when we have found it; that we have no criterion of truth, but are nevertheless guided by the idea of truth as a *regulative principle* (as Kant or Peirce might have said); and that, though there are no general criteria by which we can recognize truth – except perhaps tautological truth – there are something like criteria of progress towards the truth (as I shall explain presently).

The status of truth in the objective sense, as correspondence to the facts, and its role as a regulative principle, may be compared to that of a mountain peak which is permanently, or almost permanently, wrapped in clouds. The climber may not merely have difficulties in getting there – he may not know when he gets there, because he may be unable to distinguish, in the clouds, between the main summit and some subsidiary peak. Yet this does not affect the objective existence of the summit, and if the climber tells us 'I have some doubts whether I reached the actual summit', then he does, by implication, recognize the objective existence of the summit. The very idea of error, or of doubt (in its normal straightforward sense) implies the idea of an objective truth which we may fail to reach.

Though it may be impossible for the climber ever to make sure that he has reached the summit, it will often be easy for him to realize that he has not reached it (or not yet reached it); for example, when he is turned back by an overhanging wall. Similarly, there will be cases when we are quite sure that we have not reached the truth. Thus while coherence, or consistency, is no criterion of truth, simply because even demonstrably consistent systems may be false in fact, incoherence or inconsistency do establish falsity; so, if we are lucky, we may discover inconsistencies and use them to establish the falsity of some of our theories.[5]

In 1944, when Tarski published the first English outline of his investigations into the theory of truth (which he had published in Poland in 1933), few philosophers would have dared to make assertions like those of Xenophanes; and it is interesting that the volume in which Tarski's paper was published also contained two subjectivist papers on truth.[6]

Though things have improved since then, subjectivism is still rampant in the philosophy of science, and especially in the field of probability theory. The subjectivist theory of probability, which interprets degrees of probability as degrees of rational belief, stems directly from the subjectivist approach to truth – especially from the coherence theory. Yet it is still embraced by philosophers who have accepted Tarski's theory of truth. At least some of them, I suspect, have turned to probability theory in the hope that it would give them what they had originally expected from a subjectivist or epistemological theory of the attainment of truth *through verification*; that is, a theory of rational and justifiable belief, based upon observed instances.[7]

It is an awkward point in all these subjectivist theories that they are irrefutable (in the sense that they can too easily evade any criticism). For it is always possible to uphold the view that everything we say about the world, or everything we print about logarithms, should be replaced by a belief-statement. Thus we may replace the statement 'Snow is white' by 'I believe that snow is white' or perhaps even by 'In the light of all the available evidence I believe that it is rational to believe that snow is white'. The possibility of replacing any assertion about the objective world by one of these subjectivist circumlocutions is trivial, though in the case of the assertions expressed in logarithm tables – which might well be produced by machines – somewhat unconvincing. (It may be mentioned in passing that the subjectivist interpretation of logical probability links these subjectivist replacements, exactly as in the case of the coherence theory of truth, with an approach which, on closer analysis, turns out to be essentially 'syntactic' rather than 'semantic' – although it can of course always be presented within the framework of a 'semantical system'.)

It may be useful to sum up the relationships between the objectivist and subjectivist theories of scientific knowledge with the help of a little table:

OBJECTIVIST OR LOGICAL OR ONTOLOGICAL THEORIES	SUBJECTIVIST OR PSYCHOLOGICAL OR EPISTEMOLOGICAL THEORIES
truth as correspondence with the facts	*truth as property of our state of mind – or knowledge or belief*
objective probability (inherent in the situation, and testable by statistical tests)	*subjective probability (degree of rational belief based upon our total knowledge)*
objective randomness (statistically testable)	*lack of knowledge*
equiprobability (physical or situational symmetry)	*lack of knowledge*

In all these cases I am inclined to say not only that these two approaches should be distinguished, but also that the subjectivist approach should be discarded as a lapse, as based on a mistake – though perhaps a tempting mistake. There is, however, a similar table in which the epistemological (right hand) side is not based on a mistake:

truth	*conjecture*
testability	*empirical test*
explanatory or predictive power	*degree of corroboration (that is, report of the results of tests)*
verisimilitude	

III

Like many other philosophers I am at times inclined to classify philosophers as belonging to two main groups – those with whom I disagree, and those who agree with me. I also call them the verificationists or the justificationist philosophers of knowledge (or of belief), and the falsificationists or critical philosophers of knowledge (or of conjectures). I may mention in passing a third group with whom I also disagree. They may be called the disappointed justificationists – the irrationalists and sceptics.

The members of the first group – the verificationists or justificationists – hold, roughly speaking, that whatever cannot be supported by positive reasons is unworthy of being believed, or even of being taken into serious consideration.

On the other hand, the members of the second group – the falsificationists – say, roughly speaking, that what cannot (at present) in principle be overthrown by criticism is (at present) unworthy of being seriously considered; while what can in principle be so overthrown and yet resists all our critical efforts to do so may quite possibly be false, but is at any rate not unworthy of being seriously considered and perhaps even of being believed – though only tentatively.

Verificationists, I admit, are eager to uphold that most important tradition of rationalism – the fight of reason against superstition and arbitrary authority. For they demand that we should accept a belief *only if it can be justified by positive evidence*; that is to say, *shown* to be true, or, at least, to be highly probable. In other words, they demand that we should accept a belief only if it can be *verified*, or probabilistically *confirmed*.

Falsificationists (the group of fallibilists to which I belong) believe – as most irrationalists also believe – that they have discovered logical arguments which show that the programme of the first group cannot be carried out: that we can never give positive reasons which justify the belief that a theory is true. But, unlike irrationalists, we falsificationists believe that we have also discovered a way to realize the old ideal of distinguishing rational science from various forms of superstition, in spite of the breakdown of the original inductivist or justificationist programme. We hold that this ideal can be realized, very simply, by recognizing that the rationality of science lies not in its habit of appealing to empirical evidence in support of its dogmas – astrologers do so too – but solely in the *critical approach* – in an attitude which, of course, involves the critical use, among other arguments, of empirical evidence (especially in refutations). For us, therefore, science has nothing to do with the quest for certainty or probability or reliability. We are not interested in establishing scientific theories as secure, or certain, or probable. Conscious of our fallibility we are interested only in criticizing them and testing them, in the hope of finding out where we are mistaken; of learning from our mistakes; and, if we are lucky, of proceeding to better theories.

Considering their view about the positive or negative function of argument in science, the first group – the justificationists – may be also nicknamed the 'positivists' and the second – the group to which I belong – the critics or the 'negativists'. These are, of course, mere nicknames. Yet they may perhaps suggest some of the reasons why some people believe that only the positivists or verificationists are seriously interested in truth and in the search for truth, while we, the critics or negativists, are flippant about the search for truth, and addicted to barren and destructive criticism and to the propounding of views which are clearly paradoxical.

This mistaken picture of our views seems to result largely from the adoption of a justificationist programme, and of the mistaken subjectivist approach to truth which I have described.

For the fact is that we too see science as the search for truth, and that, at least since Tarski, we are no longer afraid to say so. Indeed, it is only with respect to this aim, the discovery of truth, that we can say that though we are fallible, we hope to learn from our mistakes. It is only the idea of truth which allows us to speak sensibly of mistakes and of rational criticism, and which makes rational discussion possible – that is to say, critical discussion in search of mistakes with the serious purpose of eliminating as many of these mistakes as we can, in order to get nearer the truth. Thus the very idea of error – and of fallibility – involves the idea of an objective truth as the standard of which we may fall short. (It is in this sense that the idea of truth is a *regulative* idea.)

Thus we accept the idea that the task of science is the search for truth, that is, for true theories (even though as Xenophanes pointed out we may never get them, or know them *as true* if we get them). Yet we also stress that *truth is not the only aim of science*. We want more than mere truth; what we look for is *interesting truth* – truth which is hard to come by. And in the natural sciences (as distinct from mathematics) what we look for is truth which has a high degree of explanatory power, in a sense which implies that it is logically improbable truth.

For it is clear, first of all, that we do not merely want truth – we want more truth, and new truth. We are not content with 'twice two equals four', even though it is true: we do not resort to reciting the multiplication table if we are faced with a difficult problem in topology or in physics. Mere truth is not enough; what we look for are *answers to our problems*. The point has been well put by the German humorist and poet Busch, of Max-and-Moritz fame, in a little nursery rhyme – I mean a rhyme for the epistemological nursery:[8]

> Twice two equals four: 'tis true,
> But too empty, and too trite.
> What I look for is a clue
> To some matters not so light.

Only if it is an answer to a problem – a difficult, a fertile problem, a problem of some depth – does a truth, or a conjecture about the truth, become relevant to science. This is so in pure mathematics, and it is so in the natural sciences. And in the latter, we have something like a logical measure of the depth or significance of the problem in the increase of logical improbability or explanatory power of the proposed new answer, as compared with the best theory or conjecture previously proposed in the field. This logical measure is essentially the same thing which I have described above as the logical criterion of potential satisfactoriness and of progress.

My description of this situation might tempt some people to say that truth does not, after all, play a very big role with us negativists even as a regulative principle. There can be no doubt, they will say, that negativists (like myself) much prefer an attempt to solve an interesting problem by a bold conjecture, *even if it soon turns out to be false*, to any recital of a sequence of true but uninteresting assertions. Thus it does not seem, after all, as if we negativists had much use for the idea of truth. Our ideas of scientific progress and of attempted problem-solving do not seem very closely related to it.

This, I believe, would give quite a mistaken impression of the attitude of our group. Call us negativists, or what you like: but you should realize that we are as much interested in truth as anybody – for example, as the members of a court of justice. When the judge tells a witness that he should speak 'The truth, the *whole truth*, and nothing but the truth', then what he looks for is as much of the *relevant truth* as the witness may be able to offer. A witness who likes to wander off into irrelevancies is unsatisfactory as a witness, even though these irrelevancies may be truisms, and thus part of 'the whole truth'. It is quite obvious that what the judge – or anybody else – wants when he asks for 'the whole truth' is as much *interesting and relevant* true information as can be got; and many perfectly candid witnesses have failed to disclose some important information simply because they were unaware of its relevance to the case.

Thus when we stress, with Busch, that we are not interested in mere truth but in interesting and relevant truth, then, I contend, we only emphasize a point which everybody accepts. And if we are interested in bold conjectures, even if these should soon turn out to be false, then this interest is due to our methodological conviction that only with the help of such bold conjectures can we hope to discover interesting and relevant truth.

There is a point here which, I suggest, it is the particular task of the logician to analyse. 'Interest', or 'relevance', in the sense here intended, can be *objectively* analysed; it is relative to our problems; and it depends on the explanatory power, and thus on the content or improbability, of the information. The measures alluded to earlier are precisely such measures as take account of some *relative content* of the information – its content relative to a hypothesis or to a problem.

I can therefore gladly admit that falsificationists like myself much prefer an attempt to solve an interesting problem by a bold conjecture, *even (and especially) if it soon turns out to be false*, to any recital of a sequence of irrelevant truisms. We prefer this because we believe that this is the way in which we can learn from our mistakes; and that in finding that our conjecture was false, we shall have learnt much about the truth, and shall have got nearer to the truth.

I therefore hold that both ideas – the idea of truth, in the sense of correspondence with facts, and the idea of content (which may be measured by the same measure as testability) – play about equally important roles in our considerations, and that both can shed much light on the idea of progress in science.

IV

Looking at the progress of scientific knowledge, many people have been moved to say that even though we do not know how near we are to or how far we are from the truth, we can, and often do, *approach more and more closely to the truth*. I myself have sometimes said such things in the past, but always with a twinge of bad conscience. Not that I believe in being over-fussy about what we say: as long as we speak as clearly as we can, yet do not pretend that what we are saying is clearer than it is, and as long as we do not try to derive apparently exact consequences from dubious or vague premisses, there is no harm whatever in occasional vagueness, or in voicing every now and then our feelings and general intuitive impressions about things. Yet whenever I used to write, or to say, something about science as getting nearer to the truth, or as a kind of approach to truth, I felt that I really ought to be writing 'Truth', with a capital 'T', in order to make quite clear that a vague and highly metaphysical notion was involved here, in contradistinction to Tarski's 'truth' which we can with a clear conscience write in the ordinary way with small letters.[9]

It was only quite recently that I set myself to consider whether the idea of truth involved here was really so dangerously vague and metaphysical after all. Almost at once I found that it was not, and that there was no particular difficulty in applying Tarski's fundamental idea to it.

For there is no reason whatever why we should not say that one theory corresponds better to the facts than another. This simple initial step makes everything clear: there really is no barrier here between what at first sight appeared to be Truth with a capital 'T' and truth in a Tarskian sense.

But can we really speak about *better* correspondence? Are there such things as *degrees* of truth? Is it not dangerously misleading to talk as if Tarskian truth were located somewhere in a kind of metrical or at least topological space so that we can sensibly say of two theories – say an earlier theory t_1 and a later theory t_2, that t_2 has superseded t_1, or progressed beyond t_1, by approaching more closely to the truth than t_1?

I do not think that this kind of talk is at all misleading. On the contrary, I believe that we simply cannot do without something like this idea of a better or worse approximation to truth. For there is no doubt whatever that we can say, and often want to say, of a theory t_2 that it corresponds better to the facts, or that as far as we know it seems to correspond better to the facts, than another theory t_1.

I shall give here a somewhat unsystematic list of six types of case in which we should be inclined to say of a theory t_1 that it is superseded by t_2 in the sense that t_2 seems – as far as we know – to correspond better to the facts than t_1, in some sense or other.

(1) t_2 makes more precise assertions than t_1, and these more precise assertions stand up to more precise tests.

(2) t_2 takes account of, and explains, more facts than t_1 (which will include for example the above case that, other things being equal, t_2's assertions are more precise).

(3) t_2 describes, or explains, the facts in more detail than t_1.

(4) t_2 has passed tests which t_1 has failed to pass.

(5) t_2 has suggested new experimental tests, not considered before t_2 was designed (and not suggested by t_1, and perhaps not even applicable to t_1); and t_2 has passed these tests.

(6) t_2 has unified or connected various hitherto unrelated problems.

If we reflect upon this list, then we can see that the *contents* of the theories t_1 and t_2 play an important role in it. (It will be remembered that the *logical content* of a statement or a theory *a* is the class of all statements which follow logically from *a*, while I have defined the *empirical content* of *a* as the class of all basic statements which contradict *a*.[10] For in our list of six cases, the empirical content of theory t_2 exceeds that of theory t_1.

This suggests that we combine here the ideas of truth and of content into one – the idea of a degree of better (or worse) correspondence to truth or of greater (or less) likeness or similarity to truth; or to use a term already mentioned above (in contradistinction to probability) the idea of (degrees of) *verisimilitude*.

It should be noted that the idea that every statement or theory is not only either true or false but has, independently of its truth value, some degree of verisimilitude, does not give rise to any multivalued logic – that is, to a logical system with more than two truth values, true and false; though some of the things the defenders of multivalued logic are hankering after seem to be realized by the theory of verisimilitude (and related theories).

V

Once I had seen the problem it did not take me long to get to this point. But strangely enough, it took me a long time to put two and two together, and to proceed from here to a very simple *definition of verisimilitude* in terms of truth and of content. (We can use either logical or empirical content, and thus obtain two closely related ideas of verisimilitude which however merge into one if we consider here only empirical theories, or empirical aspects of theories.)

Let us consider the *content* of a statement *a*; that is, the class of all the logical consequences of *a*. If *a* is true, then this class can consist only of true statements, because truth is always transmitted from a premiss to all its consequences. But if *a* is false, then its content will always consist of both true and false consequences. (Example: 'It always rains on Sundays' is false, but its consequence that it rained last Sunday happens to be true.) Thus whether a statement is true or false, *there may be more truth, or less truth, in what it says*, according to whether its content consists of a greater or a lesser number of true statements.

Let us call the class of the true logical consequence of a the 'truth content' of a (a German term '*Wahrheitsgehalt*' – reminiscent of the phrase 'there is truth in what you say' – of which 'truth content' may be said to be a translation, has been intuitively used for a long time); and let us call the class of the false consequences of a – but only these – the 'falsity content' of a. (The 'falsity content' is not, strictly speaking, a 'content', because it does not contain any of the true consequences of the false statements which form its elements. Yet it is possible to define its *measure* with the help of two contents.) These terms are precisely as objective as the terms 'true' or 'false' and 'content' themselves. Now we can say:

Assuming that the truth content and the falsity content of two theories t_1 and t_2 are comparable, we can say that t_2 is more closely similar to the truth, or corresponds better to the facts, than t_1, if and only if either

(1) *the truth content but not the falsity content of t_2 exceeds that of t_1,*

(2) *the falsity content of t_1, but not its truth content, exceeds that of t_2.*

If we work with the (perhaps fictitious) assumption that the content and truth content of a theory a are in principle *measurable*, then we can go slightly beyond this definition and can define $Vs(a)$, that is to say, a measure of the *verisimilitude* or *truthlikeness* of a. The simplest definition will be

$$Vs(a) = Ct_T(a) - Ct_F(a)$$

where $Ct_T(a)$ is a measure of the truth content of a, and $Ct_F(a)$ is a measure of the falsity content of a. (A slightly more complicated but in some respects preferable definition can also be formulated.[11]) It is obvious that $Vs(a)$ satisfies our two demands, according to which $Vs(a)$ should increase (1) if $Ct_T(a)$ increases while $Ct_F(a)$ does not, or (2) if $Ct_F(a)$ decreases while $Ct_T(a)$ does not.

VI

Three non-technical points may be made. The first is that our idea of approximation to truth, or of verisimilitude, has the same objective character and the same ideal or regulative character as the idea of objective or absolute *truth*. It is *not an epistemological or an epistemic idea* – no more than truth or content. (In Tarski's terminology, it is obviously a 'semantic' idea, like truth, or like logical consequence, and, therefore, content.) Accordingly, we have here again to distinguish between the question 'What do you intend to say if you say that the theory t_2 has a higher degree of verisimilitude than the theory t_1?', and the question 'How do you know that the theory t_2 has a higher degree of verisimilitude than the theory t_1?'

We have so far answered only the first of these questions. The answer to the second question depends on it, and is exactly analogous to the answer to the analogous (absolute rather than comparative) question about truth: 'I do *not* know – I only guess. But I can examine my guess critically, and if it withstands severe criticism, then this fact may be taken as a good critical reason in favour of it.'

My second point is this. Verisimilitude is so defined that maximum verisimilitude would be achieved only by a theory which is not only true, but completely comprehensively true: if it corresponds to *all* facts, as it were, and, of course, only to *real* facts. This is of course a much more remote and unattainable ideal than a mere correspondence with *some* facts (as in, say, 'Snow is usually white').

But all this holds only for the maximum degree of verisimilitude, and not for the *comparison of theories with respect to their degree of verisimilitude*. This comparative use of the idea is its main point; and the idea of a higher or lower degree of verisimilitude seems less remote and more applicable and therefore perhaps more important for the analysis of scientific methods than the – in itself much more fundamental – idea of absolute truth itself.

This leads me to my third point. Let me first say that I do not suggest that the explicit introduction of the idea of verisimilitude will lead to any changes in the theory of method. On the contrary, I think that my theory of testability or corroboration by empirical tests is the methodological theory that gives point to this new metalogical idea. The only improvement is one of clarification. Thus I have often said that we prefer the theory t_2 which has passed certain severe tests to the theory t_1 which has failed these tests, because a false theory is certainly worse than one which, for all we know, may be true.

To this we can now add that after t_2 has been refuted in its turn, we can still say that it is better than t_1, for although both have been shown to be false, the fact that t_2 has withstood tests which t_1 did not pass may be a good indication that the falsity content of t_1 exceeds that of t_2 while its truth content does not. Thus we may still give preference to t_2, even after its falsification, because we have reason to think that it agrees better with the facts than did t_1.

All cases where we accept t_2 because of experiments which were crucial between t_2 and t_1 seem to be of this kind, and especially all cases where the experiments were found by trying to think out, with the help of t_2, cases where t_2 leads to other results than did t_1. Thus Newton's theory allowed us to predict some deviations from Kepler's laws. Its success in this field established that it did not fail in cases which refuted Kepler's: at least the now known falsity content of Kepler's theory was not part of Newton's, while it was pretty clear that the truth content could not have shrunk, since Kepler's theory followed from Newton's as a 'first approximation'.

Similarly, a theory t_2 which is more precise than t_1 can now be shown to have – always provided its falsity content does not exceed that of t_1 – a higher degree of verisimilitude than t_1. The same will hold for t_2 whose numerical assertions, though false, come nearer to the true numerical values than those of t_1.

Ultimately, the idea of verisimilitude is most important in cases where we know that we have to work with theories which are *at best* approximations – that is to say, theories of which we actually know that they cannot be true. (This is often the case in the social sciences.) In these cases we can still speak of better or worse approximations to the truth (and we therefore do not need to interpret these cases in an instrumentalist sense).

VII

It always remains possible, of course, that we shall make mistakes in our relative appraisal of two theories, and the appraisal will often be a controversial matter. This point can hardly be overemphasized. Yet it is also important that in principle, and as long as there are no revolutionary changes in our background knowledge, the relative appraisal of our two theories, t_1 and t_2, will remain stable. More particularly, our preferences need not change, as we have seen, if we eventually refute the better of the two theories. Newton's dynamics, for example, even though we may regard it as refuted, has of course maintained its superiority over Kepler's and Galileo's theories. The reason is its greater content or explanatory power. Newton's theory continues to explain more facts than did the others; to explain them with greater precision; and to unify the previously unconnected problems of celestial and terrestrial mechanics. The reason for the stability of relative appraisals such as these is quite simple: the logical relation between the theories is of such a character that, first of all, there exist with respect to them those crucial experiments, and these, when carried out, went against Newton's predecessors. And secondly, it is of such a character that the later refutations of Newton's theory could not support the older theories: they either did not affect them, or (as with the perihelion motion of Mercury) they could be claimed to refute the predecessors also.

I hope that I have explained the idea of better agreement with the facts, or of degrees of verisimilitude, sufficiently clearly for the purpose of this brief survey.

15 Propensities, Probabilities, and the Quantum Theory (1957)

In this paper, I propose briefly to put forth and to explain the following theses, and to indicate the manner of their defence.

(1) The solution of the problem of interpreting probability theory is fundamental for the interpretation of quantum theory; for quantum theory is a probabilistic theory.

(2) The idea of a statistical interpretation is correct, but is lacking in clarity.

(3) As a consequence of this lack of clarity, the usual interpretation of probability in physics *oscillates* between two extremes: an *objectivist* purely statistical interpretation and a *subjectivist* interpretation in terms of our incomplete knowledge, or of the available information.

(4) In the orthodox Copenhagen interpretation of quantum theory we find the same oscillation between an objectivist and subjectivist interpretation: *the famous intrusion of the observer into physics*.

(5) As opposed to all this, a revised or reformed statistical interpretation is here proposed. It is called the *propensity interpretation of probability*.

(6) The propensity interpretation is a purely objectivist interpretation. It eliminates the oscillation between objectivist and subjectivist interpretations, and with it the intrusion of the subject into physics.

(7) The idea of propensities is 'metaphysical', in exactly the same sense as forces or fields of forces are metaphysical.

(8) It is also 'metaphysical' in another sense: in the sense of providing a coherent programme for physical research.

These are my theses. I begin by explaining what I call the propensity interpretation of probability theory.[1]

I Objectivist and Subjectivist Interpretations of Probability

Let us assume that we have two dice: one is a *regular* die of homogeneous material, the other is *loaded*, in such a way that in long sequences of throws the side marked '6' comes uppermost in about 1/4 of the throws. We say, in this case, that the probability of throwing a 6 is 1/4.

Now the following line of arguing seems attractive.

We ask what we *mean* by saying that the probability is 1/4; and we may arrive at the answer: what we *mean* precisely, is that the relative frequency, or the statistical frequency, of the results in long sequences is 1/4. Thus probability is relative frequency in the long run. This is the statistical interpretation.

The statistical interpretation has been often criticized because of the difficulties of the phrase 'in the long run'. I will *not* discuss this question.[2] Instead I will discuss the question of *the probability of a single event*. This question is of importance in connection with quantum theory because the ψ-function determines the probability of a *single electron* to take up a certain state, under certain conditions.

Thus we ask ourselves now what it *means* to say 'The probability of throwing 6 *with the next throw* of this loaded die is 1/4.'

From the point of view of the *statistical interpretation*, this can only mean one thing: 'The next throw is a *member of a sequence* of throws, and the relative frequency within this sequence is 1/4.'

At first sight, this answer seems satisfactory. But we can ask the following awkward question.

What if the sequence consists of throws of a *loaded* die, with one or two throws of a *regular* die occurring in between the others? Clearly, we shall say about the throws with the regular die that their probability is different from 1/4, in spite of the fact that these throws are members of a sequence of throws with the frequency 1/4.

This simple objection is of fundamental importance. It can be answered in various ways. I shall mention two of these answers, one leading to a *subjectivist interpretation*, the other to the *propensity interpretation*.

The first or subjectivist answer is this. 'You have assumed in your question', the subjectivist may address me, 'that *we know* that the one die is loaded, the other regular, and also that *we know* whether the one or the other is used at a certain place in the sequence of throws. In view of this information, we shall of course attribute the proper probabilities to the various single throws. For probability, as your own objection shows, is not simply a frequency in a sequence. Admittedly, observed frequencies are important as providing us with valuable *information*. But we must use *all* our information. The probability is our assessment, in the light *of all we know*, of reasonable betting odds. It is a measure which depends essentially upon our incomplete information, and *it is a measure of the incompleteness of our information*: if our information about the conditions under which the die will be thrown were sufficiently precise, then there would be no difficulty in predicting the result with certainty.'

This is the subjectivist's answer, and I shall take it as a characterization of the subjectivist position which I shall not discuss further in this paper, although I shall mention it in various places.[3]

Now what will the defender of an objectivist interpretation say to our fundamental objection? Most likely he will say (as I myself used to say for a long time) the following.

'To make a statement about probability is to propose a *hypothesis*. It is a hypothesis about frequencies in a sequence of events. In proposing this hypothesis, we can make use of all sorts of things – of past experience, or of inspiration: it does not matter *how we get* it: all that matters is *how we test it*. Now in the case mentioned, we all agree on the frequency hypothesis, and we all agree that the frequency of 1/4 will not be affected by having one or two throws with a regular die in between the throws with a loaded die. As to the regular throws, *if* we consider them merely as belonging to this sequence, we have to attribute to them, strange as it may sound, the probability of 1/4, even though they are throws with a regular die. And if, on the other hand, we attribute to them the probability of 1/6, then we do so because of the hypothesis that in *another* sequence – one of throws with the regular die – the frequency will be 1/6.'

This is the objectivist's defence of the purely statistical interpretation, or of the frequency interpretation, and *as far as it goes* I still agree with it.

But I now think it strange that I did not press my question further. For it seems clear to me now that this answer of mine, or of the objectivist's, implies the following. In attributing probabilities to sequences, we consider as decisive the *conditions under which the sequence is produced*. In assuming that a sequence of throws of a loaded die will be different from a sequence of throws of a regular die, we attribute the probability to the *experimental conditions*. But this leads to the following result.

Even though probabilities may be said to be frequencies, we believe that these *frequencies will depend on the experimental arrangement*.

But with this, we come to a new version of the objectivist interpretation. It is as follows.

Every experimental arrangement is *liable to produce*, if we repeat the experiment very often, a sequence with frequencies which depend upon this particular experimental arrangement. These virtual frequencies may be called probabilities. But since the probabilities turn out to depend upon the experimental arrangement, they may be looked upon as *properties of this arrangement*. *They characterize the disposition, or the propensity*, of the experimental arrangement to give rise to certain characteristic frequencies *when the experiment is often repeated*.

II The Propensity Interpretation

We thus arrive at the propensity interpretation of probability.[4] It differs from the purely statistical or frequency interpretation only in this – that it considers the probability as a characteristic property of the experimental arrangement rather than as a property of a sequence.

The main point of this change is that we now take as fundamental *the probability of the result of a single experiment*, with respect to its *conditions*, rather than the frequency of results in a sequence of experiments. Admittedly, if we wish to *test* a probability statement, we have to test an experimental sequence. But now the probability statement is not a statement *about* this sequence: it is a statement *about* certain properties of the experimental conditions, of the experimental set-up. (Mathematically, the change corresponds to the transition from the frequency theory to the measure-theoretical approach.)

A statement about propensities may be compared with a statement about the strength of an electric field. We can test this statement only if we introduce a test body and measure the effect of the field upon this body. But the statement which we test speaks about the field rather than about the body. It speaks about certain *dispositional properties* of the field. And just as we can consider the field as physically real, so we can consider the propensities as physically real. They are *relational* properties of the experimental set-up. For example, the propensity 1/4 *is not a property of our loaded die*. This can be seen at once if we consider that in a very weak gravitational field, the load will have little effect – the propensity of throwing a 6 may decrease from 1/4 to very nearly 1/6. In a strong gravitational field, the load will be more effective and the same die will exhibit a propensity of 1/3 or 1/2. The tendency or disposition or propensity is therefore, as a relational property of the experimental set-up, something more abstract than, say, a Newtonian force with its simple rules of vectorial addition. *The propensity distribution attributes weights to all possible results of the experiment*. Clearly, it can be represented by a vector in the *space of possibilities*.

III Propensity and Quantum Theory

The main thing about the propensity interpretation is that *it takes the mystery out of quantum theory, while leaving probability and indeterminism in it*. It does so by pointing out that all the apparent mysteries would also involve thrown dice, or tossed pennies – *exactly* as they do electrons. In other words, it shows that quantum theory is a probability theory just as any theory of any other game of chance, such as the bagatelle board (pin board).

In our interpretation, Schrödinger's ψ-function determines the propensities of the states of the electron. We therefore have no 'dualism' of particles and waves. The electron is a particle, but its wave theory is a propensity theory which attributes weights to the electron's possible states. The waves in configuration space are waves of weights, or waves of propensities.

Let us consider Dirac's example of a photon and a polarizer. According to Dirac, we have to say that the photon is in both possible states at once, half in each; even though it is indivisible, and though we can find it, or observe it, in only one of its possible states.

We can translate this as follows. The theory describes, and gives weights to, all the possible states – in our case, two. The photon will be in one state only. The situation is exactly the same as with a tossed penny. Assume that we have tossed the penny, and that we are shortsighted and have to bend down before we can observe which side is upmost. The probability formalism tells us then that each of the possible states has a probability of 1/2. So we can say that the penny is half in one state, and half in the other. And when we bend down to observe it, the Copenhagen spirit will inspire the penny to make a quantum jump into one of its two eigenstates. For nowadays a quantum jump is said by Heisenberg to be the same as a reduction of the wave packet. And by 'observing' the penny, we induce exactly what in Copenhagen is called a 'reduction of the wave packet'.

The famous two-slit experiment allows exactly the same analysis. If we shut one slit, we interfere with the possibilities, and therefore get a different ψ-function, and a different probability distribution of the possible results. *Every change in the experimental arrangement such as the shutting of a slit, will lead to a different distribution of weights to the possibilities* (just as will the shifting of a pin on a pin board). That is, we obtain a different ψ-function, determining a different distribution of the propensities.

There is nothing peculiar about the role of the observer: he does not come in at all. What 'interferes' with the ψ-function are only changes of experimental arrangements.

The opposite impression is due to an oscillation between an objectivist and a subjectivist interpretation of probability. It is the subjectivist interpretation which drags in our knowledge, and its changes, while we ought to speak only of experimental arrangements, and the results of experiments.

IV Metaphysical Considerations

I have stressed that the propensities are not only as objective as the experimental arrangements but also *physically real* – in the sense in which forces, and fields of forces, are *physically real*. Nevertheless they are *not* pilot-waves in ordinary space, but weight functions of possibilities, that is to say, vectors in possibility space. (Bohm's 'quantum-mechanical potential' would become here a propensity to accelerate, rather than an accelerating force. This would give full weight to the Pauli/Einstein criticism of the pilot-wave theory of de Broglie and Bohm.) We are quite used to the fact that such abstract things as, for example, degrees of freedom, have a very real influence on our results, and are in so far something physically real. Or consider the fact that, compared with the mass of the sun, the masses of the planets are negligible, and that compared with the masses of the planets, those of their moons are also negligible. This is an abstract, a relational fact, not attributable to any planet or to any point in space, but a relational property of the whole solar system. Nevertheless, there is every reason to believe that it is one of the 'causes' of the stability of the solar system. Thus abstract relational facts can be 'causes' and in that sense physically real.

It seems to me that by stressing that the ψ-function describes physical realities, we may be able to bridge the gap between those who rightly stress the statistical character of modern physics and those who, like Einstein and Schrödinger, insist that physics has to describe an objective physical reality. The two points of view are incompatible on the subjectivist assumption that statistical laws describe our own imperfect state of knowledge. They become compatible if only we realize that these statistical laws describe propensities, that is to say, objective relational properties of the physical world.

Beyond this, the propensity interpretation seems to offer a new metaphysical interpretation of physics (and incidentally also of biology and psychology). For we can say that all physical (and psychological) properties are dispositional. That a surface is coloured red means that it has the disposition to reflect light of a certain wave length. That a beam of light has a certain wave length means that it is disposed to behave in a certain manner if surfaces of various colours, or prisms, or spectographs, or slotted screens, etc., are put in its way.

Aristotle put the propensities as potentialities *into* the things. Newton's was the first *relational* theory of physical dispositions and his gravitational theory led, almost inevitably, to a theory of fields of forces. I believe that the propensity interpretation of probability may take this development one step further.

Part III Metaphysics

16 Metaphysics and Criticizability (1958)

In order to avoid right from the start the danger of getting lost in generalities, it might be best to explain at once, with the help of five examples, what I mean by a *philosophical or metaphysical theory*.

A typical example of a philosophical theory is Kant's doctrine of *determinism*, with respect to the world of experience. Though Kant was an indeterminist at heart, he said in the *Critique of Practical Reason*[1] that full knowledge of our psychological and physiological conditions and of our environment would make it possible to predict our future behaviour with the same certainty with which we can predict an eclipse of the sun or of the moon.

In more general terms, one could formulate the determinist doctrine as follows [see also selection 20, section II, below].

The future of the empirical world (or of the phenomenal world) is completely predetermined by its present state, down to its smallest detail.

Another philosophic theory is *idealism*, for example, Berkeley's or Schopenhauer's; we may perhaps express it here by the following thesis: 'The empirical world is my idea', or '*The world is my dream*'. [See also selection 17 below.]

A third philosophic theory – and one that is very important today – is epistemological *irrationalism*, which might be explained as follows.

Since we know from Kant that human reason is incapable of grasping, or knowing, the world of things-in-themselves, we must either give up hope of ever knowing it, or else try to know it otherwise than by means of our reason; and since we cannot and will not give up this hope, we can only use irrational or supra-rational means, such as instinct, poetic inspiration, moods, or emotions.

This, irrationalists claim, is possible because in the last analysis we are ourselves such things-in-themselves; thus if we can manage somehow to obtain an intimate and immediate knowledge of ourselves, we can thereby find out what things-in-themselves are like.

This simple argument of irrationalism is highly characteristic of most nineteenth-century post-Kantian philosophers; for example of the ingenious Schopenhauer, who in this way discovered that since we, as things-in-themselves, are *will*, will must be the thing-in-itself. The world, as a thing-in-itself, is *will*, while the world as phenomenon is an *idea*. Strangely enough this obsolescent philosophy, dressed up in new clothes, has once again become the latest fashion, although, or perhaps just because, its striking similarity to old post-Kantian ideas has remained hidden (so far as anything may remain hidden under the emperor's new clothes). Schopenhauer's philosophy is nowadays propounded in obscure and impressive language, and his self-revealing intuition that man, as a thing-in-itself, is ultimately *will*, has now given place to the self-revealing intuition that man may so utterly bore himself that his very boredom proves that the thing-in-itself is Nothing – that it is Nothingness, Emptiness-in-itself. I do not wish to deny a certain measure of originality to this existentialist variant of Schopenhauer's philosophy: its originality is proved by the fact that Schopenhauer could never have thought so poorly of his powers of self-entertainment. What he discovered in himself was will, activity, tension, excitement – roughly the opposite of what some existentialists discovered: the utter boredom of the bore-in-himself bored by himself. Yet Schopenhauer is no longer the fashion: the great fashion of our post-Kantian and post-rationalist era is what Nietzsche ('haunted by premonitions and suspicious of his own progeny') rightly called 'European nihilism'.[2]

Yet all this is only by the way. We now have before us a list of five philosophical theories.

First, determinism: the future is contained in the present, in as much as it is fully determined by the present.

Second, idealism: the world is my dream.

Third, irrationalism: we have irrational or supra-rational experiences in which we experience ourselves as things-in-themselves; and so have some kind of knowledge of things-in-themselves.

Fourth, voluntarism: in our own volitions we know ourselves as wills. The thing-in-itself is the will.

Fifth, nihilism: in our boredom we know ourselves as nothings. The thing-in-itself is Nothingness.

So much for our list. I have chosen my examples in such a way that I can say of each one of these five theories, after careful consideration, that I am convinced that it is false. To put it more precisely; I am *first* of all an indeterminist, *secondly* a realist, *thirdly* a rationalist. As regards my fourth and fifth examples, I gladly admit – with Kant and other critical rationalists – that we cannot possess anything like full knowledge of the real world with its infinite richness and beauty. Neither physics nor any other science can help us to this end. Yet I am sure the voluntarist formula, 'The world is will', cannot help us either. And as to our nihilists and existentialists who bore themselves (and perhaps others), I can only pity them. They must be blind and deaf, poor things, for they speak of the world like a blind man of Perugino's colours or a deaf man of Mozart's music.

Why then have I made a point of selecting for my examples a number of philosophical theories that I believe to be false? Because I hope in this way to put more clearly the problem contained in the following important statement.

Although I consider each one of these five theories to be *false*, I am nevertheless convinced that each of them is *irrefutable*.

Listening to this statement you may well wonder how I can possibly hold a theory to be *false* and *irrefutable* at one and the same time – I who claim to be a rationalist. For how can a rationalist say of a theory that it is false and irrefutable? Is he not bound, as a rationalist, to refute a theory before he asserts that it is false? And conversely, is he not bound to admit that if a theory is irrefutable, it is true?

With these questions I have at last arrived at our problem.

The last question can be answered fairly simply. There have been thinkers who believed that the truth of a theory may be inferred from its irrefutability. Yet this is an obvious mistake, considering that there may be two incompatible theories which are equally irrefutable – for example, determinism and its opposite, indeterminism. Now since two incompatible theories cannot both be true, we see from the fact that both theories are irrefutable that irrefutability cannot entail truth.

To infer the truth of a theory from its irrefutability is therefore inadmissible, no matter how we interpret irrefutability. For normally 'irrefutability' would be used in the following two senses:

The first is a purely logical sense: we may use 'irrefutable' to mean the same as 'irrefutable by purely logical means'. But this would mean the same as 'consistent'. Now it is quite obvious that the truth of a theory cannot possibly be inferred from its consistency.

The second sense of 'irrefutable' refers to refutations that make use not only of logical (or analytic) but also of empirical (or synthetic) assumptions; in other words, it admits empirical refutations. In this second sense, 'irrefutable' means the same as 'not empirically refutable', or more precisely 'compatible with any possible empirical statement' or 'compatible with every possible experience'.

Now both the logical and the empirical irrefutability of a statement or a theory can easily be reconciled with its falsehood. In the case of logical irrefutability this is clear from the fact that every empirical statement and its negation must both be *logically* irrefutable. For example, the two statements, 'Today is Monday', and, 'Today is not Monday', are both logically irrefutable; but from this it follows immediately that there exist false statements which are logically irrefutable.

With empirical irrefutability the situation is a little different. The simplest examples of empirically irrefutable statements are so-called strict or pure existential statements. Here is an example of a strict or pure existential statement: 'There exists a pearl which is ten times larger than the next largest pearl.' If in this statement we restrict the words 'There exists' to some finite region in space and time, then it may of course become a refutable statement. For example, the following statement is obviously empirically refutable: 'At this moment and in this box here there exist at least two pearls one of which is ten times larger than the next largest pearl in this box.' But then this statement is no longer a strict or pure existential statement: rather it is a *restricted* existential statement. A strict or pure existential statement applies to the whole universe, and it is irrefutable simply because there can be no method by which it could be refuted. For even if we were able to search our entire universe, the strict or pure existential statement would not be refuted by our failure to discover the required pearl, seeing that it might always be hiding in a place where we are not looking.

Examples of empirically irrefutable existential statements which are of greater interest are the following.

'There exists a completely effective cure for cancer, or, more precisely, there is a chemical compound which can be taken without ill effect, and which cures cancer.' Needless to say, this statement must not be interpreted as meaning that such a chemical compound is actually *known* or that it will be discovered within a given time.

Similar examples are: 'There exists a cure for any infectious disease' and 'There exists a Latin formula which, if pronounced in proper ritual manner, cures all diseases.'

Here we have an empirically irrefutable statement that few of us would hold to be true. The statement is irrefutable because it is obviously impossible to try out every conceivable Latin formula in combination with every conceivable manner of pronouncing it. Thus there always remains the logical possibility that there might be, after all, a magical Latin formula with the power of curing all diseases.

Even so, we are justified in believing that this irrefutable existential statement is false. We certainly cannot *prove* its falsehood; but everything we know about diseases tells against its being true. In other words, though we cannot establish its falsity, the conjecture that there is no such magical Latin formula is much more reasonable than the irrefutable conjecture that such a formula does exist.

I need hardly add that through almost 2000 years learned men have believed in the truth of an existential statement very much like this one; this is why they persisted in their search for the philosopher's stone. Their failure to find it does not prove anything – precisely because existential propositions are irrefutable.

Thus the logical or empirical irrefutability of a theory is certainly not a sufficient reason for holding the theory to be true, and hence I have vindicated my right to believe, at the same time, that these five philosophical theories are irrefutable, and that they are false.

Some twenty five years ago I proposed to distinguish empirical or scientific theories from non-empirical or non-scientific ones precisely by defining the empirical theories as the refutable ones and the non-empirical theories as the irrefutable ones. My reasons for this proposal were as follows. Every serious test of a theory is an attempt to refute it. Testability is therefore the same as refutability, or falsifiability. And since we should call 'empirical' or 'scientific' only such theories as can be empirically tested, we may conclude that it is the possibility of an empirical refutation which distinguishes empirical or scientific theories. [See selection 8 above.]

If this 'criterion of refutability' is accepted, then we see at once that *philosophical* theories, or metaphysical theories, will be *irrefutable by definition.*

My assertion that our five philosophical theories are irrefutable may now sound almost trivial. At the same time it will have become obvious that though I am a rationalist I am in no way obliged to refute these theories before being entitled to call them 'false'. And this brings us to the crux of our problem:

If philosophical theories are all irrefutable, how can we ever distinguish between true and false philosophical theories?

This is the serious problem which arises from the *irrefutability of philosophical theories.*

In order to state the problem more clearly, I should like to reformulate it as follows.

We may distinguish here between three types of theory.

First, logical and mathematical theories.

Second, empirical and scientific theories.

Third, philosophical or metaphysical theories.

How can we, in each of these groups, distinguish between true and false theories?

Regarding the first group the answer is obvious. Whenever we find a mathematical theory of which we do not know whether it is true or false we test it, first superficially and then more severely, by trying to refute it. If we are unsuccessful we then try to prove it or to refute its negation. If we fail again, doubts as to the truth of the theory may have cropped up again, and we shall again try to refute it, and so on, until we either reach a decision or else shelve the problem as too difficult for us.

The situation could also be described as follows. Our task is the testing, the critical examination, of two (or more) rival theories. We solve it by trying to refute them – either the one or the other – until we come to a decision. In mathematics (but only in mathematics) such decisions are generally *final*: invalid proofs that escape detection are rare.

If we now look at the empirical sciences, we find that we follow, as a rule, fundamentally the same procedure. Once again we test our theories: we examine them critically, we try to refute them. The only important difference is that now we can also make use of empirical arguments in our critical examinations. But these empirical arguments occur only together with other critical considerations. Critical thought as such remains our main instrument. Observations are used only if they fit into our critical discussion.

Now if we apply these considerations to philosophical theories, our problem can be reformulated as follows:

Is it possible to examine irrefutable philosophical theories *critically*? If so, what can a critical discussion of a theory consist of, if not of *attempts to refute the theory*?

In other words, is it possible to assess an irrefutable theory rationally – which is to say, critically? And what reasonable argument can we adduce for and against a theory which we know to be neither demonstrable nor refutable?

In order to illustrate these various formulations of our problem by examples, we may first refer again to the problem of determinism. Kant knew perfectly well that we are unable to predict the future actions of a human being as accurately as we can predict an eclipse. But he explained the difference by assuming that we know far less about the present conditions of a man – about his wishes and fears, his feelings and his motives – than about the present state of the solar system. Now this assumption contains, implicitly, the following hypothesis:

'*There exists* a true description of the present state of this man which would suffice (in conjunction with true natural laws) for the prediction of his future actions.'

This is of course again a purely existential statement, and it is thus irrefutable. Can we, in spite of this fact, discuss Kant's argument rationally and critically?

As a second example we may consider the thesis: 'The world is my dream.' Though this thesis is clearly irrefutable, few will believe in its truth. But can we discuss it rationally and critically? Is not its irrefutability an insurmountable obstacle to any critical discussion?

As to Kant's doctrine of determinism, it might perhaps be thought that the critical discussion of it might begin by saying to him: 'My dear Kant, it simply is not enough to assert that *there exists* a true description that is sufficiently detailed to enable us to predict the future. What you must do is tell us exactly what this description would consist of, so that we may test your theory empirically.' This speech, however, would be tantamount to the assumption that philosophical – that is, irrefutable – theories can never be discussed and that a responsible thinker *is bound* to replace them by empirically testable theories, in order to make a rational discussion possible.

I hope that our *problem* has by now become sufficiently clear; so I will now proceed to *propose a solution* of it.

My solution is this: if a philosophical theory were no more than an isolated assertion about the world, flung at us with an implied 'take it or leave it' and without a hint of any connection with anything else, then it would indeed be beyond discussion. But the same might be said of an empirical theory also. Should anybody present us with Newton's equations, or even with his arguments, without explaining to us first what the problems were which his theory was meant to solve, then we should not be able to discuss its truth rationally – no more than the truth of the *Book of Revelation*. Without any knowledge of the results of Galileo and Kepler, of the problems that were resolved by these results, and of Newton's problem of explaining Galileo's and Kepler's solutions by a unified theory, we should find Newton's theory just as much beyond discussion as any metaphysical theory. In other words every *rational* theory, no matter whether scientific or philosophical, is rational in so far as it tries to *solve certain problems*. A theory is comprehensible and reasonable only in its relation to a given *problem situation*. and it can be rationally discussed only by discussing this relation.

Now if we look upon a theory as a proposed solution to a set of problems, then the theory immediately lends itself to critical discussion – even if it is non-empirical and irrefutable. For we can now ask questions such as: Does it solve the problem? Does it solve it better than other theories? Has it perhaps merely shifted the problem? Is the solution simple? Is it fruitful? Does it perhaps contradict other philosophical theories needed for solving other problems?

Questions of this kind show that a critical discussion even of irrefutable theories may well be possible.

Once again let me refer to a specific example: the idealism of Berkeley or Hume (which I have replaced by the simplified formula 'The world is my dream'). It is notable that these authors were far from wishing to offer us so extravagant a theory. This may be seen from Berkeley's repeated insistence that his theories were really in agreement with sound common sense.[3] Now if we try to understand the *problem situation* which induced them to propound this theory, then we find that Berkeley and Hume believed that all our knowledge was reducible to *sense impressions* and to associations between *memory images*. This assumption led these two philosophers to adopt idealism; and in the case of Hume, in particular, very unwillingly. Hume was an idealist only because he failed in his attempt to reduce realism to *sense impressions*.

It is therefore perfectly *reasonable* to criticize Hume's idealism by pointing out that his sensualistic theory of knowledge and of learning was in any case inadequate, and that there are less inadequate theories of learning which have no unwanted idealistic consequences.

In a similar way we could now proceed to discuss Kant's determinism rationally and critically. Kant was in his fundamental intention an indeterminist: even though he believed in determinism with respect to the phenomenal world as an unavoidable consequence of Newton's theory, he never doubted that man, as a moral being, was not determined. Kant never succeeded in solving the resulting conflict between his theoretical and practical philosophy in a way that satisfied himself completely, and he despaired of ever finding a real solution.

In the setting of this *problem situation* it becomes possible to criticize Kant's determinism. We may ask, for example, whether it really follows from Newton's theory. Let us conjecture for a moment that it does not. [See selection 20, section III, below.] I do not doubt that a clear proof of the truth of this conjecture would have persuaded Kant to renounce his doctrine of determinism – even though this doctrine happens to be irrefutable and even though he would not, for this very reason, have been logically compelled to renounce it.

Similarly with irrationalism. It first entered rational philosophy with Hume – and those who have read Hume, that calm analyst, cannot doubt that this was not what he intended. Irrationalism was the unintended consequence of Hume's conviction that *we do in fact learn* by Baconian induction coupled with Hume's logical proof that *it is impossible to justify induction rationally*. 'So much the worse for rational justification' was a conclusion which Hume, of necessity, was compelled to draw from this situation. He accepted this irrational conclusion with the integrity characteristic of the real rationalist who does not shrink from an unpleasant conclusion if it seems to him unavoidable.

Yet in this case it was not unavoidable, though it seemed to Hume to be so. We are not in fact the Baconian induction machines that Hume believed us to be. Habit or custom does not play the role in the process of learning which Hume assigned to it. And so Hume's problem dissolves and with it his irrationalist conclusion.

The situation of post-Kantian irrationalism is somewhat similar. Schopenhauer in particular was genuinely opposed to irrationalism. He wrote with only *one* desire: to be understood; and he wrote more lucidly than any other German philosopher. His striving to be understood made him one of the few great masters of the German language.

Yet Schopenhauer's problems were those of Kant's metaphysics – the problem of determinism in the phenomenal world, the problem of the thing-in-itself, and the problem of our own membership of a world of things-in-themselves. He solved these problems – *problems transcending all possible experience* – in his typically rational manner. But the solution was *bound* to be irrational. For Schopenhauer was a Kantian and as such he believed in the Kantian limits of reason: he believed that the limits of human reason coincided with the *limits of possible experience*.

But here again there are other possible solutions. Kant's problems can and must be revised; and the direction that this revision should take is indicated by his fundamental idea of critical, or self-critical, rationalism. The discovery of a philosophical problem can be something final; it is made once, and for all time. But the solution of a philosophical problem is never final. It cannot be based upon a final proof or upon a final refutation: this is a consequence of the irrefutability of philosophical theories. Nor can the solution be based upon the magical formulae of inspired (or bored) philosophical prophets. Yet it may be based upon the conscientious and critical examination of a problem situation and its underlying assumptions, and of the various possible ways of resolving it.

17 Realism (1970)

Realism is essential to common sense. Common sense, or enlightened common sense, distinguishes between appearance and reality. (This may be illustrated by examples such as 'Today the air is so clear that the mountains appear much nearer than they really are.' Or perhaps, 'He appears to do it without effort, but he has confessed to me that the tension is almost unbearable.') But common sense also realizes that appearances (say, a reflection in a looking glass) have a sort of reality; in other words, that there can be a surface reality – that is, an appearance – and a depth reality. Moreover, there are many sorts of real things. The most obvious sort is that of foodstuffs (I conjecture that they produce the basis of the feeling of reality), or more resistant objects (*objectum* = what lies in the way of our action) like stones, and trees, and humans. But there are many sorts of reality which are quite different, such as our subjective decoding of our experiences of foodstuffs, stones, and trees, and human bodies. The taste and weight of foodstuffs and of stones involve another sort of reality, and so do the properties of trees and human bodies. Examples of other sorts of this many-sorted universe are: a toothache, a word, a language, a highway code, a novel, a governmental decision; a valid or invalid proof; perhaps forces, fields of forces, propensities, structures; and regularities. (My remarks here leave it entirely open whether, and how, these many sorts of objects can be related to each other.)

My thesis is that realism is neither demonstrable nor refutable. Realism like anything else outside logic and finite arithmetic is not demonstrable; but while empirical scientific theories are refutable [see selection 8 above], realism is not even refutable. (It shares this irrefutability with many philosophical or 'metaphysical' theories, in particular also with idealism [as pointed out in selection 16].)

But it is arguable, and the weight of the arguments is overwhelmingly in its favour.

Common sense is clearly on the side of realism; there are, of course, even before Descartes – in fact ever since Heraclitus – a few hints of doubt whether or not *our ordinary world is perhaps just our dream*. But even Descartes and Locke were realists. A philosophical theory competing with realism did not seriously start before Berkeley, Hume, and Kant.[1] Kant, incidentally, even provided a proof for realism. But it was not a valid proof; and I think it important that we should be clear why no valid proof of realism can exist.

In its simplest form, idealism says: the world (which includes the present reader) is just my dream. Now it is clear that this theory (though you will know that it is false) is not refutable: whatever you, the reader, may do to convince me of your reality – talking to me, or writing a letter, or perhaps kicking me – it cannot possibly assume the force of a refutation; for I would continue to say that I am dreaming that you are talking to me, or that I received a letter, or felt a kick. (One might say that these answers are all, in various ways, immunizing stratagems [of the kind described on pp.125f. above]. This is so, and it is a strong argument against idealism. But again, that it is a self-immunizing theory does not refute it.)

Thus idealism is irrefutable; and this means, of course, that realism is indemonstrable. But I am prepared to concede that realism is not only indemonstrable but, like idealism, irrefutable also; that no describable event, and no conceivable experience, can be taken as an effective refutation of realism.[2] Thus there will be in this issue, as in so many, no conclusive argument. *But there are arguments in favour of realism*; or, rather, *against idealism*.

(1) Perhaps the stongest argument consists of a combination of two: (*a*) that realism is part of common sense, and (*b*) that all the alleged *arguments* against it not only are philosophical in the most derogatory sense of this term, but are at the same time based upon an uncritically accepted part of common sense; that is to say, upon that mistaken part of the commonsense theory of knowledge which I have called the 'bucket theory of the mind' [see selection 7, section IV, above].

(2) Although science is a bit out of fashion today with some

people, for reasons which are, regrettably, far from negligible, we should not ignore its relevance to realism, despite the fact that there are scientists who are not realists, such as Ernst Mach or, in our own time, Eugene P. Wigner;[3] their arguments fall very clearly in the class just characterized in (1)(*b*). Let us here forget about Wigner's argument from atomic physics. We can then assert that almost all, if not all, physical, chemical, or biological theories imply realism, in the sense that if they are true, realism must also be true. This is one of the reasons why some people speak of 'scientific realism'. It is quite a good reason. Because of its (apparent) lack of testability, I myself happen to prefer to call realism 'metaphysical' rather than 'scientific'.[4]

However one may look at this, there are excellent reasons for saying that *what we attempt in science is to describe and* (*so far as possible*) *explain reality*. We do so with the help of conjectural theories; that is, theories which we hope are true (or near the truth), but which we cannot establish as certain or even as probable (in the sense of the probability calculus), even though they are the best theories which we are able to produce, and may therefore be called 'probable' as long as this term is kept free from any association with the calculus of probability.

There is a closely related and excellent sense in which we can speak of 'scientific realism': the procedure we adopt may lead (as long as it does not break down, for example because of anti-rational attitudes) to success, in the sense that our conjectural theories tend progressively to come nearer to the truth; that is, to true descriptions of certain facts, or aspects of reality.

(3) But even if we drop all arguments drawn from science, there remain the arguments from language. Any discussion of realism, and especially all arguments against it, have to be formulated in some language. But human language is essentially descriptive (and argumentative),[5] and an unambiguous description is always realistic: it is *of* something – of some state of affairs which may be real or imaginary. Thus if the state of affairs is imaginary, then the description is simply false and its negation is a true description of reality, in Tarski's sense. This does not logically refute idealism or solipsism; but it makes it at least irrelevant. Rationality, language, description, argument, are all about some reality, and they address themselves to an audience. All this presupposes

realism. Of course, this argument for realism is logically no more conclusive than any other, because I may merely dream that I am using descriptive language and arguments; but this argument for realism is nevertheless strong and *rational*. It is as strong as reason itself.

(4) To me, idealism appears absurd, for it also implies something like this: that it is my mind which creates this beautiful world. But I know I am not its creator. After all, the famous remark 'Beauty is in the eye of the beholder', though perhaps not an utterly stupid remark, means no more than that there is a problem of the *appreciation* of beauty. I know that the beauty of Rembrandt's self-portraits is not in my eye, nor that of Bach's Passions in my ear. On the contrary, I can establish to my satisfaction, by opening and closing my eyes and ears, that my eyes and ears are not good enough to take in all the beauty that is there. Moreover, there are people who are better judges – better able than I to appreciate the beauty of pictures and of music. Denying realism amounts to megalomania (the most widespread occupational disease of the professional philosopher).

(5) Out of many other weighty though inconclusive arguments I wish to mention only one. It is this. If realism is true – more especially, something approaching scientific realism – then the reason for the impossibility of proving it is obvious. The reason is that our subjective knowledge, even perceptual knowledge, consists of dispositions to act, and is thus a kind of tentative adaptation to reality; and that we are searchers, at best, and at any rate fallible. There is no guarantee against error. At the same time, the whole question of the truth and falsity of our opinions and theories clearly becomes pointless if there is no reality, only dreams or illusions.

To sum up, I propose to accept realism as the only sensible hypothesis – as a conjecture to which no sensible alternative has ever been offered. I do not wish to be dogmatic about this issue any more than about any other. But I think I know all the epistemological arguments – they are mainly subjectivist – which have been offered in favour of alternatives to realism, such as positivism, idealism, phenomenalism, phenomenology, and so on, and although I am not an enemy of the discussion of *isms* in philosophy, I regard all the philosophical *arguments* which (to my knowledge) have ever been offered in favour of my list of *isms* as clearly mistaken. Most of them are the result of the mistaken quest for certainty, or for secure foundations on which to build. And all of them are typical philosophers' mistakes in the worst sense of this term: they are all derivatives of a mistaken though commonsensical theory of knowledge which does not stand up to any serious criticism.

I will conclude what I have to say about realism with the opinion of the two men whom I regard as the greatest of our time: Albert Einstein and Winston Churchill.

'I do not see', writes Einstein, 'any "metaphysical danger" in our acceptance of things – that is, of the objects of physics . . . together with the spatiotemporal structures which pertain to them.'[6]

This was Einstein's opinion after a careful and sympathetic analysis of a brilliant attempt at refuting naïve realism due to Bertrand Russell.

Winston Churchill's views are very characteristic and, I think, a very fair comment on a philosophy which may since have changed its colours, crossing the floor of the house from idealism to realism, but which remains as pointless as ever it was: 'Some of my cousins who had the great advantage of University education', Churchill writes, 'used to tease me with arguments to prove that nothing has any existence except what we think of it. . .' He continues:[7]

> I always rested upon the following argument which I devised for myself many years ago. . . [Here] is this great sun standing apparently on no better foundation than our physical senses. But happily there is a method, apart altogether from our physical senses, of testing the reality of the sun. . . . astronomers . . . predict by [mathematics and] pure reason that a black spot will pass across the sun on a certain day. You . . . look, and your sense of sight immediately tells you that their calculations are vindicated. . . . *We have taken what is called in military map-making 'a cross bearing'*. We have got *independent testimony* to the reality of the sun. *When my metaphysical friends tell me that the data on which the astronomers made their calculations . . . were necessarily obtained originally through the evidence of their senses, I say 'No'. They might, in theory at any rate, be obtained by automatic calculating-machines set in motion by the light falling*

> *upon them without admixture of the human senses at any stage*. . . . I . . . reaffirm with emphasis . . . that the sun is real, and also that it is hot – in fact as hot as Hell, and that if the metaphysicians doubt it they should go there and see.

I may perhaps add that I regard Churchill's argument, especially the important passages which I have put in italics, not only as a valid criticism of the idealistic and subjectivistic arguments, but as the philosophically soundest and most ingenious argument against subjectivist epistemology that I know. I am not aware of any philosopher who has not ignored this argument (apart from some of my students whose attention I have drawn to it). The argument is highly original; first published in 1930 it is one of the earliest philosophical arguments making use of the possibility of automatic observatories and calculating machines (programmed by Newtonian theory). And yet, forty years after its publication, Winston Churchill is still quite unknown as an epistemologist: his name does not appear in any of the many anthologies on epistemology, and it is also missing even from the *Encyclopedia of Philosophy*.

Of course Churchill's argument is merely an excellent refutation of the specious arguments of the subjectivists: *he does not prove realism*. For the idealist can always argue that he is dreaming the debate, with calculating machines and all. Yet I regard this argument as silly, because of its universal applicability. At any rate, until some philosopher should produce some entirely new argument, I suggest that subjectivism and idealism may in future be ignored.

18 Cosmology and Change (1958)

I

In this paper I speak as an amateur, as a lover of the beautiful story of the Presocratics. I am not a specialist or an expert: I am completely out of my depth when an expert begins to argue which words or phrases Heraclitus might, and which he could not possibly, have used. Yet when some expert replaces a beautiful story, based on the oldest texts we possess, by one which – to me at any rate – no longer makes any sense, then I feel that even an amateur may stand up and defend an old tradition. Thus I will at least look into the expert's arguments, and examine their consistency. This seems a harmless occupation to indulge in; and if an expert or anybody else should take the trouble to refute my criticism I shall be pleased and honoured.[1]

I shall be concerned with the cosmological theories of the Presocratics, but only to the extent to which they bear upon the development of *the problem of change*, as I call it, and only to the extent to which they are needed for understanding the approach of the Presocratic philosophers to the problem of knowledge – their practical as well as their theoretical approach. For it is of considerable interest to see how their practice as well as their theory of knowledge is connected with the cosmological and theological questions which they posed to themselves. Theirs was not a theory of knowledge that began with the question, 'How do I know that this is an orange?' or, 'How do I know that the object I am now perceiving is an orange?' Their theory of knowledge started from problems such as, 'How do we know that the world is made of water?' or, 'How do we know that the world is full of gods?' or, 'How can we know anything about the gods?'

There is a widespread belief, somewhat remotely due, I think, to the influence of Francis Bacon, that one should study the problems of the theory of knowledge in connection with our knowledge of an orange rather than our knowledge of the cosmos. I dissent from this belief, and it is one of the main purposes of my paper to convey to you some of my reasons for dissenting. At any rate it is good to remember from time to time that our Western science – and there seems to be no other – did not start with collecting observations of oranges, but with bold theories about the world.

II

Traditional empiricist epistemology and the traditional historiography of science are both deeply influenced by the Baconian myth that all science starts from observation and then slowly and cautiously proceeds to theories. That the facts are very different can be learnt from studying the early Presocratics. Here we find bold and fascinating ideas, some of which are strange and even staggering anticipations of modern results, while many others are wide of the mark, from our modern point of view; but most of them, and the best of them, have nothing to do with observation. Take for example some of the theories about the shape and position of the earth. Thales said, we are told, 'that the earth is supported by water on which it rides like a ship, and when we say that there is an earthquake, then the earth is being shaken by the movement of the water'. No doubt Thales had observed earthquakes as well as the rolling of a ship before he arrived at his theory. But the point of his theory was to *explain* the support or suspension of the earth, and also earthquakes, by the conjecture that the earth floats on water; and for this conjecture (which so strangely anticipates the modern theory of continental drift) he could have had no basis in his observations.

We must not forget that the function of the Baconian myth is to explain why scientific statements are *true*, by pointing out that observation is the '*true source*' of our scientific knowledge. Once we realize that all scientific statements are hypotheses, or guesses, or conjectures, and that the vast majority of these conjectures (including Bacon's own) have turned out to be false, the Baconian myth becomes irrelevant. For it is pointless to argue that the conjectures of science – those which have proved to be false as well as those which are still accepted – all start from observation.

However this may be, Thales's beautiful theory of the support or suspension of the earth and of earthquakes, though in no sense based upon observation, is at least inspired by an empirical or observational analogy. But even this is no longer true of the theory proposed by Thales's great pupil, Anaximander. Anaximander's theory of the suspension of the earth is still highly intuitive, but it no longer uses observational analogies. In fact it may be described as counterobservational. According to Anaximander's theory, 'The earth ... is held up by nothing, but remains stationary owing to the fact that it is equally distant from all other things. Its shape is ... like that of a drum. ... We walk on one of its flat surfaces, while the other is on the opposite side.' The drum, of course, is an observational analogy. But the idea of the earth's free suspension in space, and the explanation of its stability, have no analogy whatever in the whole field of observable facts.

In my opinion this idea of Anaximander's is one of the boldest, most revolutionary, and most portentous ideas in the whole history of human thought. It made possible the theories of Aristarchus and Copernicus. But the step taken by Anaximander was even more difficult and audacious than the one taken by Aristarchus and Copernicus. To envisage the earth as freely poised in midspace, and to say 'that it remains motionless because of its equidistance or equilibrium' (as Aristotle paraphrases Anaximander), is to anticipate to some extent even Newton's idea of immaterial and invisible gravitational forces.[2]

III

How did Anaximander arrive at this remarkable theory? Certainly not by observation but by reasoning. His theory is an attempt to solve one of the problems to which his teacher and kinsman Thales, the founder of the Milesian or Ionian School, had offered a solution before him. I therefore conjecture that Anaximander arrived at his theory by criticizing Thales's theory. This conjecture can be supported, I believe, by a consideration of the structure of Anaximander's theory.

Anaximander is likely to have argued against Thales's theory (according to which the earth was floating on water) on the following lines. Thales's theory is a specimen of a type of theory which if consistently developed would lead to an infinite regress. If we explain the stable position of the earth by the assumption that it is supported by water – that it is floating on the ocean (*okeanos*) – should we not have to explain the stable position of the ocean by an analogous hypothesis? But this would mean looking for a support for the ocean, and then for a support for this support. This method of explanation is unsatisfactory: first, because we solve our problem by creating an exactly analogous one; and also for the less formal and more intuitive reason that in any such system of supports or props failure to secure any one of the lower props must lead to the collapse of the whole edifice.

From this we see intuitively that the stability of the world cannot be secured by a system of supports or props. Instead Anaximander appeals to the internal or structural symmetry of the world, which ensures that there is no preferred direction in which a collapse can take place. He applies the principle that where there are no differences there can be no change. In this way he explains the stability of the earth by the equality of its distances from all other things.

This, it seems, was Anaximander's argument. It is important to realize that it abolishes, even though not quite consciously perhaps, and not quite consistently, the idea of an absolute direction – the absolute sense of 'upwards' and 'downwards'. This is not only contrary to all experience but notoriously difficult to grasp. Anaximenes ignored it, it seems, and even Anaximander himself did not grasp it completely. For the idea of an equal distance from all other things should have led him to the theory that the earth has the shape of a globe. Instead he believed that it had the shape of a drum, with an upper and a lower flat surface. Yet it looks as if the remark, 'We walk on one of its flat surfaces, while the other is on the opposite side', contained a hint that there was no absolute upper surface, but that on the contrary the surface on which we happened to walk was the one we might *call* the upper.

What prevented Anaximander from arriving at the theory that the earth was a globe rather than a drum? There can be little doubt:

it was *observational experience* which taught him that the surface of the earth was, by and large, flat. Thus it was a speculative and critical argument, the abstract critical discussion of Thales's theory, which almost led him to the true theory of the shape of the earth; and it was observational experience which led him astray.

IV

There is an obvious objection to Anaximander's theory of symmetry, according to which the earth is equally distant from all other things. The asymmetry of the universe can be easily seen from the existence of sun and moon, and especially from the fact that sun and moon are sometimes not far distant from each other, so that they are on the same side of the earth, while there is nothing on the other side to balance them. It appears that Anaximander met this objection by another bold theory – his theory of the hidden nature of the sun, the moon, and the other heavenly bodies.

He envisages the rims of two huge chariot wheels rotating round the earth, one twenty seven times the size of the earth, the other eighteen times its size. Each of these rims or circular pipes is filled with fire, and each has a breathing hole through which the fire is visible. These holes we call the sun and the moon respectively. The rest of the wheel is invisible, presumably because it is dark (or misty) and far away. The fixed stars (and presumably the planets) are also holes on wheels which are nearer to the earth than the wheels of the sun and the moon. The wheels of the fixed stars rotate on a common axis (which we now call the axis of the earth) and together they form a sphere round the earth, so the postulate of equal distance from the earth is (roughly) satisfied. This makes Anaximander also a founder of the *theory of the spheres*.[3]

V

There can be no doubt whatever that Anaximander's theories are critical and speculative rather than empirical: and considered as approaches to truth his critical and abstract speculations served him better than observational experience or analogy.

But, a follower of Bacon may reply, this is precisely why Anaximander was not a scientist. This is precisely why we speak of early Greek *philosophy* rather than of early Greek *science*. Philosophy is speculative: everybody knows this. And as everybody knows, science begins only when the speculative method is replaced by the observational method, and when deduction is replaced by induction.

Yet there is the most perfect possible continuity of thought between the theories of the Presocratics and the later developments in physics. Whether they are called philosophers, or pre-scientists, or scientists, matters very little, I think. But I do assert that Anaximander's theory cleared the way for the theories of Aristarchus, Copernicus, Kepler, and Galileo. It is not that he merely 'influenced' these later thinkers; 'influence' is a very superficial category [see also p.61 above]. I would rather put it like this: Anaximander's achievement is valuable in itself, like a work of art. Besides, his achievement made other achievements possible, among them those of the great scientists mentioned.

But are not Anaximander's theories false, and therefore non-scientific? They are false, I admit; but so are many theories, based upon countless experiments, which modern science accepted until recently, and whose scientific character nobody would dream of denying, even though they are now believed to be false. (An example is the theory that the typical chemical properties of hydrogen belong only to one kind of atom – the lightest of all atoms.) There were historians of science who tended to regard as unscientific (or even as superstitious) any view no longer accepted at the time they were writing; but this is an untenable attitude. A false theory may be as great an achievement as a true one. And many false theories have been more helpful in our search for truth than some less interesting theories which are still accepted. For false theories can be helpful in many ways; they may for example suggest some more or less radical modifications, and they may stimulate criticism. Thus Thales's theory that the earth floats on water re-appeared in a modified form in Anaximenes, and in more recent times in the form of Wegener's theory of continental drift. How Thales's theory stimulated Anaximander's criticism has been shown already.

Anaximander's theory, similarly, suggested a modified theory – the theory of an earth globe, freely poised in the centre of the universe, and surrounded by spheres on which heavenly bodies were mounted. And by stimulating criticism it also led to the theory that the moon shines by reflecting light; to the Pythagorean theory of a central fire; and ultimately to the heliocentric world system of Aristarchus and Copernicus.

VI

I believe that the Milesians, like their oriental predecessors who took the world for a tent, envisaged the world as a kind of house, the home of all creatures – our home. Thus there was no need to ask what it was for. But there was a real need to inquire into its architecture. The questions of its structure, its groundplan, and its building material, constitute the three main problems of Milesian cosmology. There is also a speculative interest in its origin, the question of cosmogony. It seems to me that the cosmological interest of the Milesians far exceeded their cosmogonical interest, especially if we consider the strong cosmogonical tradition, and the almost irresistible tendency to describe a thing by describing how it has been made, and thus to present a cosmological account in a cosmogonical form. The cosmological interest must be very strong, as compared with the cosmogonical one, if the presentation of a cosmological theory is even partially free from these cosmogonical trappings.

I believe that it was Thales who first discussed the architecture of the cosmos – its structure, groundplan, and building material. In Anaximander we find answers to all three questions. I have briefly mentioned his answer to the question of structure. As to the question of the groundplan of the world, he studied and expounded this too, as indicated by the tradition that he drew the first map of the world. And of course he had a theory about its building material – the 'endless' or 'boundless' or 'unbounded' or 'unformed' – the '*apeiron*'.

In Anaximander's world all kinds of *changes* were going on. There was a fire which needed air and breathing holes, and these were at times blocked up ('obstructed'), so that the fire was smothered:[4] this was his theory of eclipses, and of the phases of the moon. There were winds, which were responsible for the changing weather. And there were the vapours, resulting from the drying up of water and air, which were the cause of the winds and of the 'turnings' of the sun (the solstices) and of the moon.

We have here the first hint of what was soon to come: of the *general problem of change*, which became the central problem of Greek cosmology, and which ultimately led, with Leucippus and Democritus, to a *general theory of change* that was accepted by modern science almost up to the beginning of the twentieth century. (It was given up only with the breakdown of Maxwell's models of the ether, an historic event that was little noticed before 1905.)

This *general problem of change* is a philosophical problem; indeed in the hands of Parmenides and Zeno it almost turns into a logical one. *How is change possible* – logically possible, that is? How can a thing change, without losing its identity? If it remains the same, it does not change; yet if it loses its identity, then it is no longer that thing which has changed.

VII

The exciting story of the development of the problem of change appears to me in danger of being completely buried under the mounting heap of the minutiae of textual criticism. The story cannot, of course, be fully told in one short paper, and still less in one of its many sections. But in briefest outline, it is this.

For Anaximander, our own world, our own cosmic edifice, was only one of an infinity of worlds – an infinity without bounds in space and time. This system of worlds was eternal, and so was motion. There was thus no need to explain motion, no need to offer a *general* theory of change (in the sense in which we shall find a general problem and a general theory of change in Heraclitus; see below). But there was a need to explain the well-known changes occurring in our world. The most obvious changes – the changes of day and night, of winds and of weather, of the seasons, from sowing to harvesting, and of the growth of plants and animals and men – all were connected with the contrast of temperatures, with the opposition between the hot and the cold, and with that between the dry and the wet. 'Living creatures came into being from moisture evaporated by the sun', we are told; and the hot and the cold also administer to the genesis of our own world edifice. The hot and the cold were also responsible for the vapours and winds which in their turn were conceived as the agents of almost all other changes.

Anaximenes, a pupil of Anaximander and his successor, developed these ideas in much detail. Like Anaximander he was interested in the oppositions of the hot and the cold and of the moist and the dry, and he explained the transitions between these opposites by a theory of condensation and rarefaction. Like Anaximander he believed in eternal motion and in the action of the winds; and it seems not unlikely that one of the two main points in which he deviated from Anaximander was reached by a criticism of the idea that what was completely boundless and formless (the *apeiron*) could yet be in motion. At any rate, he replaced the *apeiron* by air – something that was almost boundless and formless, and yet, according to Anaximander's old theory of vapours, not only capable of motion, but the main agent of motion and change. A similar unification of ideas was achieved by Anaximenes's theory that 'the sun consists of earth, and that it gets very hot owing to the rapidity of its motion'. The replacement of the more abstract theory of the unbounded *apeiron* by the less abstract and more commonsense theory of air is matched by the replacement of Anaximander's bold theory of the stability of the earth by the more commonsense idea that the earth's 'flatness is responsible for its stability; for it. . . . covers like a lid the air beneath it'. Thus the earth rides on air as the lid of a pot may ride on steam, or as a ship may ride on water; Thales's question and Thales's answer are both re-instituted, and Anaximander's epochmaking argument is not understood. Anaximenes is an eclectic, a systematizer, an empiricist, a man of common sense. Of the three great Milesians he is least productive of revolutionary new ideas; he is the least philosophically minded.

The three Milesians all looked on our world as our home. There was movement, there was change in this home, there were hot and cold, fire and moisture. There was a fire in the hearth, and on it a kettle with water. The house was exposed to the winds, and a bit draughty, to be sure; but it was home, and it meant security and stability of a sort. But for Heraclitus the house was on fire.

There was no stability left in the world of Heraclitus. 'Everthing is in flux, and nothing is at rest.' *Everything* is in flux, even the beams, the timber, the building material of which the world is made: earth and rocks, or the bronze of a cauldron – they are all in flux. The beams are rotting, the earth is washed away and blown away, the very rocks split and wither, the bronze cauldron turns into green patina, or into verdigris: 'All things are in motion all the time, even though ... this escapes our senses', as Aristotle expressed it. Those who do not know and do not think believe that only the fuel is burned, while the bowl in which it burns remains unchanged;[5] for we do not see the bowl burning. And yet it burns; it is eaten up by the fire it holds. We do not *see* our children grow up, and change, and grow old, but they do.

Thus there are no solid bodies. Things are not really things, they are processes, they are in flux. They are like fire, like a flame which, though it may have a definite shape, is a process, a stream of matter, a river. All things are flames: fire is the very building material of our world; and the apparent stability of things is merely due to the laws, the measures, which the processes in our world are subject to.

This, I believe, is Heraclitus's story; it is his 'message', the 'true word' (the *logos*), to which we ought to listen: 'Listening not to me but to the true account, it is wise to admit that all things are one': they are 'an everlasting fire, flaring up in measures, and dying down in measures'.

I know very well that the traditional interpretation of Heraclitus's philosophy here restated is not generally accepted at present. But the critics have put nothing in its place – nothing, that is, of philosophical interest.[6] Here I wish only to stress that Heraclitus's philosophy, by appealing to thought, to the word, to argument, to reason, and by pointing out that we are living in a world of things whose changes escape our senses, though we *know* that they do change, created two new problems – *the problem of change* and *the problem of knowledge*. These problems were the more urgent as his own account of change was difficult to understand. But this, I believe, is due to the fact that he saw more clearly than his predecessors the difficulties that were involved in the very idea of change.

For all change is the change of something: change presupposes something that changes. And it presupposes that, while changing, this something must remain the same. We may say that a green leaf changes when it turns brown; but we do not say that the green leaf changes when we substitute for it a brown leaf. It is essential to the idea of change that the thing which changes retains its identity while changing. And yet it must become something else: it was green, and it becomes brown; it was moist, and it becomes dry; it was hot, and it becomes cold.

Thus every change is the transition of a thing into something with, in a way, opposite qualities (as Anaximander and Anaximenes had seen). And yet, while changing, the changing thing must remain identical with itself.

This is the problem of change. It led Heraclitus to a theory which (partly anticipating Parmenides) distinguishes between reality and appearance. 'The real nature of things loves to hide itself. An unapparent harmony is stronger than the apparent one.' Things are *in appearance* (and for us) opposites, but in truth (and for God) they are the same.[7]

> Life and death, being awake and being asleep, youth and old age, all these are the same ... for the one turned round is the other and the other turned round is the first. ... The path that leads up and the path that leads down are the same path. ... Good and bad are identical. ... For God all things are beautiful and good and just, but men assume some things to be unjust, and others to be just. ... It is not in the nature or character of man to possess true knowledge, though it is in the divine nature.

Thus in truth (and for God) the opposites are identical; it is only to man that they appear as non-identical. And all things are one – they are all part of the process of the world, the everlasting fire.

This theory of change appeals to the 'true word', to the *logos*, to reason; nothing is more real for Heraclitus than change. Yet his doctrine of the oneness of the world, of the identity of opposites, and of appearance and reality threatens his doctrine of the reality of change.

For change is the transition from one opposite to the other. Thus if in truth the opposites are identical, though they appear different, then change itself might be only apparent. If in truth, and for God, all things are one, there might, in truth, be no change.

This consequence was drawn by Parmenides, the pupil (*pace* Burnet and others) of the monotheist Xenophanes, who said of the one God: 'He always remains in the same place, never moving. It is not fitting that He should go to different places at different times. . . . He is in no way similar to mortal men, neither in body nor in thought.'[8]

Xenophanes's pupil Parmenides taught that the real world was one, and that it always remained in the same place, never moving. It was not *fitting* that it should go to different places at different times. It was in no way similar to what it appeared to be to mortal men. The world was one, an undivided whole, without parts, homogeneous and motionless: motion was impossible in such a world. In truth there was no change. The world of change was an illusion.

Parmenides based this theory of an unchanging reality on something like a logical proof; a proof which can be presented as proceeding from the single premiss, 'What is not is not'. From this we can derive that the nothing – that which is not – does not exist; a result which Parmenides interprets to mean that the void does not exist. Thus the world is full: it consists of one undivided block, since any division into parts could only be due to separation of the parts by the void. (This is 'the well-rounded truth' which the goddess revealed to Parmenides.) In this full world there is no room for motion.

Only the delusive belief in the reality of opposites – the belief that not only *what is* exists but also *what is not* – leads to the illusion of a world of change.

Parmenides's theory may be described as the first hypothetico-deductive theory of the world. The atomists took it as such; and they asserted that it was refuted by experience, since motion does exist. Accepting the formal validity of Parmenides's argument, they inferred from the falsity of his conclusion the falsity of his premiss. But this meant that the nothing – the void, or empty space – existed. Consequently there was now no need to assume that 'what is' – the full, that which fills some space – had no parts; for its parts could now be separated by the void. Thus there are many parts, each of which is 'full': there are full particles in the world, separated by empty space, and able to move in empty space, each of them being 'full', undivided, indivisible, and unchanging. Thus what exist are *atoms and the void*. In this way the atomists arrived at a *theory of change* – a theory that dominated scientific thought until 1900. It is the theory that *all change, and especially all qualitative change, has to be explained by the spatial movement of unchanging bits of matter – by atoms moving in the void.*

The next great step in our cosmology and the theory of change was made when Maxwell, developing certain ideas of Faraday's, replaced this theory by a theory of changing intensities of fields.

19 Natural Selection and Its Scientific Status (1977)

I Darwin's Natural Selection versus Paley's Natural Theology

The first edition of Darwin's *Origin of Species* was published in 1859. In a reply to a letter from John Lubbock, thanking Darwin for an advance copy of his book, Darwin made a remarkable comment about William Paley's book *Natural Theology*, which had been published half a century before. Darwin wrote: 'I do not think I hardly ever admired a book more than Paley's "Natural Theology". I could almost formerly have said it by heart.' Years later in his autobiography Darwin wrote of Paley that 'The careful study of [his] works . . . was the only part of the academical course [in Cambridge] which . . . was of the least use to me in the education of my mind.'[1]

I have started with these quotations because the problem posed by Paley became one of Darwin's most important problems. It was *the problem of design*.

The famous *argument from design* for the existence of God was at the centre of Paley's theism. If you find a watch, Paley argued, you will hardly doubt that it was designed by a watchmaker. So if you consider a higher organism, with its intricate and purposeful organs such as the eyes, then, Paley argued, you are bound to conclude that it must have been designed by an intelligent creator. This is Paley's argument from design. Prior to Darwin, the theory of special creation – the theory that each species was designed by the Creator – had been widely accepted, not only in the University of Cambridge, but also elsewhere, by many of the best scientists. There were of course alternative theories in existence, such as Lamarck's; and Hume had earlier attacked, somewhat feebly, the argument from design; but Paley's theory was in those days the one most seriously entertained by serious scientists.

It is almost unbelievable how much the atmosphere changed as a consequence of the publication, in 1859, of the *Origin of Species*. The place of an argument that really had no status whatever in science has been taken by an immense number of the most impressive and well-tested scientific results. Our whole outlook, our picture of the universe, has changed, as never before.

Although Darwin destroyed Paley's argument from design by showing that what appeared to Paley as purposeful design could as well be explained as the result of chance and of natural selection, he was most modest and undogmatic in his claims. He had a correspondence about divine design with Asa Gray of Harvard, and wrote to Gray, one year after the *Origin of Species*: '. . . .about Design. I am conscious that I am in an utterly hopeless muddle. I cannot think that the world, as we see it, is the result of chance; and yet I cannot look at each separate thing as the result of Design.' And a year later Darwin wrote to Gray: 'With respect to Design, I feel more inclined to show a white flag than to fire. . . . [a] shot. . . . You say that you are in a haze; I am in thick mud; . . . yet I cannot keep out of the question.'[2]

To me it seems that the question may not be within the reach of science. And yet I do think that science has taught us a lot about the evolving universe that bears in an interesting way on Paley's and Darwin's problem of creative design.

I think that science suggests to us (tentatively of course) a picture of a universe that is inventive[3] or even creative; of a universe in which *new things* emerge, on *new levels*.

There is, on the first level, the theory of the emergence of heavy atomic nuclei in the centre of big stars, and, on a higher level, the evidence for the emergence somewhere in space of organic molecules.

On the next level, there is the emergence of life. Even if the origin of life should one day become reproducible in the laboratory, life creates something that is utterly new in the universe: the peculiar activity of organisms; especially the often purposeful actions of animals; and animal problem solving. All organisms are constant problem solvers; even though they are not conscious of most of the problems they are trying to solve.

On the next level, the great step is the emergence of conscious states. With the distinction between conscious states and unconscious states, again something utterly new and of the greatest importance enters the universe. It is a new world: the world of conscious experience.

On the next level, this is followed by the emergence of the products of the human mind, such as the works of art; and also the works of science; especially scientific theories.

I think that scientists, however sceptical, are bound to admit that the universe, or nature, or whatever we may call it, is creative. For it has produced creative men: it has produced Shakespeare and Michelangelo and Mozart, and thus indirectly their works. It has produced Darwin, and so created the theory of natural selection. Natural selection has destroyed the proof for the miraculous specific intervention of the Creator. But it has left us with the marvel of the creativeness of the universe, of life, and of the human mind. Although science has nothing to say about a personal creator, the fact of the emergence of novelty, and of creativity, can hardly be denied. I think that Darwin himself, who could not 'keep out of the question', would have agreed that, though natural selection was an idea which opened up a new world for science, it did not remove, from the picture of the universe that science paints, the marvel of creativity; nor did it remove the marvel of freedom: the freedom to create; and the freedom of choosing our own ends and our own purposes.

II Natural Selection and Its Scientific Status

When speaking here of Darwinism, I shall speak always of today's theory – that is Darwin's own theory of natural selection supported by the Mendelian theory of heredity, by the theory of the mutation and recombination of genes in a gene pool, and by the decoded genetic code. This is an immensely impressive and powerful theory. The claim that it completely explains evolution is of course a bold claim, and very far from being established. All scientific theories are conjectures, even those that have successfully passed many severe and varied tests. The Mendelian underpinning of modern Darwinism has been well tested, and so has the theory of evolution which says that all terrestrial life has evolved from a few primitive unicellular organisms, possibly even from one single organism.

However, Darwin's own most important contribution to the theory of evolution, his theory of natural selection, is difficult to test. There are some tests, even some experimental tests; and in some cases, such as the famous phenomenon known as 'industrial melanism', we can observe natural selection happening under our very eyes, as it were. Nevertheless, really severe tests of the theory of natural selection are hard to come by, much more so than tests of otherwise comparable theories in physics or chemistry.

The fact that the theory of natural selection is difficult to test has led some people, anti-Darwinists and even some great Darwinists, to claim that it is a tautology. A tautology like 'All tables are tables' is not, of course, testable; nor has it any explanatory power. It is therefore most surprising to hear that some of the greatest contemporary Darwinists themselves formulate the theory in such a way that it amounts to the tautology that those organisms that leave most offspring leave most offspring. C.H. Waddington says somewhere (and he defends this view in other places) that 'Natural selection ... turns out ... to be a tautology'.[4] However, he attributes at the same place to the theory an 'enormous power. ... of explanation'. Since the explanatory power of a tautology is obviously zero, something must be wrong here.

Yet similar passages can be found in the works of such great Darwinists as Ronald Fisher, J.B.S. Haldane, and George Gaylord Simpson; and others.

I mention this problem because I too belong among the culprits. Influenced by what these authorities say, I have in the past described the theory as 'almost tautological', and I have tried to explain how the theory of natural selection could be untestable (as is a tautology) and yet of great scientific interest. My solution was that the doctrine of natural selection is a most successful metaphysical research programme. It raises detailed problems in many fields, and it tells us what we would expect of an acceptable solution of these problems.[5]

I still believe that natural selection works in this way as a research programme. Nevertheless, I have changed my mind about the testability and the logical status of the theory of natural selection; and I am glad to have an opportunity to make a recantation. My recantation may, I hope, contribute a little to the understanding of the status of natural selection.

What is important is to realize the explanatory task of natural selection; and especially to realize *what* can be explained *without* the theory of natural selection.

We may start from the remark that, for sufficiently small and reproductively isolated populations, the Mendelian theory of genes and the theory of mutation and recombination together suffice to predict, *without natural selection*, what has been called 'genetic drift'. If you isolate a small number of individuals from the main population and prevent them from interbreeding with the main population, then, after a time, the distribution of genes in the gene pool of the new population will differ somewhat from that of the original population. This will happen even if selection pressures are completely absent.

Moritz Wagner, a contemporary of Darwin, and of course a pre-Mendelian, was aware of this situation. He therefore introduced a theory of *evolution by genetic drift*, made possible by reproductive isolation through geographical separation.

In order to understand the task of natural selection, it is good to remember Darwin's reply to Wagner.[6] Darwin's main reply to Wagner was: if you have no natural selection, you cannot explain the evolution of the apparently designed organs, like the eye. Or in other words, without natural selection, you cannot solve Paley's problem.

In its most daring and sweeping form, the theory of natural selection would assert that *all* organisms, and especially *all* those highly complex organs whose existence might be interpreted as evidence of design and, in addition, *all* forms of animal behaviour, have evolved as the result of natural selection; that is, as the result of chancelike inheritable variations, of which the useless ones are weeded out, so that only the useful ones remain. If formulated in this sweeping way, the theory is not only refutable, but actually refuted. For *not all* organs serve a *useful* purpose: as Darwin himself points out, there are organs like the tail of the peacock, and behavioural programmes like the peacock's display of his tail, which cannot be explained by their *utility*, and therefore not by natural selection. Darwin explained them by the preference of the other sex, that is, by sexual selection. Of course one can get round this refutation by some verbal manoeuvre: one can get round any refutation of any theory. But then one does get near to rendering the theory tautological. It seems far preferable to admit that *not* everything that evolves is *useful*, though it is astonishing how many things are; and that in conjecturing what is the *use* of an organ or a behavioural programme, we conjecture a possible explanation by natural selection: of *why* it evolved in the way it has, and perhaps even of *how* it evolved. In other words, it seems to me that like so many theories in biology, evolution by natural selection is not strictly universal, though it seems to hold for a vast number of important cases.

According to Darwin's theory, sufficiently invariant selection pressures may turn the otherwise random genetic drift into a drift that has the appearance of being purposefully directed. In this way, the selection pressures, if there are any, will leave their imprint upon the genetic material. (It may be mentioned, however, that there are selection pressures that can operate successfully over very short periods: one severe epidemic may leave alive only those who are genetically immune.)

I may now briefly sum up what I have said so far about Darwin's theory of natural selection.

The theory of natural selection may be so formulated that it is far from tautological. In this case it is not only testable, but it turns out to be not strictly universally true. There seem to be exceptions, as with so many biological theories; and considering the random character of the variations on which natural selection operates, the occurrence of exceptions is not surprising. Thus not all phenomena of evolution are explained by natural selection alone. Yet in every particular case it is a challenging research programme to show how far natural selection can possibly be held responsible for the evolution of a particular organ or behavioural programme.

It is of considerable interest that the idea of natural selection can be generalized. In this connection it is helpful to discuss the relation between selection and instruction. While Darwin's theory is selectionist, the theistic theory of Paley is instructionist. It is the Creator who, by His design, moulds matter, and instructs it which shape to take. Thus Darwin's selectionist theory can be regarded as a theory that explains by selection something that looks like instruction. Certain invariant features of the environment leave their imprint on the genetic material as if they had moulded it; while in fact, they selected it.

Many years ago I visited Bertrand Russell in his rooms at Trinity College and he showed me a manuscript of his in which there was not a single correction for many pages. With the help of his pen, he had instructed the paper. This is very different indeed from what I do. My own manuscripts are full of corrections – so full that it is easy to see that I am working by something like trial and error; by more or less random fluctuations from which I select what appears to me fitting. We may pose the question whether Russell did not do something similar, though only in his mind, and perhaps not even consciously, and at any rate very rapidly. For indeed, what seems to be instruction is frequently based upon a roundabout mechanism of selection, as illustrated by Darwin's answer to the problem posed by Paley.

I suggest that we might try out the conjecture that something like this happens in many cases. We may indeed conjecture that Bertrand Russell produced almost as many trial formulations as I do, but that his mind worked more quickly than mine in trying them out and rejecting the non-fitting verbal candidates. Einstein somewhere says that he produced and rejected an immense number of hypotheses before hitting on (and first rejecting) the equations of general relativity. Clearly, the method of production and selection is one that operates with negative feedback. [See also pp.83-6 above.]

One of the important points about this roundabout method of selection is that it throws light on the problem of downward causation to which Donald Campbell and Roger Sperry have called attention.[7]

We may speak of downward causation whenever a higher structure operates causally upon its substructure. The difficulty of understanding downward causation is this. We think we can understand how the substructures of a system co-operate to affect the whole system; that is to say, we think that we understand upward causation. But the opposite is very difficult to envisage. For the set of substructures, it seems, interacts causally in any case, and there is no room, no opening, for an action from above to interfere. It is this that leads to the heuristic demand that we explain everything in terms of molecular or other elementary particles (a demand that is sometimes called 'reductionism').

I suggest that downward causation can sometimes at least be explained as *selection* operating on the randomly fluctuating elementary particles. The randomness of the movements of the elementary particles – often called 'molecular chaos' – provides, as it were, the opening for the higher-level structure to interfere. A random movement is accepted when it fits into the higher level structure; otherwise it is rejected.

I think that these considerations tell us a lot about natural selection. While Darwin still worried that he could not explain variation, and while he felt uneasy about being forced to look at it as chancelike, we can now see that the chancelike character of mutations, which may go back to quantum indeterminacy, explains how the abstract invariances of the environment, the somewhat abstract selection pressures, can, by selection, have a downward effect on the concrete living organism – an effect that may be amplified by a long sequence of generations linked by heredity.

The selection of a kind of behaviour out of a randomly offered repertoire may be an act of choice, even an act of free will. I am an indeterminist; and in discussing indeterminism I have often regretfully pointed out [for example, in selection 20, section VII, below] that quantum indeterminacy does not seem to help us; for the amplification of something like, say, radioactive disintegration processes would not lead to human action or even animal action, but only to random movements. I have changed my mind on this issue.[8] A choice process may be a selection process, and the *selection* may be *from* some repertoire of random events, *without being random in its turn*. This seems to me to offer a promising solution to one of our most vexing problems, and one by downward causation.

20 Indeterminism and Human Freedom (1965)

1 Of Clouds and Clocks

The central purpose of my lecture is to try to put simply and forcefully before you the ancient problems referred to in my title. But first I must say something about *clouds* and *clocks*.

My clouds are intended to represent physical systems which, like gases, are highly irregular, disorderly, and more or less unpredictable. I shall assume that we have before us a schema or arrangement in which a very disturbed or disorderly cloud is placed on the left. At the other extreme of our arrangement, on its right, we may place a very reliable pendulum clock, a precision clock, intended to represent physical systems which are regular, orderly, and highly predictable in their behaviour.

According to what I may call the commonsense view of things, some natural phenomena, such as the weather, or the coming and going of clouds, are hard to predict: we speak of the 'vagaries of the weather'. On the other hand, we speak of 'clockwork precision' if we wish to describe a highly regular and predictable phenomenon.

There are lots of things, natural processes and natural phenomena, which we may place between these two extremes – the clouds on the left, and the clocks on the right. The changing seasons are somewhat unreliable clocks, and may therefore be put somewhere towards the right, though not too far. I suppose we shall easily agree to put animals not too far from the clouds on the left, and plants somewhat nearer to the clocks. Among the animals, a young puppy will have to be placed further to the left than an old dog. Motor cars, too, will find their place somewhere in our arrangement, according to their reliability: a Cadillac, I suppose, is pretty far over to the right, and even more so a Rolls-Royce, which will be quite close to the best of the clocks. Perhaps furthest to the right should be placed the *solar system.*[1]

As a typical and interesting example of a cloud I shall make some use here of a cloud or cluster of small flies or gnats. Like the individual molecules in a gas, the individual gnats which together form a cluster of gnats move in an astonishingly irregular way. It is almost impossible to follow the flight of any one individual gnat, even though each of them may be quite big enough to be clearly visible.

Apart from the fact that the velocities of the gnats do not show a very wide spread, the gnats present us with an excellent picture of the irregular movement of molecules in a gas cloud, or of the minute drops of water in a storm cloud. There are, of course, differences. The cluster does not dissolve or diffuse, but it keeps together fairly well. This is surprising, considering the disorderly character of the movement of the various gnats; but it has its analogue in a sufficiently big gas cloud (such as our atmosphere, or the sun) which is kept together by gravitational forces. In the case of the gnats, their keeping together can be easily explained if we assume that, although they fly quite irregularly in all directions, those that find that they are getting away from the crowd turn back towards that part which is densest.

This assumption explains how the cluster keeps together even though it has no leader, and no structure – only a random statistical distribution resulting from the fact that each gnat does exactly what he likes, in a lawless or random manner, together with the fact that he does not like to stray too far from his comrades.

I think that a philosophical gnat might claim that the gnat society is a great society or at least a good society, since it is the most egalitarian, free, and democratic society imaginable.

However, as the author of a book on *The Open Society*, I would deny that the gnat society is an open society. For I take it to be one of the characteristics of an open society that it cherishes, apart from a democratic form of government, the freedom of association, and that it protects and even encourages the formation of free subsocieties, each holding different opinions and beliefs. But every reasonable gnat would have to admit that in his society this kind of pluralism is lacking.

I do not intend, however, to discuss today any of the social or political issues connected with the problem of freedom; and I intend to use the cluster of gnats not as an example of a *social* system, but rather as my main illustration of a cloudlike *physical* system, as an example or paradigm of a highly irregular or disordered cloud.

Like many physical, biological, and social systems, the cluster of gnats may be described as a 'whole'. Our conjecture that it is kept together by a kind of attraction which its densest part exerts on individual gnats straying too far from the crowd shows that there is even a kind of action or control which this 'whole' exerts upon its elements or parts. [See the remarks on downward causation on pp.245f. above.] Nevertheless, this 'whole' can be used to dispel the widespread 'holistic' belief that a 'whole' is *always* more than a mere sum of its parts. I do not deny that it may sometimes be so.[2] Yet the cluster of gnats is an example of a whole that is indeed nothing but the sum of its parts – and in a very precise sense; for not only is it completely described by describing the movements of all the individual gnats, but the movement of the whole is, in this case, precisely the (vectorial) sum of the movements of its constituent members, divided by the number of the members.

An example (in many ways similar) of a biological system or 'whole' which exerts some control over the highly irregular movements of its parts would be a picnicking family – parents with a few children and a dog – roaming the woods for hours, but never straying far from the family car (which acts as a centre of attraction, as it were). This system may be said to be even more cloudy – that is, less regular in the movement of its parts – than our cloud of gnats.

I hope you will now have before you an idea of my two prototypes or paradigms, the clouds on the left and the clocks on the right, and of the way in which we can arrange many kinds of things, and many kinds of systems, between them. I am sure you have caught some vague, general idea of the arrangement, and you need not worry if your idea is still a bit foggy, or cloudy.

II Physical Determinism

The arrangement I have described is, it seems, quite acceptable to common sense; and more recently, in our own time, it has become acceptable even to physical science. It was not so, however, during the preceding 250 years: the Newtonian revolution, one of the greatest revolutions in history, led to the rejection of the commonsense arrangement which I have tried to present to you. For one of the things which almost everybody[3] thought had been established by the Newtonian revolution was the following staggering proposition:

All clouds are clocks – even the most cloudy of clouds.

This proposition, 'All clouds are clocks', may be taken as a brief formulation of the view which I shall call '*physical determinism*'.

The physical determinist who says that all clouds are clocks will also say that our commonsense arrangement, with the clouds on the left and the clocks on the right, is misleading, since *everything* ought to be placed on the extreme right. He will say that, with all our common sense, we arranged things *not according to their nature, but merely according to our ignorance*. Our arrangement, he will say, reflects merely the fact that we know in some detail how the parts of a clock work, or how the solar system works, while we do not have any knowledge about the *detailed* interaction of the particles that form a gas cloud, or an organism. And he will assert that, once we have obtained this knowledge, we shall find that gas clouds or organisms are as clocklike as our solar system.

Newton's theory did not, of course, tell the physicists that this was so. In fact, it did not treat at all of clouds. It treated especially of planets, whose movements it explained as due to some very simple laws of nature; also of cannon balls, and of the tides. But its immense success in these fields turned the physicists' heads; and surely not without reason.

Before the time of Newton and his predecessor, Kepler, the movements of the planets had escaped many attempts to explain or even to describe them fully. Clearly, they somehow participated in the unvarying general movement of the rigid system of the fixed stars; yet they deviated from the movement of that system almost like single gnats deviating from the general movement of a cluster of gnats. Thus the planets, not unlike living things, appeared to be in a position intermediate between clouds and clocks. Yet the success of Kepler's and even more of Newton's theory showed that those thinkers had been right who had suspected that the planets were in fact perfect clocks. For their movements turned out to be precisely predictable with the help of Newton's theory; predictable in all those details which had previously baffled the astronomers by their apparent irregularity.

Newton's theory was the first really successful scientific theory in human history; and it was tremendously successful. Here was real knowledge; knowledge beyond the wildest dreams of even the boldest minds. Here was a theory which explained precisely not only the movements of *all* the stars in their courses, but also, just as precisely, the movements of bodies on earth, such as falling apples, or projectiles, or pendulum clocks. And it even explained the tides.

All openminded men – all those who were eager to learn, and who took an interest in the growth of knowledge – were converted to the new theory. Most openminded men, and especially most scientists, thought that in the end it would explain everything, including not only electricity and magnetism, but also clouds, and even living organisms. Thus physical determinism – the doctrine that all clouds are clocks – became the ruling faith among enlightened men; and everybody who did not embrace this new faith was held to be an obscurantist or a reactionary.[4]

III Indeterminism

Among the few dissenters[5] was Charles Sanders Peirce, the great American mathematician and physicist and, I believe, one of the greatest philosophers of all time. He did not question Newton's theory; yet as early as 1892 he showed that this theory, even if true, does not give us any valid reason to believe that clouds are perfect clocks. Though in common with all other physicists of his time he believed that the world was a clock that worked according to Newtonian laws, he rejected the belief that this clock, or any other, was *perfect*, down to the smallest detail. He pointed out that at any rate we could not possibly claim to know, from experience, of anything like a perfect clock, or of anything even faintly approaching that absolute perfection which physical determinism assumed. I may perhaps quote one of Peirce's brilliant comments: '... one who is behind the scenes' (Peirce speaks here as an experimentalist) '... knows that the most refined comparisons [even] of masses [and] lengths, ... far surpassing in precision all other [physical] measurements, ... fall behind the accuracy of bank accounts, and that the ... determinations of physical constants ... are about on a par with an upholsterer's measurements of carpets and curtains....'[6] From this Peirce concluded that we were free to conjecture that there was a certain *looseness or imperfection* in all clocks, and that this allowed an *element of chance* to enter. Thus Peirce conjectured that the world was not only ruled by the *strict Newtonian laws*, but that it was also at the same time ruled by *laws of chance*, or of randomness, or of disorder: by laws of statistical *probability*. This made the world an interlocking system of clouds and clocks, so that even the best clock would, *in its molecular structure*, show some degree of cloudiness. So far as I know Peirce was the first post-Newtonian physicist and philosopher who thus dared to adopt the view that to some degree *all clocks are clouds*; or in other words, that *only clouds exist*, though clouds of very different degrees of cloudiness.

Peirce supported this view by pointing out, no doubt correctly, that all physical bodies, even the jewels in a watch, were subject to molecular heat motion,[7] a motion similar to that of the molecules of a gas, or of the individual gnats in a cluster of gnats.

These views of Peirce's were received by his contemporaries with little interest. Apparently only one philosopher noticed them; and he attacked them.[8] Physicists seem to have ignored them; and even today most physicists believe that if we had to accept the classical mechanics of Newton as true, we should be compelled to accept physical determinism, and with it the proposition that all clouds are clocks. It was only with the downfall of classical physics and with the rise of the new quantum theory that physicists were prepared to abandon physical determinism.

Now the tables were turned. Indeterminism, which up to 1927 had been equated with obscurantism, became the ruling fashion; and some great scientists, such as Max Planck, Erwin Schrödinger, and Albert Einstein, who hesitated to abandon determinism, were considered old fogies,[9] although they had been in the forefront of the development of quantum theory. I myself once heard a brilliant young physicist describe Einstein, who was then still alive and hard at work, as 'antediluvian'. The deluge that was supposed to have swept Einstein away was the new quantum theory, which had risen during the years from 1925 to 1927, and to whose advent at most seven people had made contributions comparable to those of Einstein.

IV The Nightmare of the Physical Determinist

Arthur Holly Compton was among the first who welcomed the new quantum theory and Heisenberg's new physical indeterminism of 1927. In 1931 he became also one of the first to examine the human and, more generally, the biological implications of this new indeterminism.[10] And now it became clear why he had welcomed the new theory so enthusiastically: it solved for him not only problems in physics but also biological and philosophical problems, and among the latter especially problems connected with ethics.

To show this, I shall quote the striking opening passage of Compton's *The Freedom of Man*:

> The fundamental question of morality, a vital problem in religion, and a subject of active investigation in science: Is man a free agent?
>
> If ... the atoms of our bodies follow physical laws as immutable as the motions of the planets, why try? What difference can it make how great the effort if our actions are already predetermined by mechanical laws ... ?

Compton describes here what I shall call '*the nightmare of the physical determinist*'. A deterministic physical clockwork mechanism is, above all, completely self-contained: in the perfect deterministic physical world there is simply no room for any outside intervention. Everything that happens in such a world is physically predetermined, including all our movements and therefore all our actions. Thus all our thoughts, feelings, and efforts can have no practical influence upon what happens in the physical world: they are, if not mere illusions, at best superfluous byproducts ('epiphenomena') of physical events.

In this way, the daydream of the Newtonian physicist who hoped to prove all clouds to be clocks had threatened to turn into a nightmare; and the attempt to ignore this had led to something like an intellectual split personality. Compton, I think, was grateful to the new quantum theory for rescuing him from this difficult intellectual situation. Thus he writes, in *The Freedom of Man*: 'The physicist has rarely . . . bothered himself with the fact that if . . . completely deterministic . . . laws . . . apply to man's actions, he is himself an automaton.' And in *The Human Meaning of Science* he expresses his relief:

> In my own thinking on this vital subject I am thus in a much more satisfied state of mind than I could have been at any earlier stage of science. If the statements of the laws of physics were assumed correct, one would have had to suppose (as did most philosophers) that the feeling of freedom is illusory, or if [free] choice were considered effective, that the statements of the laws of physics were . . . unreliable. The dilemma has been an uncomfortable one. . . .

Later in the same book Compton sums up the situation crisply in the words: '. . . it is no longer justifiable to use physical law as evidence against human freedom.'

These quotations from Compton show clearly that before Heisenberg he had been harassed by what I have here called the nightmare of the physical determinist, and that he had tried to escape from this nightmare by adopting something like an intellectual split personality. Or as he himself puts it: 'We [physicists] have preferred merely to pay no attention to the difficulties. . . .'[11] Compton welcomed the new theory which rescued him from all this.

I believe that the only form of the problem of determinism which is worth discussing seriously is exactly that problem which worried Compton: the problem which arises from a physical theory which describes the world as a *physically complete* or a *physically closed* system.[12] By a physically closed system I mean a set or system of physical entities, such as atoms or elementary particles or physical forces or fields of forces, which interact with each other – and *only* with each other – in accordance with definite laws of interaction that do not leave any room for interaction with, or interference by, anything outside that closed set or system of physical entities. It is this 'closure' of the system that creates the deterministic nightmare.[13]

v Psychological Determinism

I should like to digress here for a minute in order to contrast the problem of physical determinism, which I consider to be of fundamental importance, with the far from serious problem which many philosophers and psychologists, following Hume, have substituted for it.

Hume interpreted determinism (which he called 'the doctrine of necessity', or 'the doctrine of constant conjunction') as the doctrine that 'like causes always produce like effects' and that 'like effects necessarily follow from like causes'. Concerning human actions and volitions he held, more particularly, that 'a spectator can commonly infer our actions from our motives and character; and even where he cannot, he concludes in general, that he might, were he perfectly acquainted with every circumstance of our situation and temper, and the most secret springs of our ... disposition. Now this is the very essence of necessity ....'[14] Hume's successors put it thus: our actions, or our volitions, or our tastes, or our preferences, are *psychologically* 'caused' by preceding experiences ('motives'), and ultimately by our heredity and environment.

But this doctrine which we may call *philosophical* or *psychological* determinism is not only a very different affair from *physical* determinism, but it is also one which a physical determinist who understands the matter at all can hardly take seriously. For the thesis of philosophical determinism, that 'Like effects have like causes' or that 'Every event has a cause', is so vague that it is perfectly compatible with physical *in*determinism.

Indeterminism – or more precisely, physical indeterminism – is merely the doctrine that *not all* events in the physical world are predetermined with absolute precision, in all their infinitesimal details. Apart from this, it is compatible with practically any degree of regularity you like, and it does not, therefore, entail the view that there are 'events without causes'; simply because the terms 'event' and 'cause' are vague enough to make the doctrine that every event has a cause compatible with physical indeterminism. While physical determinism demands complete and infinitely precise physical predetermination and the absence of *any* exception whatever, physical indeterminism asserts no more than that determinism is false, and that there are *at least some* exceptions, here or there, to precise predetermination.

Thus even the formula 'Every observable or measurable *physical* event has an observable or measurable *physical* cause' is still compatible with physical indeterminism, simply because no measurement can be infinitely precise: for the salient point about physical determinism is that, based on Newton's dynamics, it asserts the existence of a world of absolute mathematical precision. And although in so doing it goes beyond the realm of possible observation (as was seen by Peirce), it nevertheless is testable, in principle, with any desired degree of precision; and it actually withstood surprisingly precise tests.

By contrast, the formula 'Every event has a cause' says nothing about precision; and if, more especially, we look at the laws of psychology, then there is not even a suggestion of precision. This holds for a 'behaviourist' psychology as much as for an 'introspective' or 'mentalist' one. In the case of a mentalist psychology this is obvious. But even a behaviourist may *at the very best* predict that, under given conditions, a rat will take twenty to twenty two seconds to run a maze: he will have no idea how, by specifying more and more precise experimental conditions, he could make predictions which become more and more precise – and, *in principle, precise without limit*. This is so because behaviourist 'laws' are not, like those of Newtonian physics, differential equations, and because every attempt to introduce such differential equations would lead beyond behaviourism into physiology, and thus ultimately into physics; so it would lead us back to the problem of *physical determinism*.

As noted by Laplace, physical determinism implies that every physical event in the distant future (or in the distant past) is predictable (or retrodictable) with any desired degree of precision, provided we have sufficient knowledge about the present state of the physical world. The thesis of a philosophical (or psychological) determinism of Hume's type, on the other hand, asserts even in its strongest interpretation no more than that any *observable* difference between two events is related by some as yet perhaps unknown law to some difference – an observable difference perhaps – in the preceding state of the world; obviously a very much weaker assertion, and incidentally one which we could continue to uphold even if most of our experiments, performed under conditions which are, *in appearance*, 'entirely equal', should yield different results. This was stated very clearly by Hume himself. 'Even when these contrary experiments are entirely equal', he writes, 'we remove not the notion of causes and necessity, but . . . conclude, that the [apparent] chance . . . lies only in . . . our imperfect knowledge, not in the things themselves, which are in every case equally necessary [i.e., determined], tho' to appearance not equally constant or certain.'[15]

This is why a Humean philosophical determinism and, more especially, a psychological determinism, lack the sting of physical determinism. For in Newtonian physics things really looked as if any apparent looseness in a system was in fact merely due to our ignorance, so that, should we be fully informed about the system, any appearance of looseness would disappear. Psychology, on the other hand, never had this character.

Physical determinism, we might say in retrospect, was a daydream of omniscience which seemed to become more real with every advance in physics until it became an apparently inescapable nightmare. But the corresponding daydreams of the psychologists were never more than castles in the air: they were Utopian dreams of attaining equality with physics, its mathematical methods, and its powerful applications; and perhaps even of attaining superiority, by moulding men and societies. (While these totalitarian dreams are not serious from a scientific point of view, they are very dangerous politically [see especially selections 23 and 24 below].[16])

VI Criticism of Physical Determinism

I have called physical determinism a nightmare. It is a nightmare because it asserts that the whole world with everything in it is a huge automaton, and that we are nothing but little cogwheels, or at best sub-automata, within it.

It thus destroys, in particular, the idea of creativity. It reduces to a complete illusion the idea that in preparing this lecture I have used my brain to create *something new*. There was no more in it, according to physical determinism, than that certain parts of my body put down black marks on white paper: any physicist with sufficient detailed information could have written my lecture by the simple method of predicting the precise places on which the physical system consisting of my body (including my brain, of course, and my fingers) and my pen would put down those black marks.

Or to use a more impressive example: if physical determinism is right, then a physicist who is completely deaf and who has never heard any music could write all the symphonies and concertos written by Mozart or Beethoven, by the simple method of studying the precise physical states of their bodies and predicting where they would put down black marks on their lined paper. And our deaf physicist could do even more: by studying Mozart's or Beethoven's bodies with sufficient care he could write scores which were never actually written by Mozart or Beethoven, but which they would have written had certain external circumstances of their lives been different: if they had eaten lamb, say, instead of chicken, or drunk tea instead of coffee.

All this could be done by our deaf physicist if supplied with a sufficient knowledge of purely physical conditions. There would be no need for him to know anything about the theory of music – though he might be able to predict what answers Mozart or Beethoven would have written down under examination conditions if presented with questions on the theory of counterpoint.

I believe that all this is absurd;[17] and its absurdity becomes even more obvious, I think, when we apply this method of physical prediction to a determinist.

For according to determinism, any theories – such as, say, determinism – are held because of a certain physical structure of the holder (perhaps of his brain). Accordingly we are deceiving ourselves (and are physically so determined as to deceive ourselves) whenever we believe that there are such things as arguments or reasons which make us accept determinism. Or in other words, physical determinism is a theory which, if it is true, is not arguable, since it must explain all our reactions, including what appear to us as beliefs based on arguments, as due to *purely physical conditions*. Purely physical conditions, including our physical environment, make us say or accept whatever we say or accept; and a well-trained physicist who does not know any French, and who has never heard of determinism, would be able to predict what a French determinist would say in a French discussion on determinism; and of course also what his indeterminist opponent would say. But this means that if we believe that we have accepted a theory like determinism because we were swayed by the logical force of certain arguments, then we are deceiving ourselves, according to physical determinism; or more precisely, we are in a physical condition which determines us to deceive ourselves.

Hume saw much of this, even though it appears that he did not quite see what it meant for his own arguments; for he confined himself to comparing the determinism of '*our judgments*' with that of '*our actions*', saying that '*we have not more liberty in the one than in the other*'.[18]

Considerations such as these may perhaps be the reason why there are so many philosophers who refuse to take the problem of physical determinism seriously and dismiss it as a 'bogy'.[19] Yet the doctrine that *man is a machine* was argued most forcefully and seriously in 1751, long before the theory of evolution became generally accepted, by de La Mettrie; and the theory of evolution gave the problem an even sharper edge, by suggesting that there may be no clear distinction between living matter and dead matter.[20] And in spite of the victory of the new quantum theory, and the conversion of so many physicists to indeterminism, de La Mettrie's doctrine that man is a machine has today perhaps more defenders than ever before among physicists, biologists, and philosophers; especially in the form of the thesis that man is a computer.[21]

For if we accept a theory of evolution (such as Darwin's) then even if we remain sceptical about the theory that life emerged from inorganic matter we can hardly deny that there must have been a time when abstract and non-physical entities, such as reasons and arguments and scientific knowledge, and abstract rules, such as rules for building railways or bulldozers or sputniks or, say, rules of grammar or of counterpoint, did not exist, or at any rate had no effect upon the physical universe. It is difficult to understand how the physical universe could produce abstract entities such as rules, and then could come under the influence of these rules, so that these rules in their turn could exert very palpable effects upon the physical universe. [See section III of selection 4 above.]

There is, however, at least one perhaps somewhat evasive but at any rate easy way out of this difficulty. We can simply deny that these abstract entities exist and that they can influence the physical universe. And we can assert that what do exist are our brains, and that these are machines like computers; that the allegedly abstract rules are physical entities, exactly like the concrete physical punch-cards by which we 'programme' our computers; and that the existence of anything non-physical is just 'an illusion', perhaps, and at any rate unimportant, since everything would go on as it does even if there were no such illusions.

According to this way out, we need not worry about the 'mental' status of these illusions. They may be universal properties of all things: the stone which I throw may have the illusion that it jumps, just as I have the illusion that I throw it; and my pen, or my computer, may have the illusion that it works because of its interest in the problems which it thinks that it is solving – and which I think I am solving – while in fact there is nothing of any significance going on except purely physical interactions.

You may see from all this that the problem of physical determinism which worried Compton is indeed a serious problem. It is not just a philosophical puzzle, but it affects at least physicists, biologists, behaviourists, psychologists, and computer engineers.

Admittedly, quite a few philosophers have tried to show (following Hume or Schlick) that it is merely a verbal puzzle, a puzzle about the use of the word 'freedom'. But these philosophers have hardly seen the difference between the problem of physical determinism and that of philosophical determinism; and either they are determinists like Hume, which explains why for them 'freedom' is 'just a word', or they have never had that close contact with the physical sciences or with computer engineering which would have impressed upon them that we are faced with more than a merely verbal puzzle.

VII Indeterminism Is Not Enough

Like Compton I am among those who take the problem of physical determinism seriously, and like Compton I do not believe that we are mere computing machines (though I readily admit that we can learn a great deal from computing machines – even about ourselves). Thus, like Compton, I am a *physical indeterminist*: physical indeterminism, I believe, is a necessary prerequisite for any solution of our problem. We have to be indeterminists; yet I shall try to show that indeterminism is not enough.

With this statement, *indeterminism is not enough*, I have arrived, not merely at a new point, but at the very heart of my problem.

The problem may be explained as follows.

If determinism is true, then the whole world is a perfectly running flawless clock, including all clouds, all organisms, all animals, and all men. If, on the other hand, Peirce's or Heisenberg's or some other form of indeterminism is true, then sheer *chance* plays a major role in our physical world. *But is chance really more satisfactory than determinism?*

The question is well known. Determinists like Schlick have put it in this way: '... freedom of action, responsibility, and mental sanity, cannot reach beyond the realm of causality: they stop where chance begins ... a higher degree of randomness ... [simply means] a higher degree of irresponsibility.'[22]

I may perhaps put this idea of Schlick's in terms of an example I have used before: to say that the black marks made on white paper which I produced in preparation for this lecture were just the result of *chance* is hardly more satisfactory than to say that they were physically predetermined. In fact, it is even less satisfactory. For some people may perhaps be quite ready to believe that the text of my lecture can be in principle completely explained by my physical heredity, and my physical environment, including my upbringing, the books I have been reading, and the talks I have listened to; but hardly anybody will believe that what I am reading to you is the result of nothing but chance – just a random sample of English words, or perhaps of letters, put together without any purpose, deliberation, plan, or intention.

The idea that the only alternative to determinism is just sheer chance was taken over by Schlick, together with many of his views on the subject, from Hume, who asserted that 'the removal' of what he called 'physical necessity' must always result in 'the same thing with *chance*. As objects must either be conjoin'd or not, . . . 'tis impossible to admit of any medium betwixt chance and an absolute necessity.'[23]

I shall in a moment argue against this important doctrine according to which the only alternative to determinism is sheer chance. Yet I must admit that the doctrine seems to hold good for the quantum-theoretical models which have been designed to explain, or at least to illustrate, the possibility of human freedom. This seems to be the reason why these models are so very unsatisfactory.

Compton himself designed such a model, though he did not particularly like it. It uses quantum indeterminacy, and the unpredictability of a quantum jump, as a model of a human decision of great moment. It consists of an amplifier which amplifies the effect of a single quantum jump in such a way that it may either cause an explosion or destroy the relay necessary for bringing the explosion about. In this way one single quantum jump may be equivalent to a major decision. But in my opinion the model has no similarity to any *rational decision*. It is, rather, a model of a kind of decision-making where people who cannot make up their minds say: 'Let us toss a penny.' In fact, the whole apparatus for amplifying a quantum jump seems rather unnecessary: tossing a penny, and deciding on the result of the toss whether or not to pull a trigger, would do just as well. And there are of course computers with built-in penny-tossing devices for producing random results, where such are needed.

It may perhaps be said that some of our decisions *are* like penny tosses: they are snap decisions, taken without deliberation, since we often do not have enough time to deliberate. A driver or a pilot has sometimes to take a snap decision like this; and if he is well trained, or just lucky, the result may be satisfactory; otherwise not.

I admit that the quantum-jump model may be a model for such snap decisions; and I even admit that it is conceivable that something like the amplification of a quantum jump may actually happen in our brains if we make a snap decision. But are snap decisions really so very interesting? Are they characteristic of human behaviour – of *rational* human behaviour?

I do not think so; and I do not think that we shall get much further with quantum jumps. They are just the kind of examples which seem to lend support to the thesis of Hume and Schlick that perfect chance is the only alternative to perfect determinism. What we need for understanding rational human behaviour – and indeed, animal behaviour – is something *intermediate* in character between perfect chance and perfect determinism – something intermediate between perfect clouds and perfect clocks.

Hume's and Schlick's ontological thesis that there cannot exist anything intermediate between chance and determinism seems to me not only highly dogmatic (not to say doctrinaire) but clearly absurd; and it is understandable only on the assumption that they believed in a complete determinism in which chance has no status except as a symptom of our ignorance. (But even then it seems to me absurd, for there is, clearly, something like partial knowledge, or partial ignorance.) For we know that even highly reliable clocks are not really perfect, and Schlick (if not Hume) must have known that this is largely due to factors such as friction – that is to say, to statistical or chance effects. And we also know that our clouds are not perfectly chancelike, since we can often predict the weather quite successfully, at least for short periods.

VIII Compton's Problem

Thus we shall have to return to our old arrangement with clouds on the left and clocks on the right and animals and men somewhere in between.

But even after we have done so (and there are some problems to be solved before we can say that this arrangement is in keeping with presentday physics), even then we have at best only made room for our main question.

For obviously what we want is to understand how such non-physical things as *purposes, deliberations, plans, decisions, theories, intentions*, and *values*, can play a part in bringing about physical changes in the physical world. That they do this seems to be obvious, *pace* Hume and Laplace and Schlick. It is clearly untrue that all those tremendous physical changes brought about hourly by our pens, or pencils, or bulldozers, can be explained in purely physical terms, either by a deterministic physical theory, or (by a stochastic theory) as due to chance.

Compton was well aware of this problem, as the following charming passage from his Terry Lectures shows:[24]

> It was some time ago when I wrote to the secretary of Yale University agreeing to give a lecture on November 10 at 5 p.m. He had such faith in me that it was announced publicly that I should be there, and the audience had such confidence in his word that they came to the hall at the specified time. But consider the great physical improbability that their confidence was justified. In the meanwhile my work called me to the Rocky Mountains and across the ocean to sunny Italy. A phototropic organism [such as I happen to be, would not easily] . . . tear himself away from there to go to chilly New Haven. The possibilities of my being elsewhere at this moment were infinite in number. Considered as a physical event, the probability of meeting my engagement would have been fantastically small. Why then was the audience's belief justified? . . . They knew my purpose, and it was my purpose [which] determined that I should be there.

Compton shows here very beautifully that mere physical indeterminism is not enough. We have to be indeterminists, to be sure; but we must also try to understand how men, and perhaps animals, can be 'influenced' or 'controlled' by such things as aims, or purposes, or rules, or agreements.

This then is our central problem.[25]

21 The Mind-Body Problem (1977)

1 World 3 and the Mind-Body Problem

It is one of the central conjectures of *The Self and Its Brain* that the consideration of world 3 [see selection 4 above] can throw some new light on the mind-body problem. I will briefly state three arguments.

The first argument is as follows.

(1) World 3 objects are abstract (even more abstract than physical forces), but none the less real; for they are powerful tools for changing world 1. (I do not wish to imply that this is the only reason for calling them real, or that they are nothing but tools.)

(2) World 3 objects have an effect on world 1 only through human intervention, the intervention of their makers; more especially, through being grasped, which is a world 2 process, a mental process, or more precisely, a process in which world 2 and world 3 interact.

(3) We therefore have to admit that both world 3 objects and the processes of world 2 are real – even though we may not like this admission, out of deference, say, to the great tradition of materialism.

I think that this is an acceptable argument – though, of course, it is open to someone to deny any one of its assumptions. He may deny that theories are abstract, or deny that they have an effect on world 1, or claim that abstract theories can directly affect the physical world. (I think, of course, that he would have a difficult time in defending any of these views.)

The second argument partly depends upon the first. If we admit the interaction of the three worlds, and thus their reality, then the interaction between worlds 2 and 3, which we can to some extent understand, can perhaps help us a little towards a better understanding of the interaction between worlds 1 and 2, a problem that is part of the mind-body problem.

For one kind of interaction between worlds 2 and 3 ('grasping') can be interpreted as a making of world 3 objects and as a matching of them by critical selection; and something similar seems to be true for the visual perception of a world 1 object. This suggests that we should look upon world 2 as active – as productive and critical (making and matching). But we have reason to think that some unconscious neurophysiological processes achieve precisely this. This makes it perhaps a little easier to 'understand' that conscious processes may act along similar lines: it is, up to a point, 'understandable' that conscious processes perform tasks similar to those performed by nervous processes.

A third argument bearing on the mind-body problem is connected with the status of human language.

The capacity to learn a language – and even a strong need to learn a language – are, it appears, part of the genetic make-up of man. By contrast, the actual learning of a particular language, though influenced by unconscious inborn needs and motives, is not a gene regulated process and therefore not a natural process, but a cultural process, a world 3 regulated process. Thus language learning is a process in which genetically based dispositions, evolved by natural selection, somewhat overlap and interact with a conscious process of exploration and learning, based on cultural evolution. This supports the idea of an interaction between world 3 and world 1; and in view of our earlier arguments, it supports the existence of world 2.

Several eminent biologists[1] have discussed the relationship between genetic evolution and cultural evolution. Cultural evolution, we may say, continues genetic evolution by other means: by means of world 3 objects.

It is often stressed that man is a tool-making animal, and rightly so. If by tools material physical bodies are meant, it is, however, of considerable interest to notice that none of the human tools is genetically determined, not even the stick. The only tool that seems to have a genetic basis is language. Language is non-material, and appears in the most varied physical shapes – that is to say, in the form of very different systems of physical sounds.

There are behaviourists who do not wish to speak of 'language', but only of the 'speakers' of one or the other particular language. Yet there is more to it than that. All normal men speak; and speech is of the utmost importance for them; so much so that even a deaf, dumb and blind little girl like Helen Keller acquired with enthusiasm, and speedily, a substitute for speech through which she obtained a real mastery of the English language and of literature. Physically, her language was vastly different from spoken English; but it had a one-to-one correspondence with written or printed English. There can be no doubt that she would have acquired any other language in place of English. Her urgent though unconscious need was for language – language in the abstract.

As shown by their numbers and their differences, the various languages are manmade: they are cultural world 3 objects, though they are made possible by capabilities, needs, and aims which have become genetically entrenched. Every normal child acquires a language through much active work, pleasurable and perhaps also painful. The intellectual achievement that goes with it is tremendous. This effort has, of course, a strong feedback effect on the child's personality, on his relations to other persons, and on his relations to his material environment.

Thus we can say that the child is, partly, the product of his achievement. He is himself, to some extent, a world 3 product. Just as the child's mastery and consciousness of his material environment are extended by his newly acquired ability to speak, so also is his consciousness of himself. The self, the personality, emerges in interaction with the other selves and with the artefacts and other objects of his environment. All this is deeply affected by the acquisition of speech; especially when the child becomes conscious of his name, and when he learns to name the various parts of his body; and, most important, when he learns to use personal pronouns.

Becoming a fully human being depends on a maturation process in which the acquisition of speech plays an enormous part. One learns not only to perceive, and to interpret one's perceptions, but also to be a person, and to be a self. I regard the view that our perceptions are 'given' to us as a mistake: they are 'made' by us, they are the result of active work. Similarly I regard it as a mistake to overlook the fact that the famous Cartesian argument 'I think, therefore I am' presupposes language, and the ability to use the pronoun (to say nothing of the formulation of the highly sophisticated problem which this argument is supposed to settle). When Kant suggests that the thought 'I think' must be able to accompany all our perceptions and experiences, he does not seem to have thought of a child (or of himself) in his pre-linguistic or pre-philosophical state.[2]

II Materialism and the Autonomous World 3

What does world 3 look like from a materialistic point of view? Obviously, the bare existence of aeroplanes, airports, bicycles, books, buildings, cars, computers, gramophones, lectures, manuscripts, paintings, sculptures and telephones presents no problem for any form of physicalism or materialism. While to the pluralist these are the material instances, the embodiments, of world 3 objects, to the materialist they are simply parts of world 1.

But what about the objective logical relations which hold between theories (whether written down or not), such as incompatibility, mutual deducibility, partial overlapping, etc.? The radical materialist replaces world 2 objects (subjective experiences) by brain processes. Especially important among these are dispositions for verbal behaviour: dispositions to assent or reject, to support or refute; or merely to consider – to rehearse the pros and cons. Like most of those who accept world 2 objects (the 'mentalists'), materialists usually interpret world 3 contents as if they were 'ideas in our minds': but the radical materialists try, further, to interpret 'ideas in our minds' – and thus also world 3 objects – as brain-based dispositions to verbal behaviour.

Yet neither the mentalist nor the materialist can in this way do justice to world 3 objects, especially to the contents of theories, and to their objective logical relations.

World 3 objects just are not 'ideas in our minds', nor are they dispositions of our brains to verbal behaviour. And it does not help if one adds to these dispositions the embodiments of world 3, as mentioned in the first paragraph of this section. For none of these copes adequately with the *abstract* character of world 3 objects, and especially with the *logical relations* existing between them.[3]

As an example, Frege's *Grundgesetze* was written, and partly printed, when he deduced, from a letter written by Bertrand Russell, that there was a self-contradiction involved in its foundation. This self-contradiction had been there, objectively, for years. Frege had not noticed it: it had not been 'in his mind'. Russell only noticed the problem (in connection with quite a different manuscript) at a time when Frege's manuscript was complete. Thus there existed for years a theory of Frege's (and a similar more recent one of Russell's) which were objectively inconsistent without anyone's having an inkling of this fact, or without anyone's brain state disposing him to agree to the suggestion 'This manuscript contains an inconsistent theory'.

To sum up, world 3 objects and their properties and relations cannot be reduced to world 2 objects. Nor can they be reduced to brain states or dispositions; not even if we were to admit that all mental states and processes can be reduced to brain states and processes. This is so despite the fact that we can regard world 3 as the product of human minds.

Russell did not invent or produce the inconsistency, but he *discovered* it. (He invented, or produced, a way of showing or proving that the inconsistency was there.) Had Frege's theory not been objectively inconsistent, he could not have applied Russell's inconsistency proof to it, and he would not have thus convinced himself of its untenability. Thus a state of Frege's mind (and no doubt also a state of Frege's brain) were the result, partly, of the objective fact that this theory was inconsistent: he was deeply upset and shaken by his discovery of this fact. This, in turn, led to his writing (a physical world 1 event) the words, '*Die Arithmetik ist ins Schwanken geraten*' ('Arithmetic is tottering'). Thus there is interaction between (1) the physical, or partly physical, event of Frege's receiving Russell's letter; (2) the objective hitherto unnoticed fact, belonging to world 3, that there was an inconsistency in Frege's theory; and (3) the physical, or partly physical, event of Frege's writing his comment on the (world 3) status of arithmetic.

These are some of the reasons why I hold that world 1 is not causally closed, and why I assert that there is interaction (though an indirect one) between world 1 and world 3. It seems to me clear that this interaction is mediated by mental, and partly even conscious, world 2 events.

The physicalist, of course, cannot admit any of this.

I believe that the physicalist is also prevented from solving another problem: he cannot do justice to the higher functions of language.

This criticism of physicalism relates to the analysis of the functions of language that was introduced by my teacher, Karl Bühler. He distinguished three functions of language: (1) the expressive function; (2) the signalling or release function; and (3) the descriptive function. I have discussed Bühler's theory in various places [for example, section IV of selection 4 above], and I have added to his three functions a fourth – (4) the argumentative function. Now I have argued elsewhere[4] that the physicalist is only able to cope with the first and the second of these functions. As a result, if faced with the descriptive and the argumentative functions of language, the physicalist will always see only the first two functions (which are also always present), with disastrous results.

In order to see what is at issue, it is necessary to discuss briefly the theory of the functions of language.

In Bühler's analysis of the act of speech he differentiates between the *speaker* (or, as Bühler also calls him, the *sender*) and the person spoken to, the *listener* (or the *receiver*). In certain special ('degenerate') cases the receiver may be missing, or he may be identical with the sender. The four functions here discussed (there are others, such as command, exhortation, advice – compare also Austin's 'performative utterances'[5]) are based on relations between (1) the sender, (2) the receiver, (3) some other objects or states of affairs which, in degenerate cases, may be identical with (1) or (2). On the next page I will give a table of the functions in which the lower functions are placed lower and the higher functions higher. The following comments may be made on this table:

(1) The expressive function consists in an outward expression of an inner state. Even simple instruments such as a thermometer or a traffic light 'express' their states in this sense. However, not only instruments, but also animals (and sometimes plants) express their inner state in their behaviour. And so do men, of course. In fact,

		functions	values	
		(4) Argumentative Function	validity/ invalidity	man
		(3) Descriptive Function	falsity/ truth	
animals, plants	perhaps bees[6]	(2) Signalling Function	efficiency/ inefficiency	
		(1) Expressive Function	revealing/ not revealing	

any action we undertake, not merely the use of a language, is a form of self-expression.

(2) The signalling function (Bühler calls it also the 'release function') presupposes the expressive function, and is therefore on a higher level. The thermometer may signal to us that it is very cold. The traffic light is a signalling instrument (though it may continue to work during hours where there may not always be cars about). Animals, especially birds, give danger signals; and even plants signal (for example to insects); and when our self-expression (whether linguistic or otherwise) leads to a reaction, in an animal or in a man, we can say that it was taken as a signal.

(3) The descriptive function of language presupposes the two latter functions. What characterizes it, however, is that over and above expressing and communicating (which may become quite unimportant aspects of the situation), it makes statements that can be *true* or *false*: the standards of truth and falsity are introduced. (We may distinguish a lower half of the descriptive function where false descriptions are beyond the animal's (the bee's?) power of abstraction. A thermograph would also belong here, for it describes the truth unless it breaks down.)

(4) The argumentative function adds argument to the three lower functions, with its values of *validity* and *invalidity*.

Now, functions (1) and (2) are almost always present in human language; but they are as a rule unimportant, at least when compared with the descriptive and argumentative functions.

However, when the radical physicalist and the radical behaviourist turn to the analysis of human language, they cannot get beyond the first two functions.[7] The physicalist will try to give a physical explanation – a causal explanation – of language phenomena. This is equivalent to interpreting language as expressive of the state of the speaker, and therefore as having the expressive function alone. The behaviourist, on the other hand, will concern himself also with the social aspect of language – but this will be taken, essentially, as affecting the behaviour of others; as 'communication', to use a vogue word; as the way in which speakers respond to one another's 'verbal behaviour'. This amounts to seeing language as expression and communication.

But the consequences of this are disastrous. For if all language is seen as merely expression and communication, then one neglects all that is characteristic of human language in contradistinction to animal language: its ability to make true and false statements, and to produce valid and invalid arguments. This, in its turn, has the consequence that the physicalist is prevented from accounting for the difference between propaganda, verbal intimidation, and rational argument.

III Epiphenomenalism

From a Darwinian point of view, we are led to speculate about the survival value of mental processes. For example we might regard pain as a warning signal. More generally, Darwinists ought to regard 'the mind', that is to say mental processes and dispositions for mental actions and reactions, as analogous to a bodily organ (closely linked with the brain, presumably) which has evolved under the pressure of natural selection. It functions by helping the adaptation of the organism.[8] The Darwinian view must be this: consciousness and more generally the mental processes are to be regarded (and, if possible, to be explained) as the product of evolution by natural selection.

The Darwinian view is needed, especially, for understanding intellectual mental processes. Intelligent actions are actions adapted to foreseeable events. They are based upon foresight, upon expectation; as a rule, upon short term *and* long term expectation, and upon the comparison of the expected results of several possible moves and countermoves. Here *preference* comes in, and with it, the making of decisions, many of which have an instinctual basis. This may be the way in which emotions enter the world 2 of mental processes and experiences; and why they sometimes 'become conscious', and sometimes not.

The Darwinian view also explains at least partly the first emergence of a world 3 of products of the human mind: the world of tools, of instruments, of languages, of myths, and of theories. (This much can be of course also admitted by those who are reluctant, or hesitant, to ascribe 'reality' to entities such as problems and theories, and also by those who regard world 3 as a part of world 1 and/or world 2.) The existence of the cultural world 3 and of cultural evolution may draw our attention to the fact that there is a great deal of systematic coherence within both world 2 and world 3; and that this can be explained – partly – as the systematic result of selection pressures. For example, the evolution of language can be explained, it seems, only if we assume that even a primitive language can be helpful in the struggle for life, and that the emergence of language has a feedback effect: linguistic capabilities are competing; they are being selected for their biological effects; which leads to higher levels in the evolution of language.

We can summarize this in the form of the following four principles of which the first two, it seems to me, must be accepted especially by those who are inclined towards physicalism or materialism.

(1) The theory of natural selection is the only theory known at present which can explain the emergence of purposeful processes in the world and, especially, the evolution of higher forms of life.

(2) Natural selection is concerned with *physical survival* (with the frequency distribution of competing genes in a population). It is therefore concerned, essentially, with the explanation of world 1 effects.

(3) If natural selection is to account for the emergence of the world 2 of subjective or mental experiences, the theory must explain the manner in which the evolution of world 2 (and of world 3) systematically provides us with instruments for survival.

(4) Any explanation in terms of natural selection is partial and incomplete. For it must always assume the existence of many (and

of partly unknown) competing mutations, and of a variety of (partly unknown) selection pressures.

These four principles may be briefly referred to as the Darwinian point of view. I shall try to show here that the Darwinian point of view clashes with the doctrine usually called 'epiphenomenalism'.

Epiphenomenalism admits the existence of mental events or experiences – that is, of a world 2 – but asserts that these mental or subjective experiences are causally ineffective byproducts of physiological processes, which alone are causally effective. In this way the epiphenomenalist can accept the physicalistic principle of the closedness of world 1, together with the existence of a world 2. Now the epiphenomenalist must insist that world 2 is indeed irrelevant; that only physical processes matter. If a man reads a book, the decisive thing is not that it influences his opinions, and provides him with information. These are all irrelevant epiphenomena. What matters is solely the change in his brain structure that affects his disposition to act. These dispositions are indeed, the epiphenomenalist will say, of the greatest importance for survival: it is only here that Darwinism comes in. The subjective experiences of reading and thinking exist, but they do not play the role we usually attribute to them. Rather, this mistaken attribution is the result of our failure to distinguish between our experiences and the crucially important impact of our reading upon the dispositional properties of the brain structure. The subjective experiential aspects of our perceptions while reading do not matter; nor do the emotional aspects. All this is fortuitous, casual rather than causal.

It is clear that this epiphenomenalist view is unsatisfactory. It admits the existence of a world 2, but denies it any biological function. It therefore cannot explain, in Darwinian terms, the evolution of world 2. And it is forced to deny what is plainly a most important fact – the tremendous impact of this evolution (and of the evolution of world 3) upon world 1.

I think that this argument is decisive.

To put the matter in biological terms, there are several closely related systems of controls in higher organisms: the immune system, the endocrinal system, the central nervous system, and what we call the 'mental system'. There is little doubt that the last two of these are closely linked. But so are the others, if perhaps less closely. The mental system has, clearly, its evolutionary and functional history, and its functions have increased with the evolution from lower to higher organisms. It thus has to be linked with the Darwinian point of view. But epiphenomenalism cannot provide any link.

22 The Self (1977)

I Selves

Before starting my remarks about the self, I wish to state clearly and unambiguously that I am convinced that *selves exist*.

This statement might seem somewhat superfluous in a world in which overpopulation is one of the great social and moral problems. Obviously, people exist; and each of them is an individual self, with feelings, hopes and fears, sorrows and joys, dreads and dreams, which we can only guess since they are known only to the person himself or herself.

All this is almost too obvious to be written down. But it must be said. For some great philosophers have denied it. David Hume was one of the first who was led to doubt the existence of his own self; and he had many followers.

Hume was led to his somewhat strange position by his empiricist theory of knowledge. He adopted the commonsense view (a view which I regard as mistaken [see selection 7, section IV above]) that all our knowledge is the result of sense experience. (This overlooks the tremendous amount of knowledge which we inherit and which is built into our sense organs and our nervous system; our knowledge how to react, how to develop, and how to mature.[1]) Hume's empiricism led him to the doctrine that we can know nothing but our sense impressions and the 'ideas' derived from sense impressions. On this basis he argued that *we cannot have anything like an idea of self*; and that, therefore, there cannot be such a thing as the self.

Thus in the section '*Of Personal Identity*' of his *Treatise*,[2] he argues against 'some philosophers who imagine we are every moment intimately conscious of what we call our SELF'; and he says of these philosophers that 'Unluckily all these positive assertions are contrary to that very experience, which is pleaded for them, nor have we any idea of *self*. . . . For from what impression cou'd this idea be deriv'd? This question 'tis impossible to answer without a manifest contradiction and absurdity. . . .'

These are strong words, and they have made a strong impression on philosophers: from Hume to our own time the existence of a self has been regarded as highly problematical.

Yet Hume himself, in a slightly different context, asserts the existence of selves just as emphatically as he here denies it. Thus he writes, in Book II of the *Treatise*:[3]

''Tis evident, that the idea, or rather impression of ourselves is always intimately present with us, and that our consciousness gives us so lively a conception of our own person, that 'tis not possible to imagine, that anything can in this particular go beyond it.'

This positive assertion of Hume's amounts to the same position that he attributes in the more famous negative passage quoted before to 'some philosophers', and that he there emphatically declares to be manifestly contradictory and absurd.

But there are lots of other passages in Hume supporting the idea of selves, especially under the name of 'character'. Thus we read:[4]

'There are also characters peculiar to different . . . persons. . . . The knowledge of these characters is founded on the observation of an uniformity in the actions, that flow from them. . . .'

Hume's official theory (if I may call it so) is that the self is no more than the sum total (the bundle) of its experiences. [See section IV below for a criticism of this theory.] He argues – in my opinion, rightly – that talk of a 'substantial' self does not help us much. Yet he again and again describes actions as 'flowing' from a person's character. In my opinion we do not need more in order to be able to speak of a self.

Hume, and others, take it that if we speak of the self as a substance, then the properties (and the experiences) of the self may be said to 'inhere' in it. I agree with those who say that this way of speaking is not illuminating. We may, however, speak of 'our' experiences, using the possessive pronoun. This seems to me perfectly natural; and it need not give rise to speculations about an ownership relation. I may say of my cat that it 'has' a strong character without thinking that this way of talking expresses an ownership relation (in the reverse direction to the one suggested when I speak of 'my' body). Some theories – such as the ownership theory – are incorporated in our language. We do not, however, have to accept as true the theories that are incorporated in our language, even though this fact may make it difficult to criticize them. If we decide that they are seriously misleading, we may be led to change the aspect of our language in question; otherwise, we may continue to use it, and simply bear in mind the fact that it should not be taken too literally (for example the 'new' moon). All this, however, should not prevent us from always trying to use the plainest language we can.

II Learning to be a Self

In this section my thesis is that we – that is to say our personalities, our selves – are anchored in all the three worlds, and especially in world 3.

It seems to me of considerable importance that we are not born as selves, but that we have to learn that we are selves; in fact we have to learn to be selves. This learning process is one in which we learn about world 1, world 2, and especially world 3.

Much has been written (by Hume, by Kant, by Ryle, and many others) about the question whether one can observe one's self. I regard the question as badly formulated. We can – and this is important – know quite a bit about our selves; but knowledge is not always (as so many people believe) based on observation. Both pre-scientific knowledge and scientific knowledge are largely based on action and on thought: on problem solving. Admittedly, observations do play a role, but this role is that of posing problems to us, and of helping us to try out, and weed out, our conjectures.

Moreover, our powers of observing are primarily directed to our environment. Even in experiments with optical illusions[5] what we observe is an environmental object, and to our surprise we find that it *seems* to have certain properties while we *know* that it does not have them. We know this in a world 3 sense of 'know': we have well-tested world 3 theories which tell us, for example, that a printed picture does not change, physically, while being looked at. We can say that the background knowledge which we possess, dispositionally, plays an important role in the way in which we interpret our observational experience. It has also shown by experiments that some of this background knowledge is culturally acquired.[6]

This is why, when we try to live up to the command 'observe yourself!', the outcome is usually so meagre. The reason is not, in the first instance, a special elusiveness of the ego (even though there is something in Ryle's contention[7] that it is almost impossible to observe oneself as one is 'now'). For if you are told 'observe the room you are sitting in' or 'observe your body', the result is also likely to be pretty meagre.

How do we obtain self-knowledge? Not by self-observation, I suggest, but by becoming selves, and by developing theories about ourselves. Long before we attain consciousness and knowledge of ourselves, we have, normally, become aware of other persons, usually our parents. There seems to be an inborn interest in the human face: experiments by R.L. Fantz[8] have shown that even very young babies fixate a schematic representation of a face for longer periods than a similar yet 'meaningless' arrangement. These and other results suggest that very young children develop an interest in and a kind of understanding of other persons. I suggest that a consciousness of self begins to develop through the medium of other persons: just as we learn to see ourselves in a mirror, so the child becomes conscious of himself by sensing his reflection in the mirror of other people's consciousness of himself. (I am very critical of psychoanalysis, but it seems to me that Freud's emphasis upon the formative influence of social experiences in early childhood was correct.) For example, I am inclined to suggest that when the child tries actively 'to draw attention to himself' it is part of this learning process. It seems that children, and perhaps primitive people, live through an 'animistic' or 'hylozoistic' stage in which they are inclined to assume of a physical body that it is animate – that it is a person[9] – until this theory is refuted by the passivity of the thing.

To put it slightly differently, the child learns to know his environment; but persons are the most important objects within his environment; and through their interest in him – and through learning about his own body – he learns in time that he is a person himself.

This is a process whose later stages depend much upon language.

But even before the child acquires a mastery of language, the child learns to be called by his name, and to be approved or disapproved of. And since approval and disapproval are largely of a cultural or world 3 character, one may even say that the very early and apparently inborn response of the child to a smile already contains the primitive pre-linguistic beginning of his anchorage in world 3.

In order to be a self, much has to be learnt; especially a sense of time, with oneself extending into the past (at least into 'yesterday') and into the future (at least into 'tomorrow'). But this involves *theory*; at least in its rudimentary form as an expectation:[10] there is no self without theoretical orientation, both in some primitive space and some primitive time. So the self is, partly, the result of the active exploration of the environment, and of the grasp of a temporal routine, based upon the cycle of day and night. (This will no doubt be different with Eskimo children.)[11]

The upshot of all this is that I do not agree with the theory of the 'pure self'. The philosophical term 'pure' is due to Kant and suggests something like 'prior to experience' or 'free from (the contamination of) experience'; and so the term 'pure self' suggests a theory which I think is mistaken: that the ego was there prior to experience, so that all experiences were, from the beginning, accompanied by the Cartesian and Kantian 'I think' (or perhaps by 'I am thinking'; at any rate by a Kantian 'pure apperception'). Against this, I suggest that being a self is partly the result of inborn dispositions and partly the result of experience, especially social experience. The newborn child has many inborn ways of acting and of responding, and many inborn tendencies to develop new responses and new activites. Among these tendencies is a tendency to develop into a person conscious of himself. But in order to achieve this, much must happen. A human child growing up in social isolation will fail to attain a full consciousness of self.[12]

Thus I suggest that not only perception and language have to be learnt – actively – but even the task of being a person; and I further suggest that this involves not merely a close contact with the world 2 of other persons, but also a close contact with the world 3 of language and of theories such as a theory of time (or something equivalent).[13]

What would happen to a human child growing up without *active* participation in social contacts, without other people, and without language? There are some such tragic cases known. As an indirect answer to our question, I will refer to a report by Eccles of a very important experiment comparing the experiences of an active and a non-active kitten. The non-active kitten learns nothing. I think that the same must happen to a child deprived of active experience in the social world.[14]

There is a most interesting recent report which bears on this issue. Scientists at Berkeley operated with two groups of rats, one living in an enriched environment and one living in a impoverished environment. The first were kept in a large cage, in social groups of twelve, with an assortment of playthings that were changed daily. The others were living alone in standard laboratory cages. The main result was that the animals living in the enriched environment had a heavier cerebral cortex than the impoverished ones. It appears that the brain grows through activity, through having to solve problems actively.[15] (The increment resulted from a proliferation of dendritic spines on cortical cells and of glial cells.)

III The Biological Function of Conscious and of Intelligent Activity

I propose that the evolution of consciousness, and of conscious intelligent effort, and later that of language and of reasoning – and of world 3 – should be considered teleologically, as we consider the evolution of bodily organs: as serving certain purposes, and as having evolved under certain selection pressures. [Compare section III of the previous selection.]

The problem can be put as follows. Much of our purposeful behaviour (and presumably of the purposeful behaviour of animals) happens without the intervention of consciousness.[16] What, then, are the biological achievements that are helped by consciousness?

I suggest as a first reply: the solution of *problems of a non-routine kind*. Problems that can be solved by routine do not need consciousness. This may explain why intelligent speech (or still better, writing) is such a good example of a conscious achievement (of course, it has its unconscious roots). As has been often stressed, it is one of the characteristics of human language that we constantly produce new *sentences* – sentences never before formulated – and understand them. As opposed to this major achievement, we constantly make use of *words* (and, of course, of phonemes) which are used routinely, again and again, though in a most varied context. A fluent speaker produces most of these words unconsciously, without paying attention to them, except where the choice of the best word may create a problem – a new problem, not solved by routine. '. . .new situations and the new responses they prompt are kept in the light of consciousness', Erwin Schrödinger writes; 'old and well practised ones are no longer so [kept].'[17]

A closely related idea concerning the function of consciousness is the following. Consciousness is needed to select, critically, new expectations or theories – at least on a certain level of abstraction. If any one expectation or theory is invariably successful, under certain conditions, its application will after a time turn into a matter of routine, and become unconscious. But an unexpected event will attract attention, and thus consciousness. We may be unconscious of the ticking of a clock, but 'hear' that it has stopped ticking.

We cannot know, of course, how far animals are conscious. But novelty can excite their attention; or more precisely, it can excite behaviour which, because of its similarity to human behaviour, many observers will describe as 'attention', and interpret as conscious.

But the role of consciousness is perhaps clearest where an aim or purpose (perhaps even an unconscious or instinctive aim or purpose) can be achieved by *alternative means*, and when two or more means are tried out, after deliberation. It is the case of making a new decision. (Of course, the classical case is Köhler's chimpanzee Sultan who fitted a bamboo stick into another, after many attempts to solve the problem of obtaining fruit out of his reach: a detour strategy in problem solving.) A similar situation is the choice of a non-routine programme, or of a new aim, such as the decision whether or not to accept an invitation to lecture, in addition to much work in hand. The acceptance letter, and the entry into the engagement calendar, are world 3 objects, anchoring our action programme; and the general principles we may have developed for accepting or rejecting such invitations are also programmes, also belonging to world 3, though perhaps on a higher hierarchical level.

IV The Integrative Unity of Consciousness

From the biological point of view it is, especially in the case of the higher animals, the individual organism that is fighting for its existence; that is relaxing; that is acquiring new experiences and skills; that is suffering; and that is ultimately dying. In the case of the higher animals it is the central nervous system which 'integrates' (to use Sherrington's phrase[18]) all the activities of the individual animal (and, if I may say so, all its 'passivities' which will include *some* 'reflexes'). Sherrington's famous idea of 'the integrative action of the nervous system' is perhaps best illustrated by the innumerable nervous actions which have to co-operate in order to keep a man standing quietly upright, at rest.

A great many of these integrative actions are automatic and unconscious. But some are not. To these belong, especially, the selection of means to certain (often unconscious) ends, that is to say, the making of decisions, the selection of programmes.

Decision making or programming is clearly a biologically important function of whatever the entity is that rules, or controls, the behaviour of animals or men. It is essentially an integrative action, in Sherrington's sense: it relates the behaviour at different instants of time to expectations; or in other words, it relates present behaviour to impending or future behaviour. And it directs *attention*, by selecting what are relevant objects, and what is to be ignored.

As a wild conjecture I suggest that it is out of four biological functions that consciousness emerges: pain, pleasure, expectation and attention. Perhaps attention emerges out of primitive experiences of pain and pleasure. But attention is, as a phenomenon, almost identical with consciousness: even pain may sometimes disappear if attention is distracted and focused elsewhere.

The question arises: how far can we explain the individual unity of our consciousness, or our selfhood, by an appeal to the biological situation? I mean by an appeal to the fact that we are animals,

animals in whom the instinct for individual survival has developed, as well as, of course, an instinct for racial survival.

Konrad Lorenz writes of the sea urchin that its 'non-centralized nervous system . . . makes it impossible for such animals to inhibit completely one of a number of potentially possible ways of behaviour, and thus to "decide" in favour of an alternative way. But such a decision (as shown so convincingly by Erich von Holst in the case of the earth worm) is the most fundamental and the most important achievement of a brainlike central nervous organ.'[19] In order to achieve this, the relevant situation must be signalled to the central organ in an adequate manner (that is to say, both in a realistic manner and, by suppressing the irrelevant aspects of the situation, in an idealizing manner). Thus a unified centre must inhibit some of the possible ways of behaviour and only allow one single way at a time to proceed: a way, Lorenz says, 'which in the situation just existing can contribute to survival. . . . The greater the number of possible ways of behaviour, the higher the achievement which is required from the central organ.'

Thus (1) the individual organism – the animal – is a unit; (2) each of the various ways of behaving – the items of the behavioural repertoire – is a unit, the whole repertoire forming a set of mutually exclusive alternatives; (3) the central organ of control must act as a unit (or rather, it will be more successful if it does).

Together these three points, (1), (2), and (3), make even of the animal an active, problem solving *agent*: the animal is always actively attempting to control its environment, in either a positive sense, or, when it is 'passive', in a negative sense. In the latter case it is undergoing or suffering the actions of an (often hostile) environment that is largely beyond its control. Yet even if it is merely contemplating, it is actively contemplating: it is never merely the sum of its impressions, or of its experiences. Our mind (and, I venture to suggest, even the animal mind) are never a mere 'stream of consciousness', a stream of experiences. Rather, our active attention is focused at every moment on just the relevant aspects of the situation, selected and abstracted by our perceiving apparatus, into which a selection programme is incorporated; a programme which is adjusted to our available repertoire of behavioural responses.

When discussing Hume [in section I above] we considered the

view that there is no self beyond the stream of our experiences; so that the self is nothing but a bundle of the experiences. This doctrine, which has been so often re-asserted, seems to me not only untrue but actually refuted by the experiments of Penfield,[20] who stimulated what he called the 'interpretative cortex' of the exposed brain in his patients and thereby managed to make them re-experience most vividly some of their past experiences. Nevertheless, the patients fully retained their awareness that they were lying on the operating table in Montreal. Their consciousness of self was not affected by their perceptual experiences, but was based on their knowledge of the localization of their bodies.

The importance of this localization (of the question 'Where am I?' on recovering from a fit) is that we cannot act coherently without it. It is part of our self-identity that we try to know where we are, in space and time: that we relate ourselves to our past and the immediate future, with its aims and purposes; and that we try to orientate ourselves in space.

All this is well understandable from a biological point of view. The central nervous system had from its beginning the main function of *steering* or *piloting* the moving organism. A knowledge of its location (the location of one's body image) relative to the biologically most relevant aspects of the environment is a crucial prerequisite of this piloting function of the central nervous system. Another such prerequisite is the centralized unity of the steering organ, of the decision maker who will, wherever possible, devolve some of his task upon a hierarchically lower authority, upon one of the many unconscious integrative mechanisms. To these devolved tasks belong not only executive tasks (such as keeping the body's balance) but even the acquisition of information: information is selectively filtered before it is admitted to consciousness.[21] An example of this is the selectivity of perception; another is the selectivity of memory.

I do not think that what I have said here or in the preceding sections clears up any mystery; but I do think that we need not regard as mysterious either the individuality, or the unity, or the uniqueness of the self, or our personal identity; at any rate not as more mysterious than the existence of consciousness, and ultimately that of life, and of individualized organisms. The emergence of full consciousness, capable of self-reflection, which seems to be linked to the human brain and to the descriptive function of language, is indeed one of the greatest of miracles. But if we look at the long evolution of individuation and of individuality, at the evolution of a central nervous system, and at the uniqueness of individuals (due partly to genetic uniqueness and partly to the uniqueness of their experience), then the fact that consciousness and intelligence and unity are linked to the biological individual organism (rather than, say, to the germ plasm) does not seem so surprising. For it is in the individual organism that the germ plasm – the genome, the programme for life – has to stand up to tests.

Part IV Social Philosophy

23 Historicism (1936)

I The Methods of the Social Sciences

Scientific interest in social and political questions is hardly less old than scientific interest in cosmology and physics; and there were periods in antiquity (I have Plato's political theory in mind, and Aristotle's collection of constitutions) when the science of society might have seemed to have advanced further than the science of nature. But with Galileo and Newton, physics became successful beyond expectation, far surpassing all the other sciences; and since the time of Pasteur, the Galileo of biology, the biological sciences have been almost equally successful. But the social sciences do not as yet seem to have found their Galileo.

In these circumstances, students who work in one or another of the social sciences are greatly concerned with problems of method; and much of their discussion of these problems is conducted with an eye upon the methods of the more flourishing sciences, especially physics. It was, for instance, a conscious attempt to copy the experimental method of physics which led, in the generation of Wundt, to a reform in psychology; and since J.S. Mill, repeated attempts had been made to reform on somewhat similar lines the method of the social sciences. In the field of psychology, these reforms may have had some measure of success, despite a great many disappointments. But in the theoretical social sciences, outside economics, little else but disappointment has come from these attempts. When these failures were discussed, the question was soon raised whether the methods of physics were really applicable to the social sciences. Was it not perhaps the obstinate belief in their applicability that was responsible for the much-deplored state of these studies?

The query suggests a simple classification of the schools of thought interested in the methods of the less successful sciences.

According to their views on the applicability of the methods of physics, we may classify these schools as *pro-naturalistic* or as *anti-naturalistic*; labelling them 'pro-naturalistic' or 'positive' if they favour the application of the methods of physics to the social sciences, and 'anti-naturalistic' or 'negative' if they oppose the use of these methods.

Whether a student of method upholds anti-naturalistic or pro-naturalistic doctrines, or whether he adopts a theory combining both kinds of doctrines, will largely depend on his views about the character of the science under consideration, and about the character of its subject matter. But the attitude he adopts will also depend on his views about the methods of physics. I believe this latter point to be the most important of all. And I think that the crucial mistakes in most methodological discussions arise from some very common misunderstandings of the methods of physics. In particular, I think they arise from a misinterpretation of the logical form of its theories, of the methods of testing them, and of the logical function of observation and experiment.[1] My contention is that these misunderstandings have serious consequences; that the sometimes conflicting arguments and doctrines, anti-naturalistic as well as pro-naturalistic, are indeed based upon a misunderstanding of the methods of physics. Here, however, I will confine myself to the explanation of a characteristic approach in which both kinds of doctrines are combined.

This approach which I propose first to explain, and then [and in selection 24] to criticize, I call 'historicism'. It is often encountered in discussions on the method of the social sciences; and it is often used without critical reflection, or even taken for granted. What I mean by 'historicism' will be explained at length. It will be enough if I say here that I mean by 'historicism' an approach to the social sciences which assumes that *historical prediction* is their principal aim, and which assumes that this aim is attainable by discovering the 'rhythms' or the 'patterns', the 'laws' or the 'trends' that underlie the evolution of history. Since I am convinced that such historicist doctrines of method are at bottom responsible for the unsatisfactory state of the theoretical social sciences (other than economic theory), my presentation of these doctrines is certainly not unbiased. But I have tried hard to make a case in favour of historicism in order to give point to my subsequent criticism. I have tried to present historicism as a well-considered and close-knit philosophy. And I have not hesitated to construct arguments in its support which have never, to my knowledge, been brought forward by historicists themselves. I hope that, in this way, I have succeded in building up a position really worth attacking. In other words, I have tried to perfect a theory which has often been put forward, but perhaps never in a fully developed form. This is why I have deliberately chosen the somewhat unfamiliar label 'historicism'. By introducing it I hope I shall avoid merely verbal quibbles: for nobody, I hope, will be tempted to question whether any of the arguments here discussed really or properly or essentially belong to historicism, or what the word 'historicism' really or properly or essentially means.[2]

II Historical Laws

A non-experimental observational basis for a science is, in a certain sense of the term, always 'historical' in character. That is so even with the observational basis of astronomy. The facts on which astronomy is based are contained in the records of the observatory, records which inform us, for instance, that at such and such a date (hour, second) the planet Mercury has been observed by Mr So-and-so in a certain position. In short, they give us a 'register of events in order of time', or a chronicle of observations.

Similarly, the observational basis of sociology can be given only in the form of a chronicle of events, namely of political or social happenings. This chronicle of political and other important happenings in social life is what one customarily calls 'history'. History in this narrow sense is the basis of sociology.

It would be ridiculous to deny the importance of history in this narrow sense as an empirical basis for social science. But one of the characteristic claims of historicism which is closely associated with its denial of the applicability of the experimental method [see also section III of the next selection], is that history, political and social, is the *only* empirical source of sociology. Thus the historicist visualizes sociology as a theoretical and empirical discipline whose empirical basis is formed by a chronicle of the facts of history alone, and whose aim is to make forecasts, preferably large-scale forecasts. Clearly, *these forecasts must also be of a historical character*, since their testing by experience, their verification or refutation, must be left to future history. Thus the making and testing of large-scale historical forecasts is the task of sociology as seen by historicism. In brief, the historicist claims that *sociology is theoretical history*.

But at the same time the historicist holds that the method of generalization is inapplicable to social science, and that we must not assume uniformities of social life to be invariably valid through space and time, since they usually apply only to a certain cultural or historical period. Thus social laws – if there are any real social laws – must have a somewhat different structure from the ordinary generalizations based on uniformities. Real social laws would have to be 'generally' valid. But this can only mean that they apply to the whole of human history, covering all of its periods rather than merely some of them. But there can be no social uniformities which hold good beyond single periods. Thus the only universally valid laws of society must be the laws which *link up the successive periods*. They must be *laws of historical development* which determine the transition from one period to another. This is what historicists mean by saying that the only real laws of sociology are historical laws.

III Historical Prophecy versus Social Engineering

As indicated, these historical laws (if they can be discovered) would permit the prediction of even very distant events, although not with minute exactness of detail. Thus the doctrine that real sociological laws are historical laws (a doctrine mainly derived from the limited validity of social uniformities) leads back, independently of any attempt to emulate astronomy, to the idea of 'large-scale forecasts'. And it makes this idea more concrete, for it shows that these forecasts have the character of historical prophecies.

Sociology thus becomes, to the historicist, an attempt to solve the old problem of foretelling the future; not so much the future of the individual as that of groups, and of the human race. It is the science of things to come, of impending developments. If the attempt to furnish us with political foresight of scientific validity were to succeed, then sociology would prove to be of the greatest value to politicians, especially to those whose vision extends beyond the exigencies of the present, to politicians with a sense of historic destiny. Some historicists, it is true, are content to predict only the next stages of the human pilgrimage, and even these in very cautious terms. But one idea is common to them all – that sociological study should help to reveal the political future, and that it could thereby become the foremost instrument of farsighted practical politics.

From the point of view of the pragmatic value of science, the significance of scientific predictions is clear enough. It has not always been realized, however, that two different kinds of prediction can be distinguished in science, and accordingly two different ways of being practical. We may predict (1) the coming of a typhoon, a prediction which may be of the greatest practical value because it may enable people to take shelter in time; but we may also predict (2) that if a certain shelter is to stand up to a typhoon, it must be constructed in a certain way, for instance, with ferroconcrete buttresses on its north side.

These two kinds of predictions are obviously very different although both are important and fulfil age-old dreams. In the one case we are told about an event which we can do nothing to prevent. I shall call such a prediction a 'prophecy'. Its practical value lies in our being warned of the predicted event, so that we can sidestep it or meet it prepared (possibly with the help of predictions of the other kind).

Opposed to these are predictions of the second kind which we can describe as *technological* predictions since predictions of this kind form a basis of *engineering*. They are, so to speak, constructive, intimating the steps open to us *if* we want to achieve certain results. The greater part of physics (nearly the whole of it apart from astronomy and meteorology) makes predictions of such a form that, considered from a practical standpoint, they can be described as technological prediction. The distinction between these two sorts of prediction roughly coincides with the lesser or greater importance of the part played by designed experiment, as opposed to mere patient observation, in the science concerned. The typical experimental sciences are capable of making technological predictions, while those employing mainly non-experimental observations produce prophecies.

I do not wish to be taken as implying that all sciences, or even all scientific predictions, are fundamentally practical – that they are necessarily either prophetic or technological and cannot be anything else. I only want to draw attention to a distinction between the two kinds of prediction and the sciences corresponding to them. In choosing the terms 'prophetic' and 'technological', I certainly wish to hint at a feature they exhibit if looked at from the pragmatic standpoint; but my use of this terminology is neither intended to mean that the pragmatic point of view is necessarily superior to any other, nor that scientific interest is limited to pragmatically important prophecies and to predictions of a technological character. If we consider astronomy, for example, then we have to admit that its findings are mainly of theoretical interest even though they are not valueless from a pragmatic point of view; but as 'prophecies' they are all akin to those of meteorology whose value for practical activities is quite obvious.

It is worth noting that this difference between the prophetic and the engineering character of sciences does not correspond to the difference between long-term and short-term predictions. Although most engineering predictions are short-term there are also long-term technological predictions, for instance, about the lifetime of an engine. Again, astronomical prophecies may be either short-term or long-term, and most meteorological prophecies are comparatively short-term.

The difference between these two practical aims – prophesying and engineering – and the corresponding difference in the structure of relevant scientific theories, will be seen [in the next selection] to be one of the major points in our methodological analysis. For the moment I only wish to stress that historicists, quite consistently with their belief that sociological experiments are useless and impossible, argue for historical prophecy – the prophecy of social, political and institutional developments – and against social engineering, as the practical aim of the social sciences. The idea of social engineering, the planning and construction of institutions, with the aim, perhaps, of arresting or of controlling or of quickening impending social developments, appears to some historicists as possible. To others, this would seem an almost impossible undertaking, or one which overlooks the fact that political planning, like all social activity, must stand under the superior sway of historical forces. [See especially selection 26.]

IV The Theory of Historical Development

These considerations have taken us to the very heart of the body of arguments which I propose to call 'historicism', and they justify the choice of this label. Social science is nothing but history: this is the thesis. Not, however, history in the traditional sense of a mere chronicle of historical facts. The kind of history with which historicists wish to identify sociology looks not only backwards to the past but also forwards to the future. It is the study of the operative forces and, above all, of the laws of social development. Accordingly, it could be described as historical theory, or as theoretical history, since the only universally valid social laws have been identified as historical laws. They must be laws of process, of change, of development – not the pseudolaws of apparent constancies or uniformities. According to historicists, sociologists must try to get a general idea of the *broad trends* in accordance with which social structures change. But besides this, they should try to understand the causes of this process, the working of the forces responsible for change. They should try to formulate hypotheses about general trends underlying social development in order that men may adjust themselves to impending changes by deducing prophecies from these laws.

The historicist's notion of sociology can be further clarified by following up the distinction I have drawn between the two different kinds of prognosis – and the related distinction between two classes of science. In opposition to the historicist methodology, we could conceive of a methodology which aims at a *technological social science*. Such a methodology would lead to the study of the general laws of social life with the aim of finding all those facts which would be indispensable as a basis for the work of everyone seeking to reform social institutions. There is no doubt that such facts exist. We know many Utopian systems, for instance, which are impracticable simply because they do not consider such facts sufficiently. The technological methodology we are considering would aim at furnishing means of avoiding such unrealistic constructions. It would be anti-historicist, but by no means anti-historical. Historical experience would serve it as a most important source of information. But, instead of trying to find laws of social development, it would look for the various laws which impose limitations upon the construction of social institutions, or for other uniformities (though these, the historicist says, do not exist).

As well as using counterarguments of a kind already mentioned, the historicist could question the possibility and the utility of such a social technology in another way. Let us assume, he could say, that a social engineer has worked out a plan for a new social structure, backed by the kind of sociology you have envisaged. This plan we suppose to be both practical and realistic in the sense that it does not conflict with the known facts and laws of social life; and we even assume that the plan is backed by an equally practicable further plan for transforming society as it is at present into the new structure. Even so, historicist arguments can show that such a plan would deserve no serious consideration. It would still remain an unrealistic and Utopian dream, just because it does not take account of the laws of historical development. Social revolutions are not brought about by rational plans, but by social forces, for instance, by conflicts of interests. The old idea of a powerful philosopher king who would put into practice some carefully thought-out plans was a fairy tale invented in the interest of a landowning aristocracy. The democratic equivalent of this fairy tale is the superstition that enough people of good will may be persuaded by rational argument to take planned action. History shows that the social reality is quite different. The course of historical development is never shaped by theoretical constructions, however excellent, although such schemes might, admittedly, exert some influence, along with many other less rational (or even quite irrational) factors. Even if such a rational plan coincides with the interests of powerful groups it will never be realized in the way in which it was conceived, in spite of the fact that the struggle for its realization would then become a major factor in the historical process. The real outcome will always be very different from the rational construction. It will always be the resultant of the momentary constellation of contesting forces. Furthermore, under no circumstances could the outcome of rational planning become a stable structure; for the balance of forces is bound to change. All social engineering, no matter how much it prides itself on its realism and on its scientific character, is doomed to remain a Utopian dream.

So far, the historicist would continue, the argument has been directed against the practical possibility of social engineering backed by some theoretical social science, and not against the idea of such a science itself. It can easily be extended, however, so as to prove the impossibility of any theoretical social science of the technological kind. We have seen that practical engineering ventures must be doomed to failure on account of very important sociological facts and laws. But this implies not only that such a venture has no practical value but also that it is theoretically unsound, since it overlooks the only really important social laws – the laws of development. The 'science' upon which it was allegedly based must have missed these laws too, for otherwise it would never have furnished the basis for such unrealistic constructions. Any social science which does not teach the impossibility of rational social construction is entirely blind to the most important facts of social life, and must overlook the only social laws of real validity and of real importance. Social sciences seeking to provide a background for social engineering cannot, therefore, be true descriptions of social facts. They are impossible in themselves.

The historicist will claim that besides this decisive criticism there are other reasons for rejecting technological sociologies. One reason is, for example, that they neglect such aspects of the social development as the emergence of novelty. The idea that we can construct new social structures rationally on a scientific basis implies that we can bring into existence a new social period more or less precisely in the way we have planned it. Yet if the plan is based on a science that covers social facts, it cannot account for intrinsically new features, only for newness of arrangement.[3] But we know that a new period will have its own intrinsic novelty – an argument which must render any detailed planning futile, and any science upon which it is grounded untrue.

These historicist considerations can be applied to all social sciences, including economics. Economics, therefore cannot give us any valuable information concerning social reform. Only a pseudo-economics can seek to offer a background for rational economic planning. Truly scientific economics can merely help to reveal the driving forces of economic development through different historical periods. It may help us to foresee the outlines of future periods, but it cannot help us to develop and put into operation any detailed plan for any new period. What holds for the other social sciences must hold for economics. Its ultimate aim can only be 'to lay bare the economic law of motion of human society' (Marx).

v Criticism of Historicism: Is There a Law of Evolution?

The belief that it is the task of the social sciences to lay bare the *law of evolution of society* in order to foretell its future might be perhaps described as the central historicist doctrine. For it is this view of a society moving through a series of periods that gives rise, on the one hand, to the contrast between a changing social and an unchanging physical world, and thereby to anti-naturalism. On the other hand, it is the same view that gives rise to the pro-naturalistic – and scientistic – belief in so-called 'natural laws of succession'; a belief which, in the days of Comte and Mill, could claim to be supported by the long-term predictions of astronomy, and more recently, by Darwinism. Indeed, the recent vogue of historicism might be regarded as merely part of the vogue of evolutionism – a philosophy that owes its influence largely to the somewhat sensational clash between a brilliant scientific hypothesis concerning the history of the various species of animals and plants on earth, and an older metaphysical theory which, incidentally, happened to be part of an established religious belief.[4]

What we call the evolutionary hypothesis is an explanation of a host of biological and palaeontological observations – for instance, of certain similarities between various species and genera – by the assumption of the common ancestry of related forms.[5] This hypothesis is not a universal law, even though certain universal laws of nature, such as laws of heredity, segregation, and mutation, enter with it into the explanation. It has, rather, the character of a particular (singular or specific) historical statement. (It is of the same status as the historical statement: 'Charles Darwin and Francis Galton had a common grandfather.') The fact that the evolutionary hypothesis is not a universal law of nature but a particular (or, more precisely, singular) historical statement about the ancestry of a number of terrestrial plants and animals is somewhat obscured by the fact that the term 'hypothesis' is so often used to characterize the status of universal laws of nature. But we should not forget that we quite frequently use this term in a different sense. For example, it would undoubtedly be correct to describe a tentative medical diagnosis as a hypothesis, even though such a hypothesis is of a singular and historical character rather than of the character of a universal law. In other words, the fact that all laws of nature are hypotheses must not distract our attention from the fact that not all hypotheses are laws, and that more especially historical hypotheses are, as a rule, not universal but singular statements about one individual event, or a number of such events.

But can there be a *law* of evolution? Can there be a scientific law in the sense intended by T.H. Huxley when he wrote: '. . .he must be a half-hearted philosopher who . . . doubts that science will sooner or later . . . become possessed of the law of evolution of organic forms – of the unvarying order of that great chain of causes and effects of which all organic forms, ancient and modern, are the links. . .'?[6]

I believe that the answer to this question must be 'No', and that the search for the law of the 'unvarying order' in evolution cannot possibly fall within the scope of scientific method, whether in biology or in sociology. My reasons are very simple. The evolution of life on earth, or of human society, is a unique historical process. Such a process, we may assume, proceeds in accordance with all kinds of causal laws, for example, the laws of mechanics, of chemistry, of heredity and segregation, of natural selection, etc. Its description, however, is not a law, but only a singular historical statement. Universal laws make assertions concerning some unvarying order, as Huxley puts it, i.e. concerning all processes of a certain kind; and although there is no reason why the observation of one single instance should not incite us to formulate a universal law, nor why, if we are lucky, we should not even hit upon the truth, it is clear that any law, formulated in this or in any other way, must be *tested* by new instances before it can be taken seriously by science. But we cannot hope to test a universal hypothesis nor to find a natural law acceptable to science if we are for ever confined to the observation of one unique process. Nor can the observation of one unique process help us to foresee its future development. The most careful observation of *one* developing caterpillar will not help us to predict its transformation into a butterfly. As applied to the history of human society – and it is with this that we are mainly concerned here – our argument has been formulated by H.A.L. Fisher in these words: 'Men ... have discerned in history a plot, a rhythm, a predetermined pattern ... I can see only one emergency following upon another ..., *only one great fact with respect to which, since it is unique, there can be no generalizations....*'[7]

How can this objection be countered? There are, in the main, two positions which may be taken up by those who believe in a law of evolution. They may (1) deny our contention that the evolutionary process is unique; or (2) assert that in an evolutionary process, even if it is unique, we may discern a trend or tendency or direction, and that we may formulate a hypothesis which states this trend, and test this hypothesis by future experience. The two positions (1) and (2) are not exclusive of each other.

Position (1) goes back to an idea of great antiquity – the idea that the life-cycle of birth, childhood, youth, maturity, old age, and death applies not only to individual animals and plants, but also to societies, races, and perhaps even to 'the whole world'. Of this doctrine I shall say only that it is merely one of the many instances of metaphysical theories seemingly confirmed by facts – facts which, if examined more closely, turn out to be selected in the light of the very theories they are supposed to test.[8]

As for position (2), the belief that we may discern, and extrapolate, the trend or direction of an evolutionary movement, it may first be mentioned that this belief has influenced and has been used to support some of the cyclical hypotheses which represent position (1). Yet the idea of the movement of society itself – the idea that society, like a physical body, can move *as a whole* along a certain path and in a certain direction – is merely a holistic confusion.[9] The hope, more especially, that we may some day find the 'laws of motion of society', just as Newton found the laws of motion of physical bodies, is nothing but the result of these misunderstandings. Since there is no motion of society in any sense similar or analogous to the motion of physical bodies, there can be no such laws.

But, it will be said, the existence of trends or tendencies in social change can hardly be questioned: every statistician can calculate such trends. Are these trends not comparable with Newton's law of inertia? The answer is: trends exist, or more precisely, the assumption of trends is often a useful statistical device. *But trends are not laws.* A statement asserting the existence of a trend is existential, not universal. (A universal law, on the other hand, does not assert existence; on the contrary: as will be shown [in section I of selection 24], it asserts the impossibility of something or other.[10]) And a statement asserting the existence of a trend at a certain time and place would be a singular historical statement, not a universal law. The practical significance of this logical situation is considerable: while we may base scientific predictions on laws, we cannot (as every cautious statistician knows) base them merely on the existence of trends. A trend (we may again take population growth as an example) which has persisted for hundreds or even thousands of years may change within a decade, or even more rapidly than that.

It is important to point out that *laws and trends are radically different things*. (A law, however, may assert that under certain circumstances (initial conditions) certain trends will be found; moreover, after a trend has been so explained, it is possible to formulate a law corresponding to the trend.) There is little doubt that the habit of confusing trends with laws, together with the intuitive observation of trends (such as technical progress), inspired the central doctrines of evolutionism and historicism – the doctrines of the inexorable laws of biological evolution and of the irreversible laws of motion of society. And the same confusions and intuitions also inspired Comte's doctrine of laws of succession – a doctrine which is still very influential.

The distinction, famous since Comte and Mill, between *laws of coexistence*, alleged to correspond to statics, and *laws of succession*, alleged to correspond to dynamics, can admittedly be interpreted in a reasonable way; i.e. as a distinction between laws that do not involve the concept of *time*, and laws into whose formulation *time* enters (for instance, laws that speak of velocities).[11] But this is not quite what Comte and his followers had in mind. When speaking of laws of succession, Comte thought of laws determining the succession of a 'dynamic' series of phenomena in the order in which we observe them. Now it is important to realize that 'dynamic' laws of succession, as Comte conceived them, do not exist. They certainly do not exist within dynamics. (I *mean* dynamics.) The closest approach to them in the field of natural science – and what he probably had in mind – are natural periodicities like the seasons, the phases of the moon, the recurrence of eclipses, or perhaps the swings of a pendulum. But these periodicities, which in physics would be described as dynamical (though stationary), would be, in Comte's sense of these terms, 'static' rather than 'dynamic'; and in any case they can hardly be called laws (since they depend upon the special conditions prevailing in the solar system). I will call them 'quasilaws of succession'.

The crucial point is this: although we may assume that any actual succession of phenomena proceeds according to the laws of nature, it is important to realize that practically *no sequence of, say, three or more causally connected concrete events proceeds according to any single law of nature*. If the wind shakes a tree and Newton's apple falls to the ground, nobody will deny that these events can be described in terms of causal laws. But there is no single law, such as that of gravity, nor even a single definite set of laws, to describe the actual or concrete succession of causally connected events; apart from gravity, we should have to consider the laws explaining wind pressure; the jerking movements of the branch; the tension in the apple's stalk; the bruise suffered by the apple on impact; all of which is succeeded by chemical processes resulting from the bruise, etc. The idea that any concrete sequence or succession of events (apart from such examples as the movement of a pendulum or a solar system) can be described or explained by any one law, or by any one definite set of laws, is simply mistaken. There are neither laws of succession, nor laws of evolution.

Yet Comte and Mill did envisage their historical laws of succession as laws determining a sequence of historical events in the order of their actual occurrence. This may be seen from the manner in which Mill speaks of a method that 'consists in attempting, by a study and analysis of the general facts of history, to discover . . . the law of progress; which law, once ascertained, must . . . enable us to predict future events, *just as after a few terms of an infinite series in algebra we are able to detect the principle of regularity in their formation, and to predict the rest of the series to any number of terms we please.*' Mill himself is critical of this method; but his criticism fully admits the possibility of finding laws of succession analogous to those of a mathematical sequence, even though he expressed doubts whether 'the order of succession ... which history presents to us' may be sufficiently 'rigidly uniform' to be compared with a mathematical sequence.[12]

Now we have seen that there are no *laws* that determine the succession of such a 'dynamic' series of events.[13] On the other hand, there may be *trends* which are of this 'dynamic' character; for example, population increase. It may therefore be suspected that Mill had such trends in mind when he spoke of 'laws of succession'. And this suspicion is confirmed by Mill himself when he describes his historical law of progress as a *tendency*. Discussing this 'law', he expresses his 'belief ... that the general *tendency* is, and will continue to be, saving occasional and temporary exceptions, one of improvement – *a tendency towards a better and happier state*. This ... is ... a theorem of the science' (viz. of the social science). That Mill should seriously discuss the question whether 'the phenomena of human society' revolve 'in an orbit' or whether they move, progressively, in 'a trajectory'[14] is in keeping with this fundamental confusion between laws and trends, as well as with the holistic idea that society can 'move' as a whole – say, like a planet.

In order to avoid misunderstandings, I wish to make it clear that I believe that both Comte and Mill have made great contributions to the philosophy and methodology of science: I am thinking, especially, of Comte's emphasis on laws and scientific prediction, of his criticism of an essentialist theory of causality; and of his and Mill's doctrine of the unity of scientific method. Yet their doctrine of historical laws of succession is, I believe, little better than a collection of misapplied metaphors.

24 Piecemeal Social Engineering (1944)

1 The Technological Approach to Sociology

In discussing historicism, a doctrine of method with which I disagree, it will be useful to deal briefly with those methods which, in my opinion, have been successful, and whose further and more conscious development I recommend, so as to reveal to the reader my own bias and to clarify the point of view that underlies my criticism. For convenience, I shall label these methods '*piecemeal technology*'.

The term 'social technology' (and even more the term 'social engineering' which will be introduced in the next section) are likely to arouse suspicion, and to repel those whom they remind of the 'social blueprints' of the collectivist planners, or perhaps even of the 'technocrats'. I realize this danger, and so I have added the word 'piecemeal', both to offset undesirable associations and to express my conviction that 'piecemeal tinkering' (as it is sometimes called), combined with critical analysis, is the main way to practical results in the social as well as in the natural sciences. The social sciences have developed very largely through the criticism of proposals for social improvements or, more precisely, through attempts to find out whether or not some particular economic or political action is likely to produce an expected, or desired, result.[1] This approach, which might indeed be called the classical one, is what I have in mind when I refer to the technological approach to social science, or to 'piecemeal social technology'.

Technological problems in the field of social science may be of a 'private' or of a 'public' character. For example, investigations into the technique of business administration, or into the effects of improved working conditions upon output, belong to the first group. Investigations into the effects of prison reform or universal health insurance, or of the stabilization of prices by means of tribunals, or of the introduction of new import duties, etc., upon, say, the equalization of incomes, belong to the second group; and so do some of the most urgent practical questions of the day, such as the possibility of controlling trade cycles; or the question whether centralized 'planning', in the sense of state management of production, is compatible with an effective democratic control of the administration; or the question of how to export democracy to the Middle East.

This emphasis upon the practical technological approach does not mean that any of the theoretical problems that may arise from the analysis of the practical problems should be excluded. On the contrary, it is one of my main points that the technological approach is likely to prove fruitful in giving rise to significant problems of a purely theoretical kind. But besides helping us in the fundamental task of selecting problems, the technological approach imposes a discipline on our speculative inclinations (which, especially in the field of sociology proper, are liable to lead us into the region of metaphysics); for it forces us to submit our theories to definite standards, such as standards of clarity and practical testability. My point about the technological approach might perhaps be made by saying that sociology (and perhaps even the social sciences in general) should look, not indeed for 'its Newton or its Darwin',[2] but rather for its Galileo, or its Pasteur.

This and my previous references [in selection 23, section I] to an analogy between the methods of the social and the natural sciences are likely to provoke as much opposition as our choice of terms like 'social technology' and 'social engineering' (this in spite of the important qualification expressed by the word 'piecemeal'). So I had better say that I fully appreciate the importance of the fight against a dogmatic methodological naturalism or 'scientism' (to use Professor Hayek's term). Nevertheless I do not see why we should not make use of this analogy as far as it is fruitful, even though we recognize that it has been badly misused and misrepresented in certain quarters. Besides, we can hardly offer a stronger argument against these dogmatic naturalists than one that shows that some of the methods they attack are fundamentally the same as the methods used in the natural sciences.

A prima facie objection against what we call the technological approach is that it implies the adoption of an 'activist' attitude towards the social order, and that it is therefore liable to prejudice us against the anti-interventionist or 'passivist' view: the view that if we are dissatisfied with existing social or economic conditions, it is because we do not understand how they work and why active intervention could only make matters worse. Now I must admit that I am certainly out of sympathy with this 'passivist' view, and that I even believe that a policy of *universal* anti-interventionism is untenable – even on purely logical grounds, since its supporters are bound to recommend political intervention aimed at preventing intervention. Nevertheless, the technological approach as such is neutral in this matter (as indeed it ought to be), and by no means incompatible with anti-interventionism. On the contrary, I think that anti-interventionism involves a technological approach. For to assert that interventionism makes matters worse is to say that certain political actions would not have certain effects – to wit, not the desired ones; and it is one of the most characteristic tasks of any technology to *point out what cannot be achieved*.

It is worth while to consider this point more closely. As I have shown elsewhere,[3] every natural law can be expressed by asserting that *such and such a thing cannot happen*; that is to say, by a sentence in the form of the proverb: 'You can't carry water in a sieve.' For example, the law of conservation of energy can be expressed by: 'You cannot build a perpetual motion machine'; and that of entropy by: 'You cannot build a machine which is a hundred per cent efficient.' This way of formulating natural laws is one which makes their technological significance obvious and it may therefore be called the '*technological form*' of a natural law. If we now consider anti-interventionism in this light, then we see at once that it may well be expressed by sentences of the form: 'You cannot achieve such and such results', or perhaps, 'You cannot achieve such and such ends without such and such concomitant effects.' But this shows that anti-interventionism can be called a typically *technological doctrine*.

It is not, of course, the only one in the realm of social science. On the contrary, the significance of our analysis lies in the fact that it draws attention to a really fundamental similarity between the natural and the social sciences. I have in mind the existence of sociological laws or hypotheses which are analogous to the laws or hypotheses of the natural sciences. Since the existence of such sociological laws or hypotheses (other than so called 'historical laws') has often been doubted,[4] I will now give a number of examples: 'You cannot introduce agricultural tariffs and at the same time reduce the cost of living.' – 'You cannot, in an industrial society, organize consumers' pressure groups as effectively as you can organize certain producers' pressure groups.' – 'You cannot have a centrally planned society with a price system that fulfils the main functions of competitive prices.' – 'You cannot have full employment without inflation.' Another group of examples may be taken from the realm of power politics: 'You cannot introduce a political reform without causing some repercussions which are undesirable from the point of view of the ends aimed at' (therefore, look out for them). – 'You cannot introduce a political reform without strengthening the opposing forces, to a degree roughly in ratio to the scope of the reform.' (This may be said to be the technological corollary of 'There are always interests connected with the status quo.') – 'You cannot make a revolution without causing a reaction.' To these examples we may add two more, which may be called 'Plato's law of revolutions' (from the eighth book of the *Republic*) and 'Lord Acton's law of corruption', respectively: 'You cannot make a successful revolution if the ruling class is not weakened by internal dissension or defeat in war.' – 'You cannot give a man power over other men without tempting him to misuse it – a temptation which roughly increases with the amount of power wielded, and which very few are capable of resisting.'[5] Nothing is here assumed about the strength of the available evidence in favour of these hypotheses, whose formulations certainly leave much room for improvement. They are merely examples of the kind of statements which a piecemeal technology may attempt to discuss, and to substantiate.

II Piecemeal versus Utopian Engineering

Notwithstanding the objectionable associations which attach to the term 'engineering',[6] I shall use the term 'piecemeal social engineering' to describe the practical application of the results of piecemeal technology. The term is useful since there is need for a term covering social activities, private as well as public, which, in order to realize some aim or end, consciously utilize all available technological knowledge (including, if it can be obtained, knowledge concerning the limitations of knowledge, as explained in the previous note). Piecemeal social engineering resembles physical engineering in regarding the *ends* as beyond the province of technology. (All that technology may say about ends is whether or not they are compatible with each other or realizable.) In this it differs from historicism, which regards the ends of human activities as dependent on historical forces and so within its province.

Just as the main task of the physical engineer is to design machines and to remodel and service them, the task of the piecemeal social engineer is to design social institutions, and to reconstruct and run those already in existence. The term 'social institution' is used here in a very wide sense, to include bodies of a private as well as of a public character. Thus I shall use it to describe a business, whether it is a small shop or an insurance company, and likewise a school, or an 'educational system', or a police force, or a Church, or a law court. The piecemeal technologist or engineer recognizes that *only a minority of social institutions are consciously designed while the vast majority have just 'grown', as the undesigned results of human actions.*[7] But however strongly he may be impressed by this important fact, as a technologist or engineer he will look upon them from a 'functional' or 'instrumental' point of view.[8] He will see them as means to certain ends, or as convertible to the service of certain ends; as machines rather than as organisms. This does not mean, of course, that he will overlook the fundamental differences between institutions and physical instruments. On the contrary, the technologist should study the differences as well as the similarities, expressing his results in the form of hypotheses. And indeed, it is not difficult to formulate hypotheses about institutions in technological form as is shown by the following example: 'You cannot construct foolproof institutions, that is to say, institutions whose functioning does not very largely depend upon persons: institutions, at best, can reduce the uncertainty of the personal element, by assisting those who work for the aims for which the institutions are designed, and on whose personal initiative and knowledge success largely depends. (Institutions are like fortresses. They must be well designed *and* properly manned.)'[9]

The characteristic approach of the piecemeal engineer is this. Even though he may perhaps cherish some ideals which concern society 'as a whole' – its general welfare, perhaps – he does not believe in the method of redesigning it as a whole. Whatever his ends, he tries to achieve them by small adjustments and re-adjustments which can be continually improved upon. His ends may be of diverse kinds, for example, the accumulation of wealth or of power by certain individuals, or by certain groups; or the distribution of wealth and power; or the protection of certain 'rights' of individuals or groups, etc. Thus public or political social engineering may have the most diverse tendencies, totalitarian as well as liberal. (Examples of far-reaching liberal programmes for piecemeal reform have been given by W. Lippmann, under the title 'The Agenda of Liberalism'.[10]) The piecemeal engineer knows, like Socrates, how little he knows. He knows that we can learn only from our mistakes. Accordingly, he will make his way, step by step, carefully comparing the results expected with the results achieved, and always on the look-out for the unavoidable unwanted consequences of any reform; and he will avoid undertaking reforms of a complexity and scope which make it impossible for him to disentangle causes and effects, and to know what he is really doing.

Such 'piecemeal tinkering' does not agree with the political temperament of many 'activists'. Their programme, which too has been described as a programme of 'social engineering', may be called 'holistic' or 'Utopian engineering'.

Holistic or Utopian social engineering, as opposed to piecemeal social engineering, is never of a 'private' but always of a 'public' character. It aims at remodelling the 'whole of society' in accordance with a definite plan or blueprint; it aims at 'seizing the key positions'[11] and at extending 'the power of the State ... until the State becomes nearly identical with society', and it aims, furthermore, at controlling from these 'key positions' the historical forces that mould the future of the developing society: either by arresting this development, or else by foreseeing its course and adjusting society to it.

It may be questioned, perhaps, whether the piecemeal and the holistic approaches here described are fundamentally different, considering that we have put no limits to the scope of a piecemeal approach. As this approach is understood here, constitutional reform, for example, falls well within its scope; nor shall I exclude the possibility that a series of piecemeal reforms might be inspired by one general tendency, for example, a tendency towards a greater equalization of incomes. In this way, piecemeal methods may lead to changes in what is usually called the 'class structure of society'. Is there any difference, it may be asked, between these more ambitious kinds of piecemeal engineering and the holistic or Utopian approach? And this question may become even more pertinent if we consider that, when trying to assess the likely consequences of some proposed reform, the piecemeal technologist must do his best to estimate the effects of any measure upon the 'whole' of society.

In answering this question, I shall not attempt to draw a precise line of demarcation between the two methods, but I shall try to bring out the very different points of view from which the holist and the piecemeal technologist look upon the task of reforming society. The holists reject the piecemeal approach as being too modest. Their rejection of it, however, does not quite square with their practice; for in practice they always fall back on a somewhat haphazard and clumsy although ambitious and ruthless application of what is essentially a piecemeal method without its cautious and self-critical character. The reason is that, in practice, the holistic method turns out to be impossible; the greater the holistic changes attempted, the greater are their unintended and largely unexpected repercussions, forcing upon the holistic engineer the expedient of piecemeal *improvisation*. In fact, this expedient is more characteristic of centralized or collectivistic planning than of the more modest and careful piecemeal intervention; and it continually leads the Utopian engineer to do things which he did not intend to do; that is to say, it leads to the notorious phenomenon of *unplanned planning*. Thus the difference between Utopian and piecemeal engineering turns out, in practice, to be a difference not so much in scale and scope as in caution and in preparedness for unavoidable surprises. One could also say that, in practice, the two *methods* differ in other ways than in scale and scope – in opposition to what we are led to expect if we compare the two *doctrines* concerning the proper methods of rational social reform. Of these two doctrines, I hold that the one is true, while the other is false and liable to lead to mistakes which are both avoidable and grave. Of the two methods, I hold that one is possible, while the other simply does not exist: it is impossible.

One of the differences between the Utopian or holistic approach and the piecemeal approach may therefore be stated in this way: while the piecemeal engineer can attack his problem with an open mind as to the scope of the reform, the holist cannot do this; for he has decided beforehand that a complete reconstruction is possible and necessary. This fact has far-reaching consequences. It prejudices the Utopianist against certain sociological hypotheses which state limits to institutional control; for example, the one mentioned above in this section, expressing the uncertainty due to the personal element, the 'human factor'. By a rejection *a priori* of such hypotheses, the Utopian approach violates the principles of scientific method. On the other hand, problems connected with the uncertainty of the human factor must force the Utopianist, whether he likes it or not, to try to control the human factor by institutional means, and to extend his programme so as to embrace not only the transformation of society, according to plan, but also the transformation of man.[12] 'The political problem, therefore, is to *organize human impulses* in such a way that they will direct their energy to the right strategic points, and steer the total process of development in the desired direction.' It seems to escape the wellmeaning Utopianist that this programme implies an admission of failure, even before he launches it. For it substitutes for his demand that we build a new society, fit for men and women to live in, the demand that we 'mould' these men and women to fit into his new society. This, clearly, removes any possibility of testing the success or failure of the new society. For those who do not like living in it only admit thereby that they are not yet fit to live in it; that their 'human impulses' need further 'organizing'. But without the possibility of tests, any claim that a 'scientific' method is being employed evaporates. The holistic approach is incompatible with a truly scientific attitude.

III The Holistic Theory of Social Experiments

Holistic thinking is particularly detrimental in its influence upon the historicist theory of social experiments. Although the piecemeal technologist will agree with the historicist view that large-scale or holistic social experiments, if at all possible, are extremely unsuitable for scientific purposes, he will emphatically deny the assumption, common to both historicism and Utopianism, that social experiments, in order to be realistic, must be of the character of Utopian attempts at remodelling the whole of society.

It is convenient to begin our criticism with the discussion of a very obvious objection to the Utopian programme, namely that we do not possess the experimental knowledge needed for such an undertaking. The blueprints of the physical engineer are based on an experimental technology; all the principles that underlie his activities are tested by practical experiments. But the holistic blueprints of the social engineer are not based on any comparable practical experience. Thus the alleged analogy between physical engineering and holistic social engineering breaks down; holistic planning is rightly described as 'Utopian', since the scientific basis of its plans is simply nowhere.

Faced with this criticism, the Utopian engineer is likely to admit the need for practical experience, and for an experimental technology. But he will claim that we shall never know anything about these matters if we shrink from making social experiments, or, what in his view amounts to the same thing, from holistic engineering. We must make a beginning, he will argue, using whatever knowledge we possess, be it great or small. If we have some knowledge of aircraft designing today, it is only because some pioneer who did not possess this knowledge dared to design an aircraft and to try it out. Thus the Utopianist may even contend that the holistic method which he advocates is nothing but the experimental method applied to society. For he holds, in common with the historicist, that small-scale experiments, such as an experiment in socialism carried out in a factory or in a village or even in a district, would be quite inconclusive; such isolated 'Robinson Crusoe experiments' cannot tell us anything about modern social life in the 'Great Society'. They even deserve the nickname 'Utopian' in the (Marxist) sense in which this term implies the neglect of historical tendencies. (The implication in this case would be that the tendency towards an increasing interdependence of social life is being neglected.)

We see that Utopianism and historicism agree in the view that *a social experiment (if there is such a thing) could be of value only if carried out on a holistic scale*. This widely held prejudice involves the belief that we are seldom in the position to carry out 'planned experiments' in the social field, and that, for an account of the results of 'chance experiments', so far carried out in this field, we have to turn to *history*.[13]

I have two objections against this view: (1) that it overlooks those *piecemeal experiments* which are fundamental for all social knowledge, pre-scientific as well as scientific; (2) that *holistic experiments* are unlikely to contribute much to our experimental knowledge; and that they can be called 'experiments' only in the sense in which this term is synonymous with *an action whose outcome is uncertain*, but not in the sense in which this term is used to denote *a means of acquiring knowledge, by comparing the results obtained with the results expected*.

Concerning (1) it may be pointed out that the holistic view of social experiments leaves unexplained the fact that we possess a very great deal of experimental knowledge of social life. There is a difference between an experienced and an unexperienced business man, or organizer, or politician, or general. It is a difference in their social experience; and in experience gained not merely through observation, or by reflecting upon what they have observed, but by efforts to achieve some practical aim. It must be admitted that the knowledge attained in this way is usually of a pre-scientific kind, and therefore more like knowledge gained by casual observation than knowledge gained by carefully designed scientific experiments; but this is no reason for denying that the knowledge in question is based on experiment rather than on mere observation. A grocer who opens a new shop is conducting a social experiment; and even a man who joins a queue before a theatre gains experimental technological knowledge which he may utilize by having his seat reserved next time, which again is a social experiment. And we should not forget that only practical experiments have taught buyers and sellers on the markets the lesson that prices are liable to be lowered by every increase of supply, and raised by every increase of demand.

Examples of piecemeal experiments on a somewhat larger scale would be the decision of a monopolist to change the price of his product; the introduction, whether by a private or a public insurance company, of a new type of health or employment insurance; or the introduction of a new sales tax, or of a policy to combat trade cycles. All these experiments are carried out with practical rather than scientific aims in view. Moreover, experiments have been carried out by some large firms with the deliberate aim of increasing their knowledge of the market (in order to increase profits at a later stage, of course) rather than with the aim of increasing their profits immediately.[14] The situation is very similar to that of physical engineering and to the pre-scientific methods by which our technological knowledge in matters such as the building of ships or the art of navigation was first acquired. There seems to be no reason why these methods should not be improved on, and ultimately replaced by a more scientifically minded technology; that is to say, by a more systematic approach in the same direction, based on critical thought as well as on experiment.

According to this piecemeal view, there is no clearly marked division between the pre-scientific and the scientific experimental approaches, even though the more and more conscious application of scientific, that is to say, of critical methods, is of great importance. Both approaches may be described, fundamentally, as utilizing the method of trial and error. We try; that is, we do not merely register an observation, but make active attempts to solve some more or less practical and definite problems. And we make progress if, and only if, we are prepared to *learn from our mistakes*: to recognize our errors and to utilize them critically instead of persevering in them dogmatically. Though this analysis may sound trivial, it describes, I believe, the method of all empirical sciences. This method assumes a more and more scientific character the more freely and consciously we are prepared to risk a trial, and the more critically we watch for the mistakes we always make. And this formula covers not only the method of experiment, but also the relationship between theory and experiment. All theories are trials; they are tentative hypotheses, tried out to see whether they work;

and all experimental corroboration is simply the result of tests undertaken in a critical spirit, in an attempt to find out where our theories err.[15]

For the piecemeal technologist or engineer these views mean that, if he wishes to introduce scientific methods into the study of society and into politics, what is needed most is the adoption of a critical attitude, and the realization that not only trial but also error is necessary. And he must learn not only to expect mistakes, but consciously to search for them. We all have an unscientific weakness for being always in the right, and this weakness seems to be particularly common among professional and amateur politicians. But the only way to apply something like scientific method in politics is to proceed on the assumption that there can be no political move which has no drawbacks, no undesirable consequences. To look out for these mistakes, to find them, to bring them into the open, to analyse them, and to learn from them, this is what a scientific politician as well as a political scientist must do. Scientific method in politics means that the great art of convincing ourselves that we have not made any mistakes, of ignoring them, of hiding them, and of blaming others for them, is replaced by the greater art of accepting the responsibilty for them, of trying to learn from them, and of applying this knowledge so that we may avoid them in the future.

We now turn to point (2), the criticism of the view that we can learn from holistic experiments, or more precisely, from measures carried out on a scale that approaches the holistic dream (for holistic experiments in the radical sense that they remodel 'the whole of society' are logically impossible). Our main point is very simple: it is difficult enough to be critical of our own mistakes, but it must be nearly impossible for us to persist in a critical attitude towards those of our actions which involve the lives of many men. To put it differently, it is very hard to learn from very big mistakes.

The reasons for this are twofold; they are technical as well as moral. Since so much is done at a time, it is impossible to say which particular measure is responsible for any of the results; or rather, if we do attribute a certain result to a certain measure, then we can do so only on the basis of some theoretical knowledge gained previously, and not from the holistic experiment in question. This experiment does not help us to attribute particular results to particular measures; all we can do is to attribute the 'whole result' to it; and whatever this may mean, it is certainly difficult to assess. Even the greatest efforts to secure a well-informed, independent, and critical statement of these results are unlikely to prove successful. But the chances that such efforts will be made are negligible; on the contrary, there is every likelihood that free discussion about the holistic plan and its consequences will not be tolerated. The reason is that every attempt at planning on a very large scale is an undertaking which must cause considerable inconvenience to many people, to put it mildly, and over a considerable span of time. Accordingly there will always be a tendency to oppose the plan, and to complain about it. To many of these complaints the Utopian engineer will have to turn a deaf ear if he wishes to get anywhere at all; in fact, it will be part of his business to suppress unreasonable objections. But with them he must invariably suppress reasonable criticism too. And the mere fact that expressions of dissatisfaction will have to be curbed reduces even the most enthusiastic expression of satisfaction to insignificance. Thus it will be difficult to ascertain the facts, i.e. the repercussions of the plan on the individual citizen; and without these facts scientific criticism is impossible.

But the difficulty of combining holistic planning with scientific methods is still more fundamental than has so far been indicated. The holistic planner overlooks the fact that it is easy to centralize power but impossible to centralize all that knowledge which is distributed over many individual minds, and whose centralization would be necessary for the wise wielding of centralized power [see note 6 to this selection]. But this fact has far-reaching consequences. Unable to ascertain what it is in the minds of so many individuals, he must try to simplify his problems by eliminating individual differences: he must try to control and stereotype interests and beliefs by education and propaganda.[16] But this attempt to exercise power over minds must destroy the last possibility of finding out what people really think, for it is clearly incompatible with the free expression of thought, especially of critical thought. Ultimately, it must destroy knowledge; and the greater the gain in power, the greater will be the loss of knowledge. (Political power and social knowledge may thus be discovered to be 'complementary' in Bohr's sense of the term. And it may even turn out to be the only clear illustration of this elusive but fashionable term.)[17]

All these remarks are confined to the problem of scientific method. They tacitly grant the colossal assumption that we need not question the fundamental benevolence of the planning Utopian engineer, who is vested with an authority which at least approaches dictatorial powers. Tawney concludes a discussion of Luther and his time with the words: 'Sceptical as to the existence of unicorns and salamanders, the age of Machiavelli and Henry VIII found food for its credulity in the worship of that rare monster, the God-fearing Prince.'[18] Replace here the words 'unicorns and salamanders' by 'the God-fearing Prince'; replace the two names by those of some of their more obvious modern counterparts, and the phrase 'the God-fearing Prince' by 'the benevolent planning authority': and you have a description of the credulity of our own time. This credulity will not be challenged here; yet it may be remarked that, assuming the unlimited and unvarying benevolence of the powerful planners, our analysis shows that it may be impossible for them ever to find out whether the results of their measures tally with their good intentions.

I do not believe that any corresponding criticism of the piecemeal method can be offered. This method can be used, more particularly, in order to search for, and fight against, the greatest and most urgent evils of society, rather than to seek, and to fight for, some ultimate good (as holists are inclined to do). But a systematic fight against definite wrongs, against concrete forms of injustice or exploitation, and avoidable suffering such as poverty or unemployment, is a very different thing from the attempt to realize a distant ideal blueprint of society. Success or failure is more easily appraised, and there is no inherent reason why this method should lead to an accumulation of power and to the suppression of criticism. Also, such a fight against concrete wrongs and concrete dangers is more likely to find the support of a great majority than a fight for the establishment of a Utopia, ideal as it may appear to the planners. This may perhaps throw some light on the fact that in democratic countries defending themselves against aggression, sufficient support may be forthcoming for the necessary far-reaching measures (which may even take on the character of holistic planning) *without suppression of public criticism*, while in countries preparing for an attack or waging an aggressive war, public criticism as a rule must be suppressed, in order that public support may be mobilized by presenting aggression as defence.

We may now turn back to the Utopianist's claim that his method is the true experimental method applied to the field of sociology. This claim, I think, is dispelled by our criticism. This can be further illustrated by the analogy between physical and holistic engineering. It may be admitted that physical machines can be successfully planned by way of blueprints, and with them, even a whole plant for their production, etc. But all this is possible only because many piecemeal experiments have been carried out beforehand. Every machine is the result of a great many small improvements. Every model must be 'developed' by the method of trial and error, by countless small adjustments. The same holds for the planning of the production plant. The apparently holistic plan can succeed only because we have made all kinds of small mistakes already; otherwise there is every reason to expect that it would lead to big mistakes.

Thus the analogy between physical and social engineering, if looked into more closely, turns against the holist and in favour of the piecemeal social engineer. The expression 'social engineering', which alludes to this analogy, has been usurped by the Utopianist without a shadow of right.

25 The Paradoxes of Sovereignty (1945)

> The wise shall lead and rule, and the ignorant shall follow.
>
> PLATO

Plato's idea of justice demands, fundamentally, that the natural rulers should rule and the natural slaves should slave.[1] It is part of the historicist demand that the state, in order to arrest all change, should be a copy of its Idea, or of its true 'nature'. This theory of justice indicates very clearly that Plato saw the fundamental problem of politics in the question: *Who shall rule the state?*

I

It is my conviction that by expressing the problem of politics in the form 'Who should rule?' or 'Whose will should be supreme?', etc., Plato created a lasting confusion in political philosophy. It is indeed analogous to the confusion he created in the field of moral philosophy by his identification [discussed in selection 27] of collectivism and altruism. It is clear that once the question 'Who should rule?' is asked, it is hard to avoid some such reply as 'the best' or 'the wisest' or 'the born ruler' or 'he who masters the art of ruling' (or, perhaps, 'The General Will' or 'The Master Race' or 'The Industrial Workers' or 'The People'). But such a reply, convincing as it may sound – for who would advocate the rule of 'the worst' or 'the greatest fool' or 'the born slave'? – is, as I shall try to show, quite useless.

First of all, such a reply is liable to persuade us that some fundamental problem of political theory has been solved. But if we approach political theory from a different angle, then we find that far from solving any fundamental problems, we have merely skipped over them, by assuming that the question 'Who should rule?' is fundamental. For even those who share this assumption of Plato's admit that political rulers are not always sufficiently 'good' or 'wise' (we need not worry about the precise meaning of these terms), and that it is not at all easy to get a government on whose goodness and wisdom one can implicitly rely. If that is granted, then we must ask whether political thought should not face from the beginning the possibility of bad government; whether we should not prepare for the worst leaders, and hope for the best. But this leads to a new approach to the problem of politics, for it forces us to replace the question: *Who should rule?* by the new[2] question: *How can we so organize political institutions that bad or incompetent rulers can be prevented from doing too much damage?*

Those who believe that the older question is fundamental, tacitly assume that political power is 'essentially' unchecked. They assume that someone has the power – either an individual or a collective body, such as a class. And they assume that he who has the power can, very nearly, do what he wills, and especially that he can strengthen his power, and thereby approximate it further to an unlimited or unchecked power. They assume that political power is, essentially, sovereign. If this assumption is made, then, indeed, the question 'Who is to be the sovereign?' is the only important question left.

I shall call this assumption the *theory of (unchecked) sovereignty*, using this expression not for any particular one of the various theories of sovereignty, proffered more especially by such writers as Bodin, Rousseau, or Hegel, but for the more general assumption that political power is practically unchecked, or for the demand that it ought to be so; together with the implication that the main question left is to get this power into the best hands. This theory of sovereignty is tacitly assumed in Plato's approach, and has played its role ever since. It is also implicitly assumed, for instance, by those modern writers who believe that the main problem is: Who should dictate? The capitalists or the workers?

Without entering into a detailed criticism, I wish to point out that there are serious objections against a rash and implicit acceptance of this theory. Whatever its speculative merits may appear to be, it is certainly a very unrealistic assumption. No political power has ever been unchecked, and as long as men remain human (as long as the 'Brave New World' has not materialized), there can be no absolute and unrestrained political power. So long as one man cannot accumulate enough physical power in his hands to dominate all others, just so long must he depend upon his helpers. Even the most powerful tyrant depends upon his secret police, his henchmen and his hangmen. This dependence means that his power, great as it may be, is not unchecked, and that he has to make concessions, playing one group off against another. It means that there are other political forces, other powers besides his own, and that he can exert his rule only by utilizing and pacifying them. This shows that even the extreme cases of sovereignty are never cases of pure sovereignty. They are never cases in which the will or the interest of one man (or, if there were such a thing, the will or the interest of one group) can achieve his aim directly, without giving up some of it in order to enlist powers which he cannot conquer. And in an overwhelming number of cases, the limitations of political power go much further than this.

I have stressed these empirical points, not because I wish to use them as an argument, but merely in order to avoid objections. My claim is that every theory of sovereignty omits to face a more fundamental question – the question, namely, whether we should not strive towards institutional control of the rulers by balancing their powers against other powers. This *theory of checks and balances* can at least claim careful consideration. The only objections to this claim, as far as I can see, are (1) that such a control is *practically* impossible, or (2) that it is *essentially* inconceivable since political power is essentially sovereign.[3] Both of these dogmatic objections are, I believe, refuted by the facts; and with them fall a number of other influential views (for instance, the theory that the only alternative to the dictatorship of one class is that of another class).

In order to raise the question of institutional control of the rulers, we need not assume more than that governments are not always good or wise. But since I have said something about historical facts, I think I should confess that I feel inclined to go a little beyond this assumption. I am inclined to think that rulers have rarely been above the average, either morally or intellectually, and often below it. And I think that it is reasonable to adopt, in politics, the principle of preparing for the worst, as well as we can, though we should, of course, at the same time try to obtain the best. It appears to me madness to base all our political efforts upon the faint hope that we shall be successful in obtaining excellent, or even competent, rulers. Strongly as I feel in these matters, I must insist, however, that my criticism of the theory of sovereignty does not depend on these more personal opinions.

Apart from these personal opinions, and apart from the above mentioned empirical arguments against the general theory of sovereignty, there is also a kind of logical argument which can be used to show the inconsistency of any of the particular forms of the theory of sovereignty; more precisely, the logical argument can be given different but analogous forms to combat the theory that the wisest should rule, or else the theories that the best, or the law, or the majority, etc., should rule. One particular form of this logical argument is directed against a too naïve version of liberalism, of democracy, and of the principle that the majority should rule; and it is somewhat similar to the well-known '*paradox of freedom*' which was used first, and with success, by Plato. In his criticism of democracy, and in his story of the rise of the tyrant, Plato raises implicitly the following question: What if it is the will of the people that they should not rule, but a tyrant instead? The free man, Plato suggests, may exercise his absolute freedom, first by defying the laws and ultimately by defying freedom itself and by clamouring for a tyrant.[4] This is not just a far-fetched possibility; it has happened a number of times; and every time it has happened, it has put in a hopeless intellectual position all those democrats who adopt, as the ultimate basis of their political creed, the principle of majority rule or a similar form of the principle of sovereignty. On the one hand, the principle they have adopted demands from them that they should oppose any but the majority rule, and therefore the new tyranny; on the other hand, the same principle demands from them that they should accept any decision reached by the majority, and thus the rule of the new tyrant. The inconsistency of their theory must, of course, paralyse their actions.[5] Those of us democrats who demand the institutional control of the rulers by the ruled, and especially the right of dismissing the government by a majority vote, must therefore base these demands upon better grounds than a self-contradictory theory of sovereignty. (That this is possible will be briefly shown in the next section.)

Plato, we have seen, came near to discovering the paradoxes of freedom and of democracy. But what Plato and his followers overlooked is that all the other forms of the theory of sovereignty give rise to analogous inconsistencies. *All theories of sovereignty are paradoxical.* For instance, we may have selected 'the wisest' or 'the best' as a ruler. But 'the wisest' in his wisdom may find that not he but 'the best' should rule, and 'the best' in his goodness may perhaps decide that 'the majority' should rule. It is important to notice that even that form of the theory of sovereignty which demands the 'Kingship of the Law' is open to the same objection. This, in fact, was seen very early, as Heraclitus's remark[6] shows: 'The law can demand, too, that the will of One Man must be obeyed.'

In summing up this brief criticism, one can, I believe, assert that the theory of sovereignty is in a weak position, both empirically and logically. The least that can be demanded is that it must not be adopted without careful consideration of other possibilities.

II

And indeed, it is not difficult to show that a theory of democratic control can be developed which is free of the paradox of sovereignty. The theory I have in mind is one which does not proceed, as it were, from a doctrine of the intrinsic goodness or righteousness of a majority rule, but rather from the baseness of tyranny; or more precisely, it rests upon the decision, or upon the adoption of the proposal, to avoid and to resist tyranny.

For we may distinguish two main types of government. The first type consists of governments which we can get rid of without bloodshed – for example, by way of general elections; that is to say, the social institutions provide means by which the rulers may be dismissed by the ruled, and the social traditions[7] ensure that these institutions will not easily be destroyed by those who are in power. The second type consists of governments which the ruled cannot get rid of except by way of a successful revolution – that is to say, in most cases, not at all. I suggest the term 'democracy' as a shorthand label for a government of the the first type, and the term 'tyranny' or 'dictatorship' for the second. This, I believe, corresponds closely to traditional usage. But I wish to make clear that no part of my argument depends on the choice of these labels; and should anybody reverse this usage (as is frequently done nowadays), then I should simply say that I am in favour of what he calls 'tyranny', and object to what he calls 'democracy'; and I should reject as irrelevant any attempt to discover what 'democracy' 'really' or 'essentially' means, for example, by translating the term into 'the rule of the people'. (For although 'the people' may influence the actions of their rulers by the threat of dismissal, they never rule themselves in any concrete, practical sense. [See also p. 96 above.])

If we make use of the two labels as suggested, then we can now describe, as the principle of a democratic policy, the proposal to create, develop, and protect, political institutions for the avoidance of tyranny. This principle does not imply that we can ever develop institutions of this kind which are faultless or foolproof, or which ensure that the policies adopted by a democratic government will be right or good or wise – or even necessarily better or wiser than the policies adopted by a benevolent tyrant. (Since no such assertions are made, the paradox of democracy is avoided.) What may be said, however, to be implied in the adoption of the democratic principle is the conviction that the acceptance of even a bad policy in a democracy (as long as we can work for a peaceful change) is preferable to the submission to a tyranny, however wise or benevolent. Seen in this light, the theory of democracy is not based upon the principle that the majority should rule; rather, the various equalitarian methods of democratic control, such as general elections and representative government, are to be considered as no more than well-tried and, in the presence of a widespread traditional distrust of tyranny, reasonably effective institutional safeguards against tyranny, always open to improvement, and even providing methods for their own improvement.

He who accepts the principle of democracy in this sense is therefore not bound to look upon the result of a democratic vote as an authoritative expression of what is right. Although he will accept a decision of the majority, for the sake of making the democratic institutions work, he will feel free to combat it by democratic means, and to work for its revision. And should he live to see the day when the majority vote destroys the democratic institutions, then this sad experience will tell him only that there does not exist a foolproof method of avoiding tyranny. But it need not weaken his decision to fight tyranny, nor will it expose his theory as inconsistent.

26 Marx's Theory of the State (1945)

I

The legal or juridico-political system – the system of legal institutions enforced by the state – has to be understood, according to Marx, as one of the superstructures erected upon, and giving expression to, the actual productive forces of the economic system; Marx speaks[1] in this connection of 'juridical and political superstructures'. It is not, of course, the only way in which the economic or material reality and the relations between the classes which correspond to it make their appearance in the world of ideologies and ideas. Another example of such a superstructure would be, according to Marxist views, the prevailing moral system. This, as opposed to the legal system, is not enforced by state power, but sanctioned by an ideology created and controlled by the ruling class. The difference is, roughly, one between persuasion and force (as Plato[2] would have said); and it is the state, the legal or political system, which uses force. It is, as Engels[3] puts it, 'a special repressive force' for the coercion of the ruled by the rulers. 'Political power, properly so called,' says the *Manifesto*, 'is merely the organized power of one class for oppressing another.'[4] A similar description is given by Lenin: 'According to Marx, the state is an organ of class *domination*, an organ for the oppression of one class by another; its aim is the creation of an "order" which legalizes and perpetuates this oppression. . . .'[5] The state, in brief, is just part of the machinery by which the ruling class carries on its struggle.

Before proceeding to develop the consequences of this view of the state, it may be pointed out that it is partly an institutional and partly an essentialist theory. It is institutional in so far as Marx tries to ascertain what practical functions legal institutions have in social life. But it is essentialist in so far as Marx neither inquires into the variety of ends which these institutions may possibly serve (or be made to serve), nor suggests what institutional reforms are necessary in order to make the state serve those ends which he himself might deem desirable. Instead of making his demands or proposals concerning the functions which he wants the state, the legal institutions or the government to perform, he asks, '*What is* the state?'; that is to say, he tries to discover the *essential* function of legal institutions. It has been shown before [in selection 6 above] that such a typically essentialist question cannot be answered in a satisfactory way; yet this question, undoubtedly, is in keeping with Marx's essentialist and metaphysical approach which interprets the field of ideas and norms as the mere appearance on the face of an economic reality.

What are the consequences of this theory of the state? The most important consequence is that all politics, all legal and political institutions as well as all political struggles, can never be of primary importance. *Politics is impotent.* It can never alter decisively the economic reality. The main if not the only task of any enlightened political activity is to see that the alterations in the juridico-political cloak keep pace with the changes in the social reality, that is to say, in the means of production and in the relations between the classes; in this way, such difficulties as must arise if politics lags behind these developments can be avoided. Or in other words, political developments are either superficial, unconditioned by the deeper reality of the social system, in which case they are doomed to be unimportant, and can never be of real help to the suppressed and exploited; or else they give expression to a change in the economic background and the class situation, in which case they are of the character of volcanic eruptions, of complete revolutions which can perhaps be foreseen, as they arise from the social system, and whose ferocity might then be mitigated by non-resistance to the eruptive forces, but which can be neither caused nor suppressed by political action.

These consequences show again the unity of Marx's historicist system of thought. Yet considering that few movements have done as much as Marxism to stimulate interest in political action, the theory of the fundamental impotence of politics appears somewhat paradoxical. (Marxists might, of course, meet this remark with either of two arguments. The one is that in the theory expounded, political action *has* its function; for even though the workers' party cannot, by its actions, improve the lot of the exploited masses, its fight awakens class consciousness and thereby prepares for the revolution. This would be the argument of the radical wing. The other argument, used by the moderate wing, asserts that there may exist historical periods in which political action can be directly helpful; the periods, namely, in which the forces of the two opposing classes are approximately in equilibrium. In such periods, political effort and energy may be decisive in achieving very significant improvements for the workers. – It is clear that this second argument sacrifices some of the fundamental positions of the theory, but without realizing this, and consequently without going to the root of the matter.)

It is worth noting that according to Marxist theory, the workers' party can hardly make political mistakes of any importance, as long as the party continues to play its assigned role, and to press the claims of the workers energetically. For political mistakes cannot materially affect the actual class situation, and even less the economic reality on which everything else ultimately depends.

Another important consequence of the theory is that, in principle, all government, even democratic government, is a dictatorship of the ruling class over the ruled. 'The executive of the modern state', says the *Manifesto*, 'is merely a committee for managing the economic affairs of the whole bourgeoisie. . . .'[6] What we call a democracy is, according to this theory, nothing but that form of class dictatorship which happens to be most convenient in a certain historical situation. (This doctrine does not agree very well with the class equilibrium theory of the moderate wing mentioned above.) And just as the state, under capitalism, is a dictatorship of the bourgeoisie, so, after the social revolution, it will at first be a dictatorship of the proletariat. But this proletarian state must lose its function as soon as the resistance of the old bourgeoisie has broken down. For the proletarian revolution leads to a one-class society, and therefore to a classless society in which there can be no class dictatorship. Thus the state, deprived of any function, must disappear. '*It withers away*', as Engels said.[7]

II

The contrast between the legal and the social system is most clearly developed in *Capital*. In one of its theoretical parts, Marx approaches the analysis of the capitalist economic system by using the simplifying and idealizing assumption that the legal system is perfect in every respect. Freedom, equality before the law, justice, are all assumed to be guaranteed to everybody. There are no privileged classes before the law. Over and above that, he assumes that not even in the economic realm is there any kind of 'robbery'; he assumes that a 'just price' is paid for all commodities, including the labour power which the worker sells to the capitalist on the labour market. The price for all these commodities is 'just', in the sense that all commodities are bought and sold in proportion to the average amount of labour needed for their reproduction (or using Marx's terminology, they are bought and sold according to their true 'value').[8] Of course, Marx knows that all this is an oversimplification, for it is his opinion that the workers are hardly ever treated as fairly as that; in other words, that they are usually cheated. But arguing from these idealized premises, he attempts to show that even under so excellent a legal system, the economic system would function in such a way that the workers would not be able to enjoy their freedom. In spite of all this 'justice', they would not be very much better off than slaves.[9] For if they are poor, they can only sell themselves, their wives, and their children on the labour market, for as much as is necessary for the reproduction of their labour power. That is to say, for the whole of their labour power, they will not get more than the barest means of existence. This shows that exploitation is not merely robbery. It cannot be eliminated by merely legal means. (And Proudhon's criticism that 'property is theft' is much too superficial.[10])

In consequence of this, Marx was led to hold that the workers cannot hope much from the improvement of a legal system which as everybody knows grants to rich and poor alike the freedom of sleeping on park benches, and which threatens them alike with punishment for the attempt to live 'without visible means of support'. In this way Marx arrived at what may be termed (in Hegelian language) the distinction between *formal* and *material* freedom. Formal[11] or legal freedom, although Marx does not rate it low, turns out to be quite insufficient for securing to us that freedom which he considered to be the aim of the historical development of mankind. What matters is real, i.e. economic or material, freedom. This can be achieved only by an equal emancipation from drudgery. For this emancipation, 'the shortening of the labour day is the fundamental prerequisite'.

III

What have we to say to Marx's analysis? Are we to believe that politics, or the framework of legal institutions, is intrinsically impotent to remedy such a situation, and that only a complete social revolution, a complete change of the 'social system', can help? Or are we to believe the defenders of an unrestrained 'capitalist' system who emphasize (rightly, I think) the tremendous benefit to be derived from the mechanism of free markets, and who conclude from this that a truly free labour market would be of the greatest benefit to all concerned?

I believe that the injustice and inhumanity of the unrestrained 'capitalist system' described by Marx cannot be questioned: but it can be interpreted in terms of what we called [in the previous selection] the *paradox of freedom*. Freedom, we have seen, defeats itself, if it is unlimited. Unlimited freedom means that a strong man is free to bully one who is weak and to rob him of his freedom. This is why we demand that the state should limit freedom to a certain extent, so that everyone's freedom is protected by law. Nobody should be at the *mercy* of others, but all should have a *right* to be protected by the state.

Now I believe that these considerations, originally meant to apply to the realm of brute force, of physical intimidation, must be applied to the economic realm also. Even if the state protects its citizens from being bullied by physical violence (as it does, in principle, under the system of unrestrained capitalism), it may defeat our ends by its failure to protect them from the misuse of economic power. In such a state, the economically strong is still free to bully one who is economically weak, and to rob him of his freedom. Under these circumstances, unlimited economic freedom can be just as self-defeating as unlimited physical freedom, and economic power may be nearly as dangerous as physical violence; for those who possess a surplus of food can force those who are starving into a 'freely' accepted servitude, without using violence. And assuming that the state limits its activities to the suppression of violence (and to the protection of property), a minority which is economically strong may in this way exploit the majority of those who are economically weak.

If this analysis is correct,[12] then the nature of the remedy is clear. It must be a *political* remedy – a remedy similar to the one which we use against physical violence. We must construct social institutions, enforced by the power of the state, for the protection of the economically weak from the economically strong. The state must see to it that nobody need enter into an inequitable arrangement out of fear of starvation, or economic ruin.

This, of course, means that the principle of non-intervention, of an unrestrained economic system, has to be given up; if we wish freedom to be safeguarded, then we must demand that the policy of unlimited economic freedom be replaced by the planned economic intervention of the state. We must demand that unrestrained *capitalism* give way to an *economic interventionism.*[13] And this is precisely what has happened. The economic system described and criticized by Marx has everywhere ceased to exist. It has been replaced, not by a system in which the state begins to lose its functions and consequently 'shows signs of withering away', but by various interventionist systems, in which the functions of the state in the economic realm are extended far beyond the protection of property and of 'free contracts'.

IV

I should like to characterize the point here reached as the most central point in my analysis of Marxism. It is only here that we can begin to realize the significance of the clash between historicism and social engineering [discussed in selection 24], and its effect upon the policy of the friends of the open society.

Marxism claims to be more than a science. It does more than make a historical prophecy. It claims to be the basis for practical political action. It criticizes existing society, and it asserts that it can lead the way to a better world. But according to Marx's own theory, we cannot at will alter the economic reality by, for example, legal reforms. Politics can do no more than 'shorten and lessen the birth pangs'.[14] This, I think, is an extremely poor political programme, and its poverty is a consequence of the third-rate place which it attributes to political power in the hierarchy of powers. For according to Marx, the real power lies in the evolution of machinery; next in importance is the system of economic class relationships; and the least important influence is that of politics.

A directly opposite view is implied in the position we have reached in our analysis. It considers political power as fundamental. Political power, from this point of view, can control economic power. This means an immense extension of the field of political activities. We can ask what we wish to achieve and how to achieve it. We can, for instance, develop a rational political programme for the protection of the economically weak. We can make laws to limit exploitation. We can limit the working day; but we can do much more. By law, we can insure the workers (or better still, all citizens) against disability, unemployment, and old age. In this way we can make impossible such forms of exploitation as are based upon the helpless economic position of a worker who must yield to anything in order not to starve. And when we are able by law to guarantee a livelihood to everybody willing to work, and there is no reason why we should not achieve that, then the protection of the freedom of the citizen from economic fear and economic intimidation will approach completeness. From this point of view, political power is the key to economic protection. Political power and its control are everything. Economic power must not be permitted to dominate political power; if necessary, it must be fought and brought under control by political power.

From the point of view reached, we can say that Marx's disparaging attitude towards political power not only means that he neglects to develop a theory of the most important potential means of bettering the lot of the economically weak, but also that he neglects the greatest potential danger to human freedom. His naïve view that, in a classless society, state power would lose its function and 'wither away' shows very clearly that he never grasped the paradox of freedom, and that he never understood the function which state power could and should perform, in the service of freedom and humanity. (Yet this view of Marx stands witness to the fact that he was, ultimately, an individualist, in spite of his collectivist appeal to class consciousness.) In this way, the Marxian view is analogous to the liberal belief that all we need is 'equality of opportunity'. We certainly need this. But it is not enough. It does not protect those who are less gifted, or less ruthless, or less lucky, from becoming objects of exploitation for those who are more gifted, or ruthless, or lucky.

Moreover, from the point of view we have reached, what Marxists describe disparagingly as 'mere formal freedom' becomes the basis of everything else. This 'mere formal freedom', i.e. democracy, the right of the people to judge and to dismiss their government, is the only known device by which we can try to protect ourselves against the misuse of political power [see section II to selection 25 above]; it is the control of the rulers by the ruled. And since political power can control economic power, political democracy is also the only means for the control of economic power by the ruled. Without democratic control, there can be no earthly reason why any government should not use its political and economic power for purposes very different from the protection of the freedom of its citizens.

V

It is the fundamental role of 'formal freedom' which is overlooked by Marxists who think that formal democracy is not enough and wish to supplement it by what they usually call 'economic democracy'; a vague and utterly superficial phrase which obscures the fact that 'merely formal freedom' is the only guarantee of a democratic economic policy.

Marx discovered the significance of economic power; and it is understandable that he exaggerated its status. He and the Marxists see economic power everywhere. Their argument runs: he who has the money has the power; for if necessary, he can buy guns and even gangsters. But this is a roundabout argument. In fact, it contains an admission that the man who has the gun has the power. And if he who has the gun becomes aware of this, then it may not be long until he has both the gun and the money. But under an unrestrained capitalism, Marx's argument applies, to some extent; for a rule which develops institutions for the control of guns and gangsters but not of the power of money is liable to come under the influence of this power. In such a state, an uncontrolled gangsterism of wealth may rule. But Marx himself, I think, would have been the first to admit that this is not true of all states; that there have been times in history when, for example, all exploitation was looting, directly based upon the power of the mailed fist. And today there will be few to support the naïve view that the 'progress of history' has once and for all put an end to these more direct ways of exploiting men, and that, once formal freedom has been achieved, it is impossible for us to fall again under the sway of such primitive forms of exploitation.

These considerations should be sufficient for refuting the dogmatic doctrine that economic power is more fundamental than physical power, or the power of the state. The dogma that economic power is at the root of all evil must be discarded. Its place must be taken by an understanding of the dangers of *any* form of uncontrolled power. Money as such is not particularly dangerous. It becomes dangerous only if it can buy power, either directly, or by enslaving the economically weak who must sell themselves in order to live.

We must think in these matters in even more materialist terms, as it were, than Marx did. We must realize that the control of physical power and of physical exploitation remains the central political problem. In order to establish this control, we must establish 'merely formal freedom'. Once we have achieved this, and have learnt how to use it for the control of political power, everything rests with us. We must not blame anybody else any longer, nor cry out against the sinister economic demons behind the scenes. For in a democracy, we hold the keys to the control of the demons. We can tame them. We must realize this and use the keys; we must construct institutions for the democratic control of economic power, and for our protection from economic exploitation.

Much has been made by Marxists of the possibility of buying votes, either directly or by buying propaganda. But closer consideration shows that we have here a good example of the power-political situation analysed above. Once we have achieved formal freedom, we can control vote buying in every form. There are laws to limit the expenditure on electioneering, and it rests entirely with us to see that much more stringent laws of this kind are introduced. The legal system can be made a powerful instrument for its own protection. In addition, we can influence public opinion, and insist upon a much more rigid moral code in political matters. All this we can do; but we must first realize that social engineering of this kind is our task, that it is in our power, and that we must not wait for economic earthquakes miraculously to produce a new economic world for us, so that all we shall have to do will be to unveil it, to remove the old political cloak.

VI

Of course, in practice Marxists never fully relied on the doctrine of the impotence of political power. So far as they had an opportunity to act, or to plan action, they usually assumed, like everybody else, that political power can be used for the control of economic power. But their plans and actions were never based on a clear refutation of their original theory, nor upon any well-considered view of that most fundamental problem of all politics: the control of the controller, of the dangerous accumulation of power represented in the state. They never realized the full significance of democracy as the only known means to achieve this control.

As a consequence they never realized the danger inherent in a policy of increasing the power of the state. Although they abandoned more or less unconsciously the doctrine of the impotence of politics, they retained the view that state power presents no important problem, and that it is bad only if it is in the hands of the bourgeoisie. They did not realize that *all* power, and political power at least as much as economic power, is dangerous. Thus they retained their formula of the dictatorship of the proletariat. They did not understand the principle that all large-scale politics must be institutional, not personal; and when clamouring for the extension of state powers (in contrast to Marx's view of the state) they never considered that the wrong persons might one day get hold of these extended powers. This is part of the reason why, as far as they proceeded to consider state intervention, they planned to give the state practically limitless powers in the economic realm. They retained Marx's holistic and

Utopian belief that only a brand new 'social system' can improve matters.

I have criticized this Utopian and Romantic approach to social engineering [in selection 24].[15] But I wish to add here that economic intervention, even the piecemeal methods advocated here, will tend to increase the power of the state. Interventionism is therefore extremely dangerous. This is not a decisive argument against it; state power must always remain a dangerous though necessary evil. But it should be a warning that if we relax our watchfulness, and if we do not strengthen our democratic institutions while giving more power to the state by interventionist 'planning', then we may lose our freedom. And if freedom is lost, everything is lost, including 'planning'. For why should plans for the welfare of the people be carried out if the people have no power to enforce them? Only freedom can make security secure.

We thus see that there is not only a paradox of freedom but also a paradox of state planning. If we plan too much, if we give too much power to the state, then freedom will be lost, and that will be the end of planning.

Such considerations lead us back to our plea for piecemeal, and against Utopian or holistic, methods of social engineering. And they lead us back to our demand that measures should be planned to fight concrete evils rather than to establish some ideal good [see especially pp. 317f. above]. State intervention should be limited to what is really necessary for the protection of freedom.

But it is not enough to say that our solution should be a minimum solution; that we should be watchful; and that we should not give more power to the state than is necessary for the protection of freedom. These remarks may raise problems, but they do not show a way to a solution. It is even conceivable that there is no solution; that the acquisition of new economic powers by a state – whose powers, as compared to those of its citizens, are always dangerously great – will make it irresistible. So far, we have shown neither that freedom can be preserved, nor how it can be preserved.

Under these circumstances it may be useful to remember our earlier considerations concerning the question of the control of political power and the paradox of freedom.

VII

If we now look back at Marx's theory of the impotence of politics and of the power of historical forces, then we must admit that it is an imposing edifice. It is the direct result of his sociological method; of his economic historicism, of the doctrine that the development of the economic system, or of man's metabolism, determines his social and political development. The experience of his time, his humanitarian indignation, and the need of bringing to the oppressed the consolation of a prophecy, the hope, or even the certainty, of their victory, all this is united in one grandiose philosophic system, comparable or even superior to the holistic systems of Plato and Hegel. It is only due to the accident that he was not a reactionary that the history of philosophy takes so little notice of him and assumes that he was mainly a propagandist. The reviewer of *Capital* who wrote: 'At the first glance . . . we come to the conclusion that the author is one of the greatest among the idealist philosophers, in the German, that is to say, the bad sense of the word "idealist". But in actual fact, he is enormously more realistic than any of his predecessors . . .',[16] this reviewer hit the nail on the head. Marx was the last of the great holistic system builders. We should take care to leave it at that, and not to replace his by another Great System. What we need is not holism. It is piecemeal social engineering.

27 Individualism versus Collectivism (1945)

The problem of individualism and collectivism is closely related to that of equality and inequality. Before going on to discuss it, a few terminological remarks seem to be necessary.

The term 'individualism' can be used (according to *The Oxford English Dictionary*) in two different ways: (1) in opposition to collectivism, and (2) in opposition to altruism. There is no other word to express the former meaning, but several synonyms for the latter, for example 'egoism' or 'selfishness'. This is why in what follows I shall use the term 'individualism' *exclusively* in sense (1), using terms like 'egoism' or 'selfishness' if sense (2) is intended. A little table may be useful:

(1) *Individualism*	is opposed to	(1′) *Collectivism.*
(2) *Egoism*	is opposed to	(2′) *Altruism.*

Now these four terms describe certain attitudes, or demands, or decisions, or proposals, for codes of normative laws. Though necessarily vague, they can, I believe, be easily illustrated by examples and so be used with a precision sufficient for our present purpose. Let us begin with collectivism.[1] Plato's demand that the individual should subserve the interests of the whole, whether this be the universe, the city, the tribe, the race, or any other collective body, is illustrated by the following passage.[2] 'The part exists for the sake of the whole, but the whole does not exist for the sake of the part. . . . You are created for the sake of the whole and not the whole for the sake of you.' This quotation not only illustrates holism and collectivism, but also conveys its strong emotional appeal of which Plato was conscious (as can be seen from the preamble to the passage). The appeal is to various feelings, e.g. the longing to belong to a group or a tribe; and one factor in it is the moral appeal for altruism and against selfishness, or egoism. Plato suggests that if you cannot sacrifice your interests for the sake of the whole, then you are selfish.

Now a glance at our little table will show that this is not so. Collectivism is not opposed to egoism, nor is it identical with altruism or unselfishness. Collective or group egoism, for instance class egoism, is a very common thing (Plato knew[3] this very well), and this shows clearly enough that collectivism as such is not opposed to selfishness. On the other hand, an anti-collectivist, i.e. an individualist, can, at the same time, be an altruist; he can be ready to make sacrifices in order to help other individuals. One of the best examples of this attitude is perhaps Dickens. It would be difficult to say which is the stronger, his passionate hatred of selfishness or his passionate interest in individuals with all their human weaknesses; and this attitude is combined with a dislike, not only of what we now call collective bodies or collectives (and, quite wrongly, Parliament as well), but even of a genuinely devoted altruism, if directed towards anonymous groups rather than concrete individuals. (I remind the reader of Mrs Jellyby in *Bleak House*, 'a lady devoted to public duties'.) These illustrations, I think, explain sufficiently clearly the meaning of our four terms; and they show that any of the terms in our table can be combined with either of the two terms that stand in the other line (which gives four possible combinations).

Now it is interesting that for Plato, and for most Platonists, an altruistic individualism (as for instance that of Dickens) cannot exist. According to Plato, the only alternative to collectivism is egoism; he simply identifies all altruism with collectivism, and all individualism with egoism. This is not a matter of terminology, of mere words, for instead of four possibilities, Plato recognized only two. This has created considerable confusion in speculation on ethical matters, even down to our own day.

Plato's identification of individualism with egoism furnishes him with a powerful weapon for his defence of collectivism as well as for his attack upon individualism. In defending collectivism, he can appeal to our humanitarian feeling of unselfishness; in his attack, he can brand all individualists as selfish, as incapable of devotion to anything but themselves. This attack, although aimed by Plato against individualism in our sense, i.e. against the rights of human individuals, reaches of course only a very different target, egoism. But this difference is constantly ignored by Plato and by most Platonists.

Why did Plato try to attack individualism? I think he knew very well what he was doing when he trained his guns upon this position, for individualism, perhaps even more than equalitarianism, was a stronghold in the defences of the new humanitarian creed. The emancipation of the individual was indeed the great spiritual revolution which had led to the breakdown of tribalism and to the rise of democracy. Plato's uncanny sociological intuition shows itself in the way in which he invariably discerned the enemy wherever he met him.

Individualism was part of the old intuitive idea of justice. That justice is not, as Plato would have it, the health and harmony of the state, but rather a certain way of treating individuals, is emphasized by Aristotle, it will be remembered, when he says 'justice is something that pertains to persons'.[4] This individualistic element had been emphasized by the generation of Pericles. Pericles himself made it clear that the laws must guarantee equal justice 'to all alike in their private disputes'; but he went further. 'We do not feel called upon', he said, 'to nag at our neighbour if he chooses to go his own way.' (Compare this with Plato's remark[5] that the state does not produce men 'for the purpose of letting them loose, each to go his own way . . .'.) Pericles insists that this individualism must be linked with altruism: 'We are taught . . . never to forget that we must protect the injured'; and his speech culminates in a description of the young Athenian who grows up 'to a happy versatility, and self-reliance'.

This individualism, united with altruism, has become the basis of our western civilization. It is the central doctrine of Christianity ('love your neighbour', say the Scriptures, not 'love your tribe'); and it is the core of all ethical doctrines which have grown from our civilization and stimulated it. It is also, for instance, Kant's central practical doctrine ('always recognize that human individuals are ends, and do not use them as mere means to your ends'). There is no other thought which has been so powerful in the moral development of man.

Plato was right when he saw in this doctrine the enemy of his caste state; and he hated it more than any other of the 'subversive' doctrines of his time. In order to show this even more clearly, I shall quote two passages from the *Laws*[6] whose truly astonishing hostility towards the individual is, I think, too little appreciated. The first of them is famous as a reference to the *Republic*, whose 'community of women and children and property' it discusses. Plato describes here the constitution of the *Republic* as 'the highest form of the state'. In this highest state, he tells us, 'there is common property of wives, of children, and of all chattels. And everything possible has been done to eradicate from our life everywhere and in every way all that is private and individual. So far as it can be done, even those things which nature herself has made private and individual have somehow become the common property of all. Our very eyes and ears and hands seem to see, to hear, and to act, as if they belonged not to individuals but to the community. All men are moulded to be unanimous in the utmost degree in bestowing praise and blame, and they even rejoice and grieve about the same things, and at the same time. And all the laws are perfected for unifying the city to the utmost.' Plato goes on to say that 'no man can find a better criterion of the highest excellence of a state than the principles just expounded'; and he describes such a state as 'divine', and as the 'model' or 'pattern' or 'original' of the state, i.e. as its Form or Idea. This is Plato's own view of the *Republic*, expressed at a time when he had given up hope of realizing his political ideal in all its glory.

The second passage, also from the *Laws*, is, if possible, even more outspoken. It should be emphasized that the passage deals primarily with military expeditions and with military discipline, but Plato leaves no doubt that these same militarist principles should be adhered to not only in war, but also 'in peace, and from the earliest childhood on'. Like other totalitarian militarists and admirers of Sparta, Plato urges that the all-important requirements of military discipline must be paramount, even in peace, and that they must determine the whole life of all citizens; for not only the full citizens (who are all soldiers) and the children, but also the very beasts must spend their whole life in a state of permanent and total mobilization.[7] 'The greatest principle of all', he writes, 'is that nobody, whether male or female, should ever be without a leader. Nor should the mind of anybody be habituated to letting him do anything at all on his own initiative, neither out of zeal, nor even playfully. But in war and in the midst of peace – to his leader he shall direct his eye, and follow him faithfully. And even in the smallest matters he should stand under leadership. For example, he should get up, or move, or wash, or take his meals[8] . . . only if he has been told to do so. . . . In a word, he should teach his soul, by long habit, never to dream of acting independently, and to become utterly incapable of it. In this way the life of all will be spent in total community. There is no law, nor will there ever be one, which is superior to this, or better and more effective in ensuring salvation and victory in war. *And in times of peace, and from the earliest childhood on* should it be fostered – this habit of ruling others, and of being ruled by others. And every trace of anarchy should be utterly eradicated from *all the life of all the men*, and even of the wild beasts which are subject to men.'

These are strong words. Never was a man more in earnest in his hostility towards the individual. And this hatred is deeply rooted in the fundamental dualism of Plato's philosophy; he hated the individual and his freedom just as he hated the varying particular experiences, the variety of the changing world of sensible things. In the field of politics, the individual is to Plato the Evil One himself.

This attitude, anti-humanitarian and anti-Christian as it is, has been consistently idealized. It has been interpreted as humane, as unselfish, as altruistic, and as Christian. E. B. England, for instance, calls[9] the first of these two passages from the *Laws* 'a vigorous denunciation of selfishness'. Similar words are used by Barker, when discussing Plato's theory of justice. He says that Plato's aim was 'to replace selfishness and civil discord by harmony', and that 'the old harmony of the interests of the State and the individual . . . is thus restored in the teachings of Plato; but restored on a new and higher level, because it has been elevated into a conscious sense of harmony'. Such statements and countless similar ones can be easily explained if we remember Plato's identification of individualism with egoism; for all these Platonists believe that anti-individualism is the same as selflessness. This illustrates my contention that this identification had the effect of a successful piece of anti-humanitarian propaganda, and that it has confused speculation on ethical matters down to our own time. But we must also realize that those who, deceived by this identification and by highsounding words, exalt Plato's reputation as a teacher of morals and announce to the world that his ethics is the nearest approach to Christianity before Christ, are preparing the way for totalitarianism and especially for a totalitarian, anti-Christian interpretation of Christianity. And this is a dangerous thing, for there have been times when Christianity was dominated by totalitarian ideas. There was an Inquisition; and, in another form, it may come again.

It may therefore be worth while to mention some further reasons why guileless people have persuaded themselves of the humaneness of Plato's intentions. One is that when preparing the ground for his collectivist doctrines, Plato usually begins by quoting a maxim or proverb (which seems to be of Pythagorean origin): 'Friends have in common all things they possess.'[10] This is, undoubtedly, an unselfish, highminded and excellent sentiment. Who could suspect that an argument starting from such a commendable assumption would arrive at a wholly anti-humanitarian conclusion? Another and important point is that there are many genuinely humanitarian sentiments expressed in Plato's dialogues, particularly in those written before the *Republic* when he was still under the influence of Socrates. I mention especially Socrates's doctrine, in the *Gorgias*, that it is worse to do injustice than to suffer it. Clearly, this doctrine is not only altruistic, but also individualistic; for in a collectivist theory of justice like that of the *Republic*, injustice is an act against the state, not against a particular man, and though a man may commit an act of injustice, only the collective can suffer from it. But in the *Gorgias* we find nothing of the kind. The theory of justice is a perfectly normal one, and the examples of injustice given by 'Socrates' (who has here probably a good deal of the real Socrates in him) are such as boxing a man's ears, injuring, or killing him. Socrates's teaching that it is better to suffer such acts than to do them is indeed very similar to Christian teaching, and his doctrine of justice fits in excellently with the spirit of Pericles.

Now the *Republic* develops a new doctrine of justice which is not merely incompatible with such an individualism, but utterly hostile towards it. But a reader may easily believe that Plato is still holding fast to the doctrine of the *Gorgias*. For in the *Republic*,

Plato frequently alludes to the doctrine that it is better to suffer than to commit injustice, in spite of the fact that this is simply nonsense from the point of view of the collectivist theory of justice proffered in this work. Furthermore, we hear in the *Republic* the opponents of 'Socrates' giving voice to the opposite theory, that it is good and pleasant to inflict injustice, and bad to suffer it. Of course, every humanitarian is repelled by such cynicism, and when Plato formulates his aims through the mouth of Socrates: 'I fear to commit a sin if I permit such evil talk about Justice in my presence, without doing my utmost to defend her',[11] then the trusting reader is convinced of Plato's good intentions, and ready to follow him wherever he goes.

The effect of this assurance of Plato's is much enhanced by the fact that it follows, and is contrasted with, the cynical and selfish speeches[12] of Thrasymachus, who is depicted as a political desperado of the worst kind. At the same time, the reader is led to identify individualism with the views of Thrasymachus, and to think that Plato, in his fight against it, is fighting against all the subversive and nihilistic tendencies of his time. But we should not allow ourselves to be frightened by an individualist bogy such as Thrasymachus (there is a great similarity between his portrait and the modern collectivist bogy of 'bolshevism') into accepting another more real and more dangerous because less obvious form of barbarism. For Plato replaces Thrasymachus's doctrine that the individual's might is right by the equally barbaric doctrine that right is everything that furthers the stability and the might of the state.

To sum up. Because of his radical collectivism, Plato is not even interested in those problems which men usually call the problems of justice, that is to say, in the impartial weighing of the contesting claims of individuals. Nor is he interested in adjusting the individual's claims to those of the state. For the individual is altogether inferior. 'I legislate with a view to what is best for the whole state', says Plato, '. . . for I justly place the interests of the individual on an inferior level of value.'[13] He is concerned solely with the collective whole as such, and justice, to him, is nothing but the health, unity, and stability of the collective body.

28 The Autonomy of Sociology (1945)

A concise formulation of Marx's opposition to psychologism (the term is due to Husserl), i.e. to the plausible doctrine that all laws of social life must be ultimately reducible to the psychological laws of 'human nature', is his famous epigram: 'It is not the consciousness of man that determines his existence – rather, it is his social existence that determines his consciousness.'[1] I may state at once that in elucidating this epigram and developing what I believe to be Marx's anti-psychologism, I am developing a view to which I subscribe myself.

As an elementary illustration, and a first step in our examination, we may refer to the problem of the so-called rules of exogamy, i.e. the problem of explaining the wide distribution, among the most diverse cultures, of marriage laws apparently designed to prevent inbreeding. Mill and his psychologistic school of sociology (it was joined later by many psychoanalysts) would try to explain these rules by an appeal to 'human nature', for instance to some sort of instinctive aversion against incest (developed perhaps through natural selection, or else through 'repression'); and something like this would also be the naïve or popular explanation. Adopting the point of view expressed in Marx's epigram, however, one could ask whether it is not the other way round, that is to say, whether the apparent instinct is not rather a product of education, the effect rather than the cause of the social rules and traditions demanding exogamy and forbidding incest.[2] It is clear that these two approaches correspond exactly to the very ancient problem whether social laws are 'natural' or 'conventional'. In a question such as the one chosen here as an illustration, it would be difficult to determine which of the two theories is the correct one, the explanation of the traditional social rules by instinct or the explanation of an apparent instinct by traditional social rules. The possibility of deciding such questions by experiment has, however, been shown in a similar case, that of the apparently instinctive aversion to snakes. This aversion has a greater semblance of being instinctive or 'natural' in that it is exhibited not only by men but also by all anthropoid apes and most monkeys as well. But experiments seem to indicate that this fear is conventional. It appears to be a product of education, not only in the human race but also for instance in chimpanzees, since both young children and young chimpanzees who have not been taught to fear snakes do not exhibit the alleged instinct.[3] This example should be taken as a warning. We are faced here with an aversion which is apparently universal, even beyond the human race. But although from the fact that a habit is not universal we might perhaps argue against its being based on an instinct (but even this argument is dangerous since there are social customs enforcing the suppression of instincts), we see that the converse is certainly not true. The universal occurrence of a certain behaviour is not a decisive argument in favour of its instinctive character, or of its being rooted in 'human nature'.

Such considerations may show how naïve it is to assume that all social laws must be derivable, in principle, from the psychology of 'human nature'. But this analysis is still rather crude. In order to proceed one step further, we may try to analyse more directly the main thesis of psychologism, the doctrine that, society being the product of interacting minds, social laws must ultimately be reducible to psychological laws, since the events of social life, including its conventions, must be the outcome of motives springing from the minds of individual men.

Against this doctrine of psychologism, the defenders of an autonomous sociology can advance *institutionalist* views.[4] They can point out, first of all, that no action can ever be explained by motive alone; if motives (or any other psychological or behaviourist concepts) are to be used in the explanation, then they must be supplemented by a reference to the general situation, and especially to the environment. In the case of human actions, this environment is very largely of a social nature; thus our actions cannot be explained without reference to our social environment, to social institutions and to their manner of functioning. It is therefore impossible, the institutionalist may contend, to reduce sociology to a psychological or behaviourist analysis of our actions; rather, every such analysis presupposes sociology, which therefore cannot wholly depend on psychological analysis. Sociology, or at least a very important part of it, must be autonomous.

Against this view, the followers of psychologism may retort that they are quite ready to admit the great importance of environmental factors, whether natural or social; but the structure (they may prefer the fashionable word 'pattern') of the social environment, as opposed to the natural environment, is manmade; and therefore it must be explicable in terms of human nature, in accordance with the doctrine of psychologism. For instance, the characteristic institution which economists call 'the market', and whose functioning is the main object of their studies, can be derived in the last analysis from the psychology of 'economic man', or, to use Mill's phraseology, from the psychological 'phenomena . . . of the pursuit of wealth'. Moreover, the followers of psychologism insist that it is because of the peculiar psychological structure of human nature that institutions play such an important role in our society, and that, once established, they show a tendency to become a traditional and a comparatively fixed part of our environment. Finally – and this is their decisive point – the *origin as well as the development* of traditions must be explicable in terms of human nature. When tracing back traditions and institutions to their origin, we must find that their introduction is explicable in psychological terms, since they have been introduced by man for some purpose or other, and under the influence of certain motives. And even if these motives have been forgotton in the course of time, then that forgetfulness, as well as our readiness to put up with institutions whose purpose is obscure, is in its turn based on human nature. Thus 'All phenomena of society are phenomena of human nature', as Mill said; and 'The Laws of the phenomena of society are, and can be, nothing but the laws of the actions and passions of human beings', that is to say, 'the laws of individual human nature. Men are not, when brought together, converted into another kind of substance. . . .'[5]

This last remark of Mill's exhibits one of the most praiseworthy aspects of psychologism, namely, its sane opposition to collectivism and holism, its refusal to be impressed by Rousseau's or

Hegel's romanticism – by a general will or a national spirit, or perhaps, by a group mind. Psychologism is, I believe, correct only in so far as it insists upon what may be called 'methodological individualism' as opposed to 'methodological collectivism';[6] it rightly insists that the 'behaviour' and the 'actions' of collectives, such as states or social groups, must be reduced to the behaviour and to the actions of human individuals. But the belief that the choice of such an individualistic method implies the choice of a psychological method is mistaken (as will be shown below), even though it may appear very convincing at first sight. And that psychologism as such moves on rather dangerous ground, apart from its commendable individualistic method, can be seen from some further passages of Mill's argument. For they show that *psychologism is forced to adopt historicist methods.* The attempt to reduce the facts of our social environment to psychological facts forces us into speculations about origins and developments. When analysing Plato's sociology (in *The Open Society and Its Enemies*, chapter 5), we had an opportunity of gauging the dubious merits of such an approach to social science. In criticizing Mill, we shall now try to deal it a decisive blow.

It is undoubtedly Mill's psychologism which forces him to adopt a historicist method; and he is even vaguely aware of the barrenness or poverty of historicism, since he tries to account for this barrenness by pointing out the difficulties arising from the tremendous complexity of the interaction of so many individual minds. '. . . while it is . . . imperative', he says, '. . . never to introduce any generalisation ... into the social science unless sufficient grounds can be pointed out for it in human nature, I do not think any one will contend that it would have been possible, setting out from the principles of human nature and from the general circumstances of the position of our species, to determine *a priori* the order in which human development must take place, and to predict, consequently, the general facts of history up to the present time'. The reason he gives is that '[after] the first few terms of the series, the influence exercised over each generation by the generations which preceded it becomes ... more and more preponderant over all other influences'. (In other words, the social environment becomes a dominant influence.) 'So long a series of actions and reactions ... could not possibly be computed by human faculties. . . .'[7]

This argument, and especially Mill's remark on 'the first few terms of the series', are a striking revelation of the weakness of the psychologistic version of historicism. If all regularities in social life, the laws of our social environment, of all institutions, etc., are ultimately to be explained by, and reduced to, the 'actions and passions of human beings', then such an approach forces upon us not only the idea of historico-causal development, but also the idea of the *first steps* of such a development. For the stress on the psychological origin of social rules or institutions can only mean that they can be traced back to a state when their introduction was dependent solely upon psychological factors, or more precisely, when it was independent of any established social institutions. Psychologism is thus forced, whether it likes it or not, to operate with the idea of a *beginning of society*, and with the idea of a human nature and a human psychology as they existed prior to society. In other words, Mill's remark concerning the 'first few terms of the series' of social development is not an accidental slip, as one might perhaps believe, but the appropriate expression of the desperate position forced upon him. It is a desperate position because this theory of a pre-social human nature which explains the foundation of society – a psychologistic version of the 'social contract' – is not only an historical myth, but also, as it were, a methodological myth. It can hardly be seriously discussed, for we have every reason to believe that man or rather his ancestor was social prior to being human (considering, for example, that language presupposes society). But this implies that social institutions, and with them, typical social regularities or sociological laws,[8] must have existed prior to what some people are pleased to call 'human nature', and to human psychology. If a reduction is to be attempted at all, it would therefore be more hopeful to attempt a reduction or interpretation of psychology in terms of sociology than the other way round.

This brings us back to Marx's epigram at the beginning [of this selection]. Men – i.e. human minds, the needs, the hopes, fears, and expectations, the motives and aspirations of human individuals – are, if anything, the product of life in society rather than its creators. [See also selection 22, section II.] It must be admitted that the structure of our social environment is manmade in a certain sense; that its institutions and traditions are the work neither of God nor of nature, but the results of human actions and decisions, and alterable by human actions and decisions. But this does not mean that they are all consciously designed, and explicable in terms of needs, hopes, or motives. On the contrary, even those which arise as the result of conscious and intentional human actions are, as a rule, *the indirect, the unintended, and often the unwanted byproducts of such actions*. 'Only a minority of social institutions are consciously designed, while the vast majority have just "grown", as the undesigned results of human actions', as I said [on p.308 above];[9] and we can add that even most of the few institutions which were consciously and successfully designed (say, a newly founded university, or a trade union) do not turn out according to plan – again because of the unintended social repercussions resulting from their intentional creation. For their creation affects not only many other social institutions but also 'human nature' – hopes, fears, and ambitions, first of those more immediately involved, and later often of all members of the society. One of the consequences of this is that the moral values of a society – the demands and proposals recognized by all, or by very nearly all, of its members – are closely bound up with its institutions and traditions, and that they cannot survive the destruction of the institutions and traditions of the society.[10]

All this holds most emphatically for the more ancient periods of social development, i.e. for the closed society, in which the conscious design of institutions is a most exceptional event, if it happens at all. Today, things may begin to be different, owing to our slowly increasing knowledge of society, i.e. owing to the study of the unintended repercussions of our plans and actions; and one day, men may even become the conscious creators of an open society, and thereby of a greater part of their own fate. (Marx himself entertained this hope.) But all this is partly a matter of degree, and although we may learn to foresee many of the unintended consequences of our actions (the main aim of all social technology), there will always be many which we did not foresee.

The fact that psychologism is forced to operate with the idea of a psychological origin of society constitutes in my opinion a decisive argument against it. But it is not the only one. Perhaps the most important criticism of psychologism is that it fails to understand the main task of the explanatory social sciences.

This task is not, as the historicist believes, the prophecy of the future course of history. It is, rather, the discovery and explanation of the less obvious dependences within the social sphere. It is the discovery of the difficulties which stand in the way of social action – the study, as it were, of the unwieldiness, the resilience or the brittleness of the social stuff, of its resistance to our attempts to mould it and to work with it.

In order to make my point clear, I shall briefly describe a theory which is widely held but which assumes what I consider the very opposite of the true aim of the social sciences; I call it the '*conspiracy theory of society*'. It is the view that an explanation of a social phenomenon consists in the discovery of the men or groups who are interested in the occurrence of this phenomenon (sometimes it is a hidden interest which has first to be revealed), and who have planned and conspired to bring it about.[11]

This view of the aims of the social sciences arises, of course, from the mistaken theory that, whatever happens in society – especially happenings such as war, unemployment, poverty, shortages, which people as a rule dislike – is the result of direct design by some powerful individuals and groups. This theory is widely held; it is older even than historicism (which, as shown by its primitive theistic form, is a derivative of the conspiracy theory). In its modern forms it is, like modern historicism, and a certain modern attitude towards 'natural laws', a typical result of the secularization of a religious superstition. The belief in the Homeric gods whose conspiracies explain the history of the Trojan War is gone. The gods are abandoned. But their place is filled by powerful men or groups – sinister pressure groups whose wickedness is responsible for all the evils we suffer from – such as the Learned Elders of Zion, or the monopolists, or the capitalists, or the imperialists.

I do not wish to imply that conspiracies never happen. On the contrary, they are typical social phenomena. They become important, for example, whenever people who believe in the conspiracy theory get into power. And people who sincerely believe that they know how to make heaven on earth are most likely to adopt the conspiracy theory, and to get involved in a counterconspiracy against non-existing conspirators. For the only explanation of their failure to produce their heaven is the evil intention of the Devil, who has a vested interest in hell.

Conspiracies occur, it must be admitted. But the striking fact which, in spite of their occurrence, disproves the conspiracy theory is that few of these conspiracies are ultimately successful. *Conspirators rarely consummate their conspiracy.*

Why is this so? Why do achievements differ so widely from aspirations? Because this is usually the case in social life, conspiracy or no conspiracy. Social life is not only a trial of strength between opposing groups: it is action within a more or less resilient or brittle framework of institutions and traditions, and it creates – apart from any conscious counteraction – many unforeseen reactions in this framework, some of them perhaps even unforeseeable.

To try to analyse these reactions and to foresee them as far as possible is, I believe, the main task of the social sciences. It is the task of analysing the unintended social repercussions of intentional human actions – those repercussions whose significance is neglected both by the conspiracy theory and by psychologism, as already indicated. An action which proceeds precisely according to intention does not create a problem for social science (except that there may be a need to explain why in this particular case no unintended repercussions occurred). One of the most primitive economic actions may serve as an example in order to make the idea of unintended consequences of our actions quite clear. If a man wishes urgently to buy a house, we can safely assume that he does not wish to raise the market price of houses. But the very fact that he appears on the market as a buyer will tend to raise market prices. And analogous remarks hold for the seller. Or to take an example from a very different field, if a man decides to insure his life, he is unlikely to have the intention of encouraging some people to invest their money in insurance shares. But he will do so nevertheless. We see here clearly that not all consequences of our actions are intended consequences; and accordingly, that the conspiracy theory of society cannot be true because it amounts to the assertion that all results, even those which at first sight do not seem to be intended by anybody, are the intended results of the actions of people who are interested in these results.

The examples given do not refute psychologism as easily as they refute the conspiracy theory, for one can argue that it is the sellers' *knowledge* of a buyer's presence in the market, and their *hope* of getting a higher price – in other words, psychological factors – which explain the repercussions described. This, of course, is quite true; but we must not forget that this knowledge and this hope are not ultimate data of human nature, and that they are, in their turn, explicable in terms of the *social situation* – the market situation.

This social situation is hardly reducible to motives and to the general laws of 'human nature'. Indeed, the interference of certain 'traits of human nature', such as our susceptibility to propaganda, may sometimes lead to deviations from the economic behaviour just mentioned. Furthermore, if the social situation is different from the one envisaged, then it is possible that the consumer, by the action of buying, may indirectly contribute to a cheapening of the article; for instance, by making its mass production more profitable. And although this effect happens to further his interest as a consumer, it may have been caused just as involuntarily as the opposite effect, and altogether under precisely similar psychological conditions. It seems clear that the social situations which may lead to such widely different unwanted or unintended repercussions must be studied by a social science which is not bound to the prejudice that 'it is . . . imperative . . . never to introduce any generalisation into the social science unless sufficient grounds can be pointed out for it in human nature', as Mill said.[12] They must be studied by an autonomous social science.

Continuing this argument against psychologism we may say that our actions are to a very large extent explicable in terms of the situation in which they occur. Of course, they are never fully explicable in terms of the situation alone; an explanation of the way in which a man, when crossing a street, dodges the cars which move on it may go beyond the situation, and may refer to his motives, to an 'instinct' of self-preservation, or to his wish to avoid pain, etc. But this 'psychological' part of the explanation is very often trivial, as compared with the detailed determination of his action by what we may call the *logic of the situation*; and besides, it is impossible to include all psychological factors in the description of the situation. The analysis of situations, the situational logic, plays a very important part in social life as well as in the social sciences. It is, in fact, the method of economic analysis. As to an example outside economics, I refer to the 'logic of power',[13] which we may use in order to explain the moves of power politics as well as the working of certain political institutions. The method of applying a situational logic to the social sciences is not based on any psychological assumption concerning the rationality (or otherwise) of 'human nature'. On the contrary: when we speak of 'rational behaviour' or of 'irrational behaviour' then we mean behaviour which is, or which is not, in accordance with the logic of that situation. In fact, the psychological analysis of an action in terms of its (rational or irrational) motives presupposes – as has been pointed out by Max Weber[14] – that we have previously developed some standard of what is to be considered as rational in the situation in question.

My arguments against psychologism should not be misunderstood. They are not, of course, intended to show that psychological studies and discoveries are of little importance for the social scientist. They mean, rather, that psychology – the psychology of the individual – is one of the social sciences, even though it is not the basis of all social science. Nobody would deny the importance for political science of psychological facts such as the craving for power, and the various neurotic phenomena connected with it. But 'craving for power' is undoubtedly a social notion as well as a psychological one: we must not forget that, if we study, for example, the first appearance in childhood of this craving, then we study it in the setting of a certain social institution, for example, that of our modern family. (The Eskimo family may give rise to rather different phenomena.) Another psychological fact which is significant for sociology, and which raises grave political and institutional problems, is that to live in the haven of a tribe, or of a 'community' approaching a tribe, is for many men an emotional necessity (especially for young people who, perhaps in accordance with a parallelism between ontogenetic and phylogenetic development, seem to have to pass through a tribal or 'American Indian' stage). That my attack on psychologism is not intended as an attack on all psychological considerations may be seen from the use I have made elsewhere[15] of such a concept as the 'strain of civilization', which is partly the result of this unsatisfied emotional need. This concept refers to certain feelings of uneasiness, and is therefore a psychological concept. But at the same time, it is a sociological concept also; for it not only characterizes these feelings as unpleasant and unsettling, etc., but relates them to a certain social situation, and to the contrast between an open and a closed society. (Many psychological concepts such as ambition or love have an analogous status.) Also, we must not overlook the great merits which psychologism has acquired by advocating a methodological individualism and by opposing a methodological collectivism; for it lends support to the important doctrine that all social phenomena, and especially the functioning of all social institutions, should always be understood as resulting from the decisions, actions, attitudes, etc., of human individuals, and that we should never be satisfied by an explanation in terms of so-called 'collectives' (states, nations, races, etc.). The mistake of psychologism is its presumption that this methodological individualism in the field of social science implies the programme of reducing all social phenomena and all social regularities to psychological phenomena and psychological laws. The danger of this presumption is its inclination towards historicism, as we have seen. That it is unwarranted is shown by the need for a theory of the unintended social repercussions of our actions, and by the need for what I have described as the logic of social situations.

In defending and developing Marx's view that the problems of society are irreducible to those of 'human nature', I have permitted myself to go beyond the arguments actually propounded by Marx. Marx did not speak of 'psychologism', nor did he criticize it systematically; nor was it Mill whom he had in mind in the epigram quoted at the beginning of this chapter. The force of this epigram is directed, rather, against 'idealism', in its Hegelian form. Yet so far as the problem of the psychological nature of society is concerned, Mill's psychologism can be said to coincide with the idealist theory combated by Marx.[16] As it happened, however, it was just the influence of another element in Hegelianism, namely Hegel's Platonizing collectivism, his theory that the state and the nation are more 'real' than the individual who owes everything to them, that led Marx to the view expounded in this chapter. (An instance of the fact that one can sometimes extract a valuable suggestion even from an absurd philosophical theory.) Thus, historically, Marx developed certain of Hegel's views concerning the superiority of society over the individual, and used them as arguments against other views of Hegel. Yet since I consider Mill a worthier opponent than Hegel, I have not kept to the history of Marx's ideas, but have tried to develop them in the form of an argument against Mill.

29 The Rationality Principle (1967)

In this paper I wish to consider the problem of *explanation in the social sciences*, and briefly to compare and contrast it with the analogous problem in the natural sciences [discussed in selection 12 above]. My thesis is that social explanations are very similar to certain physical explanations, but that the problem of explanation in the social sciences does give rise to problems that are not encountered in the natural sciences.

Let me begin by distinguishing between two kinds of problems of explanation or prediction.

(1) The first kind is the problem of explaining or predicting one or a smallish number of *singular events*. An example from the natural sciences would be, 'When will the next lunar eclipse (or, say, the next two or three lunar eclipses) occur?' An example from the social sciences would be, 'When will there be the next rise in the rate of unemployment in the Midlands, or in Western Ontario?'

(2) The second kind of problem is the problem of explaining, or predicting, a certain *kind or type* of event. An example from the natural sciences would be, 'Why do lunar eclipses occur again and again, and only when there is a full moon?' An example from the social sciences would be, 'Why is there a seasonal increase and decrease of unemployment in the building industry?'

The difference between these two kinds of problem is that the first can be solved *without constructing a model*, while the second is most easily solved *with the help of constructing a model*.

Now it seems to me that in the theoretical social sciences it is hardly ever possible to answer questions of the first kind. The theoretical social sciences operate almost always by the method of constructing *typical* situations or conditions – that is, by the method of constructing models. (This is connected with the fact that in the social sciences, there is, in Hayek's terminology, less 'explanation in detail' and more 'explanation in principle' than in the physical sciences.)

It is important to realize the close similarity of explanations in the social sciences with explanations of the second kind in the natural sciences. Suppose, in the natural sciences, we wish to explain the repeated occurrence of lunar eclipses. In this case we may construct an actual mechanical model, or refer to a perspective drawing. For our limited purpose, the model may be very rough indeed. It may consist of a fixed lamp: the sun; a little wooden earth rotating in a circle round the sun, and a little moon rotating in a circle round the earth. One thing would be essential however: the planes of the two movements must be so inclined towards each other that we obtain lunar eclipses sometimes, but not always, when the moon is full.

A critical discussion of our rough model must give rise, however, to a new problem, 'How are earth and moon propelled in the real world?'; and with this we may come to Newton's laws of motion. There is no need, however, to introduce initial conditions explicitly into our solution: as far as problems of the second kind are concerned (the explanation of *types* of events) initial conditions may be completely replaced by the construction of the model, which one might say, incorporates *typical* initial conditions. But if we wish to make the model move, or work, or, as we may say, if we wish to '*animate*' the model; that is, if we wish to represent the way in which the various *elements* of the model act upon each other, then we do need *universal laws* (in this case, the consequences of approximating Newton's laws of motion).

So much for the natural sciences. As for the social sciences, I have elsewhere [in the previous selection] proposed that we can construct our models by means of *situational analysis*, which provides us with models (rough and ready models to be sure) of typical social situations. And my thesis is that only in this way can we explain and understand what happens in society: social events.

Now if situational analysis presents us with a model, the question arises: what corresponds here to Newton's universal laws of motion which, as we have said, 'animate' the model of the solar system? Or in other words, how is the model of a social situation 'animated'?

The usual mistake made here is to assume that in the case of human society, the 'animation' of a social model has to be provided by the human *anima* or *psyche*, and that here, therefore, we have to replace Newton's laws of motion either by laws of human psychology in general, or perhaps by the laws of individual psychology pertaining to the individual characters who are involved as actors in our situation.

But this is a mistake, for more reasons than one. First of all, in our situational analysis itself we *replace* concrete psychological experiences (or desires, hopes, tendencies) by abstract and typical situational elements, such as 'aims' and 'knowledge'. Secondly, it is the central point of situational analysis that we need, in order to 'animate' it, no more than the assumption that the various persons or agents involved act *adequately, or appropriately*; that is to say, in accordance with the situation. Here we must remember, of course, that the situation, as I use the term, already contains all the relevant aims and all the available relevant knowledge, especially that of possible means for realizing these aims.

Thus there is only one animating law involved – the principle of acting appropriately to the situation; clearly an *almost empty* principle. It is known in the literature under the name '*rationality principle*', a name which has led to countless misunderstandings.

If you look upon the rationality principle from the point of view which I have here adopted, then you will find that it has little or nothing to do with the empirical or psychological assertion that man always, or in the main, or in most cases, acts rationally. Rather, it turns out to be an aspect of, or a consequence of, the methodological postulate that we should pack or cram our whole theoretical effort, our whole explanatory theory, into an analysis of the *situation*: into the *model*.

If we adopt this methodological postulate, then, as a consequence, the animating law will become a kind of zero principle. For the principle may be stated in this way: having constructed our model, our situation, we assume no more than that the actors act within the terms of the model, or that they 'work out' what was *implicit* in the situation. This, incidentally, is what the term 'situational logic' alludes to.

The adoption of the rationality principle can therefore be regarded as a byproduct of a methodological postulate. It does not play the role of an empirical explanatory theory, of a testable hypothesis. For in this field, the empirical explanatory theories or hypotheses are our various models, our various situational analyses. It is these which may be empirically more or less adequate; which may be discussed and criticized, and whose adequacy may sometimes even be tested. And it is our analysis of a concrete empirical situation which may fail some empirical test, thereby enabling us to learn from our mistakes.

Tests of a model, it has to be admitted, are not easily obtainable and usually not very clearcut. But this difficulty arises even in the physical sciences. It is connected, of course, with the fact that models are always and necessarily rough; that they are always and necessarily schematic oversimplifications. Their roughness entails a comparatively low degree of testability; for it is difficult to decide what is a discrepancy due to the necessary roughness, and what is a discrepancy indicative of a failure, a refutation of the model. Nevertheless, we can sometimes decide by tests which one of two (or more) competing models is the best. And in the social sciences, tests of a situational analysis can sometimes be provided by historical research.

But if the rationality principle does not play the role of an empirical or psychological proposition, and more especially, if it is not treated as subject on its own to any kind of tests: if tests, when available, are used to test a particular model, a particular situational analysis, of which the rationality principle forms a part; then even if a test decides that a certain model is less adequate than another one, since both operate with the rationality principle, we have no occasion to test this principle.

This remark explains, I think, why the rationality principle has been frequently declared to be *a priori* valid. And indeed, if it is not empirically refutable what else could it be but *a priori* valid?

The point is of considerable interest. Those who say that the rationality principle is *a priori* mean, of course, that it is *a priori* valid, or *a priori* true. But it seems to me quite clear that they must be mistaken. For the rationality principle seems to me clearly false – even in its weakest zero formulation which may be put like this:

'Agents always act in a manner appropriate to the situation in which they find themselves.'

I think one can see very easily that this is not so. One has only to observe a flustered driver, desperately trying to park his car when there is no parking space to be found, in order to see that we do not always act in accordance with the rationality principle. Moreover, there are obviously vast personal differences, not only in knowledge and skill – these are part of the situation – but in assessing or understanding a situation; and this means that some people will act appropriately and others not.

But a principle that is not universally true is false. Thus the rationality principle is false. I think there is no way out of this. Consequently I must deny that it is *a priori* valid.

Now if the rationality principle is false, then an explanation which consists of the conjunction of this principle and a model must also be false, even if the particular model in question is true.

But can the model be true? Can any model be true? I do not think so. Any model, whether in physics or in the social sciences, must be an oversimplification. It must omit much, and it must overemphasize much.

My views on the rationality principle have been closely questioned. I have been asked whether there is not some confusion in what I say about the status of the 'principle of acting adequately to the situation' (that is, of my own version of the 'rationality principle'); I was told, quite rightly, that I should make up my mind whether I want it to be a methodological principle, or an empirical conjecture. In the first case it would be clear that, and why, it could not be empirically tested; also why it could not be empirically false (but only part of a successful or unsuccessful methodology). In the second case, it would become part of the various social theories – the animating part of every social model. But then it would have to be part of some empirical theory, and would have to be tested along with the rest of that theory, and rejected if found wanting.

This second case is precisely the one that corresponds to my own view of the status of the rationality principle: I regard the principle of adequacy of action (that is, the rationality principle) as an integral part of every, or nearly every, testable social theory.

Now if a theory is tested, and found faulty, then we have always to decide which of its various constituent parts we shall make accountable for its failure. My thesis is that it is sound methodological policy to decide not to make the rationality principle accountable but the rest of the theory; that is, the model.

In this way it may appear that in our search for better theories we treat the rationality principle as if it were a logical or a metaphysical principle exempt from refutation: as unfalsifiable, or as *a priori* valid. But this appearance is misleading. There are, as I have indicated, good reasons to believe that the rationality principle, even in my minimum formulation, is actually false, though a good approximation to the truth. Thus it cannot be said that I treat it as *a priori* valid.

I hold, however, that it is good policy, a good methodological device, to refrain from blaming the rationality principle for the breakdown of our theory: we learn more if we blame our situational model.

The main argument in favour of this policy is that our model is far more interesting and informative, and far better testable, than the principle of the adequacy of our actions. We do not learn much in learning that this is not strictly true: we know this already. Moreover, in spite of being false, it is as a rule sufficiently near to the truth: if we can refute our theory empirically, then its breakdown will, as a rule, be pretty drastic, and though the falsity of the rationality principle may be a contributing factor, the main responsibility will normally attach to the model. Another point is this: the attempt to replace the rationality principle by another one seems to lead to complete arbitrariness in our model-building. And we must not forget that we can test a theory only as a whole, and that the test consists in finding the better of two competing theories which may have much in common; and most of them have the rationality principle in common.

But did not Churchill say, in *The World Crisis*, that wars are not won but only lost – that, in effect, they are competitions in incompetence? And does not this remark provide us with a kind of model for typical social and historical situations; *a kind of model which emphatically is not animated by the rationality principle of the adequacy of our actions, but by a principle of inadequacy*?

The answer is that Churchill's dictum means that most war

leaders are inadequate to their task, that they do not see the situation as it is, rather than that their actions cannot be understood (in good approximation at least) as adequate for the situation *as they see it*.

In order to understand their (inadequate) actions, we have therefore to reconstruct a wider view of the situation than their own. This must be done in such a way that we can see how and why the situation as they saw it (with their limited experience, their limited or overblown aims, their limited or overexcited imagination) led them to act as they did; that is to say, adequately for their inadequate view of the situational structure. Churchill himself uses this method of interpretation with great success, for example in his careful analysis of the failure of the Auchinleck/Ritchie team (in volume IV of *The Second World War*).

It is interesting to see that we employ the rationality principle to the limit of what is possible whenever we try to understand an action, even the action of a madman. We try to explain a madman's actions, as far as possible, by his aims (which may be monomaniac) and by the 'information' on which he acts, that is to say, by his convictions (which may be obsessions, that is, false theories so tenaciously held that they become practically incorrigible). In so explaining the actions of a madman we explain them in terms of our wider knowledge of a problem situation which comprises his own, narrower, view of his problem situation; and understanding his actions means seeing their adequacy according to his view – his madly mistaken view – of the problem situation.

We may in this way even try to explain how he arrived at his madly mistaken view: how certain experiences shattered his originally sane view of the world and led him to adopt another – the most rational view he could develop in accordance with the information at his disposal, so far as he found it credible; and how he had to make this new view *incorrigible*, precisely because it would break down at once under the pressure of refuting instances which would leave him (so far as he could see) stranded without any interpretation of his world: a situation to be avoided at all costs, from a rational point of view, since it would make all rational action impossible.

Freud has often been described as the discoverer of human irrationality; but this is a misinterpretation, and a very superficial one to boot. Freud's theory of the typical origin of a neurosis falls entirely into our scheme: of explanations with the help of a situational model *plus* the rationality principle. For he explains a neurosis as an attitude adopted (in early childhood) because it was the best available way out of a situation which the agent (the child, the patient) was unable to understand and cope with. Thus the adoption of a neurosis becomes a rational act – as rational, say, as the act of a man who, jumping back when confronted by the danger of being run over by a car, collides with a bicyclist. It is rational in the sense that the agent chose what appeared to him the immediately or obviously preferable or perhaps just the lesser evil – the less intolerable of two possibilities.

I shall say no more here about Freud's method of therapy than that it is even more rationalistic than his method of diagnosis or explanation; for it is based on the assumption that once a man fully understands what befell him as a child, his neurosis will pass away.

But if we thus explain everything in terms of the rationality principle, does it not become tautological? By no means; for a tautology is obviously true, whilst we make use of the rationality principle merely as a good approximation to the truth, recognizing that it is not true, but false.

But if this is so, what becomes of the distinction between rationality and irrationality? Between mental health and mental disease?

This is an important question. The main distinction, I suggest, is that a healthy person's beliefs are not incorrigible: a healthy person shows a certain readiness to correct his beliefs. He may do so only reluctantly, yet he is nevertheless ready to correct his views under the pressure of events, of the opinions held by others, and of critical arguments.

If this is so then we can say that the mentality of the man with definitely fixed views, the 'committed' man, is akin to that of the madman. It may be that all his fixed opinions are 'adequate' in the sense that they happen to coincide with the best opinion available at the time. But in so far as he is committed, he is not rational: he will resist any change, any correction; and since he cannot be in possession of the full truth (nobody is) he will resist rational correction of even wildly mistaken beliefs. And he will resist, even if their correction is widely accepted during his lifetime.

Thus when those who praise commitment and irrational faith describe themselves as irrationalists (or post-rationalists) I agree with them. *They are irrationalists*, even if they are capable of reasoning. For they take pride in rendering themselves incapable of breaking out of their shell; they make themselves prisoners of their manias. They make themselves spiritually unfree, by an action whose adoption we may explain (following the psychiatrists) as one that is rationally understandable; understandable, for example, as an action they commit owing to fear – fear of being compelled, by criticism, to surrender a view which they dare not give up since they make it (or believe they must make it) the basis of their whole life. (Commitment – even 'free commitment' – and fanaticism, which, we know, can border on madness, are thus related in the most dangerous manner.)

To sum up: we should distinguish between rationality as a personal attitude (which, in principle, all sane men are capable of sharing) and the rationality principle.

Rationality as a personal attitude is the attitude of readiness to correct one's beliefs. In its intellectually most highly developed form it is the readiness to discuss one's beliefs critically, and to correct them in the light of critical discussions with other people.

The 'rationality principle' on the other hand has nothing to do with the assumption that men are rational in this sense – that they always adopt a rational attitude. It is, rather, a minimum principle (since it assumes no more than the adequacy of our actions to our problem situations as we see them) which animates all, or almost all, our explanatory situational models, and, although we know it not to be true, we have some reason to regard as a good approximation. Its adoption reduces considerably the arbitrariness of our models; an arbitrariness which becomes capricious indeed if we try to proceed without this principle.

30 Against the Sociology of Knowledge (1945)

> Rationality, in the sense of an appeal to a universal and impersonal standard of truth, is of supreme importance . . ., not only in ages in which it easily prevails, but also, and even more, in those less fortunate times in which it is despised and rejected as the vain dream of men who lack the virility to kill where they cannot agree.
>
> BERTRAND RUSSELL[1]

It can hardly be doubted that Hegel's and Marx's historicist philosophies are characteristic products of their time – a time of social change. Like the philosophies of Heraclitus and Plato, and like those of Comte and Mill, Lamarck and Darwin, they are philosophies of change, and they witness to the tremendous and undoubtedly somewhat terrifying impression made by a changing social environment on the minds of those who live in this environment. Plato reacted to this situation by attempting to arrest all change. The more modern social philosophers appear to react very differently, since they accept, and even welcome, change; yet this love of change seems to me a little ambivalent. For even though they have given up any hope of arresting change, as historicists they try to predict it, and thus to bring it under rational control; and this certainly looks like an attempt to tame it. Thus it seems that, to the historicist, change has not entirely lost its terrors.

In our time of still more rapid change, we even find the desire not only to predict change, but to control it by centralized large-scale planning. These holistic views (which I have criticized [in selection 24]) represent a compromise, as it were, between Platonic and Marxian theories. Plato's will to arrest change, combined with Marx's doctrine of its inevitability, yield, as a kind of Hegelian 'synthesis', the demand that since it cannot be entirely arrested, change should at least be 'planned', and controlled by the state, whose power is to be vastly extended.

An attitude like this may seem, at first sight, to be a kind of rationalism; it is closely related to Marx's dream of the 'realm of freedom' in which man is for the first time master of his own fate. But as a matter of fact, it occurs in closest alliance with a doctrine which is definitely opposed to rationalism (and especially to the doctrine of the rational unity of mankind [see section II of selection 2]), one which is well in keeping with the irrationalist and mystical tendencies of our time. I have in mind the Marxist doctrine that our opinions, including our moral and scientific opinions, are determined by class interest, and more generally by the social and historical situation of our time. Under the name of 'sociology of knowledge' or 'sociologism', this doctrine has been developed recently (especially by M. Scheler and K. Mannheim[2]) as a theory of the social determination of scientific knowledge.

The sociology of knowledge argues that scientific thought, and especially thought on social and political matters, does not proceed in a vacuum, but in a socially conditioned atmosphere. It is influenced largely by unconscious or subconscious elements. These elements remain hidden from the thinker's observing eye because they form, as it were, the very place which he inhabits, his *social habitat*. The social habitat of the thinker determines a whole system of opinions and theories which appear to him as unquestionably true or self-evident. They appear to him as if they were logically and trivially true, such as, for example, the sentence 'All tables are tables'. This is why he is not even aware of having made any assumptions at all. But that he has made assumptions can be seen if we compare him with a thinker who lives in a very different social habitat; for he too will proceed from a system of apparently unquestionable assumptions, but from a very different one; and it may be so different that no intellectual bridge may exist and no compromise be possible between these two systems. Each of these different socially determined systems of assumptions is called by the sociologists of knowledge a *total ideology*.

The sociology of knowledge can be considered as a Hegelian version of Kant's theory of knowledge. For it continues on the lines of Kant's criticism of what we may term the 'passivist' theory of knowledge. I mean by this the theory of the empiricists down to and including Hume, a theory which may be described, roughly, as holding that knowledge streams into us through our senses, and that error is due to our interference with the sense-given material, or to the associations which have developed within it; the best way of avoiding error is to remain entirely passive and receptive. Against this receptacle theory of knowledge (I have called it the 'bucket theory of the mind' [see selection 7, section IV above]) Kant[3] argued that knowledge is not a collection of gifts received by our senses and stored in the mind as if it were a museum, but that it is very largely the result of our own mental activity; that we must most actively engage ourselves in searching, comparing, unifying, generalizing, if we wish to attain knowledge. We may call this theory the 'activist' theory of knowledge. In connection with it, Kant gave up the untenable ideal of a science which is free from any kind of presuppositions. (That this ideal is even self-contradictory was shown [in selection 2].) He made it quite clear that we cannot start from nothing, and that we have to approach our task equipped with a system of presuppositions which we hold without having tested them by the empirical methods of science; such a system may be called a 'categorial apparatus'.[4] Kant believed that it was possible to discover the one true and unchanging categorial apparatus, which represents as it were the necessarily unchanging framework of our intellectual outfit, i.e. human 'reason'. This part of Kant's theory was given up by Hegel, who, as opposed to Kant, did not believe in the unity of mankind. He taught that man's intellectual outfit was constantly changing, and that it was part of his social heritage; accordingly the development of man's reason must coincide with the historical development of his society, i.e. of the nation to which he belongs. This theory of Hegel's, and especially his doctrine that all knowledge and all truth are 'relative' in the sense of being determined by history, is sometimes called 'historism' (in contradistinction to 'historicism'). The sociology of knowledge or 'sociologism' is obviously very closely related to or nearly identical with it, the only difference being that, under the influence of Marx, it emphasizes that the historical development does not produce one uniform 'national spirit', as Hegel held, but rather several and sometimes opposed 'total ideologies' within one nation according to the class, the social stratum, or the social habitat, of those who hold them.

But the likeness to Hegel goes further. I have said above that according to the sociology of knowledge, no intellectual bridge or compromise between different total ideologies is possible. But this radical scepticism is not really meant quite as seriously as it sounds. There is a way out of it, and the way is analogous to the Hegelian method of superseding the conflicts which preceded him in the history of philosophy. Hegel, a spirit freely poised above the whirlpool of the dissenting philosophies, reduced them all to mere components of the highest of syntheses, of his own system. Similarly, the sociologists of knowledge hold that the 'freely poised intelligence' of an intelligentsia which is only loosely anchored in social traditions may be able to avoid the pitfalls of the total ideologies; that it may even be able to see through, and to unveil, the various total ideologies and the hidden motives and other determinants which inspire them. Thus the sociology of knowledge believes that the highest degree of objectivity can be reached by the freely poised intelligence analysing the various hidden ideologies and their anchorage in the unconscious. The way to true knowledge appears to be the unveiling of unconscious assumptions, a kind of psychotherapy, as it were, or if I may say so, a *sociotherapy*. Only he who has been socioanalysed or who has socioanalysed himself, and who is freed from this social complex, i.e. from his social ideology, can attain to the highest synthesis of objective knowledge.

In chapter 15 of *The Open Society and Its Enemies*, when dealing with 'Vulgar Marxism', I mentioned a tendency which can be observed in a group of modern philosophies, the tendency to unveil the hidden motives behind our actions. The sociology of knowledge belongs to this group, together with psychoanalysis and certain philosophies which unveil the 'meaninglessness' of the tenets of their opponents [see notes 17 and 18 to selection 6 above]. The popularity of these views lies, I believe, in the ease with which they can be applied, and in the satisfaction which they confer on those who see through things, and through the follies of the unenlightened. This pleasure would be harmless, were it not that all these ideas are liable to destroy the intellectual basis of any discussion, by establishing what I have called a 're-inforced dogmatism'. (Indeed, this is something rather similar to a 'total ideology'.) Hegelianism does it by declaring the admissibility and even fertility of contradictions. But if contradictions need not be avoided, then any criticism and any discussion become impossible since criticism always consists in pointing out contradictions either within the theory to be criticized, or between it and some facts of experience. [See also selection 16 above.] The situation with psychoanalysis is similar: the psychoanalyst can always explain away any objections by showing that they are due to the repressions of the critic. And the philosophers of meaning, again, need only point out that what their opponents hold is meaningless, which will always be true, since 'meaninglessness' can be so defined that any discussion about it is by definition without meaning.[5] Marxists, in a like manner, are accustomed to explain the disagreement of an opponent by his class bias, and the sociologists of knowledge by his total ideology. Such methods are both easy to handle and good fun for those who handle them. But they clearly destroy the basis of rational discussion, and they must lead, ultimately, to anti-rationalism and mysticism.

In spite of these dangers, I do not see why I should entirely forgo the fun of handling these methods. For just like the psychoanalysts, the people to whom psychoanalysis applies best,[6] the socioanalysts invite the application of their own methods to themselves with an almost irresistible hospitality. For is not their description of an intelligentsia which is only loosely anchored in tradition a very neat description of their own social group? And is it not also clear that, assuming the theory of total ideologies to be correct, it would be part of every total ideology to believe that one's own group was free from bias, and was indeed that body of the elect which alone was capable of objectivity? Is it not, therefore, to be expected, always assuming the truth of this theory, that those who hold it will unconsciously deceive themselves by producing an amendment to the theory in order to establish the objectivity of their own views? Can we, then, take seriously their claim that by their sociological self-analysis they have reached a higher degree of objectivity; and their claim that socioanalysis can cast out a total ideology? But we could even ask whether the whole theory is not simply the expression of the class interest of this particular group;

of an intelligentsia only loosely anchored in tradition, though just firmly enough to speak Hegelian as their mother tongue.

How little the sociologists of knowledge have succeeded in sociotherapy, that is to say, in eradicating their own total ideology, will be particularly obvious if we consider their relation to Hegel. For they have no idea that they are just repeating him; on the contrary, they believe not only that they have outgrown him, but also that they have successfully seen through him, socioanalysed him; and that they can now look at him, not from any particular social habitat, but objectively, from a superior elevation. This palpable failure in self-analysis tells us enough.

But, all joking apart, there are more serious objections. The sociology of knowledge is not only self-destructive, not only a rather gratifying object of socioanalysis, it also shows an astounding failure to understand precisely its main subject, the *social aspects of knowledge*, or rather, of scientific method. It looks upon science or knowledge as a process in the mind or 'consciousness' of the individual scientist, or perhaps as the product of such a process. If considered in this way, what we call scientific objectivity must indeed become completely ununderstandable, or even impossible; and not only in the social or political sciences, where class interests and similar hidden motives may play a part, but just as much in the natural sciences. Everyone who has an inkling of the history of the natural sciences is aware of the passionate tenacity which characterizes many of its quarrels. No amount of political partiality can influence political theories more strongly than the partiality shown by some natural scientists in favour of their intellectual offspring. If scientific objectivity were founded, as the sociologistic theory of knowledge naïvely assumes, upon the individual scientist's impartiality or objectivity, then we should have to say goodbye to it. Indeed, we must be in a way more radically sceptical than the sociology of knowledge; for there is no doubt that we are all suffering under our own system of prejudices (or 'total ideologies', if this term is preferred); that we all take many things as self-evident, that we accept them uncritically and even with the naïve and cocksure belief that criticism is quite unnecessary; and scientists are no exception to this rule, even though they may have superficially purged themselves from some of their prejudices in their particular field. But they have not purged themselves by socioanalysis or any similar method; they have not attempted to climb to a higher plane from which they can understand, socioanalyse, and expurgate their ideological follies. For by making their minds more 'objective' they could not possibly attain to what we call 'scientific objectivity'. No, what we usually mean by this term rests on different grounds.[7] It is a matter of scientific method. And, ironically enough, objectivity is closely bound up with the *social aspect of scientific method*, with the fact that science and scientific objectivity do not (and cannot) result from the attempts of an individual scientist to be 'objective', but from the *friendly-hostile co-operation of many scientists*. Scientific objectivity can be described as the intersubjectivity of scientific method. But this social aspect of science is almost entirely neglected by those who call themselves sociologists of knowledge.

Two aspects of the method of the natural sciences are of importance in this connection. Together they constitute what I may term the 'public character of scientific method'. First, there is something approaching *free criticism*. A scientist may offer his theory with the full conviction that it is unassailable. But this will not impress his fellow scientists and competitors; rather it challenges them: they know that the scientific attitude means criticizing everything, and they are little deterred even by authorities. Secondly, scientists try to avoid talking at cross purposes. (I may remind the reader that I am speaking of the natural sciences, but a part of modern economics may be included.) They try very seriously to speak one and the same language, even if they use different mother tongues. In the natural sciences this is achieved by recognizing experience as the impartial arbiter of their controversies. When speaking of 'experience' I have in mind experience of a 'public' character, like observations, and experiments, as opposed to experience in the sense of more 'private' aesthetic or religious experience; and an experience is 'public' if everybody who takes the trouble can repeat it. In order to avoid speaking at cross purposes, scientists try to express their theories in such a form that they can be tested, i.e. refuted (or else corroborated) by such experience.

This is what constitutes scientific objectivity. Everyone who has learnt the technique of understanding and testing scientific theories can repeat the experiment and judge for himself. In spite of this, there will always be some who come to judgements which are partial, or even cranky. This cannot be helped, and it does not seriously disturb the working of the various *social institutions* which have been designed to further scientific objectivity and criticism; for instance the laboratories, the scientific periodicals, the congresses. This aspect of scientific method shows what can be achieved by institutions designed to make public control possible, and by the open expression of public opinion, even if this is limited to a circle of specialists. Only political power, when it is used to suppress free criticism, or when it fails to protect it, can impair the functioning of these institutions, on which all progress, scientific, technological, and political, ultimately depends.

In order to elucidate further still this sadly neglected aspect of scientific method, we may consider the idea that it is advisable to characterize science by its methods rather than by its results.

Let us first assume that a clairvoyant produces a book by dreaming it, or perhaps by automatic writing. Let us assume, further, that years later as a result of recent and revolutionary scientific discoveries a great scientist (who has never seen that book) produces one precisely the same. Or to put it differently, we assume that the clairvoyant 'saw' a scientific book which could not then have been produced by a scientist owing to the fact that many relevant discoveries were still unknown at that date. We now ask: is it advisable to say that the clairvoyant produced a scientific book? We may assume that, if submitted at the time to the judgement of competent scientists, it would have been described as partly ununderstandable, and partly fantastic; thus we shall have to say that the clairvoyant's book was not when written a scientific work, since it was not the result of scientific method. I shall call such a result, which, though in agreement with some scientific results, is not the product of scientific method, a piece of 'revealed science'.

In order to apply these considerations to the problem of the publicity of scientific method, let us assume that Robinson Crusoe succeeded in building on his island physical and chemical laboratories, astronomical observatories, etc., and in writing a great number of papers, based throughout on observation and experiment. Let us even assume that he had unlimited time at his disposal, and that he succeeded in constructing and in describing scientific systems which actually coincide with the results accepted at present by our own scientists. Considering the character of this Crusonian science, some people will be inclined, at first sight, to assert that it is real science and not 'revealed science'. And, no doubt, it is very much more like science than the scientific book which was revealed to the clairvoyant, for Robinson Crusoe applied a good deal of scientific method. And yet, I assert that this Crusonian science is still of the 'revealed' kind; that there is an element of scientific method missing, and consequently, that the fact that Crusoe arrived at our results is nearly as accidental and miraculous as it was in the case of the clairvoyant. For there is nobody but himself to check his results; nobody but himself to correct those prejudices which are the unavoidable consequence of his peculiar mental history; nobody to help him to get rid of that strange blindness concerning the inherent possibilities of our own results which is a consequence of the fact that most of them are reached through comparatively irrelevant approaches. And concerning his scientific papers, it is only in attempts to explain his work to *somebody who has not done it* that he can acquire the discipline of clear and reasoned communication which too is part of scientific method. In one point – a comparatively unimportant one – is the 'revealed' character of the Crusonian science particularly obvious; I mean Crusoe's discovery of his 'personal equation' (for we must assume that he made this discovery), of the characteristic personal reaction time affecting his astronomical observations. Of course it is conceivable that he discovered, say, changes in his reaction time, and that he was led, in this way, to make allowances for it. But if we compare this way of finding out about reaction time, with the way in which it was discovered in 'public' science – through the contradiction between the results of various observers – then the 'revealed' character of Robinson Crusoe's science becomes manifest.

To sum up these considerations, it may be said that what we call 'scientific objectivity' is not a product of the individual scientist's impartiality, but a product of the social or public character of scientific method; and the individual scientist's impartiality is, so far as it exists, not the source but rather the result of this socially or institutionally organized objectivity of science.

Both[8] Kantians and Hegelians make the same mistake of

assuming that our presuppositions (since they are, to start with, undoubtedly indispensable instruments which we need in our active 'making' of experiences) can neither be changed by decision nor refuted by experience; that they are above and beyond the scientific methods of testing theories, constituting as they do the basic presuppositions of all thought. But this is an exaggeration, based on a misunderstanding of the relations between theory and experience in science. It was one of the greatest achievements of our time when Einstein showed that, in the light of experience, we may question and revise our presuppositions regarding even space and time, ideas which had been held to be necessary presuppositions of all science, and to belong to its 'categorial apparatus'. Thus the sceptical attack upon science launched by the sociology of knowledge breaks down in the light of scientific method. The empirical method has proved to be quite capable to taking care of itself.

But it does so not by eradicating our prejudices all at once; it can eliminate them only one by one. The classical case in point is again Einstein's discovery of our prejudices regarding time. Einstein did not set out to discover prejudices; he did not even set out to criticize our conceptions of space and time. His problem was a concrete problem of physics, the redrafting of a theory that had broken down because of various experiments which in the light of the theory seemed to contradict one another. Einstein together with most physicists realized that this meant that the theory was false. And he found that if we alter it in a point which had so far been held by everybody to be self-evident and which had therefore escaped notice, then the difficulty could be removed. In other words, he just applied the methods of scientific criticism and of the invention and elimination of theories, of trial and error. But this method does not lead to the abandonment of all our prejudices; rather, we can discover the fact that we had a prejudice only after having got rid of it.

But it certainly has to be admitted that, at any given moment, our scientific theories will depend not only on the experiments, etc., made up to that moment, but also upon prejudices which are taken for granted, so that we have not become aware of them (although the application of certain logical methods may help us to detect them). At any rate, we can say in regard to this incrustation that science is capable of learning, of breaking down some of its crusts. The process may never be perfected, but there is no fixed barrier before which it must stop short. Any assumption can, in principle, be criticized. And that anybody may criticize constitutes scientific objectivity.

Scientific results are 'relative' (if this term is to be used at all) only in so far as they are the results of a certain stage of scientific development and liable to be superseded in the course of scientific progress. But this does not mean that *truth* is 'relative'. If an assertion is true, it is true for ever. [See selection 14 above, especially sections I and II.] It only means that most scientific results have the character of hypotheses, i.e. statements for which the evidence is inconclusive, and which are therefore liable to revision at any time. These considerations (with which I have dealt more fully elsewhere), though not necessary for a criticism of the sociologists, may perhaps help to further the understanding of their theories. They also throw some light, to come back to my main criticism, on the important role which co-operation, inter-subjectivity, and the publicity of method play in scientific criticism and scientific progress.

It is true that the social sciences have not yet fully attained this publicity of method. This is due partly to the intelligence-destroying influence of Aristotle and Hegel, partly perhaps also to their failure to make use of the social instruments of scientific objectivity. Thus they are really 'total ideologies', or putting it differently, some social scientists are unable, and even unwilling, to speak a common language. But the reason is not class interest, and the cure is not a Hegelian dialectical synthesis, nor self-analysis. The only course open to the social sciences is to forget all about the verbal fireworks and to tackle the practical problems of our time with the help of the theoretical methods which are fundamentally the same in *all* sciences. I mean the methods of trial and error, of inventing hypotheses which can be practically tested, and of submitting them to practical tests. *A social technology is needed whose results can be tested by piecemeal social engineering.*

The cure here suggested for the social sciences is diametrically opposed to the one suggested by the sociology of knowledge. Sociologism believes that it is not their unpractical character, but rather the fact that practical and theoretical problems are too much intertwined in the field of social and political knowledge, that creates the methodological difficulties of these sciences. Thus we can read in a leading work on the sociology of knowledge:[9] 'The peculiarity of political knowledge, as opposed to "exact" knowledge, lies in the fact that knowledge and will, or the rational element and the range of the irrational, are inseparably and essentially interwined.' To this we can reply that 'knowledge' and 'will' are, in a certain sense, always inseparable; and that this fact need not lead to any dangerous entanglement. No scientist can know without making an effort, without taking an interest; and in his effort there is usually even a certain amount of self-interest involved. The engineer studies things mainly from a practical point of view. So does the farmer. Practice is not the enemy of theoretical knowledge but the most valuable incentive to it. Though a certain amount of aloofness may be becoming to the scientist, there are many examples to show that it is not always important for a scientist to be thus disinterested. But it *is* important for him to remain in touch with reality, with practice, for those who overlook it have to pay by lapsing into scholasticism. Practical application of our findings is thus the means by which we may eliminate irrationalism from social science, and not any attempt to separate knowledge from 'will'.

As opposed to this, the sociology of knowledge hopes to reform the social sciences by making the social scientists aware of the social forces and ideologies which unconsciously beset them. But the main trouble about prejudices is that there is no such direct way of getting rid of them. For how shall we ever know that we have made any progress in our attempt to rid ourselves from prejudice? Is it not a common experience that those who are most convinced of having got rid of their prejudices are the most prejudiced? The idea that a sociological or a psychological or an anthropological or any other study of prejudices may help us to rid ourselves of them is quite mistaken; for many who pursue these studies are full of prejudice; and not only does self-analysis not help us to overcome the unconscious determination of our views, it often leads to even more subtle self-deception. Thus we can read in the same work on the sociology of knowledge[10] the following references to its own activities: 'There is an increasing tendency towards making conscious the factors by which we have so far been unconsciously ruled.... Those who fear that our increasing knowledge of determining factors may paralyse our decisions and threaten "freedom" should put their minds at rest. For only he is truly determined who does not know the most essential determining factors but acts immediately under the pressure of determinants unknown to him'. Now this is clearly just a repetition of a pet idea of Hegel's which Engels naïvely repeated when he said: 'Freedom is the appreciation of necessity.'[11] And it is a reactionary prejudice. For are those who act under the pressure of well-known determinants, for example, of a political tyranny, made free by their knowledge? Only Hegel could tell us such tales. But that the sociology of knowledge preserves this particular prejudice shows clearly enough that there is no possible shortcut to rid us of our ideologies. (Once a Hegelian, always a Hegelian.) Self-analysis is no substitute for those practical actions which are necessary for establishing the democratic institutions which alone can guarantee the freedom of critical thought, and the progress of science.

Notes

The motto on page 7 is taken from the first two theses of Popper's paper 'The Logic of the Social Sciences', pp.87-104 of *The Positivist Dispute in German Sociology*, Heinemann Educational Books, 1976. It is quoted here by permission of the publishers.

1 The Beginnings of Rationalism

1 The fragments quoted here are respectively Xenophanes B 16, 15, 18, 35 and 34; Heraclitus B 78 and 18; and Democritus B 117 in H. Diels & W. Krantz, *Die Fragmente der Vorsokratiker*, 5th edition, 1964. [The translations are all Popper's own. An alternative translation of all the Presocratic fragments, in the same order as in Diels & Krantz, may be found in Kathleen Freeman, *Ancilla to The Pre-Socratic Philosophers*, 1948.]

2 The Defence of Rationalism

1 See *The Open Society and Its Enemies*, chapter 10, especially notes 38-41, and text.

In Pythagoras, Heraclitus, Parmenides, and Plato, mystical and rationalist elements are mixed. Plato especially, in spite of all his emphasis on 'reason', incorporated into his philosophy such a weighty mixture of irrationalism that it nearly ousted the rationalism he inherited from Socrates. This enabled the neo-Platonists to base their mysticism on Plato; and most subsequent mysticism goes back to these sources.

It may perhaps be accidental, but it is in any case remarkable that there is still a cultural frontier between Western Europe and the regions of Central Europe which coincide very nearly with those regions that did not come under the administration of Augustus's Roman Empire, and that did not enjoy the blessings of the Roman peace, i.e. of the Roman civilization. The same 'barbarian' regions are particularly prone to be affected by mysticism, even though they did not invent mysticism. Bernard of Clairvaux had his greatest successes in Germany, where later Eckhart and his school flourished, and also Boehme.

Much later Spinoza, who attempted to combine Cartesian intellectualism with mystical tendencies, rediscovered the theory of a mystical intellectual intuition, which, in spite of Kant's strong opposition, led to the post-Kantian rise of 'Idealism', to Fichte, Schelling, and Hegel. Practically all modern irrationalism goes back to the latter, as is briefly indicated in chapter 12 of *The Open Society and Its Enemies.*

2 I say 'discarded' in order to cover the views (1) that such an assumption would be false, (2) that it would be unscientific (or impermissible), though it might perhaps be accidentally true, (3) that it would be 'senseless' or 'meaningless', for example in the sense of Wittgenstein's *Tractatus* [see note 17 to selection 6, and note 4 (2) below].

3 In this and the following note a few remarks on paradoxes will be made, especially on the *paradox of the liar.* In introducing these remarks, it may be said that the so-called 'logical' and 'semantical' paradoxes are no longer merely playthings for the logicians. Not only have they proved to be important for the development of mathematics, but they are also becoming important in other fields of thought. There is a definite connection between these paradoxes and such problems as the *paradox of freedom* which [see notes 4 and 6 to selection 25, and section III of selection 26] is of considerable significance in political philosophy. In point (4) of this note, it will be briefly shown that the various *paradoxes of sovereignty* are very similar to the paradox of the liar. On the modern methods of solving these paradoxes (or perhaps better: of constructing languages in which they do not occur), I shall not make any comments here, since it would take us beyond our immediate topic.

(1) *The paradox of the liar* can be formulated in many ways. One of them is this. Let us assume that somebody says one day:

'All that I say today is a lie'; or more precisely: 'All statements I make today are false'; and that he says nothing else the whole day. Now if we ask ourselves whether he spoke the truth, this is what we find. If we start with the assumption that what he said was true, then we arrive, considering *what* he said, at the result that it must have been false. And if we start with the assumption that what he said was false, then we must conclude, considering *what* he said, that it was true.

(2) Paradoxes are sometimes called 'contradictions'. But this is perhaps slightly misleading. An ordinary contradiction (or a self-contradiction) is simply a logically false statement such as 'Plato was happy yesterday and he was not happy yesterday'. If we assume that such a sentence is false, no further difficulty arises. But of a paradox, we can assume neither that it is true *nor that it is false*, without getting involved in difficulties.

(3) There are, however, statements which are closely related to paradoxes, but which are, more strictly speaking, only self-contradictions. Take for example the statement: 'All statements are false.' If we assume this this statement is true, then we arrive, considering *what* it says, at the result that it is false. But if we assume that it is false, then we are out of the difficulty; for this assumption leads only to the result that not all statements are false, or in other words, that there are some statements – at least one – that are true. And this result is harmless; for it does not imply that our original statement is one of the true ones. (This does not imply that we can, in fact, construct a language *free of paradoxes* in which 'All statements are false' or 'All statements are true' can be formulated.)

In spite of the fact that this statement 'All propositions are false' is not really a paradox, it may be called, by courtesy 'a form of the paradox of the liar' because of its obvious resemblance to the latter; and indeed the old Greek formulation of this paradox (Epimenides the Cretan says: 'All Cretans always lie') is, in this terminology, rather 'a form of the paradox of the liar', i.e. a contradiction rather than a paradox. (See also the next note.)

(4) I shall now show briefly the similarity between the paradox of the liar and the various *paradoxes of sovereignty*, for

example, of the principle that the best or the wisest or the majority should rule.

C.H. Langford has described various ways of putting the paradox of the liar, among them the following. We consider two statements, made by two people *A* and *B*.

A says: 'What *B* says is true.'

B says: 'What *A* says is false.'

By applying the method described above, we easily convince ourselves that each of these sentences is paradoxical. Now we consider the following two sentences, of which the first is the principle that the wisest should rule:

(A) The principle says: What the wisest says under *(B)* should be law.

(B) The wisest says: What the principle states under *(A)* should not be law.

4 (1) That the principle of avoiding all presuppositions is 'a form of the paradox of the liar' in the sense of the previous note, and therefore self-contradictory, will be easily seen if we describe it like this. A philosopher starts his investigation by assuming without argument the principle: 'All principles assumed without argument are impermissible.' It is clear that if we assume that this principle is true, we must conclude, considering what it says, that it is impermissible. (The opposite assumption does not lead to any difficulty.) The remark 'a counsel of perfection' alludes to the usual criticism of this principle which was laid down, for example, by Husserl. J. Laird (*Recent Philosophy*, 1936, p.121) writes about this principle that it is 'a cardinal feature of Husserl's philosophy. Its success may be more doubtful, for presuppositions have a way of creeping in.' So far, I fully agree; but not quite with the next remark: '. . .the avoidance of all presuppositions may well be a counsel of perfection, impracticable in an inadvertent world.'

(2) We may consider at this place a few further 'principles' which are, in the sense of the previous note, 'forms of the paradox of the liar', and therefore self-contradictory.

(a) From the point of view of social philosophy, the following 'principle of sociologism' (and the analogous 'principle of

historism') are of interest. 'No statement is absolutely true, and all statements are inevitably relative to the social (or historical) habitat of their originators.' It is clear that the considerations above apply practically without alteration. For if we assume that such a principle is true, then it follows that it is not true but only 'relative to the social or historical habitat of its originator'. See also note 53 to chapter 24 of *The Open Society and Its Enemies*, and text.

(*b*) Some examples of this kind can be found in Wittgenstein's *Tractatus*. One is Wittgenstein's proposition (quoted more fully [in note 13 to selection 6]: 'The totality of true propositions is . . . the totality of the natural sciences.' Since this proposition does not belong to natural science (but, rather, to a metascience, i.e. a theory that speaks about science) it follows that it asserts its own untruth, and is therefore contradictory.

Furthermore, it is clear that this proposition violates Wittgenstein's own principle (*Tractatus*, 3.332), 'No proposition can say anything about itself. . . .'

But even this last quoted principle, which I shall call '*W*', turns out to be a form of the paradox of the liar, and to assert its own untruth. (It therefore can hardly be – as Wittgenstein believes it to be – equivalent to, or a summary of, or a substitute for, 'the whole theory of types', i.e. Russell's theory, which was designed to avoid the paradoxes by dividing expressions which look like propositions into three classes – true propositions, false propositions, and meaningless expressions or pseudopropositions.) For Wittgenstein's principle *W* may be reformulated as follows:

(W^+) Every expression (and especially one that looks like a proposition) which contains a reference to itself – by containing either its own name or an individual variable ranging over a class to which it itself belongs – is not a proposition (but a meaningless pseudoproposition).

Now let us assume that W^+ is true. Then, considering the fact that it is an expression, and that it refers to every expression, it cannot be a proposition, and is therefore *a fortiori* not true.

The assumption that it is true is therefore untenable; W^+

cannot be true. But this does not show that it must be false; for neither the assumption that it is false nor the assumption that it is a meaningless (or senseless) expression, involves us in immediate difficulties.

Wittgenstein might perhaps say that he saw this himself when he wrote (6.54 [see note 17 to selection 6]): 'My propositions are elucidatory in this way: he who understands me finally recognizes them as senseless. . . .'; in any case, we may conjecture that he would incline to describing W^+ as meaningless rather than false. I believe, however, that it is not meaningless but simply false. Or more precisely, I believe that in every formalized language (e.g. in one in which Gödel's undecidable statements can be expressed) which contains means for speaking about its own expressions and in which we have names of classes of expressions such as 'propositions' and 'non-propositions', *the formalization of a statement which, like* W^+, *asserts its own meaninglessness, will be self-contradictory and neither meaningless nor genuinely paradoxical*; it will be a meaningful proposition merely because it asserts of every expression of a certain kind that it is not a proposition (i.e. not a well-formed formula); and such an assertion will be true or false, but not meaningless, simply because to be (or not to be) a well-formed proposition is a property of expressions. For example, 'All expressions are meaningless' will be self-contradictory, but not genuinely paradoxical, and so will be the expression, 'The expression x is meaningless', if we substitute for 'x' a name of this expression. Modifying an idea of J.N. Findlay's we can write:

The expression obtained by substituting for the variable in the following expression 'The expression obtained by substituting for the variable in the following expression x the quotation name of this expression, is not a statement' the quotation name of this expression is not a statement.

And what we have just written turns out to be a self-contradictory statement. (If we write twice 'is a false statement' instead of 'is not a statement', we obtain a paradox of the liar; if we write 'is a non-demonstrable statement', we obtain a Gödelian statement in Findlay's writing.)

To sum up. Contrary to first impressions we find that a

theory which implies its own meaninglessness is not meaningless but false, since the predicate 'meaningless', as opposed to 'false', does not give rise to paradoxes. And Wittgenstein's theory is therefore not meaningless, as he believes, but simply false (or more specifically, self-contradictory).

(3) It has been claimed by some positivists that a tripartition of the expressions of a language into (i) true statements, (ii) false statements, and (iii) meaningless expressions (or, better, expressions other than well-formed statements), is more or less 'natural' and that it provides, because of their meaninglessness, for the elimination of the paradoxes and, at the same time, of metaphysical systems. The following may show that this tripartition is not enough. [See also *Conjectures and Refutations*, chapter 14.]

The General's Chief Counter-espionage Officer is provided with three boxes, labelled (i) 'General's Box', (ii) 'Enemy's Box' (to be made accessible to the enemy's spies), and (iii) 'Waste Paper', and is instructed to distribute all information arriving before 12 o'clock among these three boxes, according to whether this information is (i) true, (ii) false, or (iii) meaningless.

For a time he receives information which he can easily distribute (among it true statements of the theory of natural numbers, etc. and perhaps statements of logic such as *L*: 'From a set of true statements, no false statement can be validly derived'). The last message *M*, arriving with the last incoming mail just before 12 o'clock, disturbs him a little, for *M* reads: 'From the set of all statements placed, or to be placed, within the box labelled "General's Box", the statement "0=1" cannot validly be derived.' At first, the Chief Counter-espionage Officer hesitates whether he should not put *M* into box (ii). But since he realizes that, if put into (ii), *M* would supply the enemy with valuable true information, he ultimately decides to put *M* into (i).

But this turns out to be a big mistake. For the symbolic logicians (experts in logistic?) on the General's staff, after formalizing (and 'arithmetizing') the contents of the General's box, discover that they obtain a set of statements which contains an assertion of its own consistency; and this, according to Gödel's second theorem on decidability, leads to a contradiction, so that '0=1' can actually be deduced from the presumably true information supplied to the General.

The solution of this difficulty consists in the recognition of the fact that the tripartition claim is unwarranted, at least for ordinary languages; and we can see from Tarski's theory of truth that no definite number of boxes will suffice. At the same time we find that 'meaninglessness' in the sense of 'not belonging to the well-formed formulae' is by no means an indication of 'nonsensical talk' in the sense of 'words which just don't mean anything, although they may pretend to be deeply significant'; but to have revealed that metaphysics was just of this character was the chief claim of the positivists.

5 It appears that it was the difficulty connected with the problem of induction which led Whitehead to the disregard of argument displayed in *Process and Reality*, 1929. [In connection with the whole of this selection, and the possibility of a *comprehensive critical* rationalism, the reader's attention is drawn to the works of W.W. Bartley III, especially *The Retreat to Commitment*, 1962. See also *The Open Society and Its Enemies*, volume II, addendum I.]

6 It is a moral decision and not merely 'a matter of taste' since it is not a private affair but affects other men and their lives. The decision with which we are faced is most important from the point of view that the 'learned', who are faced with it, act as intellectual trustees for those who are not faced with it.

7 It is, I believe, perhaps the greatest strength of Christianity that it appears fundamentally not to abstract speculation but to the imagination, by describing in a very concrete manner the suffering of man.

8 Kant, the great equalitarian in regard to moral decisions, has emphasized the blessings involved in the fact of human inequality. He saw in the variety and individuality of human characters and opinions one of the main conditions of moral as well as material progress.

9 The allusion is to A. Huxley's *Brave New World*, 1932.

10 For the distinction between facts, and decisions or demands, see chapter 5 of *The Open Society and Its Enemies*. For the 'language of political demands' (or 'proposals' in the sense of L.J. Russell) see *op.cit.* chapter 6, section VI.

I should be inclined to say that the theory of the innate intellectual equality of all men is false; but since such men as Niels Bohr contend that the influence of environment is alone responsible for individual differences, and since there are no sufficient experimental data for deciding this question, 'probably false' is perhaps all that should be said.

11 See, for example, *Statesman*, 293 C-E. Another such passage is *Republic*, 409 E - 410 A. After having spoken (409 B/C) of the '*good judge ... who is good because of the goodness of his soul*', Plato continues: 'And are you not going to establish physicians and judges ... who are to look after those citizens whose physical and mental constitution is healthy and good? Those whose physical health is bad, they will leave to die. And those whose soul is badnatured and incurable, they will actually kill.' – 'Yes,' he said, 'since you have proved that this is the best thing, both for those to whom it happens, and for the state.'

12 See *Phaedo*, 89 C/D.

13 An example is H.G. Wells, who gave to the first chapter of his book, *The Common Sense of War and Peace*, 1940, the excellent title: 'Grown Men Do Not Need Leaders'.

14 For the problem and the paradox of tolerance [see note 4 to selection 25].

15 The 'world' is not rational, but it is the the task of science to rationalize it. 'Society' is not rational, but it is the task of the social engineer to rationalize it. (This does not mean, of course, that he should 'direct' it, or that centralized or collectivist 'planning' is desirable.) Ordinary language is not rational but it is our task to rationalize it, or at least to keep up its standards of clarity. The attitude here characterized could be described as '*pragmatic rationalism*'. This pragmatic rationalism is related to an uncritical rationalism and to irrationalism in a similar way as critical rationalism is related to these two. For an uncritical

rationalism may argue that the world is rational and that the task of science is to discover this rationality, while an irrationalist may insist that the world, being fundamentally irrational, should be experienced and exhausted by our emotions and passions (or by our intellectual intuition) rather than by scientific methods. As opposed to this, pragmatic rationalism may recognize that the world is not rational, but demand *that we submit or subject it to reason*, as far as possible. Using Carnap's words (*The Logical Structure of the World*, 1928, p.vi; English translation, 1967, p.xviii) one could describe what I call 'pragmatic rationalism' as 'the attitude which strives for clarity everywhere but recognizes the never fully understandable or never fully rational entanglement of the events of life.'

16 [See also note 16 to selection 6.]

3 Knowledge without Authority

1 See D. Hume, *An Enquiry concerning Human Understanding*, 1748, section V, part I; edition of L. Selby-Bigge, p.46. See also Hume's assertion that 'it is impossible for us to *think* of any thing, which we have not antecedently *felt*, either by our external or internal senses' in section VII, part I; Selby-Bigge, p.62.

2 See also *The Logic of Scientific Discovery*, appendix *x (2).

3 See D. Hume, *A Treatise of Human Nature*, 1739, Book I, part III, section IV; edition of L. Selby-Bigge, p.83. See also Hume's *Enquiry*, section X; Selby-Bigge, pp.111 ff.

4 See Immanuel Kant, *Religion Within the Limits of Pure Reason*, 2nd edition, 1794, chapter 4, part II, section 1, the first footnote.

5 See F.P. Ramsey, *The Foundations of Mathematics*, 1931, p.291.

4 Knowledge: Subjective versus Objective

1 The argument is adapted from *The Open Society and Its Enemies*, chapter 15, section III.

2 See p.32 of G. Frege, 'Über Sinn und Bedeutung', *Zeitschrift für Philosophie und philosophische Kritik* **100**, 1892, pp.25-50; the italics are mine. (Frege's paper has been translated and reprinted in several places; for example by H. Feigl on pp.85-102 of H. Feigl & W. Sellars, editors, *Readings in Philosophical Analysis*, 1949.)

3 See p.195 of A. Heyting, 'After Thirty Years', pp.194-7 of E. Nagel, P. Suppes, & A. Tarski, editors, *Logic, Methodology and Philosophy of Science*, 1962.

4 On these 'artefacts' see p.111 of F.A. von Hayek, *Studies in Philosophy, Politics and Economics*, 1967.

5 See Hayek, *op.cit.*, chapter 6, especially pp.96, 100, n.12; R. Descartes, *Discourse on Method*, edition of E.S. Haldane & G.R.T. Ross, p.89; [selection 24, section II below]; and *Objective Knowledge*, pp.253-5.

6 An example of the latter is Lakatos's 'concept-stretching refutation' in I. Lakatos, *Proofs and Refutations*, 1976, especially pp.83-99.

7 See also *Objective Knowledge*, p.243.

8 See *Conjectures and Refutations*, chapters 4 and 12, especially the references on pp.134, 293, and 295 to K. Bühler, *Sprachtheorie*, 1934. Bühler was the first to discuss the decisive difference between the lower functions and the descriptive function. I found later, as a consequence of my theory of criticism, the decisive distinction between the descriptive and the argumentative functions. See also *Objective Knowledge*, pp.235-8 [and section II of selection 21 below].

9 One of the great discoveries of modern logic was Alfred Tarski's re-establishment of the (objective) correspondence theory of truth (truth = correspondence to the facts). This theory, together with the regulative ideas of truth content and

verisimilitude, is discussed [in selection 14 below]. The present paper owes everything to Tarski's theory; but I do not of course wish to implicate Tarski in any of the crimes here committed.

10 See *Conjectures and Refutations*, p.64.

11 The theory that our beliefs may be gauged by our readiness to bet on them was regarded in 1781 as well known; see I. Kant, *Critique of Pure Reason*, 2nd edition, 1787, p.853.

12 See J.W.N. Watkins, *Hobbes's System of Ideas*, 1965, chapter VIII, especially pp.145f.; *The Logic of Scientific Discovery*, pp.420-2; and *Conjectures and Refutations*, pp.18ff., 262, 297f.

13 The error, which is traditional, is known as 'the problem of universals'. This should be replaced by 'the problem of theories', or 'the problem of the theoretical content of all human language'. See *The Logic of Scientific Discovery*, note *1 to section 4 [and also section I of selection 11 below].

Incidentally, it is clear that of the famous three positions – *universale ante rem*, *in re*, and *post rem* – the last, in its usual meaning, is anti-world-3 and tries to explain language as expression, while the first (Platonic) is pro-world-3. Interestingly enough, the (Aristotelian) middle position (*in re*) may be said either to be anti-world-3 or to ignore the problem of world 3. It thus testifies to the confusing influence of conceptualism.

14 See Aristotle, *Metaphysics*, 1072b21f. and 1074b15-1075a4. This passage (which Ross sums up: 'the divine thought must be concerned with the most divine object, which is itself') contains an implicit criticism of Plato. Its affinity with Platonic ideas is especially clear in lines 25f.: 'it thinks of that which is most divine and precious, and it does not change; for change would be change for the worse...'. (See also Aristotle, *De Anima*, 429b27ff., especially 430a4.)

15 See Plotinus, *Enneads*, II.IV.4, III.VIII.11, V.III.2-5, V.IX.5-8, VI.V.2, VI.VI.6-7. (The numbering here is that of the edition

of R. Volkmann, 1883; there are slight variations in the English translation of S. Mackenna, 1917-1930.)

16 See G.W.F. Hegel, *Enzyklopädie der philosophischen Wissenschaften*, 3rd edition, 1930, paragraph 551. (An English translation by W. Wallace is available in A.V. Miller, editor, *Hegel's Philosophy of Mind*, 1971.)

17 See *Conjectures and Refutations*, chapter 15, and *The Open Society and Its Enemies*, addendum I ('Facts, Standards and Truth: a Further Criticism of Relativism') to volume II.

18 See Lakatos, *op.cit.*, note 2 on p.54.

5 Evolutionary Epistemology

1 The formation of membrane proteins, of the first viruses, and of cells, may perhaps have been among the earliest inventions of new environmental niches; though it is possible that other environmental niches (perhaps networks of enzymes invented by otherwise naked genes) may have been invented even earlier.

2 It is an open problem whether one can speak in these terms ('in response') about the genetic level (compare my conjecture about responding mutagens in section v). Yet if there were no variations, there could not be adaptation or evolution; and so we can say that the occurrence of mutations is either partly controlled by a need for them, or functions as if it was.

3 For the use of the term 'blind' (especially in the second sense) see D.T. Campbell, 'Methodological Suggestions for a Comparative Psychology of Knowledge Processes', *Inquiry* **2**, 1959, pp.152-82; 'Blind Variation and Selective Retention in Creative Thought as in Other Knowledge Processes', *Psychological Review* **67**, 1960, pp.380-400; and 'Evolutionary Epistemology', pp.413-63 of P.A. Schilpp, editor, *The Philosophy of Karl Popper*, The Library of Living Philosophers 1974.

While the 'blindness' of trials is relative to what we have found out in the past, randomness is relative to a set of elements (forming the 'sample space'). On the genetic level these 'elements' are the four nucleotide bases; on the behavioural level they are the constituents of the organism's repertoire of behaviour. These constituents may assume different weights with respect to different needs or goals, and the weights may change through experience (lowering the degree of 'blindness').

4 On the importance of active participation, see R.Held & A. Hein, 'Movement-produced Stimulation in the Development of Visually Guided Behaviour', *Journal of Comparative and Physiological Psychology* **56**, 1963, pp.872-6; see also J.C. Eccles, *Facing Reality*, 1963, pp.66f. The activity is, at least partly, one of producing hypotheses: see J. Krechevsky, '"Hypothesis" versus "Chance" in the Pre-solution Period in Sensory Discrimination-learning', *University of California Publications in Psychology* **6**, 1932, pp.27-44 (reprinted on pp.183-97 of A.J. Riopelle, editor, *Animal Problem Solving*, 1967).

5 I may perhaps mention here some of the differences between my views and the views of the *Gestalt* school. (Of course, I accept the fact of *Gestalt* perception; I am dubious only about what may be called *Gestalt* philosophy.)

I conjecture that the unity, or the articulation, of perception is more closely dependent on the motor control systems and the efferent neural systems of the brain than on the afferent systems: that it is closely dependent on the behavioural repertoire of the organism. I conjecture that a spider or a mouse will never have insight (as had Köhler's ape) into the possible unity of the two sticks which can be joined together, because handling sticks of that size does not belong to their behavioural repertoire. All this may be interpreted as a kind of generalization of the James/Lange theory of emotions (1884; see pp.449ff. of W. James, *The Principles of Psychology*, volume II, 1890), extending the theory from our emotions to our perceptions (especially to *Gestalt* perceptions) which thus would not be 'given' to us (as in *Gestalt* theory) but rather 'made' by us, by decoding (comparatively 'given') clues. The fact that the clues may mislead (optical illusions in man;

dummy illusions in animals, etc.) can be explained by the biological need to impose our behavioural interpretations upon highly simplified clues. The conjecture that our decoding of what the senses tell us depends on our behavioural repertoire may explain part of the gulf that lies between animals and man; for through the evolution of the human language our repertoire has become unlimited.

6 See pp.99ff. of W.H. Thorpe, *Learning and Instinct in Animals*, 1956; 1963 edition, pp.100-47; W. Köhler, *The Mentality of Apes*, 1925; Penguin Books edition, 1957, pp.166ff.

7 See I.P. Pavlov, *Conditioned Reflexes*, 1927, especially pp.11f. In view of what he calls 'exploratory behaviour' and the closely related 'freedom behaviour' – both obviously genetically based – and of the significance of these for scientific activity, it seems to me that the behaviour of behaviourists who aim to supersede the value of freedom by what they call 'positive re-inforcement' may be a symptom of an unconscious hostility to science. Incidentally, what B.F. Skinner, *Beyond Freedom and Dignity*, 1972, calls 'the literature of freedom' did not arise as a result of negative re-inforcement, as he suggests. It arose, rather, with Aeschylus and Pindar, as a result of the victories of Marathon and Salamis.

8 Thus exploratory behaviour and problem solving create new conditions for the evolution of genetic systems; conditions which deeply affect the natural selection of these systems. One can say that once a certain latitude of behaviour has been attained – as it has been attained even by unicellular organisms (see especially the classic work of H.S. Jennings, *The Behaviour of the Lower Organisms*, 1906) – the initiative of the organism in selecting its ecology or habitat takes the lead, and natural selection within the new habitat follows the lead. In this way, Darwinism can simulate Lamarckism, and even Bergson's 'creative evolution'. This has been recognized by strict Darwinists. For a brilliant presentation and survey of the history, see Sir Alister Hardy, *The Living Stream*, 1965, especially lectures VI, VII, and VIII, where many references to earlier literature will be found, from James Hutton (who

died in 1797) onwards (see pp.178ff.). See also Ernst Mayr, *Animal Species and Evolution*, 1963, pp.604ff. and 611; Erwin Schrödinger, *Mind and Matter*, 1958, chapter 2; F.W. Braestrup, 'The Evolutionary Significance of Learning', *Videnskabelige Meddelelser Naturhistorisk Forening i Kjøbenhavn* **134**, 1971, pp.89-102 (with a bibliography); and *Objective Knowledge*, chapter 7.

9 Quoted by Jacques Hadamard, *The Psychology of Invention in the Mathematical Field*, 1945; Dover edition, 1954, p.48.

10 Behavioural psychologists who study 'experimenter bias' have found that some albino rats perform decidedly better than others if the experimenter is led to believe (wrongly) that the former belong to a strain selected for high intelligence: see R. Rosenthal & K.L. Fode, 'The Effect of Experimenter Bias on the Performance of the Albino Rat', *Behavioural Science* **8**, 1963, pp.183-9. The lesson drawn by the authors of this paper is that experiments should be made by 'research assistants who do not know what outcome is desired' (p.188). Like Bacon, these authors pin their hopes on the empty mind, forgetting that the expectations of the director of research may communicate themselves, without explicit disclosure, to his research assistants, just as they seem to have communicated themselves from each research assistant to his rats.

11 It is interesting that Charles Darwin in his later years believed in the occasional inheritance even of mutilations. See his *The Variation of Animals and Plants under Domestication*, volume I, 2nd edition, 1875, pp.466-70.

12 Specific mutagens (acting selectively, perhaps on some particular sequence of codons rather than on others) are not known, I understand. Yet their existence would hardly be surprising in this field of surprises; and they might explain mutational 'hot spots'. At any rate, there seems to be a real difficulty in concluding from the absence of known specific mutagens that specific mutagens do not exist. Thus it seems to me that the problem suggested in the text (the possibility of a reaction to certain strains by the production of mutagens) is still open.

13 See Ernst Gombrich, *Art and Illusion*, 1960 and later editions, in the index under 'making and matching'.

14 See N.K. Jerne, 'The Natural Selection Theory of Antibody Formation; Ten Years Later', pp.301-12 of J. Cairns *et al.*, editors, *Phage and the Origins of Molecular Biology*, 1966; also 'The Natural Selection Theory of Antibody Formation', *Proceedings of the National Academy of Sciences* **41**, 1955, pp.849-57; 'Immunological Speculations', *Annual Review of Microbiology* **14**, 1960, pp.341-58; 'The Immune System', *Scientific American* **229**, 1, 1973, pp.52-60. See also Sir Macfarlane Burnet, 'A Modification of Jerne's Theory of Anti-body Production, using the Concept of Clonal Selection', *Australian Journal of Science* **20**, 1957, pp.67-9; *The Clonal Selection Theory of Acquired Immunity*, 1959.

6 Two Kinds of Definitions

1 The motto is from p.269 of *The Foundations of Mathematics*, 1931. [In connection with this selection the reader's attention is drawn particularly to *Unended Quest*, sections 6 and 7.]

2 For Plato's, or rather Parmenides's, distinction between knowledge and opinion (a distinction which continued to be popular with more modern writers, for example with Locke and Hobbes), see *The Open Society and Its Enemies*, chapter 3, notes 22 and 26 and text; further, notes 19 to chapter 5, and 25-7 to chapter 8. For Aristotle's corresponding distinction, see, for example, *Metaphysics*, 1039b31 and *Posterior Analytics*, 88b30 ff. and 100b5.

For Aristotle's distinction between *demonstrative* and *intuitive* knowledge, see the last chapter of *Posterior Analytics* (especially 100b5-17; see also 72b18-24, 75b31, 84a31, 90a6-91a11). For the connection between demonstrative knowledge and the 'causes' of a thing which are 'distinct from its essential nature' and thereby require a middle term, see *op.cit.*, especially 93a5, 93b26. For the analogous connection between intellectual intuition and the 'indivisible form' which it grasps – the indivisible essence and individual nature which is identical with its cause – see *op. cit.*, 72b24, 77a4, 85a1, 88b35. See also *op. cit.*, 90a31: 'To know the nature of a thing is to know the reason why it is' (i.e. its cause); and 93b21: 'There are essential natures which are immediate, i.e. basic premisses.'

For Aristotle's recognition that we must stop somewhere in the regression of proofs or demonstrations, and accept certain *principles* without proof, see for example *Metaphysics*, 1006a7: 'It is impossible to prove everything, for then there would arise an infinite regression....' See also *Posterior Analytics*, 90b18-27.

3 See *Metaphysics*, 1031b7 and 1031b20. See also 996b20.

'A definition is a statement that describes the essence of a thing' (Aristotle, *Topics*, 101b36, 153a, 153a15, etc. See also *Metaphysics*, 1042a17) – 'The definition . . . reveals the essential nature' (*Posterior Analytics*, 91a1) – 'Definition is ... a statement of the nature of the thing' (*ibid.*, 93b28) – 'Only those things have essences whose formulae are definitions' (*Metaphysics*, 1030a5 f.) – 'The essence, whose formula is a definition, is also called the substance of a thing' (*ibid.*, 1017b21) – 'Clearly, then, the definition is the formula of the essence . . .' (*ibid.*, 1031a13).

Regarding these principles, i.e. the starting points or basic premisses of proofs, we must distinguish between two kinds. (1) The logical principles (see *Metaphysics*, 996b25 ff.) and (2) the premisses from which proofs must proceed and which cannot be proved in turn if an infinite regression is to be avoided (see note 2). The latter are definitions: 'The basic premisses of proofs are definitions' (*Posterior Analytics*, 90b23; see also 89a17, 90a35). See also pp.45f. of W.D. Ross, *Aristotle*, 5th edition, 1949, commenting upon *Posterior Analytics*, 73a20-74a4: 'the premises of science', Ross writes (p.46), 'will, we are told, be *per se* in either sense (*a*) or sense (*b*)'. On the previous page we learn that a premiss is necessary *per se* (or essentially necessary) in the senses (*a*) and (*b*) *if it rests upon a definition.*

4 'If it has a name, then there will be a formula of its meaning', says Aristotle (*Metaphysics*, 1030a14; see also 1030b24); and he explains that not every formula of the meaning of a name is a

definition; but if the name is one of a species of a genus, then the formula will be a definition.

It is important to note that in my use (I follow here the modern use of the word) 'definition' always refers to the whole definition sentence, while Aristotle (and others who follow him in this, e.g. Hobbes) sometimes use the word also as a synonym for 'definiens'.

Definitions are not of particulars, but only of universals (see *Metaphysics*, 1036a28) and only of essences, i.e. of something which is the species of a genus (i.e. a *last differentia*; *ibid.*, 1038a19) and an indivisible form; see also *Posterior Analytics*, 97b6 f.

5 For Plato's doctrine see *The Open Society and Its Enemies*, chapter 8, section IV.

Grote writes on p.260 of *Aristotle*, 2nd edition, 1880: 'Aristotle had inherited from Plato this doctrine of an infallible Noûs or Intellect, enjoying complete immunity from error.' Grote continues to emphasize that, as opposed to Plato, Aristotle does not despise observational experience, but rather assigns to his Nous (i.e. intellectual intuition) 'a position as terminus and correlate to the process of Induction' (*loc. cit.*, see also *op. cit.*, p.577). This is so; but observational experience has apparently only the function of priming and developing our intellectual intuition for its task, the intuition of the universal essence; and, indeed, nobody has ever explained how definitions, *which are beyond error*, can be reached by induction.

6 Aristotle's view amounts to the same as Plato's in so far as there is for both, in the last instance, no possible appeal to argument. All that can be done is to assert *dogmatically* of a certain definition that it is a true description of its essence; and if asked why this and no other description is true, all that remains is an appeal to the 'intuition of the essence'.

Aristotle speaks of induction in at least two senses – in a more heuristic sense of a method leading us to 'intuit the general principle' (see *Prior Analytics*, 67a22 f., 27b25-33, *Posterior Analytics*, 71a7, 81a38-b5, 100b4 f.) and in a more empirical sense (*Prior Analytics*, 68b15-37, 69a16, *Posterior Analytics*, 78a35, 81b5 ff., *Topics*, 105a13, 156a4, 157a34).

For 'the whole body of fact' mentioned in the next paragraph, see the end of *Posterior Analytics* (100b15 f.).

It is remarkable how similar the views of Hobbes (a nominalist but *not* a methodological nominalist) are to Aristotle's methodological essentialism. Hobbes too believes that definitions are the basic premisses of all knowledge (as opposed to opinion).

7 The quotation is from my note in *Erkenntnis* **3**, 1933, pp.426 f., now translated in *The Logic of Scientific Discovery*, pp.312-14; it is a variation and generalization of a statement on geometry made by Einstein in his 'Geometry and Experience', 1921, pp.232-46 of *Ideas and Opinions*.

8 See, for example, *Metaphysics*, 1030a6 and 14 (see note 4 above).

9 I wish to emphasize that I speak here about *nominalism versus essentialism* in a purely methodological way. I do not take up any position towards the *metaphysical* problem of universals, i.e. towards the metaphysical problem of nominalism versus essentialism (a term which I suggest should be used instead of the traditional term 'realism'); and I certainly do not advocate a metaphysical nominalism, although I advocate a methodological nominalism. [See also note 13 to selection 4 above.]

The opposition between *nominalist and essentialist definitions* made in the text is an attempt to reconstruct the traditional distinction between 'verbal' and 'real' definitions. *My main emphasis, however, is on the question of whether the definition is read from the right to the left or from the left to the right; or in other words, whether it replaces a long story by a short one, or a short story by a long one.*

10 My contention that in science *only* nominalist definitions occur (I speak here of explicit definitions only and neither of implicit nor of recursive definitions) needs some defence. It certainly does not imply that terms are not used more or less 'intuitively' in science; this is clear if only we consider that all chains of definitions must start with *undefined* terms, whose meaning can be exemplified but not defined. Further, it seems clear in science, especially in mathematics, we often first use a term,

for instance 'dimension' or 'truth', intuitively, but proceed later to define it. But this is rather a rough description of the situation. A more precise description would be this. Some of the undefined terms used intuitively can be sometimes replaced by defined terms of which it can be shown that they fulfil the intentions with which the undefined terms have been used; that is to say, to every sentence in which the undefined terms occurred (e.g., which was interpreted as analytic) there is a corresponding sentence in which the newly defined term occurs (which follows from the definition).

One certainly can say that K. Menger has recursively defined 'dimension' or that A. Tarski has defined 'truth'; but this way of expressing matters may lead to misunderstandings. What has happened is that Menger gave a purely nominal definition of classes of sets of points which he labelled '*n*-dimensional', because it was possible to replace the intuitive mathematical concept '*n*-dimensional' by the new concept in all important contexts; and the same can be said of Tarski's concept 'truth'. Tarski gave a nominal definition (or rather a method of drafting nominal definitions) which he labelled 'truth', since a system of sentences could be derived from the definition corresponding to those sentences (like the law of the excluded middle) which had been used by many logicians and philosophers in connection with what they called 'truth'.

11 The fact that a statement is true may sometimes help to explain why it appears to us as self-evident. This is the case with '2 + 2 = 4', or with the sentence 'The sun radiates light as well as heat'. But the reverse is clearly not the case. The fact that a sentence appears to some or even all of us to be 'self-evident', that is to say, the fact that some or even all of us believe firmly in its truth and cannot conceive of its falsity, is no reason why it should be true. (The fact that we are unable to conceive of the falsity of a statement is in many cases only a reason for suspecting that our power of imagination is deficient or undeveloped.) It is one of the gravest mistakes if a philosophy ever offers self-evidence as an argument in favour of the truth of a sentence; yet this is done by practically all idealist

philosophies. It shows that idealist philosophies are often systems of apologetics for some dogmatic beliefs.

The excuse that we are often in such a position that we must accept certain sentences for no better reason than that they are self-evident, is not valid. The principles of logic and of scientific method (especially the 'principle of induction' or the 'law of uniformity of nature') are usually mentioned as statements which we must accept, and which we cannot justify by anything but self-evidence. Even if this were so, it would be franker to say that we cannot justify them, and leave it at that. But, in fact, there is no need for a 'principle of induction'. [See the next selection.] And as far as the 'principles of logic' are concerned, much has been done in recent years which shows that the self-evidence theory is obsolete. (See especially R. Carnap, *Logical Syntax of Language*, 1937, and his *Introduction to Semantics*, 1942.)

12 'Science assumes the definitions of all its terms. . . .' (Ross, *Aristotle*, p.44; see *Posterior Analytics*, 76a32-36); see also note 4 above.

13 R.H.S. Crossman, *Plato To-day*, 1937; 2nd edition, 1959, p.51.

A very similar doctrine is expressed by M.R. Cohen & E. Nagel in their book, *An Introduction to Logic and Scientific Method*, 1934, p.232: 'Many of the disputes about the true nature of property, of religion, of law, . . . would assuredly disappear if the precisely defined equivalents were substituted for these words.' (See also note 15 below.)

The views concerning this problem expressed by Wittgenstein in his *Tractatus Logico-Philosophicus*, 1921/22, and by several of his followers are not as definite as those of Crossman, Cohen and Nagel. Wittgenstein is an anti-metaphysician. 'The book', he writes in the preface, 'deals with the problems of philosophy and shows, I believe, that the method of formulating these problems rests on the misunderstanding of the logic of our language.' He tries to show that metaphysics is 'simply nonsense' and tries to draw a limit, in our language, between sense and nonsense: 'The limit can . . . be drawn in languages and what lies on the other side of the limit will be simply nonsense.' According to Wittgenstein's book, propositions have sense. They are true or false. Philosophical propositions do not exist; they only look like propositions, but are, in fact, nonsensical. The limit between sense and nonsense coincides with that between natural science and philosophy: 'The totality of true propositions is the total natural science (or the totality of the natural sciences). – Philosophy is not one of the natural sciences.' *The true task of philosophy, therefore, is not to formulate propositions; it is, rather, to clarify propositions*: 'The result of philosophy is not a number of "philosophical propositions", but to make propositions clear.' Those who do not see that, and propound philosophical propositions, talk metaphysical nonsense.

14 It is important to distinguish between a logical deduction in general, and a proof or demonstration in particular. A *proof* or *demonstration* is a deductive argument by which the truth of the conclusion is finally established; this is how Aristotle uses the term, demanding (for example, in *Posterior Analytics*, 73a20 ff.) that the 'necessary' truth of the conclusion should be established; and this is how Carnap uses the term (see especially *Logical Syntax*, section 10, p.29, section 47, p.171), showing that conclusions which are 'demonstrable' in this sense are 'analytically' true. (Into the problems concerning the terms 'analytic' and 'synthetic', I shall not enter here.)

Since Aristotle, it has been clear that not all logical deductions are proofs (i.e. demonstrations); there are also logical deductions which are not proofs; for example, we can deduce conclusions from admittedly false premisses, and such deductions are not called proofs. Non-demonstrative deductions are called by Carnap 'derivations' (*loc. cit.*). It is interesting that a name for these non-demonstrative deductions has not been introduced earlier; it shows the preoccupation with proofs, a preoccupation which arose from the Aristotelian prejudice that 'science' or 'scientific knowledge' must establish all its statements, i.e. accept them either as self-evident premisses, or prove them. But the position is this. *Outside of pure logic and pure mathematics nothing can be proved.* Arguments in other sciences (and even some within mathematics, as I. Lakatos has shown) are not proofs but merely *derivations*.

It may be remarked that there is a far-reaching parallelism between the problems of *derivation* on the one side and *definition* on the other, and between the problems of the *truth of sentences*, and that of the *meaning of terms*. [See in particular the table on p.75 above.]

15 The examples are the same as those which Cohen & Nagel, *op.cit.*, pp.232f. recommend for definition. (See note 13 above.)

Some general remarks on the uselessness of essentialist definitions may be added here.

(1) The attempt to solve a factual problem by reference to definitions usually means the substitution of a merely verbal problem for the factual one. (There is an excellent example of this method in Aristotle's *Physics*, 197b6-32.) This may be shown for the following examples. (*a*) There is a factual problem: Can we return to the cage of tribalism? And by what means? (*b*) There is a moral problem: Should we return to the cage?

The philosopher of meaning, if faced by (*a*) or (*b*), will say: It all depends on what you mean by your vague terms; tell me how you define 'return', 'cage', 'tribalism', *and with the help of these definitions I may be able to decide your problem*. Against this, I maintain that if the decision can be made with the help of the definitions, if it follows from the definitions, then the problem so decided was merely a verbal problem; for it has been solved independently of facts or of moral decisions.

(2) An *essentialist* philosopher of meaning may do even worse, especially in connection with problem (*b*); he may suggest, for example, that it depends upon 'the essence' or 'the essential character' or perhaps upon 'the destiny' of our civilization whether or not we should try to return.

(3) Essentialism and the theory of definition have led to an amazing development in ethics. The development is one of increasing abstraction and loss of touch with *the basis of all ethics* – the practical moral problems, to be decided by us here and now. It leads first to the general question, 'What is good?'

or 'What is the Good?'; next to 'What does "Good" mean?' and next to 'Can the problem "What does Good mean?" be answered?' or 'Can "good" be defined?' G.E. Moore, who raised this last problem in his *Principia Ethica*, 1903, was certainly right in insisting that 'good' in the moral sense cannot be defined in 'naturalistic' terms. For, indeed, if we could, it would mean something like 'bitter' or 'sweet' or 'green' or 'red'; and it would be utterly irrelevant from the point of view of morality. Just as we need not attain the bitter, or the sweet, etc., there would be no reason to take any moral interest in a naturalistic 'good'. But although Moore was right in what is perhaps justly considered his main point, it may be held that an analysis of good or of any other concept or essence can in no way contribute to an ethical theory which bears upon the only relevant basis of all ethics, the immediate moral problem that must be solved here and now. Such an analysis can lead only to the substitution of a verbal problem for a moral one. (See also note 18(1) to chapter 5 of *The Open Society and Its Enemies*, especially upon the irrelevance of moral judgements.)

16 I have in mind the methods of 'constitution', 'implicit definition', 'definition by correlation', and 'operational definition'. The arguments of the 'operationalists' seem to be in the main sound enough; but they cannot get over the fact that in their operational definitions, or descriptions, they need universal terms which have to be taken as undefined; and to them, the problem applies again. Despite this, we can operate with these terms whose meaning we have learned 'operationally'. We use them, as it were, so that nothing depends upon their meaning or as little as possible. Our 'operational definitions' have the advantage of helping us to shift the problem into a field in which nothing or little depends on words. *Clear speaking is speaking in such a way that words do not matter.*

17 Wittgenstein teaches in the *Tractatus* (see also note 13) that philosophy cannot propound propositions, and that all philosophical propositions are in fact senseless pseudo-propositions. Closely connected with this is his doctine that the true task of philosophy is not to propound sentences but to

clarify them: 'The object of philosophy is the logical clarification of thoughts. – Philosophy is not a theory but an activity. A philosophical work consists essentially of elucidations.' (4.112)

The question arises whether this view is in keeping with Wittgenstein's fundamental aim, the destruction of metaphysics by unveiling it as meaningless nonsense. In my *The Logic of Scientific Discovery* (see especially pp.311-14) I have tried to show that Wittgenstein's method leads to a merely verbal solution and that it must give rise, in spite of its apparent radicalism, not to the destruction or to the exclusion or even to the clear demarcation of metaphysics, but to its intrusion into the field of science, and to its confusion with science. The reasons for this are simple enough.

Let us consider one of Wittgenstein's sentences, for example, 'Philosophy is not a theory but an activity'. Surely, this is not a sentence belonging to 'total natural science (or the totality of the natural sciences)'. Therefore, according to Wittgenstein (see note 13 above), it cannot belong to 'the totality of true propositions'. On the other hand, it is not a false proposition either (since if it were, its negation would have to be true, and to belong to natural science.) *Thus we arrive at the result that it must be 'meaningless' or 'senseless' or 'nonsensical'; and the same holds for most of Wittgenstein's propositions*. This consequence of his doctrine is recognized by Wittgenstein himself, for he writes (6.54): 'My propositions are elucidatory in this way: he who understands me finally recognizes them as senseless. . . .' The result is important. Wittgenstein's own philosophy is senseless, and it is admitted to be so. 'On the other hand', as Wittgenstein says in his Preface, 'the truth of the thoughts communicated here seems to me unassailable and definitive. I am, therefore, of the opinion that the problems have in essentials been finally solved.' This shows that we can communicate *unassailably and definitely true thoughts* by way of propositions which are admittedly nonsensical, and that we can solve problems 'finally' by propounding nonsense. [See also note 4 (2)(*b*) to selection 2.]

Consider what this means. It means that all the metaphysical nonsense against which Bacon, Hume, Kant, and Russell have fought for centuries may now comfortably settle down, and even frankly admit that it is nonsense. (Heidegger does so.) For now we have a new kind of nonsense at our disposal, nonsense that communicates thoughts whose truth is unassailable and definitive; in other words, *deeply significant nonsense.*

I do not deny that Wittgenstein's thoughts are unassailable and definitive. For how could one assail them? Obviously, whatever one says against them must be philosophical and therefore nonsense. And it can be dismissed as such. We are thus faced with that kind of position which I have described elsewhere, in connection with Hegel (see *Conjectures and Refutations*, p.327 [and also pp.369f. above]), as a *re-inforced dogmatism*. [See also p.138 above.]

To sum up. The anti-metaphysical theory of meaning in Wittgenstein's *Tractatus*, far from helping to combat metaphysical dogmatism and oracular philosophy, represents a re-inforced dogmatism that opens wide the door to the enemy, deeply significant metaphysical nonsense, and throws out, by the same door, the best friend, that is to say, scientific hypothesis. [See also selection 8 on the *problem of demarcation*.]

18 It appears that irrationalism in the sense of a doctrine or creed that does not propound connected and debatable arguments but rather propounds aphorisms and dogmatic statements which must be 'understood' or else left alone, will generally tend to become the property of an esoteric circle of the initiated. And, indeed, this prognosis seems to be partly corroborated by some of the publications that come from Wittgenstein's school. (I do not wish to generalize; for example, everything I have seen of F. Waismann's writing is presented as a chain of rational and exceedingly clear arguments, and entirely free from the attitude of '*take it or leave it*'.)

Some of these esoteric publications seem to be without a serious problem; to me, they appear to be subtle for subtlety's sake. It is significant that they come from a school which started by denouncing philosophy for the barren subtlety of its attempts to deal with pseudoproblems.

I may end this criticism by stating briefly that I do not think that there is much justification for fighting metaphysics in general, or that anything worthwhile will result from such a fight. It is necessary to solve the problem of the demarcation of science from metaphysics. But we should recognize that many metaphysical systems have led to important scientific results. I mention only the system of Democritus; and that of Schopenhauer which is very similar to that of Freud. And some, for instance those of Plato or Malebranche or Schopenhauer, are beautiful structures of thought. But I believe, at the same time, that we should fight those metaphysical systems which tend to bewitch and to confuse us. But clearly, we should do the same even with unmetaphysical and anti-metaphysical systems, if they exhibit this dangerous tendency. And I think that we cannot do this at one stroke. We have rather to take the trouble to analyse the systems in some detail; we must show that we understand what the author means, but that what he means is not worth the effort to understand it. (It is characteristic of all these dogmatic systems and especially of the esoteric systems that their admirers assert of all critics that 'they do not understand'; but these admirers forget that understanding must lead to agreement only in the case of sentences with a trivial content. In all other cases, one can understand *and* disagree.)

19 See A. Schopenhauer, *Die beiden Grundprobleme der Ethik*, 4th edition, 1890, p.147.

20 Simplicius, one of the best of our sources on these very doubtful matters, presents Antisthenes (*ad Arist. Categ.* 66b, 67b) as an opponent of Plato's theory of Forms or Ideas, and in fact, of the doctrine of essentialism and intellectual intuition altogether. 'I can see a horse, Plato,' Antisthenes is reported to have said, 'but I cannot see its horseness.' (A very similar argument is attributed by a lesser source, Diogenes Laertes, VI, 53, to Diogenes the Cynic, and there is no reason why the latter should not have used it too.) I think that we may rely upon Simplicius (who appears to have had access to Theophrastus), considering that Aristotle's own testimony in the *Meta-*

physics (especially at 1043b24) squares well with this anti-essentialism of Antisthenes.

I wish to add here that in spite of all my criticism I am very ready to admit Aristotle's merits. He is the founder of logic, and down to *Principia Mathematica*, all logic can be said to be an elaboration and generalization of the Aristotelian beginnings. (A new epoch in logic has indeed begun, in my opinion, though not with the so-called 'non-Aristotelian' or 'multi-valued' systems, but rather with the clear distinction between 'object language' and 'metalanguage'.) Furthermore, Aristotle has the great merit of having tried to tame idealism by his commonsense approach which insists that only individual things are 'real' (and that their 'forms' and 'matter' are aspects or abstractions). Yet this very approach is responsible for the fact that Aristotle does not even attempt to solve Plato's problem of universals [see p.166 above], i.e., the problem of explaining why certain things resemble one another and others do not. For why should there not be as many different Aristotelian essences in things as there are things?

7 The Problem of Induction

1 See M. Born, *Natural Philosophy of Cause and Chance*, 1949, p.6.

2 See, for example, sections 10 and 11 of my comment on Carnap's paper on pp.285-303 of I. Lakatos, editor, *The Problem of Inductive Logic*, 1968, and section 32 of *Unended Quest*.

3 See also appendix 1 and chapter 2 of *Objective Knowledge*.

4 D. Hume, *A Treatise of Human Nature*, Book I, part IV, the last paragraph of section II; edition of L. Selby-Bigge, p.218. David Miller has pointed out to me that Hume, by establishing and experiencing the contrast between what he believed (realism), and what he thought was true (idealism), made here – no doubt unwittingly – a first step away from his own (commonsense) characterization of knowledge as a form of belief; a step, that

is, towards recognizing the profound gulf between world 2 and world 3. Unfortunately, this discovery of Hume's itself remained within world 2, as an irritation, and failed to become an objective problem in world 3.

5 The three quotations are from Bertrand Russell, *A History of Western Philosophy*, 1946, pp.698f.; new edition, 1961, pp.645-7. (The italics are mine.)

6 See p.21 of P.F. Strawson, 'On Justifying Induction', *Philosophical Studies* **9**, 1958, pp.20f. See also Hume, *op.cit.*, Book II, part III, section III; edition of L. Selby-Bigge, p.415: 'Reason is, and ought only to be the slave of the passions....'

7 See *The Logic of Scientific Discovery*, pp.253f.

8 The Problem of Demarcation

1 See *Conjectures and Refutations*, p.110: 'From the point of view of general relativity, ... the earth rotates ... *in precisely that sense in which a bicycle wheel rotates*.'

2 See *Conjectures and Refutations*, chapter 3, notes 20-2, pp. 106f.

3 See also my paper 'The Present Significance of Two Arguments of Henri Poincaré', *Methodology and Science* **14**, 1981, pp.260-4.

4 See the index of *Conjectures and Refutations* under these names, and *Quantum Theory and the Schism in Physics*, section 20.

5 I must stress this point, because Ayer has asserted on pp.583f. of 'Philosophy and Scientific Method', *Proceedings of the XIVth International Congress of Philosophy, Vienna: 2nd to 9th September 1968*, volume I, pp.536-42, that 'In modern times two theses have held the field. According to one of them, what is required is that the hypothesis be verifiable: according to the other, that it be falsifiable.' And after outlining very briefly a history of the verifiability criterion, he writes: 'In its current form, all that it requires of a scientific hypothesis is that it

should figure non-trivially in a theory which is open to confirmation when taken as a whole.'

'In the case of the principle of falsifiability', Ayer continues, 'the process of adaptation has been less explicit. Some of its adherents still talk as if the formulation which was given to it by Professor Popper in the opening chapters of his *Logik der Forschung* [*The Logic of Scientific Discovery*] continued to hold good. The fact is, however, that Professor Popper himself found it necessary to modify it in the course of this very book.' To this I can only reply that (1) it seems to me better to introduce the necessary modifications in 'this very book' in which the proposal was made; (2) I introduced falsifiability as a criterion of demarcation on p.40 of *The Logic of Scientific Discovery* and I 'found it necessary' to outline all the various objections on the next page, in the same section, announcing my intention to discuss each of them more fully later; (3) the one difficulty which I postponed for later – the formal non-falsifiability of probability statements – was solved by a methodological proposal.

6 The term is due to Hans Albert.

7 For a fuller discussion see *The Open Society and Its Enemies*, volume II, pp.108f. [and also selection 26].

8 See *Conjectures and Refutations*, chapter 1, especially pp.35-8.

9 Scientific Method

1 J. Liebig, *Induktion und Deduktion*, 1865, was probably the first to reject the inductive method from the standpoint of natural science; his attack is directed against Bacon. P. Duhem, *The Aim and Structure of Physical Theory*, 1906 (English translation, 1954), held pronounced deductivist views. But there are also inductivist views to be found in Duhem's book, for example in the third chapter of Part I, where we are told that only experiment, induction, and generalization have produced Descartes's law of refraction (p.34). See also V. Kraft, *Die*

Grundformen der Wissenschaftlichen Methoden, 1925; and R. Carnap, *The Unity of Science*, 1934.

2 Address on Max Planck's sixtieth birthday. The passage quoted begins with the words, 'The supreme task of the physicist is to search for those highly universal laws . . .'. See A. Einstein, *The World As I See It*, 1935 (translation by A. Harris), p.125. The German word '*Einfühlung*' is difficult to translate. Harris translates as 'sympathetic understanding of experience'. Similar ideas are found earlier in J. Liebig, *op. cit.*; see also E. Mach, *Principien der Wärmerlehre*, 1896, pp.443ff.

3 For this term see chapter X of *The Logic of Scientific Discovery*, and *Realism and the Aim of Science*, Part I, chapter IV.

4 In the two years before the first publication of *The Logic of Scientific Discovery* in 1934 it was the standing criticism raised by members of the Vienna Circle against my ideas that a theory of method which was neither an empirical science nor pure logic was impossible: what was outside these two fields was sheer nonsense. (The same view was still maintained by Wittgenstein in 1946; see note 8 on p.69 of *Conjectures and Refutations*, and *Unended Quest*, section 26.) Later, the standing criticism became anchored in the legend that I proposed to replace the verifiability criterion by a falsifiability criterion of *meaning*. See *Realism and the Aim of Science*, Part I, sections 19-22, and 'Replies to My Critics', sections 1-4.

5 [See note 17 to selection 6 above.]

6 H. Gomperz, *Weltanschauungslehre*, volume I, 1905, p.35, writes: 'If we consider how infinitely problematic the concept of *experience* is . . . we may well be forced to believe that . . . enthusiastic affirmation is far less appropriate in regard to it . . . than the most careful and guarded criticism. . . .'

7 H. Dingler, *Physik und Hypothesis*, 1921; similarly, V. Kraft, *op.cit.*

8 The view, only briefly set forth here, that it is a matter for decision what is to be called 'a genuine statement' and what 'a meaningless pseudostatement' is one that I have held for years.

(Also the view that the exclusion of metaphysics is likewise a matter of decision.) However, my present criticism of positivism (and of the naturalistic view) no longer applies, as far as I can see, to Carnap's *Logical Syntax of Language*, 1934, in which he too adopts the standpoint that all such questions rest upon decisions (the 'principle of tolerance'). According to Carnap's preface, Wittgenstein has for years propounded a similar view in unpublished works. Carnap's *Logical Syntax* was published while *The Logic of Scientific Discovery* was in proof. I regret that I was unable to discuss it in my text.

9 Regarding the translation 'to prove one's mettle' for '*sich bewähren*' see the first footnote to chapter X of *The Logic of Scientific Discovery*. The concept 'better testable' is analysed in *op.cit.*, chapter VI.

10 See pp. 58ff. of K. Menger, *Moral, Wille, und Weltgestaltung*, 1934.

11 I am still inclined to uphold something like this, even though such theorems as '*degree of corroboration ≠ probability*' or my 'theorem on truth content' (see pp. 343-53 of P. K. Feyerabend & G. Maxwell, editors, *Mind, Matter, and Method*, 1966) are perhaps unexpected and not quite on the surface.

12 See *The Logic of Scientific Discovery*, chapter VIII, especially section 68 [and also selection 15 below].

13 See p. 76 of K. Menger, *Dimensionstheorie*, 1928.

14 In *The Logic of Scientific Discovery* I relegated the critical – or, if you will, the 'dialectical' – method of resolving contradictions to second place, since I was concerned with the attempt to develop the practical methodological aspects of my views. In *Die beiden Grundprobleme der Erkenntnistheorie* I have tried to take the critical path; and I have tried to show that the problems of both the classical and the modern theory of knowledge (from Hume via Kant to Russell and Whitehead) can be traced back to the problem of demarcation, that is to the problem of finding the criterion of the empirical character of science.

15 See *The Logic of Scientific Discovery*, sections 12 and 79.

10 Falsificationism versus Conventionalism

1 The chief representatives of the school are Poincaré and Duhem (*The Aim and Structure of Physical Theory*, 1906; English translation, 1954). A recent adherent is H. Dingler (among his numerous works may be mentioned: *Das Experiment*, and *Der Zusammenbruch der Wissenschaft und das Primat der Philosophie*, 1926). The German Hugo Dingler should not be confused with the Englishman Herbert Dingle. The chief representative of conventionalism in the English-speaking world is Eddington. It may be mentioned here that Duhem denies (p.188) the possibility of crucial experiments, because he thinks of them as verifications, while I assert the possibility of crucial *falsifying* experiments. See *Conjectures and Refutations*, chapter 3, especially section v.

2 This view can also be regarded as an attempt to solve the problem of induction; for the problem would vanish if natural laws were definitions, and therefore tautologies. Thus according to the views of H. Cornelius, 'Zur Kritik der Wissenschaftlichen Grundbegriffe', *Erkenntnis* **2**, 1931, pp. 191-218, the statement 'The melting point of lead is about 335°C' is part of the definition of the concept 'lead' (suggested by inductive experience) and cannot therefore be refuted. A substance otherwise resembling lead but with a different melting point would simply not be lead. But according to my view the statement of the melting point of lead is, *qua* scientific statement, synthetic. It asserts, among other things, that an element with a given atomic structure (atomic number 82) always has this melting point, whatever name we may give to this element.

K. Ajdukiewicz appears to agree with Cornelius (see 'Sprache und Sinn', *Erkenntnis* **4**, 1934, pp.100-38, as well as the work there announced, 'Das Weltbild und die Begriffsapparatur', *ibid.*, pp.259-87); he calls his standpoint 'radical conventionalism'.

3 For the problem of simplicity see *The Logic of Scientific Discovery*, chapter VII, especially section 46.

4 R. Carnap, 'Über die Aufgabe der Physik und die Anwendung des Grundsatzes der Einfachtsheit', *Kant-Studien* **28**, 1923, pp.90-107, especially p.100.

5 See p.193 of J. Black, *Lectures on the Elements of Chemistry*, volume I, 1803.

6 How degrees of falsifiability are to be estimated is explained in *The Logic of Scientific Discovery*, chapter VI.

7 *This is a mistake*, as pointed out by A. Grünbaum, 'The Falsifiability of the Lorentz-Fitzgerald Contraction Hypothesis', *British Journal for the Philosophy of Science* **10**, 1959, pp.48-50. Yet as this hypothesis is less testable than special relativity, it may illustrate *degrees of adhocness*.

8 See, for instance, pp.22ff. of H. Hahn, *Logik, Mathematik, und Naturerkennen (Einheitswissenschaft* **2**), 1933. In this connection, I only wish to say that in my view 'constituable' (i.e. empirically definable) terms do not exist at all. I am using in their place undefinable universal names which are established only by linguistic usage. [See also p.97 above, and the end of section I of selection 11.]

9 Formulations equivalent to the one given here have been put forward as criteria of the *meaningfulness of sentences* (rather than as criteria of *demarcation* applicable to theoretical *systems*) again and again after the publication of my book, even by critics who pooh-poohed my criterion of falsifiability. But it is easily seen that, if used as a criterion of *demarcation*, our present formulation is equivalent to falsifiability. For if the basic statement b_2 does not follow from b_1, but follows from b_1 in conjunction with the theory t (this is the present formulation) then this amounts to saying that the conjunction of b_1 with the negation of b_2 contradicts the theory t. But the conjunction of b_1 with the negation of b_2 is a basic statement [see section III of the next selection]. Thus our criterion demands the existence of a falsifying basic statement, i.e. it demands falsifiability in precisely my sense.

As a criterion of *meaning* (or of 'weak verifiability') it breaks down, however, for various reasons. First, because the negations of some meaningful statements would become meaningless, according to this criterion. Secondly, because the conjunction of a meaningful statement and a 'meaningless pseudosentence' would become meaningful – which is equally absurd.

If we now try to apply these two criticisms to our criterion of *demarcation*, they both prove harmless. As to the first, see *The Logic of Scientific Discovery*, section 15, especially note *2 (and *Realism and the Aim of Science*, Part I, section 22). As to the second, empirical theories (such as Newton's) may contain 'metaphysical' elements. But these cannot be eliminated by a hard and fast rule; though if we succeed in so presenting the theory that it becomes a conjunction of a testable and a non-testable part, we know, of course, that we can now eliminate one of its metaphysical components.

The preceding paragraph of this note may be taken as illustrating another *rule of method*: that after having produced some criticism of a rival theory, we should always make a serious attempt to apply this or a similar criticism to our own theory.

10 In fact, many of the 'permitted' basic statements will, in the presence of the theory, contradict each other. For example, the universal law 'All planets move in circles' (i.e., 'Any set of positions of one planet is co-circular') is trivially 'instantiated' by any set of no more than three positions of one planet; but two such 'instances' together will in most cases contradict the law.

11 The falsifying hypothesis can be of a very low level of universality (obtained, as it were, by generalizing the individual coordinates of a result of observation). Even though it is to be intersubjectively testable, it need not in fact be a strictly universal statement. Thus to falsify the statement 'All ravens are black' the intersubjectively testable statement that there is a family of white ravens in the zoo at New York would suffice. All this shows the urgency of replacing a falsified hypothesis by a better one. In most cases we have, before falsifying a hypothesis, another one up our sleeves; for the falsifying experiment is usually a *crucial experiment* designed to decide

between the two. That is to say, it is suggested by the fact that the two hypotheses differ in some respect; and it makes use of this difference to refute (at least) one of them.

The reference to accepted basic statements may seem to contain the seeds of an infinite regress. For our problem here is this. Since a hypothesis is falsified by *accepting* a basic statement, we need *methodological rules for the acceptance of basic statements*. Now if these rules in their turn refer to accepted basic statements, we may get involved in an infinite regress. To this I reply that the rules we need are merely rules for accepting basic statements that falsify a well-tested and so far successful hypothesis; and the accepted basic statements to which the rule has recourse need not be of this character. Moreover, the rule formulated in the text is far from exhaustive; it only mentions an important aspect of the acceptance of basic statements that falsify an otherwise successful hypothesis, and it will be expanded [in the next selection (especially section IV)].

Professor J. H. Woodger, in a personal communication, has raised the question: how often has an effect to be actually reproduced in order to be a '*reproducible effect*' (or a '*discovery*')? The answer is: in some cases *not even once*. If I assert that there is a family of white ravens in the New York zoo, then I assert something which can be tested *in principle*. If somebody wishes to test it and is informed, upon arrival, that the family has died, or that it has never been heard of, it is left to him to accept or reject my falsifying basic statement. As a rule, he will have means for forming an opinion by examining witnesses, documents, etc.; that is to say, by appealing to other intersubjectively testable and reproducible facts.

11 The Empirical Basis

1 J. F. Fries, *Neue oder anthropologische Kritik der Vernunft*, 1828-31.

2 See, for example, pp.102f. of J. Kraft, *Von Husserl zu Heidegger*, 1932; 2nd edition, 1957, pp. 108f.

3 I am following here almost word for word the expositions of P. Frank and H. Hahn (see notes 7 and 5 below).

4 [See note 8 of the previous selection.] 'Constituted' is Carnap's term.

5 The first two quotations are from pp.19 and 24 of H. Hahn, *Logik, Mathematik, und Naturerkennen* (*Einheitswissenschaft* **2**), 1933. The third is from p.15 of R. Carnap, *Pseudoproblems of Philosophy*, 1928; English translation, 1967, p.314 (the italics are not in the original).

6 The expression is Böhm-Bawerk's ('*Produktionsumweg*').

7 See p.1 of P. Frank, *Das Kausalgesetz und seine Grenzen*, 1932. For instrumentalism, see *Conjectures and Refutations*, chapter 3, and *Realism and the Aim of Science*, Part I, sections 12-14.

8 When writing this, I believed that it was plain enough that from Newton's theory alone, without initial conditions, nothing of the nature of an observation statement can be deducible (and therefore certainly no basic statements). Unfortunately, it turned out that this fact, and its consequences for the problem of observation statements or 'basic statements', were not appreciated by some of the critics of *The Logic of Scientific Discovery*. I may therefore add here a few remarks.

First, nothing observable follows from any pure all-statement – 'All swans are white', say. This is easily seen if we contemplate the fact that 'All swans are white' and 'All swans are black' do not, of course, contradict each other, but together merely imply that there are no swans – clearly not an observation statement, and not even one that can be 'verified'. (A unilaterally falsifiable statement like 'All swans are white', by the way, has the same logical form as 'There are no swans', for it is equivalent to 'There are no non-white swans'.)

Now if this is admitted, it will be seen at once that the singular statements which *can* be deduced from purely universal statements cannot be basic statements. I have in mind statements of the form: 'If there is a swan at the place *k*, then there is a white swan at the place *k*.' (Or, 'At *k*, there is either no swan or a white swan.') We see now at once why these 'instantial statements' (as they may be called) are not basic statements. The reason is that these instantial statements *cannot play the role of test statements* (or of potential falsifiers) which is precisely the role which basic statements are supposed to play. If we were to accept instantial statements as test statements, we should obtain for any theory (and thus both for 'All swans are white' *and* for 'All swans are black') an overwhelming number of verifications – indeed, an infinite number, once we accept as a fact that the overwhelming part of the world is empty of swans.

Since 'instantial statements' are derivable from universal ones, their negations must be potential falsifiers, and *may* therefore be basic statements (if the conditions stated below in the text are satisfied). Instantial statements, vice versa, will then be of the form of negated basic statements. It is interesting to note that basic statements (which are too strong to be derivable from universal laws alone) will have a greater informative content than their instantial negations; which means that *the content of basic statements exceeds their logical probability* (since it must exceed 1/2).

These were some of the considerations underlying my theory of the logical form of basic statements. (See *Conjectures and Refutations*, pp.386 f.)

9 See p.445 of R. Carnap, 'Die physikalische Sprache als Universalsprache der Wissenschaft', *Erkenntnis* **2**, 1932, pp.432-65; translated into English as *The Unity of Science*, 1934.

10 See p.224 of R. Carnap, 'Über Protokollsätze', *Erkenntnis* **3**, 1932, pp.215-28. This paper of Carnap's contained the first published report of my theory of tests; and the view here quoted from it was there erroneously attributed to me.

11 It seems to me that the view here upheld is closer to that of the 'critical' (Kantian) school of philosophy (perhaps in the form represented by Fries) than to positivism. Fries in his theory of our 'predilection for proofs' emphasizes that the (logical) relations holding between statements are quite different from the relation between statements and sense experiences; positiv-

ism on the other hand always tries to abolish the distinction: either all science is made part of my knowing, 'my' sense experience (monism of sense data); or sense experiences are made part of the objective scientific network of arguments in the form of protocol statements (monism of statements).

12 The Aim of Science

1 See *Conjectures and Refutations*, p.174.

2 This kind of reasoning survives in Thales; see H. Diels & W. Krantz, *Die Fragmente der Vorsokratiker*, 10th edition, volume I, p.456, line 35. It survives too in Anaximander (DK A 11 and A 28), Anaximenes (DK A 17, B 1), and Alcmaeon (DK A 5).

3 See also Newton's letters to Richard Bentley of 17 January and especially 25 February 1693. I have quoted from this letter in chapter 3, pp.106f. of *Conjectures and Refutations*, where essentialism is discussed (and criticized) more fully.

4 The term 'modified essentialism' was used as a description of my own 'third view' by a reviewer of my paper 'Three Views Concerning Human Knowledge' (chapter 3 of *Conjectures and Refutations*) in *The Times Literary Supplement* 55, 1956, p.527. In order to avoid misunderstandings, I wish to say here that my acceptance of this term should not be construed as a concession to the doctrine of 'ultimate reality', and even less as a concession to the doctrine of essentialist definitions. I fully adhere to my criticism of this doctrine [in selection 6 above].

5 As to Plato's theory of Forms or Ideas, it is 'one of its most important functions ... to explain the similarity of sensible things...'; see section V of chapter 3 of *The Open Society and Its Enemies*, in particular notes 19 and 20 and text. The failure of Aristotle's theory to perform this function is mentioned [in note 20 to selection 6] above.

6 What can be deduced from Kepler's laws (see Max Born, *Natural Philosophy of Cause and Chance*, 1949, pp. 129-33) is that, for all planets, the acceleration towards the sun equals at

any moment k/r^2, where r is the distance at that moment between the planet and the sun, and k a constant, the same for all planets. Yet this very result formally contradicts Newton's theory (except on the assumption that the masses of the planets are all equal or, if unequal, then at any rate infinitely small as compared with the mass of the sun). But in addition, it should be remembered that neither Kepler's nor Galileo's theory contains Newton's concept of *force*, which is traditionally introduced in these deductions without further ado; as if this ('occult') concept could be read off from the facts, instead of being the result of a new interpretation of the facts (that is, of the 'phenomena' described by Kepler's and Galileo's laws) in the light of a completely new theory. Only after the concept of force (and even the proportionality of gravitational and inertial mass) has been introduced is it at all possible to link the above formula for the acceleration with Newton's inverse square law of attraction (by the assumption that the planets' masses are negligible).

7 See pp. 817f. of A. Einstein, 'Über die Entwicklung unserer Anschauungen über das Wesen und die Konstitution der Strahlung', *Physikalische Zeitschrift* **10**, 1909, pp. 817-26. The abandonment of a theory of a material ether (implicit in Maxwell's failure to construct a satisfactory material model of it) may be said to give depth, in the sense analysed above, to Maxwell's theory as compared to Fresnel's; and this is, it seems to me, implicit in the quotation from Einstein's paper. Thus Maxwell's theory in Einstein's formulation is perhaps not really an example of *another* sense of 'depth'. But in Maxwell's own original form it is, I think.

13 The Growth of Scientific Knowledge

1 See the 1958 Preface to *The Logic of Scientific Discovery*.

2 See the discussion of degrees of testability, empirical content, corroborability, and corroboration in *The Logic of Scientific Discovery*, especially sections 31-46; 82-5; new appendix *ix; also the discussion of degrees of explanatory power in this

appendix, and especially the comparison of Einstein's and Newton's theories (in note 7 on p.401). In what follows, I shall sometimes refer to testability, etc., as the 'criterion of progress', without going into the more detailed distinctions mentioned.

3 See for example J. C. Harsanyi, 'Popper's Improbability Criterion for the Choice of Scientific Hypotheses', *Philosophy* **35**, 1960, pp.332-40. Incidentally, I do not propose any 'criterion' for the choice of scientific hypotheses: every choice remains a risky guess. Moreover, the theoretician's choice is the hypothesis most worthy of *further critical discussion* (rather than of *acceptance*). [See also section VIII of selection 7 above.]

4 See *The Logic of Scientific Discovery*, appendices *iv and *v.

5 *Op.cit.*, appendix *ix.

6 I have been influenced in adopting this view by Dr J. Agassi who, in a discussion in 1956, convinced me that the attitude of looking upon the finished deductive systems as an end is a relic of the long domination of Newtonian ideas (and thus, I may add, of the Platonic, and Euclidean, tradition).

14 Truth and Approximation to Truth

1 See *The Logic of Scientific Discovery*, especially section 84, and *The Open Society and Its Enemies*, volume II, pp.369-74.

2 See L. Wittgenstein, *Tractatus Logico-Philosophicus*, especially 4.0141, and also 2.161, 2.17, 2.223, and 3.11.

3 See especially section 10 of his remarkable *General Theory of Knowledge*, 2nd edition, 1925; English translation, 1974.

4 See the discussion of the 'second view' (called 'instrumentalism') in *Conjectures and Refutations*, chapter 3.

5 See A. Tarski, 'The Semantic Conception of Truth', *Philosophy and Phenomenological Research* **4**, 1943, pp.341-75, especially section 21. (Tarski's paper has been reprinted in

several places; for example on pp.52-84 of H. Feigl & W. Sellars, editors, *Readings in Philosophical Analysis*, 1949.)

6 See the volume referred to in the preceding note, especially pp.279 and 336.

7 See R. Carnap, *Logical Foundations of Probability*, 1950, p.177. See also *The Logic of Scientific Discovery*, especially section 84.

8 From W. Busch, *Schein und Sein*, 1909; Insel edition, 1952, p.28. My attention has been drawn to this rhyme by an essay on Busch as a philosopher which my late friend Julius Kraft contributed to the volume *Erziehung und Politik* (Essays for Minna Specht), 1960; see p.262. My translation makes it perhaps more like a nursery rhyme than Busch intended.

9 Similar misgivings are expressed by W. V. Quine, *Word and Object*, 1960, p.23, when he criticizes Peirce for operating with the idea of approaching to truth.

10 This definition is logically justified by the theorem that, so far as the 'empirical part' of the logical content is concerned, comparisons of empirical contents and of logical contents always yield the same results; and it is intuitively justified by the consideration that a statement *a* tells the more about our world of experience the more possible experiences it excludes (or forbids). [For basic statements see section III of selection 11 above.]

11 See the addenda to *Conjectures and Refutations*. My theory of verisimilitude has been subjected to severe and detailed criticism in recent years. For a discussion of the main points, together with references, see *Objective Knowledge*, 2nd edition, 1979, especially pp.371-4. I should like to stress here what I have in effect noted [on p.196], that the failure of my *formal* theory of verisimilitude does not in any way undermine the original methodological proposals of falsificationism.

15 Propensities, Probabilities, and the Quantum Theory

1 A full treatment of the propensity interpretation of probability and of its repercussions on quantum theory is to be found in the three volumes of *The Postscript*. See especially *Realism and the Aim of Science*, Part II, chapter III; *The Open Universe*, sections 27-30; and *Quantum Theory and the Schism in Physics*, chapter II.

2 See *The Logic of Scientific Discovery*, chapter VIII, and *Realism and the Aim of Science*, sections 21-3.

3 See *Realism and the Aim of Science*, Part II, chapter I. The subjectivist interpretation of probability is a necessary consequence of determinism. Its retention within the quantum theory is a residue of a not yet fully eliminated determinist position. See *The Open Universe*, section 29, and also *Quantum Theory and the Schism in Physics*, sections 5 and 6.

4 What we interpret is not a word, 'probability', and its 'meaning', but formal systems – the probability calculus (especially in its measure-theoretical form), and the formalism of quantum theory. For the formal treatment of probability see *The Logic of Scientific Discovery*, appendices *iv and *v.

16 Metaphysics and Criticizability

1 See I. Kant, *Critique of Practical Reason*, 6th edition, 1827, p.172.

2 See Julius Kraft, *Von Husserl zu Heidegger*, 2nd edition, 1957, pp.103f., 136f., and particularly p.130, where Kraft writes: 'Thus it is hard to understand how existentialism could ever have been considered to be something new in philosophy, from an epistemological point of view.' See also the stimulating paper by H. Tint, 'Heidegger and the "Irrational"', *Proceedings of the Aristotelian Society* **LVII**, 1956-7, pp.253-68.

3 It may also be seen from Hume's frank admission that 'whatever may be the reader's opinion at this present moment, . . . an hour hence he will be persuaded there is both an external

and internal world'; see D. Hume, *A Treatise of Human Nature*, Book I, part IV, section II; edition of L. Selby-Bigge, p.218. [For a comment see note 4 to selection 7 above.]

17 Realism

1 Positivism, phenomenalism, and also phenomenology are all of course infected by the subjectivism of the Cartesian starting point.

2 The irrefutability of realism (which I am prepared to concede) may be questioned. The great Austrian authoress Marie Ebner von Eschenbach (1830-1916) tells in some memoirs of her childhood that she suspected realism to be mistaken. Perhaps things do disappear when we look away. So she tried to catch the world in its disappearing trick by suddenly turning round, half expecting that she would see how out of nothingness things try quickly to re-assemble themselves; and she was both disappointed and relieved whenever she failed. Several comments may be made on this story. First, it is conceivable that this report of childish experimentation is not untypical, but normal and typical, and plays a part in the development of the commonsense distinction of appearance from reality. Secondly (and I am slightly inclined to favour this view) it is conceivable that the report is untypical; that most children are naïve realists, or become so before an age within their memory; and Marie von Ebner certainly was an untypical child. Thirdly, I have experienced – and not only in childhood but also as an adult – something not too far removed from it: for example, when finding something of which I had completely forgotten, I sometimes felt that if nature had let this thing disappear, nobody would have been the wiser. (There was no need for reality to show that it 'really' existed; nobody would have noticed had it not done so.) The question arises whether, if Marie had succeeded, this would have refuted realism or whether it would not merely have refuted a very special form of it. I do not feel obliged to go into this question, but rather *concede* to my opponents that realism is irrefutable. Should this

concession be wrong, then realism is even nearer to being a testable scientific theory than I originally intended to claim.

3 See E. P. Wigner, 'Remarks on the Mind-Body Question', pp.284-302 of I. J. Good, editor, *The Scientist Speculates*, 1962. For a criticism see especially sections 14-16 of E. Nelson, *Dynamical Theories of Brownian Motion*, 1967. See also the Introduction to *Quantum Theory and the Schism in Physics*, and my paper 'Particle Annihilation and the Experiment of Einstein, Podolsky, and Rosen', pp.182-98 of W. Yourgrau & A. van der Merwe, editors, *Perspectives in Quantum Theory*, 1971.

4 In section 79, p.252, of *The Logic of Scientific Discovery* I described myself as a metaphysical realist. In those days I wrongly identified the limits of science with those of arguability. [See now the previous selection.]

5 K. Bühler (partly anticipated by W. Humboldt) clearly pointed out the descriptive function of language. [See especially section II of selection 21.]

6 See pp.290f. of A. Einstein, 'Remarks on Bertrand Russell's Theory of Knowledge', pp.277-91 of P. A. Schilpp, editor, *The Philosophy of Bertrand Russell*, 1944. Schilpp's translation on p.291 is very much closer than mine, but I felt that the importance of Einstein's idea justified my attempt at a *very* free translation, which, I hope, is still faithful to what Einstein wanted to say.

7 See W. S. Churchill, *My Early Life: A Roving Commission*, 1930; quoted by permission of the Hamlyn Publishing Group from the Odhams Press edition, 1947, chapter IX, pp. 115f. (The italics are not in the original.) See also the Macmillan edition, 1944, pp.131f.

18 Cosmology and Change

1 I am glad to be able to report that Professor G.S. Kirk has indeed replied to my address; see his 'Popper on Science and

the Presocratics', *Mind* **69**, 1960, pp.318-39, and my reply on pp.153-65 of *Conjectures and Refutations*.

2 Aristotle himself understood Anaximander in this way; for he caricatures Anaximander's 'ingenious but untrue' theory by comparing the situation of its earth to that of a man who, being equally hungry and thirsty yet equidistant from food and drink, is unable to move. (*De Caelo*, 295b32. The idea has become known by the name 'Buridan's ass'.) Clearly Aristotle conceives this man as being held in equilibrium by immaterial and invisible attractive forces similar to Newtonian forces; and it is interesting that this 'animistic' or 'occult' character of his forces was deeply (though mistakenly) felt by Newton himself, and by his opponents, such as Berkeley, to be a blot on his theory. For further comments on Anaximander, see *Conjectures and Refutations*, p.413.

3 See Aristotle, *De Caelo*, 289b10-290b7.

4 I do not suggest that the smothering is due to blocking breathing-in holes: according to the phlogiston theory, for example, fire is smothered by obstructing breathing-out holes. But I do not wish to ascribe to Anaximander either a phlogiston theory of combustion, or an anticipation of Lavoisier.

5 The fragments quoted in this paragraph and the next but one are respectively Heraclitus A 4 and B 50, 30 in H. Diels & W. Krantz, *Die Fragmente der Vorsokratiker*, 5th edition, 1964. [See also note 1 to selection 1 above.]

6 I am here referring particularly to G.S. Kirk & J.E. Raven, *The Presocratic Philosophers*, 1957, which I discuss in *Conjectures and Refutations*, pp.146-8. See also *The Open Society and Its Enemies*, chapter 2.

7 The fragments quoted here are Heraclitus B 123, B 54, B 88, B 60, B 58, B 102, B 78 in H. Diels & W. Krantz, *op.cit.*

8 This quotation is from *op.cit.*, Xenophanes B 26 and 23. See also Parmenides B 7 and 8.

19 Natural Selection and Its Scientific Status

1 The quotations here are from F. Darwin, editor, *The Life and Letters of Charles Darwin*, 1887; see volume II, p.219, and volume I, p.47.

2 *Op.cit.*, volume II, pp.353 and 382.

3 See, for example, K.G. Denbigh, *The Inventive Universe*, 1975.

4 See p.385 of C.H. Waddington, 'Evolutionary Adaptation', pp.381-402 of S. Tax, editor, *Evolution After Darwin*, volume I, 1960.

5 See *Objective Knowledge*, p.241, and *Unended Quest*, sections 33 and 37.

6 Darwin, *op.cit.*, volume III, pp.158f.

7 See D.T. Campbell, '"Downward Causation" in Hierarchically Organized Biological Systems', pp.179-86 of F.J. Ayala & T. Dobzhansky, editors, *Studies in the Philosophy of Biology*, 1974; R.W. Sperry, 'A Modified Concept of Consciousness', *Psychological Review* **76**, 1969, pp.532-6, and 'Lateral Specialization in the Surgically Separated Hemispheres', pp.5-19 of F.O. Schmitt & F. G. Worden, editors, *The Neurosciences: Third Study Programme*, 1973.

8 See also p.540 of *The Self and Its Brain*.

20 Indeterminism and Human Freedom

1 For the imperfections of the solar system see note 5 below.

2 See section 23 of *The Poverty of Historicism*, where I criticize the 'holistic' criterion of a 'whole' (or '*Gestalt*') by showing that this criterion ('a whole is more than the mere sum of its parts') is satisfied even by the favourite holistic examples of non-wholes, such as a 'mere heap' of stones. (Note that I do not deny that there exist wholes; I only object to the superficiality of most 'holistic' theories.)

3 Newton himself was not among those who drew these

'deterministic' consequences from his theory; see note 5 below.

4 The conviction that determinism forms an essential part of any rational or scientific attitude was generally accepted, even by some of the leading opponents of 'materialism' (such as Spinoza, Leibniz, Kant, and Schopenhauer). I have now treated determinism and indeterminism at much greater length in *The Open Universe*.

5 Newton himself may be counted among the few dissenters, for he regarded even the solar system as *imperfect*, and consequently as likely to perish. Because of these views he was accused of impiety, of 'casting a reflection upon the wisdom of the author of nature' (as Henry Pemberton reports on p.180 of *A View of Sir Isaac Newton's Philosophy*, 1728).

6 *Collected Papers of Charles Sanders Peirce*, volume 6, 1935, 6.44, p.35. There may of course have been other physicists who developed similar views, but I know of only one apart from Newton and Peirce: Professor Franz Exner of Vienna. Schrödinger, who was his pupil, wrote about Exner's views on pp.71, 133, 142f. of *Science, Theory and Man*, 1957 (originally published as *Science and the Human Temperament*, 1935). See also note 11 below.

7 *Op.cit.*, 6.47, p.37. The passage (first published in 1892), though brief, is most interesting because it anticipates (note the remark on fluctuations in explosive mixtures) some of the discussion of macro-effects which result from the amplification of Heisenberg uncertainties. This discussion begins, it appears, with R. Lillie, 'Physical Indeterminism and Vital Action', *Science* **66**, 1927, pp.139-44. It plays a considerable part in the discussion on pp.48ff. of A. H. Compton, *The Freedom of Man*, 1935; where in note 3 on pp.51f. there is a very interesting quantitative comparison of chance effects due to molecular heat motion (the indeterminacy Peirce had in mind) and Heisenberg indeterminacy. The discussion was carried on by N. Bohr, P. Jordan, F. Medicus, L. von Bertalanffy, and many others; more recently especially also by W. Elsasser, *The Physical Foundations of Biology*, 1958.

8 I am alluding to P.Carus, 'Mr Charles S. Peirce's Onslaught on the Doctrine of Necessity', *The Monist* **2**, 1892, pp.560-82, and 'The Idea of Necessity, Its Basis and Its Scope', *The Monist* **3**, 1892, pp.68-96; Peirce replied in 'Reply to the Necessitarians. Rejoinder to Dr Carus', *The Monist* **3**, 1893, pp.526-70; *Collected Papers*, volume 6, 1935, Appendix A, pp.390-435.

9 The sudden and complete transformation of the problem situation may be gauged by the fact that to many of us old fogies it does not really seem so very long ago that empiricist philosophers (see for example M. Schlick, *General Theory of Knowledge*, 2nd edition, 1925; p.277; English translation, 1974, p.303) were physical determinists, while nowadays physical determinism is being dismissed by P.H. Nowell-Smith, a gifted and spirited defender of Schlick's, as an '*eighteenth-century bogey*' (see p.331 of 'Determinists and Libertarians', *Mind* **63**, 1954, pp.317-37, and also note 21 below). Time marches on and no doubt it will, in time, solve all our problems, bogies or non-bogies. Yet oddly enough we old fogies seem to remember the days of Planck, Einstein, and Schlick, and have much trouble in trying to convince our puzzled and muddled minds that these great determinist thinkers produced their bogies in the eighteenth century, together with Laplace who produced the most famous bogy of all (the 'superhuman intelligence' of his *A Philosophical Essay on Probabilities*, 1819, often called 'Laplace's demon'; see also note 17 below, and *The Open Universe*, section 10). Yet a still greater effort might perhaps recall, even to our failing memories, a similar eighteenth-century bogy produced by a certain Carus (not the nineteenth-century thinker referred to in the previous note but T.Lucretius Carus, who wrote *De Rerum Natura*; see especially Book II, lines 251-60).

10 See especially the passages on 'emergent evolution' on pp.90ff. of *The Freedom of Man*, 1935; see also p.73 of A.H. Compton, *The Human Meaning of Science*, 1940. [It should be noted that this selection forms part of the Second Arthur Holly Compton Memorial Lecture, presented at Washington University, St Louis, April 21 1965.]

11 The quotations in these three paragraphs come from *The Freedom of Man*, pp.26f. (see also pp.27f.); *The Human Meaning of Science*, pp.ix and 42; *The Freedom of Man*, p.27. I may perhaps remind the reader that my views differ a little from the first quoted passage because like Peirce I think it logically possible that the *laws* of a system be Newtonian (and so prima-facie deterministic) and the system nevertheless indeterministic, because the system to which the laws apply may be intrinsically imprecise, in the sense, for example, that there is no point in saying that its coordinates, or velocities, are rational (as opposed to irrational) numbers. The following remark of Schrödinger, *op. cit.*, p.143 is also very relevant: '. . .the energy-momentum theorem provides us with only *four* equations, thus leaving the elementary process to a great extent undetermined, even if it complies with them.' See also *The Open Universe*, section 13.

12 Assume that our physical world is a *physically closed* system containing chance elements. Obviously it would not be deterministic; yet purposes, ideas, hopes, and wishes could not in such a world have any influence on physical events; assuming that they exist, they would be completely redundant: they would be what are called 'epiphenomena' [see also selection 21, section III below]. Note that a deterministic physical system will be closed, but that a closed system may be indeterministic. Thus 'indeterminism is not enough', as explained in section VII below. (See also *The Open Universe*, addendum 1.)

13 Kant suffered deeply from this nightmare and failed in his attempts to escape from it; see Compton's excellent statement on 'Kant's avenue of escape' on pp.67f. of *The Freedom of Man*.

14 The quotations are from D. Hume, *A Treatise of Human Nature*, 1739, Book I, part III, section XV, and Book II, part III, section II; edition of L. Selby-Bigge, p.174 (see also p.183 and p.87) and pp.408f.

15 Hume, *op.cit.*, Book II, part III, section I; Selby-Bigge, pp.403f. It is interesting to compare this with pp.409f. (where

Hume says 'I define necessity two ways') and with his ascription to 'matter' of 'that intelligible quality, call it necessity or not' which, as he says, everybody 'must allow to belong to the will' (or 'to the actions of the mind'). In other words, Hume tries here to apply his doctrine of custom or habit, and his association psychology, to 'matter'; that is, to physics.

16 Such dreams include B. F. Skinner, *Walden Two*, 1948, a charming and benevolent but utterly naïve utopian dream of omnipotence (see especially pp.246-50 and 214f.). Aldous Huxley, *Brave New World*, 1932 (see also *Brave New World Revisited*, 1959), and George Orwell, *1984*, 1948, are well-known antidotes.

17 My deaf physicist is of course closely similar to Laplace's demon (see note 9); and I believe that his achievements are absurd, simply because non-physical aspects (aims, purposes, traditions, tastes, ingenuity) play a role in the development of the physical world; or in other words, I believe in *interactionism* [see the next selection]. S. Alexander, *Space, Time and Deity*, 1920, volume II, p.328, says of what he calls the 'Laplacean calculator': 'Except in the limited sense described, the hypothesis of the calculator is absurd.' Yet the 'limited sense' *includes* the prediction of *all* purely physical events, and would thus *include* the prediction of the positions of all the black marks written by Mozart and Beethoven. It *excludes* only the prediction of mental experience (an exclusion that corresponds closely to my assumption of the physicist's deafness). Thus what I regard as absurd, Alexander is prepared to admit. (I may say that I think it is preferable to discuss the problem of freedom in connection with the creation of music or of new scientific theories or technical inventions, rather than with ethics and ethical responsibility.)

18 D. Hume, *op.cit.*, Book III, part III, section IV; Selby-Bigge, p. 609. (The italics are mine.)

19 See note 9 above, and G. Ryle, *The Concept of Mind*, 1949, chapter III (5) ('The Bogy of Mechanism').

20 See N. W. Pirie, 'The Meaninglessness of the Terms Life and Living', pp. 11-22 of J. Needham & D. E. Green, editors, *Perspectives in Biochemistry*, 1937.

21 See for example A. M. Turing, 'Computing Machinery and Intelligence', *Mind* **59**, 1950, pp.433-60. Turing asserted that men and computers are in principle indistinguishable by their observable (behavioural) performance, and challenged his opponents to *specify* some observable behaviour or achievement of man which a computer would in principle be unable to achieve. But this challenge is an intellectual trap: by *specifying* a kind of behaviour we would lay down a specification for building a computer. Moreover, we use, and build, computers because they can do many things which we cannot do; just as I use a pen or pencil when I wish to tot up a sum I cannot do in my head. 'My pencil is more intelligent than I', Einstein used to say. But this does not establish that he is indistinguishable from his pencil. See also section 5 of chapter 12 of *Conjectures and Refutations*, and *The Open Universe*, section 22.

22 See p.183 of M. Schlick, 'Ergänzende Bemerkungen über P. Jordan's Versuch einer Quantentheoretischen Deutung der Lebenserscheinungen', *Erkenntnis* 5, 1935, pp.181-3.

23 D. Hume, *op.cit.*, Book I, part III, section XIV; Selby-Bigge, p.171. See also for example p.407: '. . .liberty . . . is the very same thing with chance'.

24 A. H. Compton, *op.cit.*, pp.53f.

25 This problem is discussed in sections XII - XIV of chapter 6 of *Objective Knowledge*, and, of course, in many of my writings on world 3 [especially selection 4 above and selection 21].

21 The Mind-Body Problem

1 See for example J. Huxley, *Evolution. The Modern Synthesis*, 1942; P.B. Medawar, *The Future of Man*, 1960; T. Dobzhansky, *Mankind Evolving*, 1962.

2 See I. Kant, *Critique of Pure Reason*, 2nd edition, 1787. [For perception, see also note 5 to selection 5 above.]

3 For a fuller discussion see *The Self and Its Brain*, Part I, section 21.

4 See *Conjectures and Refutations*, chapter 12.

5 See J. L. Austin, *How to Do Things with Words*, 1962.

6 The dancing bees *may* perhaps be said to convey factual or descriptive information. A thermograph or barograph does so in writing. It is interesting that in both cases the problem of lying does not seem to arise – although the maker of the thermograph may use it to misinform us. (For the dancing bees see K. von Frisch, *Bees: their Vision, Chemical Senses, and Language*, 1950; *The Dancing Bees*, 1955; and M. Lindauer, *Communication Among Social Bees*, 1961.)

7 See note 4.

8 See the discussion of organic evolution in *The Self and Its Brain*, Part I, section 6.

22 The Self

1 See chapter 1 of *Conjectures and Refutations*, especially p.47.

2 See D. Hume, *A Treatise of Human Nature*, 1739, Book I, part IV, section VI; Selby-Bigge edition, p.251. In Book III, Appendix (Selby-Bigge, p.634), Hume slightly mitigates his tone; yet he seems in this Appendix to have completely forgotten about his own 'positive assertions' such as those in Book II referred to in the next note.

3 *Op.cit.*, Book II, part I, section XI; Selby-Bigge, p.317. A similar passage is Book II, part II, section II (Selby-Bigge, p.339), where we read: ' 'Tis evident that . . . we are at all times intimately conscious of ourselves, our sentiments and passions . . . .'

4 *Op.cit.*, Book II, part III, section I (Selby-Bigge, p.403; see also

p.411). Elsewhere, Hume attributes to us as agents 'motives and character' from which 'a spectator can commonly infer our actions'; see for example Book II, part III, section II (Selby-Bigge, p.408). See also the Appendix (Selby-Bigge, pp.633ff.).

5 See for example pp. 366f. of E. Rubin, 'Visual Figures Apparently Incompatible with Geometry', *Acta Psychologica* **VII**, 1950, pp.365-87.

6 See J.B. Deregowski, 'Illusion and Culture', pp.161-91 of R.L. Gregory & E. Gombrich, editors, *Illusion in Nature and Art*, 1973.

7 See chapter VI (7), entitled 'The Systematic Elusiveness of the "I"', of G. Ryle, *The Concept of Mind*, 1949.

8 See R.L. Fantz, 'The Origin of Form Perception', *Scientific American* **204**, 5, 1961, pp.66-72.

9 It seems to me that P.F. Strawson is right when he suggests on p.136 of *Individuals*, 1959, that the general idea of a person must be had prior to learning the use of the word 'I'. (I doubt however whether this priority can be described as 'logical'.) He is also right, I think, when he suggests that this helps to dissolve the so-called 'problem of other minds' [see also note 5 to selection 30]. However, it is well to remember that the early tendency to interpret all things as persons (called animism or hylozoism) needs correction, from a realistic point of view: a dualistic attitude is nearer to the truth. See p.41 of W. Kneale's excellent lecture, *On Having A Mind*, 1962, and also my discussion of Strawson's ideas in section 36 of Part I of *The Self and Its Brain*.

10 See note 1.

11 The baby smiles; no doubt unconsciously. Yet it is a kind of (mental?) *action*: it is quasi-teleological, and it suggests that the baby operates with the psychologically *a priori* expectation of being surrounded by *persons*; persons who have the power of being friendly or hostile – friends or strangers. This, I would suggest, comes prior to the consciousness of self. I would

suggest the following as a conjectural schema of development: first, the category of persons; then the distinction between persons and things; then the discovery of one's own body; the learning that it is one's own; and only then the awakening to the fact of being a self.

12 See the case of Genie discussed in chapter 4 of Part II of *The Self and Its Brain.*

Since I wrote this section, Jeremy Shearmur has drawn my attention to the fact that in Part III, section II (6th and later editions, Part III, chapter I) of his *The Theory of the Moral Sentiments*, 1759, Adam Smith puts forward the idea that society is a 'mirror' which enables the individual to see and to 'think of his own character, of the propriety or demerit of his own sentiments and conduct, of the beauty or deformity of his own mind', which suggests that if it were 'possible that a human creature could grow up to manhood in some solitary place, without any communication with his own species' then he could not develop a self. Shearmur has also suggested that there are certain similarities between my ideas here and the 'social theory of the self' of Hegel, Marx and Engels, Bradley, and the American pragmatist G.H. Mead. [See note 1 to selection 28 below.]

13 I have added the words in parentheses in view of what is said about time and the Hopi Indians in B.L.Whorf, *Language, Thought, and Reality*, 1956.

14 See J.C. Eccles, *Facing Reality*, 1970, pp.66f.

15 See M.R. Rosenzweig *et al.*, 'Brain Changes in Response to Experience', *Scientific American* **226**, 2, 1972, pp.22-9; P. A. Ferchmin et al., 'Direct Contact with Enriched Environment Is Required to Alter Cerebral Weight in Rats', *Journal of Comparative and Physiological Psychology* **88**, 1975, pp.360-7; and section 41 of Part I of *The Self and Its Brain*.

16 Thus John Beloff, *The Existence of Mind*, 1962, says somewhere: '. . .all those reflex processes on which successful vision depends: lens accommodation, pupillary contraction, binocu-

lar convergence, eye movement, etc., all take place at an unconscious level.'

17 See E. Schrödinger, *Mind and Matter*, 1958, p.7; 1967 edition with *What Is Life?*, p.103. Schrödinger actually went further than this: he suggested that whenever, in any organism, a new problem arises, it will give rise to consciously attempted solutions. This theory is too strong, as was shown by Peter Medawar in a review (*Science Progress* **47**, 1959, pp.398f.) of Schrödinger's book. Medawar pointed out that the immune system is constantly faced with new problems, but it solves them unconsciously. Medawar has shown me some correspondence between Schrödinger and himself, in which Schrödinger agrees that Medawar has produced a counterexample to his thesis.

18 The phrase is due to C. Sherrington, *The Integrative Action of the Nervous System*, 1906.

19 See pp.46f. of K. Lorenz, 'Die Vorstellung einer zweckgerichteten Weltordnung', *Österreichische Akademie der Wissenschaften, phil.-historische Klasse* **113**, 1976, pp.37-51.

20 See W. Penfield, 'The Permanent Record of the Stream of Consciousness', *Acta Psychologica* **XI**, 1955, pp.47-69. See also his *The Mystery of the Mind*, 1975.

21 See chapter 2 of Part II of *The Self and Its Brain*.

23 Historicism

1 See especially *The Logic of Scientific Discovery*, sections 12-18 [and also selections 9-11 above].

2 [See, however, section 1 of A. Donagan, 'Popper's Examination of Historicism', pp.905-24 of P.A. Schilpp, editor, *The Philosophy of Karl Popper*, The Library of Living Philosophers 1974. On p.905 Donagan writes that 'Popper was disappointed in his hope of avoiding merely verbal quibbles', and he proceeds to defend him against such criticisms.]

3 See *The Poverty of Historicism*, section 3.

4 I agree with Professor C.E. Raven when, in his *Science, Religion, and the Future*, 1943, he calls this conflict 'a storm in a Victorian tea-cup'; though the force of this remark is perhaps a little impaired by the attention he pays to the vapours still emerging from the cup – to the Great Systems of Evolutionist Philosophy produced by Bergson, Whitehead, Smuts, and others.

5 Feeling somewhat intimidated by the tendency of evolutionists to suspect anyone of obscurantism who does not share their emotional attitude towards evolution as a 'daring and revolutionary challenge to traditional thought', I had better say here that I see in modern Darwinism the most successful explanation of the relevant facts. [See also selections 5 and 19 above.] A good illustration of the emotional attitude of evolutionists is C.H. Waddington's statement on p.17 of *Science and Ethics*, 1942, that 'we must accept the direction of evolution as good simply because it *is* good'; a statement which also illustrates the fact that the following revealing comment by Professor Bernal upon the Darwinian controversy (*ibid.*, p.115) is still apposite: 'It was not . . . that science had to fight an external enemy, the Church; it was that the Church . . . was within the scientists themselves.'

6 See p.214 of T.H. Huxley, *Lay Sermons*, 1880. Huxley's belief in a law of evolution is very remarkable in view of his exceedingly critical attitude towards the idea of a law of (inevitable) progress. The explanation appears to be that he not only distinguished sharply between natural evolution and progress, but that he held (rightly, I believe) that these two had little to do with each other. Julian Huxley's interesting analysis on pp.559ff. of *Evolution*, 1942, seems to me to add little to this, although it is apparently designed to establish a link between evolution and progress. For he admits that evolution, though sometimes 'progressive', is more often not so. The fact, on the other hand, that every 'progressive' development may be considered as evolutionary is hardly more than trivial. (That the succession of dominant types is progressive in his sense may

merely mean that we habitually apply the term 'dominant types' to those of the most successful types which are the most 'progressive'.)

7 See p.vii of H.A.L. Fisher, *A History of Europe*, volume I, 1935 (the italics are mine). See also p.58 of F.A. von Hayek, 'Scientism and the Study of Society', Part II, *Economica* New Series **X**, 1943, pp.34-63, where he criticizes the attempt 'to find laws where in the nature of the case they cannot be found, in the succession of the unique and singular historical phenomena'.

8 Of nearly every theory it may be said that it agrees with many facts: this is one of the reasons why a theory can be said to be corroborated only if we are unable to find refuting facts, rather than if we are able to find supporting facts. See chapter X of *The Logic of Scientific Discovery*. An example of the procedure criticized here is, I believe, Professor Toynbee's allegedly empirical investigation into the life cycle of what he calls the 'species civilization'. He seems to overlook the fact that he classifies as civilizations only such entities as conform to his *a priori* belief in life cycles. For example, on pp.147-9 of *A Study of History*, volume I, 1934, he contrasts his 'civilizations' with 'primitive societies' in order to establish his doctrine that these two cannot belong to the same 'species' although they may belong to the same 'genus'. But the only basis of this classification is an *a priori* intuition into the nature of civilizations. This may be seen from his argument that the two are obviously as different as are elephants from rabbits – an intuitive argument whose weakness becomes clear if we consider the case of a St Bernard dog and a Pekingese. But the whole question (whether or not the two belong to the same species) is inadmissible, for it is based on the scientistic method of treating collectives as if they were physical or biological bodies. Although this method has often been criticized (see, for example, F.A. von Hayek, *op.cit.*, pp.41ff.) these criticisms have never received an adequate reply.

9 The confusion created by the talk about 'motion', 'force', 'direction', etc., may be gauged by considering that Henry

Adams, the famous American historian, seriously hoped to determine the course of history by fixing the position of two points on its track – the one point located in the thirteenth century, the other in his own lifetime. He says himself of his project: 'With the help of these two points . . . he hoped to project his lines forward and backward indefinitely . . .', for, he argued, 'any schoolboy could see that man as a force must be measured by motion, from a fixed point' (*The Education of Henry Adams*, 1918, pp.434f.)

10 See section 15 of *The Logic of Scientific Discovery*, where reasons are given for considering existential statements to be *metaphysical* (in the sense of unscientific).

11 It may be worth mentioning that equilibrium economics is undoubtedly *dynamic* (in the 'reasonable' as opposed to the 'Comtean' sense of this term), even though time does not occur in its equation. For this theory does not assert that the equilibrium is anywhere realized; it merely asserts that every disturbance (and disturbances occur all the time) is followed by an adjustment – by a 'movement' towards equilibrium. In physics, statics is the theory of equilibria and *not* of movements towards equilibrium; a static system *does not move*.

12 J.S. Mill, *A System of Logic*, 8th edition, 1872, Book VI, chapter X, section 3 (the italics are mine). For Mill's theory of 'progressive effects' in general, see also Book III, chapter XV, sections 2 and 3.

Mill seems to overlook the fact that only the very simplest arithmetical and geometrical sequences are such that 'a few terms' suffice for detecting their 'principle'. It is easy to construct more complicated mathematical sequences in which thousands of terms would not suffice to discover their law of construction – *even if it is known that there is such a law*.

13 For the nearest approach to such laws, see *The Poverty of Historicism*, section 28, especially note 1 on p.129.

14 See Mill, *loc.cit.* (the italics are mine). Mill distinguishes two senses of the word 'progress'; in the wider sense, it is opposed to cyclic change but does not imply improvement. (He

discusses 'progressive change' in this sense more fully in *op.cit.*, Book III, chapter XV.) In the narrower sense, it implies improvement. He teaches that the persistence of progress in the wider sense is a question of *method* (I do not understand this point), and in the narrower sense a theorem of sociology.

24 Piecemeal Social Engineering

1 See p.123 of F.A. von Hayek, 'The Trend of Economic Thinking', *Economica* **XIII**, 1933, pp. 121-37: '. . . economics developed mainly as the outcome of the investigation and refutation of successive Utopian proposals . . . .'

2 See p.180 of M. Ginsberg, 'Sociology and Human Affairs', pp.166-80 of R.B. Cattell *et al.*, editors, *Human Affairs*, 1937. It must be admitted, however, that the success of mathematical economics shows that one social science at least has gone through its Newtonian revolution.

3 See section 15 of *The Logic of Scientific Discovery*. The theory may be contrasted with that of J.S. Mill, *A System of Logic*, 8th edition, 1872, Book V, chapter V, section 2.

4 See, for example, pp.356-9 of M.R. Cohen, *Reason and Nature*, 1931; 2nd edition, 1953. The examples in the text appear to refute this particular anti-naturalistic view.

5 A similar formulation of this 'law of corruption' is discussed by C.J. Friedrich in his very interesting and partly technological *Constitutional Government and Politics*, 1937. He says of this law that 'all the natural sciences cannot boast of a single "hypothesis" of equal importance to mankind' (p.7). I do not doubt its importance; but I think that we may find countless laws of equal importance in the natural sciences, if only we look for them among the more platitudinous rather than among the more abstract laws. (Consider such laws as that men cannot live without food, or that vertebrates have two sexes.) Professor Friedrich insists upon the anti-naturalist thesis that the 'social sciences cannot benefit from applying methods of the natural sciences to them' (*op.cit.*, p.4). But he attempts, on the other

hand, to base his theory of politics on a number of hypotheses of whose character the following passages (*op.cit.*, pp.14ff.) may give an idea: 'Consent and constraint [are] both real forces, generating power'; together, they 'determine the intensity of a political situation'; and since 'this intensity is determined by the absolute amount of consent or constraint or both, it is perhaps most readily represented by the diagonal of the parallelogram of these two forces: consent and constraint. In that case its numerical value would equal the square root of the sum of the squares of the numerical values of consent and constraint'. This attempt to apply the Pythagorean theorem to a 'parallelogram' (we are not told why it should be rectangular) of 'forces' which are too vague to be measurable, seems to me an example not of anti-naturalism but of just that kind of naturalism or 'scientism' from which, I admit, the 'social sciences cannot benefit'. It may be noted that these 'hypotheses' can hardly be expressed in technological form, while the 'law of corruption', for example, whose importance is very justly emphasized by Friedrich, can be so expressed.

For the historical background of the 'scientistic' view that the problems of political theory can be understood in terms of the 'parallelogram of forces', see note 2 to chapter 7 of *The Open Society and Its Enemies*.

6 Against the use of the term 'social engineering' (in the 'piecemeal' sense) it has been objected by Professor Hayek that the typical engineering job involves the centralization of all relevant knowledge in a single head, whereas it is typical of all truly social problems that knowledge has to be used which cannot be so centralized. (See Hayek, *Collectivist Economic Planning*, 1935, p.210.) I admit that this fact is of fundamental importance. It can be formulated by the technological hypothesis: 'You cannot centralize within a planning authority the knowledge relevant for such tasks as the satisfaction of personal needs, or the utilization of specialized skill and ability.' (A similar hypothesis may be proposed regarding the impossibility of centralizing initiative in connection with similar tasks.) The use of the term 'social engineering' may now be defended by pointing out that the engineer must use the technological

knowledge embodied in these hypotheses which inform him of the limitations of his own initiative as well as of his own knowledge.

7 The two views – either that social institutions are 'designed' or that they just 'grow' – correspond to those of the Social Contract theorists and of their critics, for example, Hume. But Hume does not give up the 'functional' or 'instrumentalist' view of social institutions, for he says that men could not do without them. This position might be elaborated into a Darwinian explanation of the instrumental character of undesigned institutions (such as language): if they have no useful function, they have no chance of surviving. According to this view, undesigned social institutions may emerge as *unintended consequences of rational actions*: just as a road may be formed without any intention to do so by people who find it convenient to use a track already existing (as Descartes observes). It need hardly be stressed, however, that the technological approach is quite independent of all questions of 'origin'.

8 For the 'functional' approach, see for example B. Malinowski, 'Anthropology as the Basis of Social Science', pp. 199-252 of R.B. Cattell *et al.*, editors, *Human Affairs*, 1937, especially pp.206ff. and 239ff.

9 This example, asserting that the efficiency of institutional 'machines' is limited, and that the functioning of institutions depends on their being supplied with proper personnel, may perhaps be compared with the principles of thermodynamics, such as the law of conservation of energy (in the form in which it excludes the possibility of a perpetual motion machine). As such, it may be contrasted with other 'scientistic' attempts to work out an analogy between the physical concept of energy and some sociological concepts such as power; see, for example, Bertrand Russell's *Power*, 1938, pp.10f., where this kind of scientistic attempt is made. I do not think that Russell's main point – that the various 'forms of power', such as wealth, propagandist power, naked power, may sometimes be 'converted' into one another – can be expressed in technological form.

10 W. Lippmann, *The Good Society*, 1937, chapter XI, pp.203ff. See also W.H. Hutt, *Plan for Reconstruction*, 1943.

11 The expression is often used by K. Mannheim in his *Man and Society in an Age of Reconstruction*, 1940; see his index, and, for example, pp.269, 295, 320, 381. This book is the most elaborate exposition of a holistic and historicist programme known to me and is therefore singled out here for criticism.

The immediately following quotation is from *ibid.*, p.337. The passage is more fully quoted in section 23 of *The Poverty of Historicism*, where it is also criticized.

12 'The Problem of Transforming Man' is a heading of a chapter in Mannheim, *op.cit.* The following quotation is from that chapter, pp.199f.

13 This was also Mill's view when he said of social experiments that 'we palpably never have the power of trying any. We can only watch those which nature produces, . . . the successions of phenomena recorded in history . . .' See *A System of Logic*, 8th edition, 1872, Book VI, chapter VII, section 2.

14 Sidney and Beatrice Webb, *Methods of Social Study*, 1932, pp.221ff., give similar examples of social experiments. They do not distinguish, however, between the two kinds of experiments which are here called 'piecemeal' and 'holistic', although their criticism of the experimental method (see p.226, 'intermixture of effects') is especially cogent as a criticism of holistic experiments (which they seem to admire). Furthermore, their criticism is combined with the 'variability argument' which I consider to be invalid; see section 25 of *The Poverty of Historicism*.

15 See selections 9-12 above, and also *Conjectures and Refutations*, chapter 15. See also, for example, p.21 of J. Tinbergen, *Statistical Testing of Business-Cycle Theories*, volume II: 'The construction of a model . . . is . . . a matter of trial and error.'

16 One of the most crucial points in Spinoza's political theory is the impossibility of knowing and of controlling what other people think. He defines 'tyranny' as the attempt to achieve the impossible, and to exercise power where it cannot be exercised.

Spinoza, it must be remembered, was not exactly a liberal; he did not believe in institutional control of power, but thought that a prince has a right to exercise his powers up to their actual limit. Yet what Spinoza calls 'tyranny', and declares to be in conflict with reason, is treated quite innocently by holistic planners as a 'scientific' problem, the 'problem of transforming men'.

17 Niels Bohr calls two approaches 'complementary' if they are (1) complementary in the usual sense and (2) exclusive of each other in the sense that the more we make use of the one the less we can use the other. Although I refer in the text mainly to *social* knowledge, it may be claimed that the accumulation (and concentration) of political power is 'complementary' to the progress of scientific knowledge in general. For the progress of science depends on free competition of thought, hence on freedom of thought, and hence, ultimately, on political freedom.

18 See p.102 at the end of section ii of chapter II of R.H. Tawney, *Religion and the Rise of Capitalism*, 1926.

25 The Paradoxes of Sovereignty

1 The motto is from *Laws*, 690 B.

2 Similar ideas have been expressed by J.S. Mill; thus he writes in *A System of Logic*, 8th edition, 1872, Book VI, chapter VIII, section 3: 'Although the actions of rulers are by no means wholly determined by their selfish interests, it is chiefly as security against those selfish interests that constitutional checks are required ....' Similarly he writes in *The Subjection of Women*, 1869; Everyman edition, p.251 (italics mine): 'Who doubts that there may be great goodness, and great happiness and great affection, under the absolute government of a good man? Meanwhile *laws and institutions require to be adapted, not to good men, but to bad.*' Much as I agree with the sentence in italics, I feel that the admission contained in the first part of the sentence is not really called for. A similar admission may

be found in an excellent passage on p.49 of his *Representative Government*, 1861, where Mill combats the Platonic ideal of the philosopher king because, *especially if his rule should be a benevolent one*, it will involve the 'abdication' of the ordinary citizen's will, and ability, to judge a policy.

It may be remarked that this admission of J.S. Mill's was part of an attempt to resolve the conflict between James Mill's *Essay on Government* and 'Macaulay's famous attack' on it (as J.S. Mill calls it; see his *Autobiography*, chapter V, One Stage Onward; 1st edition, 1873, pp. 157-61; Macaulay's criticisms were first published in the *Edinburgh Review*, March 1829, June 1829, and October 1829). This conflict played a great role in J.S. Mill's development; his attempt to resolve it determined, indeed, the ultimate aim and character of his *Logic* ('the principle chapters of what I afterwards published on the Logic of the Moral Sciences') as we hear from his *Autobiography*.

The resolution of the conflict between his father and Macaulay which J.S. Mill proposes is this. He says that his father was right in believing that politics was a deductive science, but wrong in believing that 'the type of deduction (was) that of . . . pure geometry', while Macaulay was right in believing that it was more experimental than this, but wrong in believing that it was like 'the purely experimental method of chemistry'. The true solution according to J.S. Mill (*Autobiography*, pp.159ff.) is this: the appropriate method of politics is the deductive one of dynamics – a method which he believes, is characterized by the summation of effects as exemplified in the 'principle of the Composition of Forces'. (That this idea of J.S. Mill survived at any rate down to 1937 is shown [in note 5 to selection 24] above.)

I do not think that there is very much in this analysis (which is based, apart from other things, upon a misinterpretation of dynamics and chemistry). Yet so much would seem to be defensible.

James Mill, like many before and after him, tried to 'deduce the science of government from the principles of human nature' as Macaulay said (towards the end of his first paper), and Macaulay was right, I think, to describe this attempt as 'utterly impossible'. Also, Macaulay's method could perhaps be described as more empirical, in so far as he made full use of historical facts for the purpose of refuting J. Mill's dogmatic theories. But the method which he practised has nothing to do with that of chemistry, or with that which J.S. Mill believed to be the method of chemistry (or with the Baconian inductive method which, irritated by J. Mill's syllogisms, Macaulay praised). It was simply the method of rejecting invalid logical demonstrations in a field in which nothing of interest can be logically demonstrated, and of discussing theories and possible situations, in the light of alternative theories and of alternative possibilities, and of factual historical evidence. One of the main points at issue was that J. Mill believed that he had demonstrated the necessity for monarchy and aristocracy to produce a rule of terror – a point which was easily refuted by examples. J.S. Mill's two passages quoted at the beginning of this note show the influence of this refutation.

Macaulay always emphasized that he only wanted to reject Mill's proofs, and not to pronounce on the truth or falsity of his alleged conclusions. This alone should have made it clear that he did not attempt to practise the inductive method which he praised.

3 See for instance E. Meyer's remark on p. 4 of *Geschichte des Altertums*, volume V, 1902, that 'power is, in its very essence, indivisible'.

4 See *Republic*, 562 B – 565 C. In the text I am alluding especially to 562 C: 'Does not the excess [of liberty] bring men to such a state that they badly want a tyranny?' See furthermore 563 D/E: 'And in the end, as you know well enough, they just do not take any notice of the laws, whether written or unwritten, since they want to have no despot of any kind over them. This then is the origin out of which tyranny springs.'

Other remarks of Plato's on the *paradoxes of freedom and of democracy* are: *Republic*, 564 A: 'Then too much freedom is liable to change into nothing else but too much slavery, in the individual as well as in the state. . . . Hence it is reasonable to assume that tyranny is enthroned by no other form of government than by democracy. Out of what I believe is the greatest possible excess of freedom springs what is the hardest and most savage form of slavery.' See also *Republic*, 565 C/D: 'And are not the common people in the habit of making one man their champion or party leader, and of exalting his position and making him great?' – 'This is their habit.' – 'Then it seems clear that whenever a tyranny grows up, this democratic party leadership is the origin from which it springs.'

The so-called *paradox of freedom* is the argument that freedom in the sense of absence of any restraining control must lead to very great restraint, since it makes the bully free to enslave the meek. This idea is, in a slightly different form, and with a very different tendency, clearly expressed by Plato.

Less well known is the *paradox of tolerance*: Unlimited tolerance must lead to the disappearance of tolerance. If we extend unlimited tolerance even to those who are intolerant, if we are not prepared to defend a tolerant society against the onslaught of the intolerant, then the tolerant will be destroyed, and tolerance with them. – In this formulation, I do not imply, for instance, that we should always suppress the utterance of intolerant philosophies; as long as we can counter them by rational argument and keep them in check by public opinion, suppression would certainly be most unwise. But we should claim the *right* to suppress them if necessary even by force; for it may easily turn out that they are not prepared to meet us on the level of rational argument, but begin by denouncing all argument; they may forbid their followers to listen to rational argument, because it is deceptive, and teach them to answer arguments by the use of their fists or pistols. We should therefore claim, in the name of tolerance, the right not to tolerate the intolerant. We should claim that any movement preaching intolerance places itself outside the law, and we should consider incitement to intolerance and persecution as criminal, in the same way as we should consider incitement to murder, or to kidnapping, or to the revival of the slave trade, as criminal.

Another of the less well-known paradoxes is the *paradox of democracy* or more precisely, of majority rule; i.e. the possibility that the majority may decide that a tyrant should rule. That Plato's criticism of democracy can be interpreted in the way sketched here, and that the principle of majority rule may lead to self-contradictions, was first suggested, as far as I know, by Leonard Nelson. I do not think, however, that Nelson, who, in spite of his passionate humanitarianism and his ardent fight for freedom, adopted much of Plato's political theory, and especially Plato's principle of leadership, was aware of the fact that analogous arguments can be raised against all the different particular forms of the *theory of sovereignty*.

All these paradoxes can easily be avoided if we frame our political demands in the way suggested in section II [of this selection], or perhaps in some such manner as this. We demand a government that rules according to the principles of equalitarianism and protectionism; that tolerates all who are prepared to reciprocate, i.e. who are tolerant; that is controlled by, and accountable to, the public. And we may add that some form of majority vote, together with institutions for keeping the public well informed, is the best, though not infallible, means of controlling such a government. (No infallible means exist.) [See also note 3(4) to selection 2, and note 6 below.]

5 Further remarks on this point will be found in *The Open Society and Its Enemies* chapter 19.

6 The fragment is Heraclitus B 33 in H. Diels & W. Krantz, *Die Fragmente der Vorsokratiker*, 5th edition, 1964. [See also note 1 to selection 1.]

The following remarks on the *paradoxes of freedom and of sovereignty* may possibly appear to carry the argument too far; since, however, the arguments discussed in this place are of a somewhat formal character, it may be just as well to make them more watertight, even if it involves something approaching hair splitting. Moreover, my experience in debates of this kind leads me to expect that the defenders of the leader principle, i.e. of the sovereignty of the best or the wisest, may actually offer the following counterargument: (1) if 'the wisest' should decide that the majority should rule, then he was not really wise. As a further consideration they may support this by the assertion (2) that a wise man would never establish a principle which might lead to contradictions, like that of majority rule. My reply to (2) would be that we need only to alter this decision of the 'wise' man in such a way that it becomes free from contradictions. For instance, he could decide in favour of a government bound to rule according to the principle of equalitarianism and protectionism, and controlled by majority vote. This decision of the wise man would give up the sovereignty principle; and since it would thereby become free from contradictions, it may be made by a 'wise' man. But of course, this would not free the principle that the wisest should rule from *its* contradictions. The other argument, namely (1), is a different matter. It comes dangerously close to defining the 'wisdom' or 'goodness' of a politician in such a way that he is called 'wise' or 'good' only if he is determined not to give up his power. And indeed, the only sovereignty theory which is free from contradictions would be the theory which demands that only a man who is absolutely determined to cling to his power should rule. Those who believe in the leader principle should frankly face this logical consequence of their creed. If freed from contradictions it implies, not the rule of the best or wisest, but the rule of the strong man, of the man of power.

7 See my lecture 'Towards a Rational Theory of Tradition', chapter 4 of *Conjectures and Refutations*, where I try to show that traditions play a kind of intermediate and intermediary role between *persons* (and personal decisions) and *institutions*.

26 Marx's Theory of the State

1 See the Preface to *A Contribution to 'The Critique of Political Economy'*, 1859; E. Burns, editor, *A Handbook of Marxism*, 1935, p.372.

2 For Plato's recommendation of 'both persuasion and force', see, for instance, section VII of chapter 5 of *The Open Society and Its Enemies*, and notes 5 and 10 to chapter 8.

3 See V.I. Lenin, *The State and Revolution*, 1918, chapter 1, section 4; *A Handbook of Marxism*, p.735.

4 The two quotations are from Marx & Engels, *The Communist Manifesto*, 1848; *A Handbook of Marxism*, p.46; Moscow standard edition of Marx & Engels, Series I, volume VI, p.546.

5 See Lenin, *op.cit.*, chapter 1, section 1; *A Handbook of Marxism*, p.725.

6 This quotation is from *The Communist Manifesto*, 1848; *A Handbook of Marxism*, p.25; Moscow standard edition, Series I, volume VI, p.528. The text is from Engels's Preface to the first English translation of *Capital*. I quote here the whole concluding passage of this Preface; Engels speaks there about Marx's conclusion 'that at least in Europe, England is the only country where the inevitable social revolution might be effected entirely by peaceful and legal means. He certainly never forgot to add that he hardly expected the English ruling class to submit, without a "pro-slavery rebellion", to this peaceful and legal revolution'. (See the Everyman edition of *Capital*, p.887.) This passage shows clearly that, according to Marxism, the violence or non-violence of the revolution will depend on the resistance or non-resistance of the old ruling class. See also The *Open Society and Its Enemies*, chapter 19, section I.

7 See F. Engels, *Anti-Dühring*, 1877, Part III; *A Handbook of Marxism*, p.296; Moscow edition, Special volume, p.292. See also the passages mentioned in note 5 above.

The resistance of the bourgeoisie has been broken for some years in Russia; but there are no signs of the 'withering away' of the Russian state, not even in its internal organization.

The theory of the withering away of the state is highly unrealistic, and I think that it may have been adopted by Marx and Engels mainly in order to take the wind out of their rivals' sails. The rivals I have in mind are Bakunin and the anarchists; Marx did not like to see anyone else's radicalism outdoing his own. Like Marx, they aimed at the overthrow of the existing social order, directing their attack, however, against the politico-legal, instead of the economic system. To them, the state was the fiend who had to be destroyed. But for his anarchist competitors, Marx, from his own premises, might have easily granted the possibility that the institution of the state, under socialism, might have to fulfil new and indispensable functions; namely those functions of safeguarding justice and freedom allotted to it by the great theorists of democracy.

8 Marx defines the 'value' of a commodity as the average number of labour hours necessary for its reproduction. This definition is a good illustration of his *essentialism*. For he introduces *value* in order to get at the essential reality which corresponds to what appears in the form of the *price* of a commodity. Price is a delusive kind of appearance. 'A thing may have a price without having value', writes Marx (Everyman edition of *Capital*, p.79; see also Cole's excellent remarks in his Introduction to *Capital*, especially pp. xxvii ff.).

9 For the problem of the 'wage-slaves', and Marx's analysis, the results of which are briefly sketched here, see especially *Capital*, Everyman edition, pp.153ff. and footnotes.

My presentation of Marx's analysis may be supported by quoting a statement made by Engels in his *Anti-Dühring* on the occasion of a summary of *Capital*. Engels writes (*A Handbook of Marxism*, p.269; Moscow edition, Special volume, pp.160-7): 'In other words, even if we exclude all possibility of robbery, violence, and fraud, even if we assume that all private property was originally produced by the owner's own labour; and that throughout the whole subsequent process, there was only exchange of equal values for equal values; even then the progressive development of production and exchange would necessarily bring about the present capitalist system of production; with its monopolization of the instruments of production as well as of the goods of consumption in the hands of a class weak in numbers; with its degradation into proletarian paupers of the other class comprising the immense majority; with its periodic cycle of production booms and of trade depressions; in other words, with the whole anarchy of our present system of production. The whole process is explained by purely economic causes: robbery, force, and the assumption of political interference of any kind are unnecessary at any point whatever.'

Perhaps this passage may one day convince a Vulgar Marxist that Marxism does not explain depressions by the conspiracy of 'big business'. Marx himself said (*Das Kapital*, volume II, 1885, pp.406f., italics mine): 'Capitalist production involves conditions which, *independently of good or bad intentions*, permit only a temporary relative prosperity of the working class, and always only as a forerunner of a depression.'

10 For the doctrine 'property is theft' or 'property is robbery', see also Marx's remarks on John Watts in *Capital*, Everyman edition, p.601, footnote 1.

11 For the Hegelian character of the distinction between merely 'formal' and 'actual' or 'real' freedom, or democracy, see note 62 to chapter 12 of *The Open Society and Its Enemies*. Hegel likes to attack the British constitution for its cult of merely 'formal' freedom, as opposed to the Prussian State in which 'real' freedom is 'actualized'. For the quotation at the end of this paragraph, see *Das Kapital*, volume III/2, 1894, p.355.

12 Against this analysis, it may be said that, if we assume perfect competition between the entrepreneurs as producers, and especially as buyers of labour on the labour markets (and if we further assume that there is no 'industrial reserve army' of unemployed to exert pressure on this market), then there could be no talk of exploitation of the economically weak by the economically strong, i.e. of the workers by the entrepreneurs. But is the assumption of perfect competition between the buyers on the labour markets at all realistic? Is it not true that, for example, on many local labour markets, there is only one buyer of any significance? Besides, we cannot assume that perfect competition would automatically eliminate the problem of unemployment, if for no other reason because labour cannot easily be moved.

13 For the problem of economic intervention by the state, and for a characterization of our present economic system as *interventionism*, see *The Open Society and Its Enemies*, chapters 18-20, especially note 9 to chapter 18 and text. It may be remarked

that *interventionism* as used here is the economic complement of what I have called on p.111 of *op.cit.*, chapter 6, political *protectionism*. (It is clear why the term 'protectionism' cannot be used instead of 'interventionism'.)

14 Everyman edition of *Capital*, p.864.

15 See also *The Open Society and Its Enemies*, chapter 9.

16 The review, published in the *European Messenger* of St Petersburg is quoted by Marx in the Preface to the 2nd edition of *Capital*. (See the Everyman edition of *Capital*, p.871.)

In fairness to Marx, we must say that he did not always take his own system too seriously, and that he was quite prepared to deviate a little from his fundamental scheme; he considered it as a point of view (and as such it was certainly most important) rather than as a system of dogmas.

Thus we read, on two consecutive pages of *Capital* (pp.832f.), a statement which emphasizes the usual Marxist theory of the secondary character of the legal system (or of its character as a cloak, an 'appearance'), and another statement which ascribes a very important role to the political might of the state and raises it explicitly to the rank of a full-grown *economic force*. The first of these statements, 'The author would have done well to remember that revolutions are not made by laws', refers to the industrial revolution, and to an author who asked for the enactments by which it was effected. The second statement is a comment (and one most unorthodox from the Marxist point of view) upon the methods of accumulating capital; all these methods, Marx says, 'make use of the power of the state, which is the centralized political might of society. Might is the midwife of every old society pregnant with a new one. *It is itself an economic force*.' Up to the last sentence, which I have put in italics, the passage is clearly orthodox. But the last sentence breaks through this orthodoxy.

Engels was more dogmatic. One should compare especially one of his statements in his *Anti-Dühring*, where he writes, 'The role played in history by political might as opposed to economic developments is now clear.' He contends that whenever 'political might works against economic developments, then, as a rule, with only few exceptions, it succumbs; these few exceptions are isolated cases of conquest in which barbarian conquerors ... have laid waste ... productive forces which they did not know how to use'. (*A Handbook of Marxism*, p.277.)

The dogmatism and authoritarianism of most Marxists is a really astonishing phenomenon. It just shows that they use Marxism irrationally, as a metaphysical system. It is to be found among radicals and moderates alike. E. Burns, for example, makes the surprisingly naïve statement (*A Handbook of Marxism*, p.374) that 'refutations ... inevitably distort Marx's theories'; which seems to imply that Marx's theories are irrefutable, i.e. unscientific; for every scientific theory is refutable, and can be superseded. L. Laurat, on the other hand, in *Marxism and Democracy*, 1940, p.226, says: 'In looking at the world in which we live, we are staggered at the almost mathematical precision with which the essential predictions of Karl Marx are being realized.'

Marx himself seems to have thought differently. I may be wrong in this, but I do believe in the sincerity of his statement (at the end of his Preface to the first edition of *Capital*; see p.865): 'I welcome scientific criticism, however harsh. But in the face of the prejudices of a so-called public opinion, I shall stick to my maxim ...: Follow your course, and let them chatter!'

27 Individualism versus Collectivism

1 On the term 'collectivism', a terminological comment may be made here. What H.G. Wells calls 'collectivism' has nothing to do with what I call by that name. Wells is an individualist (in my sense of the word), as is shown especially by his *Rights of Man* and his *Common Sense of War and Peace*, which contain very acceptable formulations of the demands of an equalitarian individualism. But he also believes, rightly, in the rational planning of political institutions, with the aim of furthering the freedom and the welfare of individual human beings. This he calls 'collectivism'; to describe what I believe to be the same

thing as his 'collectivism', I should use an expression like: 'rational institutional planning for freedom'. This expression may be long and clumsy, but it avoids the danger that 'collectivism' may be interpreted in the anti-individualistic sense in which it is often used, not only in the present book.

2 *Laws*, 903 C.

3 There are innumerable places in the *Republic* and in the *Laws* where Plato gives a warning against unbridled group egoism; see, for instance, *Republic*, 519 E, 466 B/C, and *Laws*, 715 B/C.

Regarding the identity often alleged to exist between collectivism and altruism, I may refer, in this connection, to the very pertinent question of Sherrington, who asks on p.388 of *Man on His Nature*, 1951: 'Are the shoal and the herd altruism?'

4 *Politics*, 1282b. See also Aristotle's remark in *Politics*, 1280a, to the effect that justice pertains to persons as well as to things.

5 This remark is from *Republic*, 519 E f.

6 The first passage is *Laws*, 793 C ff. Plato refers here to the *Republic*, and apparently especially to *Republic*, 462 A ff., 424 A and 449 E. (A list of passages on collectivism and holism can be found in note 35 to chapter 5 of *The Open Society and Its Enemies*.) The passage here quoted begins, characteristically, with a quotation of the Pythagorean maxim 'Friends have in common all things they possess'. See note 10 and text; also the 'common meals' mentioned in note 8.

7 The quotation which follows in the present paragraph is *Laws*, 942 A f. Both it and the previous passage are referred to as anti-individualistic by T. Gomperz, *Greek Thinkers*, 1905, Book V, chapter XX; German edition, volume II, p.406. See also *Laws*, 807 D/E.

We must not forget that military education in the *Laws* (as in the *Republic*) is obligatory for all those allowed to carry arms, i.e. for all citizens – for all those who have anything like civil rights (*Laws*, 753 B). All others are 'banausic', if not slaves (*Laws*, 741 E and 743 D).

It is interesting that Barker, who hates militarism, believes that Plato held similar views (*Greek Political Theory*, 1918, pp.298-301). It is true that Plato did not eulogize war, and that he even spoke against war. But many militarists have talked peace and practised war; and Plato's state is ruled by the military caste, i.e. by the wise ex-soldiers. This remark is as true for the *Laws* (see 753 B) as it is for the *Republic*.

8 Strictest legislation about meals – especially '*common meals*' – and also about drinking habits plays a considerable part in Plato; see for instance *Republic*, 416 E, 458 C, 547 D/E; *Laws*, 625 E, 633 A (where the obligatory common meals are said to be instituted with a view to war), 762 B, 780-3, 806 C f., 839 C, 842 B. Plato always emphasizes the importance of common meals, in accordance with Cretan and Spartan customs. Interesting also is the preoccupation of Plato's uncle Critias with these matters. See Critias B 33 in H. Diels & W. Krantz, *Die Fragmente der Vorsokratiker*, 5th edition, 1964. [See also note 1 to selection 1.]

With the allusion to the anarchy of the 'wild beasts', at the end of the present quotation, compare also *Republic*, 563 C.

9 See E.B. England's edition of the *Laws*, volume I, p.514, note to 739 B 8 ff. The quotations from Barker are from *op.cit.*, pp.149 and 148. Countless similar passages can be found in the writings of most Platonists. See however Sherrington's remark (quoted in note 3 above) that it is hardly correct to say that a shoal or a herd is inspired by altruism. Herd instinct and tribal egoism, and the appeal to these instincts, should not be mixed up with unselfishness.

10 See *Republic*, 424 A, 449 C; *Phaedrus*, 279 C: *Laws*, 739 C; and also *Lysis*, 207 C, and Euripides, *Oresteia*, 725.

Regarding the individualistic theory of justice and injustice in the *Gorgias*, see for instance the examples given in *Gorgias*, 468 B ff., 508 D/E. These passages probably still show Socratic influence. Socrates's individualism is most clearly expressed in his famous doctrine of the self-sufficiency of the good man; a doctrine which is mentioned by Plato in the *Republic*, 387 D/E, in spite of the fact that it flatly contradicts one of the main theses of the *Republic*, viz., that the state alone can be self-sufficient. See also *The Open Society and Its Enemies*, notes 5ff. to chapter 5 and note 56 to chapter 10.

11 *Republic*, 368 B/C.

12 See especially *Republic*, 344 A ff.

13 *Laws*, 923 B.

28 The Autonomy of Sociology

1 See Marx's Preface to *A Contribution to the Critique of Political Economy*, 1859; E. Burns, editor, *A Handbook of Marxism*, 1935, p.372; Everyman edition of *Capital*, p.xvi. See also Marx & Engels, *German Ideology*, 1847; *A Handbook of Marxism*, p.213; Moscow standard edition of Marx & Engels, Series I, volume V, p.16: 'It is not consciousness that determines life, but life that determines consciousness.'

2 See M. Ginsberg, *Sociology*, pp.130ff., who discusses this problem in a similar context, without, however, referring to Marx. For the contrast between nature and convention see especially chapter 5 of *The Open Society and Its Enemies*.

3 See, for instance, *Zoology Leaflet 10*, published by the Field Museum of Natural History, Chicago, 1929.

4 For institutionalism, see *The Open Society and Its Enemies*, especially chapter 3 (text to notes 9 and 10) and chapter 9.

5 The quotations in this paragraph are from J.S. Mill, *A System of Logic*, 8th edition, 1872, Book VI, chapter IX, section 3; *ibid.*, chapter VI, section 2; and *ibid.*, chapter VII, section 1.

6 For the opposition between 'methodological individualism' and 'methodological collectivism', see section VII, pp. 41ff. of F.A. von Hayek, 'Scientism and the Study of Society', Part II, *Economica* New Series **X**, 1943, pp.34-63.

7 These quotations are from Mill, *op.cit.*, Book VI, chapter X, section 4.

8 I am using the term 'sociological laws' to denote the natural laws of social life, as opposed to its normative laws.

9 I owe the suggestion that it was Marx who first conceived social theory as the study of the *unwanted social repercussions of nearly all our actions* to K. Polanyi, who emphasized this aspect of Marxism in private discussions in 1924.

It should be noted, however, that in spite of the aspect of Marxism which has just been mentioned and which constitutes an important point of agreement between Marx's views on method and mine, there is a considerable disagreement between Marx's and my views about the way in which these unwanted or unintended repercussions have to be analysed. For Marx is a *methodological collectivist*. He believes that it is the 'system of economic relations' as such which gives rise to the unwanted consequences – a system of institutions which, in turn, may be explicable in terms of 'means of production', but which is not analysable in terms of individuals, their relations, and their actions. As opposed to this, I hold that institutions (and traditions) must be analysed in individualistic terms – that is to say, in terms of the relations of individuals acting in certain situations, and of the unintended consequences of their actions.

Concerning the remarks in the text (in the paragraph to which this note is appended, and in some of those which follow) about the unintended social repercussions of our actions, I wish to draw attention to the fact that the situation in the physical sciences (and in the field of mechanical engineering and technology) is somewhat similar. The task of technology is here also largely to inform us about unintended consequences of what we are doing (e.g. that a bridge may become too heavy if we strengthen certain of its components). But the analogy goes even further. Our mechanical inventions do rarely turn out according to our original plans. The inventors of the motor car probably did not foresee the social repercussions of their doings, but they certainly did not foresee the purely mechanical repercussions – the many ways in which their cars broke down. And while their cars were altered in order to avoid these breakdowns, they changed beyond recognition. (And with them, some people's motives and aspirations changed also.)

10 See *The Open Society and Its Enemies*, chapter 9.

11 With my criticism of the conspiracy theory compare also *Conjectures and Refutations*, chapters 4 and 16.

12 The passage is cited in note 7 above.

13 Important contributors to the logic of power are Plato (in Books VIII and IX of the *Republic*, and in the *Laws*), Aristotle, Machiavelli, Pareto, and many others.

14 See M. Weber, *Gesammelte Aufsätze sur Wissenschaftslehre*, 1922, especially pp.408ff.

A remark may be added here concerning the often repeated assertion that the social sciences operate with a method different from that of the natural sciences, in so far as we know the 'social atoms', i.e. ourselves, by direct acquaintance, while our knowledge of physical atoms is only hypothetical. From this, it is often concluded (e.g. by Karl Menger) that the method of social science, since it makes use of our knowledge of ourselves, is psychological, or perhaps 'subjective', as opposed to the 'objective' methods of the natural sciences. To this, we may answer: There is surely no reason why we should not use any 'direct' knowledge we may have of ourselves. But such knowledge is useful in the social sciences only if we generalize, i.e. if we assume that what we know of ourselves holds good for others too. But this generalization is of a hypothetical character, and it must be tested and corrected by experience of an 'objective' kind. (Before having met anybody who does not like chocolate, some people may easily believe that everybody likes it.) Undoubtedly, in the case of 'social atoms' we are in certain ways more favourably situated than in the case of physical atoms, owing not only to our knowledge of ourselves, but also to the use of language. Yet from the point of view of scientific method, a social hypothesis suggested by self-intuition is in no different position from a physical hypothesis about atoms. The latter may also be suggested to the physicist by a kind of intuition about what atoms are like. And in both cases, this intuition is a private affair of the man who proposes the hypothesis. What is 'public', and important for science, is merely the question whether the hypotheses could be tested by experience, and whether they stood up to tests.

From this point of view, social theories are no more 'subjective' than physical ones. (And it would be clearer, for example, to speak of 'the theory of subjective values' or of 'the theory of acts of choice' than of 'the subjective theory of value'.)

15 *The Open Society and Its Enemies*, chapter 10.

16 Hegel contended that his 'Idea' was something existing 'absolutely', i.e. independently of anybody's thought. One might contend, therefore, that he did not subscribe to psychologism. Yet Marx, quite reasonably, did not take seriously this 'absolute idealism' of Hegel; he rather interpreted it as a disguised *psychologism*, and combated it as such. See *Capital*, Everyman edition, p.873 (italics mine): 'For Hegel, the *thought process* (which he even presents in disguise under the name "Idea" as an independent agent or subject) is the creator of the real.' Marx confines his attack to the doctrine that the thought process (or consciousness, or mind) creates the 'real'; and he shows that it does not even create the social reality (to say nothing about the material universe).

For the Hegelian theory of the dependence of the individual upon society, see the discussion [in selection 30] of the social, or more precisely, the interpersonal element in scientific method, as well as the corresponding discussion [in selection 2] of the interpersonal element in rationality.

30 Against the Sociology of Knowledge

1 The motto is taken from the concluding sentences, pp.107f., of 'The Ancestry of Fascism', *In Praise of Idleness*, 1935. [This reference was kindly supplied by Dr Kenneth Blackwell, Archivist to the Bertrand Russell Archives, Mills Memorial Library, McMaster University.]

2 Concerning Mannheim, see especially *Ideology and Utopia*, 1936. The terms 'social habitat' and 'total ideology' are both due to Mannheim. The idea of a 'social habitat' is Platonic.

3 For a criticism of Mannheim's *Man and Society in an Age of Reconstruction*, 1941, which combines historicist tendencies with a romantic and even mystical holism [see selection 24, section II].

4 See my interpretation in *Conjectures and Refutations*, p. 325. This is a translation of Mannheim's term (*Ideology and Utopia*, chapter II, section 1; or p.167, for example). For the 'freely poised intelligence', see *op.cit.*, p.137, where this term is attributed to Alfred Weber. For the theory of an intelligentsia loosely anchored in tradition, see *op.cit.*, pp.136-46, especially p.137.

5 The analogy between the psychoanalytic method and that of Wittgenstein is mentioned by J. Wisdom in the note on p.370 of 'Other Minds', Part I, *Mind* **49**, 1940, pp.369-402: 'A doubt such as "I can never really know what another person is feeling" may arise from more than one of these sources. This over-determination of sceptical symptoms complicates their cure. The treatment is like psychoanalytic treatment (to enlarge Wittgenstein's analogy) in that the treatment is the diagnosis and the diagnosis is the description, the very full description, of the symptoms.' And so on. (I may remark that, using the word 'know' in the ordinary sense, we can, of course, never know what another person is feeling. We can only make hypotheses about it. This solves the so-called problem. It is a mistake to speak here of doubt, and a still worse mistake to attempt to remove the doubt by a semioticoanalytic treatment.)

6 The psychoanalysts seem to hold the same of the individual psychologists, and they are probably right. See Freud's *History of the Psycho-Analytic Movement*, 1916, p. 42, where Freud records that Adler made the following remark (which fits well within Adler's individual-psychological scheme, according to which feelings of inferiority are predominantly important): 'Do you believe that it is such a pleasure for me to stand in your

shadow my whole life?' This suggests that Adler had not successfully applied his theories to himself, at that time at least. But the same seems to be true of Freud: None of the founders of psychoanalysis were psychoanalysed. To this objection, they usually replied that they had psychoanalysed themselves. But they would never have accepted such an excuse from anybody else; and, indeed, rightly so.

7 For the following analysis of scientific objectivity, see *The Logic of Scientific Discovery*, section 8.

8 I wish to apologize to the Kantians for mentioning them in the same breath as the Hegelians.

9 See K. Mannheim, *Ideology and Utopia*, p.170.

10 For these two quotations see *op.cit.*, p.169. (For simplicity's sake I translate 'conscious' for 'reflexive'.)

11 See E. Burns, editor, *A Handbook of Marxism*, 1935, p.255; Moscow standard edition, Special volume, pp.117f.: 'Hegel was the first to state correctly the relation between freedom and necessity. To him, freedom is the appreciation of necessity.' For Hegel's own formulation of his pet idea, see J. Loewenberg, editor, *Hegel: Selections*, 1929, p.213: 'The truth of necessity, therefore, is freedom'; and p.361: '. . . the *Christian* principle of self-consciousness – Freedom'; and p.362: 'The essential nature of freedom, which involves in it absolute necessity, is to be displayed as the attainment of a consciousness of itself (for it is in its very nature, self-consciousness) and it thereby realizes its existence'. And so on.

Editorial Note, Sources, and Acknowledgements

Since almost all the sources from which the selections are taken are readily available, I have thought it unnecessary to draw attention to the many minor editorial amendments to his text that Sir Karl has permitted me to make specifically for this book. These include the rephrasing of sentences for the sake of improving continuity; some streamlining of the material in the notes; alterations to spelling, punctuation, and the like in order to ensure consistency within the volume; a few stylistic and grammatical improvements; and the correction of trifling errors. Cross references have been adjusted so that, wherever possible, the reader is in the first instance directed to another part of the present book. Such references have been enclosed within square brackets, and for the most part assimilated into the text, while references to other works are banished to the notes. In general I have tried to identify English language editions of the works Popper cites, though the date assigned is normally that of the original edition. It must be made clear that the translations used here are in most cases Popper's own.

In most of the selections I have desisted from making dramatic internal cuts (to the extent, anyway, of reproducing whole sections of the original works), in the hope that Popper's text will speak more clearly than any editorial intervention. This has led, inevitably, to the occasional repetition. It should be recorded, however, that substantial cuts have been made in the notes to selection 6; and that in selections 12, 23, and 26 I have also made considerable deletions from the original material. To a lesser extent this is true of other selections, as noted below.

The date attached to each selection is that of its first appearance in some form or other: for lectures, the year of the lecture; for papers and extracts from books, the year of first publication. In some cases new material was added later, but I have suppressed explicit announcements of these additions. In particular, starred footnotes from *The Logic of Scientific Discovery* and *The Open Society and Its Enemies* appear here unstarred. Those who are interested in the details of the development of Popper's thought will have little difficulty in tracking it through his original publications.

The origins of the selections are as follows.

1 'The Beginnings of Rationalism'. This consists of sections I, XI, and XII of 'Back to the Presocratics'; this was the Presidential Address to the Aristotelian Society in 1958, and is now chapter 5 of *Conjectures and Refutations*.

2 'The Defence of Rationalism'. This consists of sections II and III of chapter 24 of *The Open Society and Its Enemies*.

3 'Knowledge without Authority'. This consists of sections XIII-XVII of 'On the Sources of Knowledge and of Ignorance'; this was the Annual Philosophical Lecture read before the British Academy in 1960, and is now the Introduction to *Conjectures and Refutations*.

4 'Knowledge: Subjective versus Objective'. This consists of sections 1-4, 5.1 and 5.2 of 'Epistemology without a Knowing Subject'; this was an address given at the Third International Congress for Logic, Methodology and Philosophy of Science in 1967, and is now chapter 3 of *Objective Knowledge*.

5 'Evolutionary Epistemology'. This consists of sections I-VI of 'The Rationality of Scientific Revolutions'; this was a Herbert Spencer Lecture given at the University of Oxford in 1973, and was published as chapter 6 of R. Harré, editor, *Problems of Scientific Revolution*, Oxford University Press 1975.

6 'Two Kinds of Definitions'. This consists of section II of chapter 11 of *The Open Society and Its Enemies*. The material in the notes has been substantially abbreviated.

7 'The Problem of Induction'. This starts with section IX of

'Philosophy of Science: A Personal Report'; this was a lecture given at Peterhouse, Cambridge, in 1953, and is now (with a different title) chapter 1 of *Conjectures and Refutations*. The rest of the selection consists of sections 13 and 14 of 'Replies to My Critics'. Some cuts have been made at the beginnings and ends of sections.

8 'The Problem of Demarcation'. This consists of sections 5-8 of 'Replies to My Critics'. Some cuts have been made at the beginnings and ends of sections.

9 'Scientific Method'. This consists of the end of section 1, sections 2 and 3, and chapter II of *The Logic of Scientific Discovery*.

10 'Falsificationism versus Conventionalism'. This consists of the the introductory material to chapter IV and sections 19-22 of *The Logic of Scientific Discovery*.

11 'The Empirical Basis'. This consists of the introductory material to chapter V and sections 25, 27-9 of *The Logic of Scientific Discovery*.

12 'The Aim of Science'. This paper was first published in *Ratio* **1**, 1957, and is now chapter 5 of *Objective Knowledge*. It is also section 15 of *Realism and the Aim of Science*. An internal cut of about four pages has been made.

13 'The Growth of Scientific Knowledge'. This consists of part of section I and sections II-VI of 'Truth, Rationality, and the Growth of Scientific Knowledge'; this was prepared for the First International Congress for Logic, Methodology and Philosophy of Science in 1960, and is now chapter 10 of *Conjectures and Refutations*.

14 'Truth and Approximation to Truth'. This consists of sections VII-XIII of 'Truth, Rationality, and the Growth of Scientific Knowledge', cited above under 13.

15 'Propensities, Probabilities, and the Quantum Theory'. This consists of the paper 'The Propensity Interpretation of the Calculus of Probability, and the Quantum Theory'; this was presented at a symposium organized by the Colston Research

Society in Bristol in 1957, and was published in S. Körner, editor, *Observation and Interpretation*, Butterworths Scientific Publications, 1957. One technical footnote has been omitted.

16 'Metaphysics and Criticizability'. This consists of section 2 of 'On the Status of Science and of Metaphysics'; this was first published in *Ratio* **1**, 1958, and is now chapter 8 of *Conjectures and Refutations*.

17 'Realism'. This consists of sections 4 and 5 of 'Two Faces of Common Sense'; this was a talk given at the London School of Economics in 1970, and is now chapter 2 of *Objective Knowledge*. One footnote has been omitted.

18 'Cosmology and Change'. This consists of sections II-IX of 'Back to the Presocratics', cited above under 1. One small internal cut has been made.

19 'Natural Selection and Its Scientific Status'. This consists of sections 1 and 2 of 'Natural Selection and the Emergence of Mind'; this was the First Darwin Lecture, delivered at Darwin College, Cambridge, in 1977, and was published in *Dialectica* **32**, 1978, being there dedicated to the memory of Professor Paul Bernays. Several cuts have been made.

20 'Indeterminism and Human Freedom'. This consists of sections II-IV and VI-XI of 'Of Clouds and Clocks'; this was the Second Arthur Holly Compton Memorial Lecture, delivered at Washington University, St Louis, in 1965, and is now chapter 6 of *Objective Knowledge*. Part of section VI has been omitted.

21 'The Mind-Body Problem'. This consists of sections 15, 17 and 20 of *The Self and Its Brain*. Some cuts have been made at the beginnings and ends of sections.

22 'The Self'. This consists of sections 29, 31, 36 and 37 of *The Self and Its Brain*. The end of section 29 has been omitted.

23 'Historicism'. This consists of the Introduction, sections 12, 14-16 and 27 of *The Poverty of Historicism*; this was first read at a private meeting in Brussels in 1936. Two substantial cuts have been made in section 27.

24 'Piecemeal Social Engineering'. This consists of sections 20, 21 and 24 of *The Poverty of Historicism*; this was first published in *Economica* **XI**, 1944, and **XII**, 1945. Some cuts have been made at the beginnings and ends of sections.

25 'The Paradoxes of Sovereignty'. This consists of part of the introductory material and sections I and II of chapter 7 of *The Open Society and Its Enemies*.

26 'Marx's Theory of the State'. This consists of chapter 17 of *The Open Society and Its Enemies*. Several internal cuts have been made.

27 'Individualism versus Collectivism'. This consists of section V of chapter 6 of *The Open Society and Its Enemies*.

28 'The Autonomy of Sociology'. This consists of chapter 14 of *The Open Society and Its Enemies*.

29 'The Rationality Principle'. This paper has not previously been published in English. A French translation was published in E.M. Claassen, editor, *Les Fondements Philosophiques des Systèmes Économiques* (*Festschrift* for Professor Jacques Rueff), Payot, 1967.

30 'Against the Sociology of Knowledge'. This consists of chapter 23 of *The Open Society and Its Enemies*.

Acknowledgements

Selections 1-3, 6, 7 (in part), 13, 14, 16, 18, 23-28 and 30 are reprinted by permission of Routledge and Kegan Paul. Selections 4, 12, 17 and 20 are reprinted by permission of Oxford University Press. Selections 9-11 are reprinted by permission of Hutchinson Educational Books. Selection 15 is reprinted by permission of the Colston Research Society and of Butterworths Scientific Publications. The editor is indebted also to the Board of Management of the Herbert Spencer Lectures for permission to reprint selection 5; to the Open Court Publishing Company for permission to reprint selections 7 (in part) and 8; to the editor of *Dialectica* for permission to reprint selection 19; and to Springer Verlag for permission to reprint selections 21 and 22.

Bibliography

Popper's main works in English are the following publications.

The Logic of Scientific Discovery, Hutchinson, 1959; 11th impression, 1982; originally published as *Logik der Forschung*, Springer, 1934.

The Poverty of Historicism, Routledge and Kegan Paul, 1957; Ark edition, 1986; originally published in *Economica*, 1944/5.

The Open Society and Its Enemies, Routledge and Kegan Paul, 1945; 5th edition, 1966.

Conjectures and Refutations, Routledge and Kegan Paul, 1963; 4th edition, 1972.

Objective Knowledge, Oxford University Press, 1972; 2nd edition, 1979.

Unended Quest, Fontana Paperbacks, 1976; Flamingo edition (with Postscript), 1986; originally published as the Intellectual Autobiography in P.A. Schilpp, editor, *The Philosophy of Karl Popper*, Open Court, 1974.

'Replies to My Critics', in P.A. Schilpp, *op. cit*.

The Self and Its Brain (with Sir John Eccles), Springer, 1977; 3rd impression, 1981; paperback edition, Routledge and Kegan Paul, 1983. Part I of this book is by Popper, Part II by Eccles, and Part III consists of dialogues between the two authors.

The Open Universe, volume II of *The Postscript*, Hutchinson, 1982.

Quantum Theory and the Schism in Physics, volume III of *The Postscript*, Hutchinson, 1982.

Realism and the Aim of Science, volume I of *The Postscript*, Hutchinson, 1983.

Available only in German at present is Popper's first book, written in 1930–2:

Die beiden Grundprobleme der Erkenntnistheorie, J.C.B. Mohr (Paul Siebeck), 1979.

Also available only in German are a recent book of essays, and two extended discussions.

Auf der Suche nach einer besseren Welt, Piper Verlag, 1984.

Offene Gesellschaft – offenes Universum (with Franz Kreuzer), Franz Deuticke Verlag, 1982.

Die Zukunft ist offen (with Konrad Lorenz), Piper Verlag, 1985.

For fuller bibliographies of Popper's works readers are referred to *Unended Quest* (Flamingo edition) and to P.A. Schilpp, *op. cit.*

The following are some of the books in English that deal descriptively and critically with Popper's work.

B. Magee, *Popper*, Fontana Paperbacks, 1973; 2nd edition, 1982.

P.A. Schilpp, editor, *The Philosophy of Karl Popper*, Open Court, 1974.

R.J. Ackermann, *The Philosophy of Karl Popper*, University of Massachusetts Press, 1976.

R. James, *Return to Reason*, Open Books, 1980.

A. O'Hear, *Karl Popper*, Routledge and Kegan Paul, 1980.

P. Levinson, editor, *In Pursuit of Truth*, Humanities, 1982.

T. E. Burke, *The Philosophy of Popper*, Manchester University Press, 1983.

Popper's ideas are also much discussed in the philosophical literature, especially in *The British Journal for the Philosophy of Science*, *Erkenntnis*, *Philosophy of Science*, and *Synthese*.

Indexes

Index of Names

Ackermann, R. J., 468
Acton, J. E. (Lord Acton), 307
Adam, 73
Adams, H., 437-8
Adler, A., 128, 460-1
Aeschylus, 393
Agassi, J., 420
Ajdukiewicz, K., 412
Albert, H., 409
Alcmaeon, 418
Alexander, S., 430
Anaximander, 14, 25, 28, 122, 228-34, 236, 418, 424f.
Anaximenes, 14, 229, 231, 234, 236, 418
Antisthenes, 100, 406
Aquinas, St Thomas, 41
Aristarchus, 119f., 228, 231
Aristotle, 29, 76, 87-97, 99f., 122f., 166, 185, 206, 228, 235, 289, 340, 376, 390, 395-8, 400-2, 406f., 418, 424f., 454, 458
Auchinleck, C., 363
Austin, J. L., 432
Ayala, F. J., 426
Ayer, A. J., 408

Bach, J. S., 223
Bacon, F. (Lord Verulam), 30, 46f., 84, 94, 218, 227, 230, 394, 405, 409, 445
Bakunin, M. A., 449
Barker, E., 342, 455
Bartley, W. W. III, 14, 386
Böhm-Bawerk, E., 416
Becquerel, H., 177
Beethoven, L. van, 258, 430
Beloff, J., 434f.
Bentham, J., 42
Bentley, R., 418
Bergson, H., 33, 134, 393, 436
Berkeley, G. (Bishop of Cloyne), 58, 60, 106, 209, 217, 221, 425
Bernal, J. D., 436
Bernard of Clairvaux, 380
Bernard, C., 84
Bernays, P., 465
Bertalanffy, L. von, 427
Selby-Bigge, L. A., 388, 407f., 423, 429-33
Birner, J., 22
Black, J., 147, 413
Blackwell, K., 459
Bodin, J., 320
Boehme, J., 380
Bohm, D., 205
Bohr, N., 118, 169, 178, 317, 387, 427, 443
Bolzano, B., 58, 68, 76
Born, M., 101f., 407, 418
Boscovič, R. J., 122, 178
Bradley, F. H., 434
Braestrup, F. W., 394
Brahe, T., 120
Briskman, L. B., 22
Broglie, L. de (Prince), 176, 205
Brouwer, L. E. J., 60f., 70
Brown, R., 424
Bühler, K., 270f., 389, 424
Buridan, J., 424
Burke, E., 33
Burnet, J., 237
Burnet, M., 86, 395
Burns, E., 448, 453, 456, 461
Busch, W., 190f., 421

Caesar, A., 380
Caesar, C. J., 49

Cairns, J., 395
Campbell, D. T., 245, 391, 426
Carnap, R., 160, 388, 400f., 407, 410f., 413, 416f., 421
Carus, P., 428
Cattell, R. B., 439, 441
Christ, J., 39, 41, 340, 342f., 386, 461
Churchill, W. S., 224f., 362f., 424
Claassen, E. M., 466
Cohen, M. R., 400, 402, 439
Cole, G. D. H., 450
Columbus, C., 177
Compton, A. H., 18, 253f., 260-4, 427, 428, 431, 465
Comte, A., 298, 301-3, 366, 438
Copernicus, N., 119f., 228, 231f.
Cornelius, H., 412
Cotes, R., 165
Critias, 455
Crossman, R. H. S., 95, 400
Crusoe, R., 312, 373f.

Darwin, C., 15, 18f., 71, 84-6, 113, 239-46, 259, 272-5, 298, 305, 366, 393f., 426, 436, 441, 465
Darwin, F., 426
Davisson, C. J., 176
Democritus, 32, 55, 233, 379, 406
Denbigh, K. G., 426
Deregowski, J. B., 433
Descartes, R., 52, 58, 122, 165, 221, 280, 380, 389, 409, 423, 441
Dickens, C., 339
Diels, H., 379, 418, 425, 447, 455
Dingle, H., 412
Dingler, H., 144-6, 410, 412
Diogenes the Cynic, 406
Diogenes Laertes, 406
Dirac, P. A. M., 178, 204
Dobzhansky, T., 426, 431
Donagan, A., 435
Duhem, P., 409, 412
Dühring, E. K., 449f., 452

Eccles, J. C., 281, 392, 434, 467
Eckhart, Master, 380
Eddington, A. S., 122, 176, 412
Einstein, A., 31, 53, 98f., 104, 111, 118, 120-2, 134, 137, 169, 176, 178, 205, 224, 245, 252f., 375, 398, 410, 419, 424, 428, 431
Elsasser, W., 176, 427
Engels, F., 326, 328, 378, 434, 449f., 452f., 456
England, E. B., 342, 455
Epimenides, 381
Ebner-Eschenbach, M. von, 423
Euclid, 177, 420
Euripedes, 455
Exner, F., 427

Fantz, R. L., 279, 433
Faraday, M., 122, 176, 238
Feigl, H., 389, 421
Ferchmin, P. A., 434
Fermat, P., 62, 156
Feyerabend, P. K., 411
Fichte, J. G., 99, 380
Findlay, J. N., 384
Fisher, H. A. L., 300, 437
Fisher, R. A., 242
Fitzgerald, G. F., 147, 413
Fleming, A., 177
Fode, K. L., 394
Frank, P., 416
Freeman, K., 379
Frege, G., 58, 60f., 269, 389
Fresnel, A., 169, 176, 419
Freud, S., 128, 279, 363f., 406, 460-1
Friedrich, C. J., 439f.
Fries, J. F., 152f., 159f., 415, 417
Frisch, K. von, 432

Galilei, G., 30f., 118, 121, 126, 168, 176, 198, 216, 231, 289, 305, 419
Galle, J. G., 176
Galton, F., 298
Gauss, C. F., 94
Genie, 434
Ginsberg, M., 439, 456
Gödel, K., 384, 386
Goldbach, C., 70
Gombrich, E. H., 86, 395, 433
Gomperz, H., 410
Gomperz, T., 454
Good, I. J., 424
Gray, A., 240
Green, D. E., 431
Gregory, R. L., 433

Grote, G., 397
Grünbaum, A., 413

Hadamard, J., 394
Hahn, H., 154, 413, 416
Haldane, E. S., 389
Haldane, J. B. S., 242
Hardy, A. 393
Harré, H. R., 463
Harris, A., 410
Harsanyi, J. C., 420
Hayek, F. von, 305, 358, 389, 437-9, 440, 456
Hegel, G. F. W., 44, 58, 76f., 94, 99, 320, 329, 337, 348, 355f., 366-71, 374, 376, 378, 380, 391, 405, 434, 451, 459, 461
Heidegger, M., 405, 415, 422
Hein, A., 392
Heisenberg, W., 204, 253f., 261, 427
Held, R., 392
Henry VIII, 317
Heraclitus, 30f., 221, 226, 233-6, 323, 366, 379, 425, 447
Hertz, H., 176
Hesiod, 122
Heyting, A., 60f., 389
Hippasus of Metapontum, 27
Hobbes, T., 390, 395, 397f.
Holst, E. von, 284
Homer, 351
Humboldt, W., 424
Hume, D., 10, 12, 46, 49, 58, 60, 101-4, 106-11, 113, 115f., 217f., 221, 239, 255-7, 260, 262f., 276-8, 284, 388, 405, 407f., 411, 422f., 429-33, 441
Husserl, E., 94, 345, 382, 415, 422
Hutt, W. H., 442
Hutton, J., 393
Huxley, A., 386, 430
Huxley, J., 431, 436
Huxley, T. H., 299, 436

James, R., 22, 468
James, W., 392
Jeffreys, H., 175
Jellyby, Mrs, 339
Jennings, H. S., 393
Jerne, N. K., 86, 395
Joan, St, 37
Jordan, P., 427, 431

Kant, I., 10, 33, 43, 52f., 58, 61, 94, 99, 101, 105, 133, 143, 185, 209-11, 215-19, 267, 278, 280, 340, 367f., 380, 386, 388, 390, 405, 411, 417, 422, 427, 429, 432, 461
Keller, H., 267
Kepler, J., 111, 118, 120f., 168, 176, 197, 216, 231, 250, 418f.
Keynes, J. M., 175
Kierkegaard, S., 86
Kirk, G. S., 424f.
Kneale, W. C., 433
Köhler, W., 82, 282, 392f.
Körner, S., 465
Kraft, J., 415, 421f.
Kraft, V., 409f.
Krantz, W., 379, 418, 425, 447, 455
Krechevsky, J., 392
Kronecker, L., 70

Laird, J., 382
Lakatos, I., 389, 391, 402, 407
Lamarck, J., 84f., 239, 366, 393
La Mettrie, J. J. de, 259
Lange, C. G., 392
Langford, C. H., 382
Laplace, P. S. de (Marquis), 175, 256, 263, 428, 430
Laurat, L., 453
Lavoisier, A. L., 177, 425
Leibniz, G. W., 105f., 122, 427
Lenin, V. I., 122, 326, 448f.
Leucippus, 233
Levinson, P., 468
Liebig, J., 409f.
Lillie, R., 427
Lindauer, M., 432
Lippmann, W., 309, 442
Locke, J., 58, 60, 221, 395
Loewenberg, J., 461
Lorentz, H. A., 147, 413
Lorenz, K., 82, 284, 435
Lubbock, J., 239
Lucretius, 428
Luther, M., 317

Macaulay, T. B. (Lord Macaulay), 444f.
Mach, E., 222, 410
Machiavelli, N., 317, 458
Mackenna, S., 391
Magee, B., 22, 468
Malebranche, N., 406
Malinowski, B., 441
Mannheim, K., 367, 442, 460f.
Marx, K., 12f., 19-21, 127f., 313, 326-35, 337, 345, 349f., 355f., 366-70, 434, 448-53, 456f., 459-61, 466
Maxwell, G., 411, 419
Maxwell, J. C., 169, 176, 178, 233, 238
Mayr, E., 394
Mead, G. H., 434
Medawar, P. B., 431, 435
Medicus, F., 427
Mendel, G., 241, 243
Menger, K., 141, 399, 411, 458
Merwe, A. van der, 424
Methuselah, 25
Meyer, E., 445
Michelangelo, 241
Michelson, A. A., 147
Mill, J., 444f.
Mill, J. S., 289, 298, 301-3, 345, 347-9, 353, 355f., 438f., 442-5, 456
Miller, A. V., 391
Miller, D. W., 114, 407
Moore, G. E., 403
Morley, E. W., 147
Mozart, W. A., 211, 241, 258, 430

Nagel, E., 389, 400, 402
Needham, J., 431
Nelson, E., 424
Nelson, L., 447
Neptune, 163
Newton, I., 21, 53, 104, 111, 118, 120-2, 124, 128f., 137, 146, 165f., 168, 176, 178, 197f., 206, 216-18, 225, 228, 250-2, 254, 256f., 289, 300-2, 305, 358f., 414, 416, 418f., 420, 426, 427, 429, 439
Nietzsche, F., 210

Örsted, H. C., 177
O'Hear, A., 22, 468
Orwell, G., 430

Paley, W., 239f., 243-5
Pareto, V., 458
Parmenides, 27, 122, 233, 236f., 425
Pasteur, L., 289, 305, 379, 395
Pauli, W., 129, 147, 205
Pavlov, I. P., 82, 393
Peirce, C. S. S., 185, 251f., 256, 261, 421, 427f.
Pemberton, H., 427
Penfield, W., 285, 435
Pericles, 340, 343
Perugino, P., 211
Pindar, 393
Pirie, N. W., 431
Planck, M., 252, 410
Plato, 20f., 26, 34, 40f., 43, 55, 68, 74-7, 87-9, 91, 93, 95, 100, 166, 177, 289, 307, 319f., 322f., 326, 337-44, 348, 355, 366, 379, 381, 387, 390, 395, 397, 406f., 418, 420, 444, 445f., 448, 454-6, 458, 460
Plotinus, 76, 390
Podolsky, B., 424
Poincaré, J. H., 147, 408, 412
Polanyi, K., 457
Popper, J. A. (Lady Popper), 22
Popper, K. R., 10-22, 379, 391, 409, 420, 424, 435, 462f., 467f.
Powell, C. F., 176
Proudhon, P. J., 329
Pythagoras, 27f., 232, 343, 379, 439, 454

Quine, W. V. O., 421

Ramsey, F. P., 56, 87, 185, 388
Raven, C. E., 436
Raven, J. E., 425
Rembrandt, 223
Riopelle, A. J., 392
Ritchie, N. M., 363
Röntgen, W. C., 177
Rosen, N., 424
Rosenthal, R., 394
Rosenzweig, M. R., 434
Ross, G. R. T., 389
Ross, W. D., 390, 396, 400

Rousseau, J. J., 320, 347
Rubin, E., 433
Rueff, J., 466
Russell, B. A. W., 57f., 60f., 101, 108f., 111f., 245, 269, 383, 405, 408, 411, 424, 441, 459
Russell, L. J., 387
Ryle, G., 278f., 430, 433

Scheler, M., 367
Schelling, F. W., 99, 380
Schilpp, P. A., 391, 424, 435, 467f.
Schlick, M., 181, 183, 260f., 263, 428, 431
Schmitt, F. O., 426
Schopenhauer, A., 99, 209f., 218, 406, 427
Schrödinger, E., 178, 203, 205, 252, 282, 394, 427, 429, 435
Sellars, W., 389, 421
Settle, T. W., 22
Shakespeare, W., 241
Shaw, G. B., 25, 37
Shearmur, J. F. G., 434
Sherrington, C., 283, 435, 454f.
Simplicius, 406
Simpson, G. G., 242
Skinner, B. F., 393, 430
Smith, A., 434
Nowell-Smith, P. H., 428
Smuts, J., 436
Socrates, 7, 25, 32, 41, 43, 86, 100, 226f., 309, 343f., 379, 418, 424f., 447, 455f.
Specht, M., 421
Spencer, H., 85, 463, 466
Sperry, R. W., 245, 426
Spinoza, B. de, 380, 427, 442f.
Stalin, J., 127
Strawson, P. F., 103, 109, 408, 433
Sultan, 282
Suppes, P. C., 389

Tarski, A., 17, 54, 181-6, 189, 192f., 195, 222, 386, 389-91, 399, 420
Tawney, R. H., 317, 443
Tax, S., 426
Thales, 14, 25f., 28f., 227-32, 234, 418
Theophrastus, 406
Thorpe, W. H., 82, 393
Thrasymachus, 344
Tinbergen, J., 442
Tint, H., 422
Toynbee, A. J., 437
Turing, A. M., 431

Victoria (Queen), 37, 436
Volkmann, R., 391

Waddington, C. H., 242, 426, 436
Wagner, M., 243
Waismann, F., 405
Wallace, A. R., 85
Wallace, W., 391
Watkins, J. W. N., 390
Watts, J., 451
Brooke-Wavell, B., 174
Webb, B., 442
Webb, S., 442
Weber, A., 460
Weber, M., 354, 458
Wegener, A., 231
Wells, H. G., 387, 453
Whewell, W., 10
Whitehead, A. N., 36, 74, 386, 411, 435
Whorf, B. L., 434
Wigner, E. P., 222, 424
Wisdom, A. J. T. D., 460
Wittgenstein, L., 25, 87, 95, 99, 138, 181, 380, 383f., 400, 403-5, 410, 420, 460
Woodger, J. H., 415
Worden, F. G., 426
Wundt, W. M., 289

Xenophanes, 28f., 31, 52, 185f., 190, 237

Yourgrau, W., 424
Yukawa, H., 176

Zeno, 233

Index of Subjects

Subjects treated in the notes have not been separately indexed except where they go beyond the accompanying text.

Ad hoc hypotheses, 128-30, 145, 163, 169
Altruism, 319, 338-40, 342
Animals, 64f., 69, 113, 240, 282, 284, 439, 454; apes, 82, 171, 282, 346, 392; Buridan's ass, 424; badgers 64; beavers, 64; bees, 271; butterflies and caterpillars, 300; cats, 82, 281; dogs, 437; earth worms, 284; elephants, 437; insects, 64, 84, 248-50, 252, 271; mice, 392; monkeys, 346; puppies, 88f., 92, 247; rabbits, 85, 437; rats, 256, 281, 394; seaserpents, 156; sea urchins, 284; snakes, 346; spiders, 63f., 84, 392; wasps, 67
Appearance and reality (see also Change), 18, 55, 119-22, 143, 220, 236, 452
Associationism, 108, 430
Astronomy (see also Solar system), 291-3, 298, 373f.
Atomism (Atomic theory), 123, 222, 233, 237f., 254, 458
Auxiliary hypotheses (see also *Ad hoc* hypotheses), 128-30, 147f.
Approximation to truth (see also Verisimilitude), 29, 120f., 122, 124, 192f., 362, 364

Bacteria, 69, 93
Basic statements, 47, 149-61, 421
Betting, 390
Biology, 64-6, 78-86, 205, 249, 274, 289, 298
Bucket theory of the mind, 105f., 221, 368
Birds, 67f., 271; blue tits, 68; peacocks, 243; ravens, 149, 157, 164, 414f.; swans, 110, 124f., 416f.

Chance (see also Randomness), 18, 252, 261-3
Chance discoveries, 55, 177, 313
Change, 17, 27, 226-38, 319, 366f.
Checks and balances, 321
Collectivism, 39, 304-19, 338-44, 347f., 355, 366
Common sense, 49, 105f., 220f., 224, 234, 250, 276
Consciousness, 58-60, 76f., 241, 266f., 279-86, 345, 369, 371, 377
Conspiracy theory of society, 351-3
Content, 16, 18, 72f., 112, 118, 124, 167-70, 173-6, 178, 180, 190-8, 411, 417
Conventions (Conventionalism; see also Immunizing stratagems), 125, 140-51, 345
Corroboration, 49, 113, 136, 140, 150f., 157, 159, 168, 176f., 188, 196, 315, 372, 411
Creativity, 86, 241, 257f., 261
Critical rationalism (see also Rationality), 9-14, 26-36, 40, 42-5, 52f., 57, 59, 63, 72, 84, 114, 189, 211, 216, 219, 230, 315f., 371-8, 379-88
Crucial experiments, 90, 119f., 127, 197f., 412, 414

Decisions, 36-9, 114f., 136-9, 141,

143-5, 159, 161, 262f., 272, 323, 350, 355
Definitions, 15, 75, 87-100, 123, 125, 141, 145f., 148, 159, 412
Demarcation, 11, 12, 16, 118-30, 143-51, 214, 413
Democracy (see also Freedom), 96, 248, 296, 305, 317, 322-5, 328, 333, 335
Depth (see also Content), 169f., 180, 190
Design, 239f., 243f.
Determinism (see Indeterminism)
Dispositions, 58, 60, 73, 155, 202f., 206, 223, 269, 278, 280
Dogmatism, 27, 44, 85, 99, 123, 126, 137, 152f., 160f., 314, 334, 400, 405, 452f.
Downward causation, 245f.

Economics, 290, 297f., 305, 307, 313, 326-37, 352-4, 372
Emergence, 71, 240f., 273, 297
Emotions, 38-41, 44f., 209, 273, 392
Empiricism, 15, 46-57, 101f., 107, 109, 227, 230, 368
Epiphenomenalism, 253, 272-5, 429
Essentialism (see also Definitions), 15, 21, 74f., 88-94, 96, 98, 100, 123, 165-7, 291, 324, 326f.
Evolution (see also Natural selection), 18f., 239-46, 259, 266, 273-5, 286, 290, 298, 303
Exogamy, 345
Experience (see also Observation, Sense experience), 139, 156, 161, 218, 276, 280, 285, 372, 375
Explanation (Explanatory power), 74, 116, 122, 160, 162-70, 179, 188, 190f., 193, 198, 222, 229, 233, 242f., 273, 346, 351, 353, 356-65

Falsification, 110, 124, 126f., 136, 141, 150-2, 157, 167, 186
Feedback, 64, 69-71, 76, 80, 245, 266, 273
Freedom (see also Democracy), 253f., 260, 322, 329f., 332-41, 336, 367, 378

Genetics, 78-86, 241-6, 266, 286, 298f.
Gestalt, 82, 426
Gravitation, 121, 124, 146, 165f., 206, 228, 248

Historicism (see also Prophecy), 19f., 166, 172, 289-304, 308, 312f., 327, 331, 334, 337, 349, 351, 366, 368
Historism, 368, 383
Holism (see also Utopianism), 249, 300, 309-18, 336f., 348

Idealism (see also Realism), 209f., 216, 355, 400
Imagination, 37, 44, 55, 83, 168, 172
Immunizing stratagems, 125-8, 130, 146f., 221, 244
Imprinting, 82
Indeterminism (see also Chance, Randomness), 11, 13, 203, 209-11, 215-18, 246-64, 378, 422
Individualism, 19-21, 39, 308f., 311, 316, 338-44, 348f., 355f.
Induction, 12, 16, 31, 84, 86, 101-17, 133, 136, 139, 152f., 168, 189, 218, 227, 231, 386, 397, 400, 412, 445
Infinite regress, 48, 50, 75, 95-7, 115, 129, 152f., 160, 229, 415
Insanity, 108f., 111f., 223, 363-5
Interventionism, 306, 331-6
Intuition, 55, 89f., 93f., 134, 168, 209f., 380, 395
Irrationalism, 33-45, 108f., 209-11, 218, 364f., 367, 370, 377, 405

Justice, 319, 326, 340, 343f.

Knowledge (see Scientific knowledge)

Language (see also World 3), 19, 59, 71-3, 83, 170, 222f., 267f., 270-3, 278-82, 349, 440
Logic (Deduction), 13, 21, 34, 61, 72, 91, 102, 107, 111, 135, 139, 141, 148, 150, 154-6, 160, 168, 177f., 194, 214, 220, 231, 237, 268f., 271f., 306, 400f., 406f.

Materialism, 13, 33, 158f., 268-72, 427

Mathematics, 62, 67, 70, 91, 156, 167, 190, 214f., 220, 269, 399, 401f.
Metaphysics (see also Demarcation), 11, 17f., 52, 101, 120f., 129, 137, 170, 199, 204-6, 209-20, 222, 224, 242, 300, 400, 404-6, 414, 453
Mind-body problem, 18, 21, 265-75
Models, 357-65
Morality, 36-9, 42, 217, 253, 315, 321, 335, 340, 342, 350, 367
Music, 13, 42, 133, 211, 258

Natural selection, 15, 18, 78-86, 239-46, 272
Negative utilitarianism, 317f.
Nihilism, 211, 344

Objectivism (Objectivity; see also World 3), 11, 17, 21, 57, 61, 63, 73, 84, 142, 199, 202, 204, 370-8, 458
Observation, 46-50, 54f., 57, 84, 89, 101f., 104, 111, 116, 120f., 158, 179, 204, 224, 226-8, 230f., 278f., 291, 372, 374

Paradoxes, 17, 20, 35, 51, 54, 108, 116, 174, 185, 189, 322-4, 327, 332, 336, 380-5
Phenomenology, 94, 223, 422
Piecemeal social engineering, 12, 20, 43, 292-5, 304-18, 327, 331, 335-7, 376-8
Politics, 11f., 18, 20, 39, 42f., 51, 95f., 249, 257, 289, 293f., 306f., 315f., 319-21, 324, 326-37, 341, 354, 371, 373, 377f.
Practical applications of science (see also Technology), 114-16, 135f., 294, 377
Preference, 111-14, 196, 272
Presupposition, 35, 382
Probability, 16f., 21, 81, 107, 136, 141, 174-6, 186-9, 194, 199-206, 222, 252, 411, 417
Problems, 55, 59, 61, 63, 65, 68, 70, 73, 77, 79f., 82, 138, 179f., 190f., 216-19, 240, 278, 281f., 284
Propensity (see also Probability), 199-206, 220
Prophecy, 291-5, 331, 337, 351
Psychoanalysis, 12, 127f., 279, 364f., 369f.
Psychologism (see also Subjectivism), 21, 153-5, 158-61, 345-56, 359, 459
Psychology, 82, 102f., 107-9, 113, 133f., 139, 147, 152, 205, 255-7, 272f., 289, 360

Quantum Theory, 17, 21, 80, 104, 199, 203-6, 246, 252-4, 259, 262

Randomness (see also Chance), 79, 81, 187, 245f., 248, 252
Rationality (see also Critical rationalism), 21, 25, 108f., 113-15, 178f., 189, 211, 214, 297
Rationality principle, 357-65
Realism, 11, 17, 105-7, 143, 170, 205f., 209-11, 216f., 220-5, 395
Regularities (see also Scientific laws), 110, 115f., 220, 255, 292, 295
Reinforced dogmatism, 369f.
Relativity, 80, 98f., 119, 148, 245, 375
Revealed science, 373f.
Revolutions, 12, 127, 307

Scientific knowledge, 10f., 60, 73, 78-86, 91-3, 99, 104, 108f., 118-23, 133-5, 137, 140f., 144, 147, 154-6, 162-8, 188, 214, 221f., 231, 241, 251, 278, 302, 368, 371-7
Scientific laws (Laws of nature), 109-11, 144, 157, 164-6, 299, 301f., 308f., 358f., 409
Scientific method (see also Testing), 37f., 90f., 133-51, 214f., 289-91, 303, 311, 315-17, 360f., 372-6, 400, 453
Scientific progress, 78, 83f., 171-80, 185, 191-8, 376-8
Self, 276-86
Sense experience (Perception), 15, 46-50, 105-7, 152-4, 156, 158f., 161, 217f., 223, 226f., 266, 268, 274, 276, 280, 285, 368
Situational logic, 21, 61, 353-65
Social institutions, 19, 295f., 308f., 326-8, 330, 346f., 349f., 354f., 373
Sociology, 291-3, 295-9, 305, 307, 311, 337, 340, 345-56

Sociology of knowledge, 366-78, 382f.
Solar system, 94, 119f., 129, 205, 224f., 228-33, 248, 250f., 302, 357-9
Subjectivism, 60-3, 105-7, 133-5, 183-8, 200-2

Technology, 293-8, 304-18
Testing (Experiments; see also Scientific method), 54, 119, 122f., 129, 134-6, 145, 148-51, 155f., 158-61, 163, 168, 172f., 178, 187, 193, 196, 201-4, 231, 241, 256, 286, 290, 299, 311-18, 360
Time and space, 280, 285, 375
Tolerance, 446
Tradition, 21, 26-30, 54f., 73, 83, 138, 323, 345-7, 350
Transference, principle of, 109f., 113
Trends, 298-303, 313
Truth, 16f., 32, 52, 54-7, 71-3, 75, 77, 110-13, 118, 121, 136, 145, 147, 170, 181-96, 222f., 227, 271f., 376, 399, 411

Unintended consequences, 69, 309, 315, 350-2, 441
Universals, 75, 148, 153f., 390, 398
Utopianism (see also Holism), 41f., 295-7, 307-18, 336

Validity (see Logic)
Verisimilitude, 16f., 72, 77, 175, 187, 192-8, 222
Voluntarism, 210f.

War, 115f., 341, 351, 362f.
World 3, 15, 18f., 58-74, 76, 265-75, 280, 282, 407